Criminal Justice, Poli<
Human Rights

Criminal Justice, Police Powers and Human Rights

Keir Starmer
Michelle Strange
Quincy Whitaker

with

Anthony Jennings QC and
Tim Owen QC

Series Editor: John Wadham

*This book has been printed digitally and produced in a standard specification
in order to ensure its continuing availability*

OXFORD
UNIVERSITY PRESS

Great Clarendon Street, Oxford OX2 6DP

Oxford University Press is a department of the University of Oxford.
It furthers the University's objective of excellence in research, scholarship,
and education by publishing worldwide in

Oxford New York

Auckland   Cape Town Dar es Salaam   Hong Kong   Karachi
Kuala Lumpur Madrid Melbourne Mexico City   Nairobi
New Delhi Shanghai Taipei Toronto
With offices in
Argentina Austria Brazil Chile Czech Republic France Greece
Guatemala Hungary Italy Japan South Korea Poland Portugal
Singapore Switzerland Thailand Turkey Ukraine Vietnam

Oxford is a registered trade mark of Oxford University Press
in the UK and in certain other countries

Published in the United States
by Oxford University Press Inc., New York

A Blackstone Press Book
© Keir Starmer, Michelle Strange, Quincy Whitaker, Anthony Jennings and Tim Owen, 2001

ISBN 978-1-84174-138-3

Printed and bound by CPI Antony Rowe, Eastbourne

Contents

Acknowledgements

All five authors would like to thank the staff and their colleagues at Doughty Street Chambers and Matrix Chambers for their support and assistance during the writing of this book. In particular, invaluable research was provided by Alison Seaman, co-ordinator of the Human Rights Unit at Doughty Street Chambers, and by Alison MacDonald, trainee barrister at Matrix Chambers.

Keir Starmer
Michelle Strange
Quincy Whitaker
Anthony Jennings QC
Tim Owen QC
20 April 2001

Abbreviations

Archbold	*Archbold on Criminal Pleading Evidence and Practice*
CCTV	closed-circuit television
CJPOA 1994	Criminal Justice and Public Order Act 1994
Convention, the	European Convention on Human Rights
CPIA 1996	Criminal Procedure and Investigations Act 1996
CSP	Communication Service Providers
ECHR	European Convention on Human Rights
European Commission	European Commission of Human Rights
European Court	European Court of Human Rights
GCHQ	Government Communications Headquarters
HRA 1998	Human Rights Act 1998
IOCA 1985	Interception of Communications Act 1985
NCIS	National Criminal Intelligence Service Authority
NCS	National Crime Squad
PACE	Police and Criminal Evidence Act 1984
PCC(S)A 2000	Powers of Criminal Courts (Sentencing) Act 2000
RIPA 2000	Regulation of Investigatory Powers Act 2000
RTA 1998	Road Traffic Act 1998

Table of Cases

Table of Primary Legislation

Table of Secondary Legislation

Table of International Instruments

Chapter One

The European Convention on Human Rights: Overview

Keir Starmer

1.1 INTRODUCTION

The European Convention for the Protection of Human Rights and Fundamental Freedoms[1] ('the Convention') is an international treaty of the Council of Europe. It was adopted in 1950, ratified by the UK in 1951 and entered into force in 1953. The unusual feature of the Convention, as an international human rights instrument, is that it provides a mechanism for individuals to enforce their Convention rights against state parties.

The Convention is divided into three sections. Section I describes and defines the rights and freedoms guaranteed under the Convention. Section II establishes the European Court of Human Rights and provides for its operation. Section III deals with miscellaneous provisions such as territorial application, reservations, denunciations, signature and ratification.

Since it was first drafted, the Convention has been amplified by a number of Protocols. One of the most important is Protocol 11, which abolished the European Commission of Human Rights. As a result, the Convention is now administered by two bodies: the European Court of Human Rights and the Committee of Ministers of the Council of Europe.

At the international level, any individual, non-governmental organisation or group of individuals can petition the European Court of Human Rights in Strasbourg alleging a violation of Convention rights. Three judges of the Court

---

[1] Cm. 8969.

sitting in committee determine whether a petition is 'admissible'. And, if so, seven judges of the Court sitting as a chamber determine the merits of the petition. Cases involving a serious question affecting the interpretation of the Convention are dealt with by a grand chamber of 11 judges.

So far as the domestic application of the Convention is concerned, Article 1 provides that:

> The High Contracting Parties shall secure to everyone within their jurisdiction the rights and freedoms defined in section I of this Convention.

For many years successive governments took the view that incorporation of the Convention was unnecessary to fulfil the requirements of Article 1. They argued that domestic law matched the Convention, or could readily be amended where it failed to do so.[2]

The Human Rights Act 1998 marks a radical departure from that approach. It is intended to give effect in domestic law to the rights and freedoms guaranteed under the Convention.

1.2   THE RIGHTS PROTECTED

The rights guaranteed by the Convention are as follows:

Article 2   The right to life and the prohibition of arbitrary deprivation of life.

Article 3   The prohibition of torture, inhuman and/or degrading treatment/ punishment.

Article 4   The prohibition of slavery and forced labour.

Article 5   The right to liberty and security of person.

Article 6   The right to a fair trial.

Article 7   The prohibition of retrospective application of the criminal law.

Article 8   The right to respect for private and family life, home and correspond-ence.

Article 9   Freedom of thought, conscience and religion, including the right to manifest religion or belief in public or private worship, teaching, practice and observance.

Article 10   Freedom of expression, including the right to receive and impart information and ideas without interference.

Article 11   Freedom of assembly and association, including the right to form and join trade unions.

Article 12   The right to marry.

---

[2] A proposition rejected by the United Nations Human Rights Committee: CCPR/C/79/Add.55 (27 July 1995).

Article 13 The right to an effective remedy in domestic law for arguable violations of the Convention.

Article 14 The prohibition of discrimination on any ground such as sex, race, colour, language, religion, political or other opinion, national or social origin, association with a national minority, property, birth or other status.

1.3 THE OPTIONAL PROTOCOLS

The UK is a party to the First Protocol to the Convention, which guarantees the right to peaceful enjoyment of possessions (First Protocol, Article 1), the right to education (First Protocol, Article 2) and the right to free elections (First Protocol, Article 3). It is also a party to the Sixth Protocol to the Convention, which abolishes the death penalty (Sixth Protocol, Article 1) save in respect of acts committed in time of war or imminent threat of war (Sixth Protocol, Article 2).

1.4 RESERVATIONS

Any contracting state may, when signing the Convention or when depositing its instrument of ratification, make a reservation in respect of any particular provision of the Convention to the extent that any law then in force in its territory is not in conformity with the provision (Article 57). The UK has entered one reservation. This relates to the right to education and makes it clear that the UK only accepts the obligation to respect the right of parents to ensure that education and teaching is in conformity with their own religious and philosophical convictions in so far as it is compatible with the provision of efficient instruction and training, and the avoidance of unreasonable public expenditure. The Human Rights Act 1998 takes effect subject to this reservation (s. 1(2)).

1.5 DEROGATIONS

In addition, with some exceptions, in times of war or other public emergency threatening the life of the nation, a contracting state may take measures derogating from its obligations under the Convention to the extent strictly required by the exigencies of the situation, provided that such measures are not inconsistent with its other obligations under international law (Article 15). The UK has entered one derogation. The derogation arose from the case of *Brogan and others* v *UK* (1988) 11 EHRR 117 in which the European Court of Human Rights held that the detention of the applicants under the Prevention of Terrorism (Temporary Provisions) Act 1984 for more than four days constituted a breach of Article 5(3) (set out below at 3.3.2) of the Convention, because they had not been brought promptly before a judicial authority. The then Government entered a derogation following the judgment in order to preserve the Secretary of State's power under the 1984 Act to extend the period of detention of persons suspected of terrorism connected with the affairs of Northern Ireland for a total of up to seven days. The validity of the derogation was subsequently upheld by the European Court of Human Rights in *Brannigan and McBride* v *UK* (1993) 17 EHRR 539. The Human Rights Act 1998 takes effect subject to this derogation (s. 1(2)).

1.6   THE CATEGORISATION OF RIGHTS

The rights protected under the Convention can be divided into three categories:

(a)   *Absolute rights*: i.e. those which cannot be restricted in any circumstances (even in times of war or other public emergency) and which are not to be balanced with any general public interest. These are Articles 2 (the right to life), 3 (the prohibition of torture, inhuman and/or degrading treatment/ punishment), 4(1) (the prohibition of slavery) and 7 (the prohibition of retrospective criminal penalties).

(b)   *Limited rights*: i.e. those in relation to which the Government can enter a derogation, but which otherwise are not to be balanced with any general public interest. These are Articles 4(2) and (3) (the prohibition of forced labour), 5 (liberty), 6 (fair trial), 9(1) (freedom of thought — but *not* freedom to manifest religion), Article 12 (the right to marry), Article 2, Protocol 1 (the right to education), Article 3, Protocol 1 (the right to free elections) and Article 1, Protocol 6 (abolition of the death penalty).

The practical difference between these rights and absolute rights is that restriction in the public interest can be justified, but only on the grounds expressly provided for within the text of the Articles themselves: e.g. Article 4(2) prohibits forced labour, but Article 4(3) then sets out a number of exceptions; similarly, the first sentence of Article 5(1) provides for the right to liberty and security of person and the second sentence then lists (exhaustively) all the circumstances in which that right can be restricted. Unless a restriction is expressly provided for in the text of the Article, the public interest cannot justify any interference with limited rights.

Strictly speaking, Article 6 (fair trial) probably falls into a category of its own. That is because the European Court has read a number of implied restrictions into Article 6: e.g. to ensure the protection of victims and vulnerable witnesses (see chapter 21). Such restrictions are limited and must be strictly necessary and proportionate. Moreover, properly understood, they *define* the scope of Article 6 and do not operate in the same way as restrictions on qualified rights. The operation of these restrictions was considered by the Privy Council in *Brown* v *Stott (Procurator Fiscal, Dunfermline)* [2001] 2 All ER 97.

(c)   *Qualified rights*: i.e. those which although set out in positive form are subject to limitation or restriction clauses which enable the general public interest to be taken into account.[3] These are Articles 8 (right to respect for private and family life), 9 (freedom to manifest religion or belief), 10 (freedom of expression), 11 (freedom of assembly), 14 (discrimination) and Article 1, Protocol 1 (the right to property).

The operation of the limitation or accommodation clauses under the third category — qualified rights — is crucial to the Strasbourg approach to the protection of Convention rights. According to the constant case law of the European Court and Commission, a limitation or restriction on these rights can only be justified if the person or body imposing the limitation or restriction can show:

(a)   That the limitation or restriction in question is 'prescribed by law'. This does not simply mean permitted under domestic law. Two of the requirements that flow from the expression 'prescribed by law' are:

    (i)   that the law must be adequately accessible, i.e. the citizen must be able to have an indication that is adequate in the circumstances of the legal rules applicable to a given case; and

    (ii)   that a norm cannot be regarded as 'law' unless formulated with sufficient precision to enable individuals to regulate their conduct[4] — individuals must be able to foresee, if necessary with appropriate advice, what activity would infringe the law.

(b)   That the limitation or restriction pursues a 'legitimate aim' — i.e. one of the aims specifically listed in Article 8(2), 9(2), 10(2) or 11(2) as the case may be. These include (i) the interests of national security, (ii) territorial integrity or public safety, (iii) the prevention of disorder or crime, or (iv) the protection of health, morals or the rights of others. They are to be interpreted narrowly.[5]

(c)   That the limitation or restriction is 'necessary in a democratic society'. To satisfy this test, the person or body imposing the limitation or restriction

---

[3] However, as the European Court of Human Rights pointed out in *Sunday Times* v *UK* (1979) 2 EHRR 245, it is not faced with a choice between two conflicting principles (an individual's right and the general public interest), but with a principle that is subject to a number of exceptions (para. 65).

[4] *Sunday Times* v *UK* (1979) 2 EHRR 245.

[5] See *Klass* v *Germany* (1978) 2 EHRR 214.

on the third category rights (i.e. qualified rights) must show that the limitation or restriction fulfils a pressing social need and that it is proportionate to the aim of responding to that need: i.e. that is it necessary and proportionate. The word 'necessary' in this context, although not synonymous with 'indispensable', is not as flexible as 'reasonable' or 'desirable'.

In some cases, it will be obvious that a measure is disproportionate. In others, a more sophisticated approach is needed, taking into account the following factors:

(i)   whether 'relevant and sufficient' reasons have been advanced in support of it;
(ii)   whether there was a less restrictive alternative;
(iii) whether there has been some measure of procedural fairness in the decision-making process;
(iv)   whether safeguards against abuse exist; and
(v)   whether the restriction in question destroys the 'very essence' of the Convention right in issue.

(d)   That the limitation or restriction is not discriminatory. In issue here are differences in treatment that have 'no objective and reasonable justification'.[6] Discrimination on grounds of sex or race is always very closely scrutinised.[7] See chapter 3.

1.7   THE STRASBOURG APPROACH TO THE PROTECTION OF HUMAN RIGHTS

A number of general principles of interpretation have emerged from the case law of the European Court and Commission. Among the most important are the following:

(a)   As an international treaty, the Convention must be interpreted according to the international law rules on the interpretation of treaties contained in the Vienna Convention on the Law of Treaties.[8] Article 31 of the Vienna Convention requires that all treaties:

> ... shall be interpreted in good faith in accordance with the ordinary meaning to be given to the terms of the treaty in their context and in light of its object and purpose.

---

[6] *Belgian Linguistic Case (No. 1)* (1967) 1 EHRR 241.
[7] See *Abdulaziz, Cabales and Balkandali* v *UK* (1985) 7 EHRR 471.
[8] Cm. 7964.

This rule has led the European Court to adopt a teleological approach, i.e. one that seeks to realise the objects and purposes of the Convention.

(b) The objects and purposes of the Convention include its role as 'an instrument for the protection of individual human beings' and the promotion of 'the ideals and values of a democratic society'.[9] And the European Court has consistently held that 'democracy' is characterised by 'pluralism, tolerance and broadmindedness'.[10]

(c) The Convention is intended to guarantee not rights that are theoretical or illusory but rights that are practical and effective.[11] This has provided a springboard for the imposition of positive obligations on state authorities and is one of the bases for the proposition that the Human Rights Act 1998 affects relations between private individuals: see chapter 2.

(d) The Convention is a 'living instrument' requiring a dynamic and evolving interpretation and therefore must be interpreted 'in the light of present day conditions'.[12] The change in the European Court's approach to issues such as corporal punishment, homosexuality and transsexuals are examples of this principle in play.

(e) The European Court is not bound by the definition of words in domestic law when interpreting the Convention. It can adopt an 'autonomous approach' by which it decides for itself the meaning of Convention words or concepts. As a result, some proceedings are deemed 'criminal' under the Convention despite the fact that they are treated as civil in domestic law. See chapter 3.

(f) In some cases, the European Court will allow states a 'margin of appreciation' in their assessment of necessity and proportionality. However, the margin of appreciation is a doctrine of international law which does not apply in domestic proceedings.[13]

---

[9] *Belgian Linguistic Case (No.1)* (1967) 1 EHRR 241.
[10] *Handyside* v *UK* (1976) 1 EHRR 737.
[11] *Artico* v *Italy* (1980) 3 EHRR 1.
[12] *Tyrer* v *UK* (1978) 2 EHRR 1.
[13] See Lord Hope's comments in *R* v *DPP, ex parte Kebilene* [1999] 3 WLR 972 at pp. 993–4.

Chapter Two

The Human Rights Act 1998: Overview

Keir Starmer

2.1 THE UK MODEL OF INCORPORATION

The Human Rights Act 1998 rests on the following five principles:

(a) All legislation (primary, subordinate and whenever enacted) must, if possible, be interpreted so as to be compatible with the Convention (HRA 1998, s. 3(1), (2)(a)).

(b) Where it simply is not possible to interpret primary legislation so as to be compatible with the Convention, the courts have no power to strike it down. However, designated courts will have power to make a 'declaration of incompatibility' which (in theory) should prompt government action (ss. 53(2)(b), 54(2)).

(c) Where it simply is not possible to interpret subordinate legislation so as to be compatible with the Convention, the courts have power to disapply it. The only exception is where primary legislation prevents the removal of any incompatibility (s. 4(4)(b)).

(d) All public authorities, including all courts and tribunals, must, if possible, act in a way which is compatible with the Convention. Public authorities include (but are not limited to) courts, tribunals and 'any person certain of whose functions are functions of a public nature' (s. 6(3)).

(e) Individuals who believe that their Convention rights have been infringed by a public authority can rely on their rights as a defence in criminal or civil proceedings or as the basis of an appeal. Alternatively, they can seek judicial review, or, if no other legal avenue is open, bring civil proceedings for damages (ss. 7, 8).

The rights protected under the Human Rights Act 1998 are those set out in Articles 2 to 12 and 14 of the Convention, Articles 1 to 3 of the First Protocol and Articles 1 and 2 of the Sixth Protocol as read with Articles 16 to 18 of the Convention (HRA 198, s. 1(1)). These rights have effect subject to any designated derogation or reservation (s. 1(2)).

Articles 1 and 13 are not included. Article 1 obliges contracting states to 'secure' Convention rights to 'everyone within their jurisdiction'. And Article 13 provides that anyone whose Convention rights are violated shall have an 'effective remedy' before a national authority. According to the Lord Chancellor, the Human Rights Act 1998 gives effect to Article 1 by securing to people in the UK the rights and freedoms of the Convention and gives effect to Article 13 by establishing a scheme under which Convention rights can be raised and remedied before UK courts.[1]

The model of incorporation established under the Human Rights Act 1998 differs from other models considered by the Government — in particular the Canadian, New Zealand and Hong Kong models — and from the approach adopted in the European Communities Act 1972.

2.2 NEW LEGISLATION

For new legislation, s. 19 of the Human Rights Act 1998 provides that the Minister in charge of a Bill in either House of Parliament must make and publish a written statement to the effect either that in his view the provisions of the Bill are compatible with Convention rights or that although he is unable to make such a statement the Government nevertheless wishes the House to proceed with the Bill.

2.3 STATUTORY INTERPRETATION: THE NEW RULE

Section 3(1) of the Human Rights Act 1998 provides that primary and subordinate legislation, whenever enacted, must as far as possible be read and given effect in a way which is compatible with Convention rights. What this means is that UK courts must strive to find a construction consistent with the intentions of Parliament and the wording of legislation which is nearest to the Convention rights.[2] Courts should proceed on the basis that Parliament is deemed to have intended its statutes to be compatible with the Convention to which the UK is

---

[1] House of Lords (Committee Stage), 18 November 1997, Hansard, col. 475. See also the Lord Chancellor's observation that:
    ... the courts may have regard to Article 13. In particular, they may wish to do so when considering the very ample provisions of [section] 8(1) [remedies].
18 November 1997, Hansard, HL, col. 477.
[2] Ibid, col. 535.

bound: the only basis for courts concluding that Parliament has failed to carry that intention into effect is where it is impossible to construe a statute so as to be compatible with the Convention.[3]

The intention underlying section 3(1) was expressed by the Lord Chancellor as follows:

> We want the courts to strive to find an interpretation of the legislation which is consistent with Convention rights as far as the language of the legislation allows and only in the last resort to conclude that the legislation is simply incompatible with them.[4]

Courts should not 'contort the meaning of words to produce implausible or incredible meanings',[5] but the Government rejected an attempt to amend section 3 so as to impose an obligation to interpret statutory provisions in accordance with the Convention only where it is 'reasonable' to do so.[6]

This new rule of construction was described in the White Paper[7] as going:

> ... far beyond the present rule which enables the courts to take the Convention into account in resolving any ambiguity in a legislative provision. The courts will be required to interpret legislation so as to uphold the Convention rights unless legislation itself is so clearly incompatible with the Convention that it is impossible to do so. (para. 2.7)

The Lord Chancellor has been enthusiastic about its scope.[8]

Section 3(1) applies to past as well as to future legislation. To the extent that it affects the meaning of a legislative provision, the courts will not be bound by previous interpretations. They will be able to build a new body of case law, taking into account the Convention rights.[9]

It is clear that, having given the courts a new interpretative tool, Parliament intends them to use it. At the Third Reading, the Lord Chancellor said:

> ... in 99% of the cases that will arise, there will be no need for judicial declarations of incompatibility.[10]

Similarly, the Home Secretary said, 'We expect that, in almost all cases, the courts will be able to interpret legislation compatibly with the Convention.'[11] An early example is *R* v *Offen* [2001] 2 All ER 154.

---

[3] Ibid.
[4] Ibid; see also the Home Secretary, HC, 3 June 1998, Hansard, cols 421–2.
[5] Ibid, col. 422.
[6] HL, 18 November 1997, Hansard, cols 533–6.
[7] *Rights Brought Home: The Human Rights Bill* (1997; Cm. 3782).
[8] 'The Development of Human Rights in Britain under an Incorporated Convention on Human Rights' [1998] Public Law 221 at p. 228.
[9] Cm. 3782, para. 2.8.
[10] HL, 5 February 1998, Hansard, col. 840.
[11] HC, 16 February 1998, Hansard, col. 780.

2.4 INTERPRETING THE HUMAN RIGHTS ACT 1998 ITSELF

Clearly, like any other legislation, the Human Rights Act 1998 must as far as possible be read and given effect in a way which is compatible with Convention rights. In addition its status, as a constitutional instrument in a larger package of constitutional reforms, calls for a generous interpretation of its provisions.

In *Minister for Home Affairs* v *Fisher* [1979] 3 All ER 21 the Privy Council considered the approach that should be taken to legislation which seeks to incorporate human rights into domestic law. Lord Wilberforce observed that the legislation there in question, the Bermuda Constitution, was based upon international human rights instruments and had been greatly influenced by the European Convention on Human Rights. It was therefore to be given:

> ... a generous interpretation avoiding what has been called 'the austerity of tabulated legalism', suitable to give individuals the full measure of the fundamental rights and freedoms referred to.

A similar approach was more recently taken in *Matadeen* v *Pointu and others* [1998] 3 WLR 18 where Lord Hoffmann explained, in the context of the protection given to human rights by the Mauritius Constitution, that the moral and political values underpinning such legislation must be taken into account.[12]

2.5 DECLARATIONS OF INCOMPATIBILITY

It is a fundamental principle of the Human Rights Act 1998 that it does not affect the validity, continuing operation or enforcement of any incompatible primary legislation or of any incompatible subordinate legislation if primary legislation prevents the removal of the incompatibility. This reflects the priority afforded to Parliamentary sovereignty by the government. In its view, the authority that Parliament derives from its democratic mandate, means that it must remain competent to make any law on any matter of its choosing.

However, where a designated court is satisfied that a provision of primary legislation is incompatible with Convention rights, or that a provision of subordinate legislation is incompatible with the Convention and the primary legislation under which it was made prevents the removal of that incompatibility, it has power under the Act to make a 'declaration of incompatibility' (s. 4). Such a declaration does not affect the validity, continuing operation or enforcement of the provision in respect of which it is made (s. 4(6)(a)). Nor does it bind the parties to the proceedings in which it is made (s. 4(6)(b)). However, it is intended to operate as a clear signal to Parliament that an incompatibility has been found.

---

[12] See also *A-G of the Gambia* v *Momodou Jobe* [1984] AC 689; *A-G of Hong Kong* v *Lee Kwong-Kut* [1993] AC 951; and *Vasquez* v *The Queen* [1994] 1 WLR 1304.

The Government envisages that a declaration of incompatibility will 'almost certainly' prompt legislative change.[13] This point was emphasised by the Lord Chancellor in the House of Lords debate on the Act.[14] The Human Rights Act 1998 therefore provides a 'fast-track' procedure for amending the law so as to bring it into conformity with the Convention.

Like all remedies under the Act, a s. 4 declaration of incompatibility is a discretionary remedy. However, it is the Government's intention that courts should generally make declarations of incompatibility when they find an Act to be incompatible with the Convention.[15] The only examples given by the Lord Chancellor where a declaration might not be made were where there may be an alternative statutory appeal route which the court thinks ought to be followed, or where there is another procedure which the court thinks the applicant should exhaust before a declaration is granted.[16]

Designated courts under the Human Rights Act 1998 — with power to make a declaration of incompatibility — are the House of Lords, the Court of Appeal, the High Court, the Judicial Committee of the Privy Council, the Courts-Martial Appeal Court and, in Scotland, the High Court of Justiciary sitting as a court of criminal appeal or the Court of Session (s. 4(5)). Unfortunately, there is no (formal) procedure by which any other court can alert Parliament to problems of compatibility.

If a court is considering whether or not to make a declaration of incompatibility the Crown has a right to be notified (s. 5(1)). A Minister or person nominated by a Minister is then entitled to be joined as a party to the proceedings (s. 5(2)) and, in criminal proceedings, may appeal (with leave) to the House of Lords against any declaration of incompatibility (s. 5(4)).

2.6 SUBORDINATE LEGISLATION

Like primary legislation, subordinate legislation[17] must also be read and given effect in a way which is compatible with Convention rights as far as possible (s. 3(1)). The major difference is that, unlike primary legislation, delegated legislation can be struck down (or simply disapplied) where it is impossible to interpret it so as to be compatible with Convention rights. This is an extension of the *ultra vires* principle. The only exception is where primary legislation prevents removal of the incompatibility (s. 3(2)(c)).

Where a provision in subordinate legislation is found to be incompatible with Convention rights, the question of severance may arise. Under the present rule,

---

[13] Cm. 3782, para. 2.9.
[14] House of Lords debate, 3 November 1997, Hansard, col. 1230.
[15] Lord Chancellor, House of Lords Committee Stage, 18 November 1997, Hansard, col. 546.
[16] Ibid.
[17] Defined in s. 21(1), HRA 1998.

severance of the offending provision is permitted so long as its removal will not result in subordinate legislation that is so different from that originally made that it cannot be assumed that, in such a form, it would ever have been made.[18]

2.7 PUBLIC AUTHORITIES

Section 6 of the Human Rights Act 1998 makes it unlawful for a public authority to act in a way which is incompatible with Convention rights, unless it is required to do so to give effect to primary legislation. In this context, 'act' includes a failure to act (s. 6(6)); but does not include a failure to legislate or make remedial orders.

The Act does not define 'public authority'. Section 6(3) expressly includes (a) courts and tribunals and (b) 'any person certain of whose functions are functions of a public nature' and expressly excludes both Houses of Parliament[19] and any person exercising functions in connection with proceedings in Parliament. The definition is in wide terms and is intended to cover central government (including executive agencies), local government, the police, immigration officers, prisons and, to the extent that they are exercising public functions, companies responsible for areas of activity which were previously in the public sector, such as the privatised utilities.[20] Introducing the HRA 1998 in the House of Lords debate, the Lord Chancellor made it clear that the Government's intention was that the Act be applied to a wide rather than a narrow range of public authorities, so as to provide as much protection as possible to those who claim that their rights have been infringed.[21]

However, in relation to a particular act, a person with some functions of a public nature is not a public authority if the nature of the act in question is private (HRA 1998, s. 6(5)). An example might be Railtrack, which has statutory public powers and functions. When carrying out its functions relating to safety, it would qualify as a public authority. But when carrying out its functions as, for instance, a property developer by engaging in private transaction such as the disposal or acquisition of land, it would not so qualify.[22] Similarly, a private security company would be exercising public functions in relation to the management of a contracted-out prison but would be acting privately when, for example, guarding commercial premises. Doctors in general practice would be public authorities in relation to their NHS functions, but not in relation to their private clients.[23]

---

[18] *DPP* v *Hutchinson* [1990] 2 AC 783.

[19] But not the House of Lords in its judicial capacity: see s. 6(4).

[20] Cm. 3782, para. 2.2.

[21] House of Lords debate, 3 November 1997, Hansard, col. 1231.

[22] This example was given by Lord Williams in debate at the House of Lords Committee Stage, 24 November 1997, Hansard, col. 758.

[23] These examples were given by the Lord Chancellor in debate at the House of Lords Committee Stage, 24 November 1997, Hansard, col. 811.

2.7.1 Proceedings against public authorities

Section 7 complements s. 6 by providing that anyone who claims that a public authority has acted (or proposes to act) in a way which is incompatible with Convention rights can either bring proceedings against that authority (s. 7(1)(a)) or rely on Convention rights in any 'legal proceedings' brought by others, but only if he is (or would be) a 'victim' within the meaning of s. 7(7).

2.8 REMEDIES: GENERAL

In relation to any act (or proposed act) of a public authority which the court finds is (or would be) unlawful, it may grant such relief or remedy, or make such order, within its jurisdiction, as it considers just and appropriate — including an award of damages (s. 8(1)). But damages may be awarded only by a court which has power to award damages, or to order the payment of compensation, in civil proceedings (s. 8(2)). No award of damages is to be made unless, taking account of all the circumstances of the case, including any other relief or remedy granted, or order made, in relation to the act in question (by that or any other court), and the consequences of any decision (of that or any other court) in respect of that act, the court is satisfied that the award is necessary to afford just satisfaction to the person in whose favour it is made (s. 8(3)).

In deciding whether to make such an award and in calculating the amount, courts will be required to take into account the principles applied by the European Court of Human Rights in relation to its own awards of compensation (s. 8(4)). Article 41 (formerly Article 50) of the Convention provides that if the European Court finds that there has been a violation of the Convention, or the Protocols made under it, and if the internal law of the contracting state concerned allows only partial reparation to be made, the Court shall, if necessary, afford just satisfaction to the injured party.

2.9 REMEDIES: JUDICIAL ACTS

Where individuals claim that their Convention rights have been infringed by a judicial act, they must bring their claim by way of an appeal (HRA 1998, s. 9(1)). But this does not expand the scope for judicial review of courts (s. 9(2)).

Judicial acts in this context include the acts of members of tribunals, justices of the peace, clerks and other officers entitled to exercise the jurisdiction of the courts (s. 9(5)). They also include acts done on the instructions, or on behalf of such individuals (s. 9(5)).

In respect of judicial acts done in good faith, damages may not be awarded otherwise than to compensate a person to the extent required by Article 5(5) of the

Convention (s. 9(3)). And any award of damages in respect of a judicial act done in good faith is to be made against the Crown, but only if the Minister responsible for the court concerned, or nominated person or government department, is joined as a party (s. 9(4), (5)).

2.10 THE OBLIGATION TO TAKE STRASBOURG CASE LAW INTO ACCOUNT

The Human Rights Act 1998 does not make decisions of the European Court or Commission of Human Rights binding in domestic law. But it does include a strong provision in relation to the interpretation of Convention rights. Section 2(1) requires that any court or tribunal determining a question in connection with a Convention right 'must take into account':

- judgments, decisions, declarations and advisory opinions of the European Court of Human Rights;
- decisions of the European Commission on Human Rights under what were[24] Articles 31 (opinion on the merits), 26 (exhaustion of domestic remedies) or 27(2) (admissibility); and
- decisions of the Committee of Ministers of the Council of Europe

whenever made or given, so far as, in the opinion of the court or tribunal, they are relevant to the proceedings in which that question has arisen. What that means is that, where relevant, domestic courts should apply Convention jurisprudence and its principles to the cases before them.[25]

There is nothing in the 1998 Act itself to suggest that the requirement in section 2(1) is limited to judgments, decisions or opinions relating to the United Kingdom. And, at the Committee Stage, the Lord Chancellor made it clear that s. 2 was intended to require courts to take account of Strasbourg decisions regardless of the identity of the respondent state.[26]

The circumstances in which domestic courts might depart from existing Strasbourg decisions are not clear. At the Committee Stage, the Lord Chancellor said:

> The Bill would of course permit United Kingdom courts to depart from existing Strasbourg decisions and upon occasion it might well be appropriate to do so and it is possible that they might give a successful lead to Strasbourg. For example, it would permit the United Kingdom courts to depart from Strasbourg decisions where there has

[24] The ECHR was fundamentally amended on 11 November 1998 when Protocol 11 came into force.
[25] Lord Chancellor, HL, 18 November 1997, Hansard, col. 515.
[26] House of Lords Committee Stage, 18 November 1997, Hansard, col. 513.

been no precise ruling on the matter and Commission opinion which does so has not taken into account subsequent Strasbourg case law.[27]

Clearly, therefore, in so far as domestic courts seek to reconcile inconsistent Strasbourg case law and/or plug the gaps in Strasbourg jurisprudence, they will be on safe ground; assuming they do so according to the most recently articulated principles of the European Court. However, any court which simply ignores or declines to follow clear Strasbourg case law runs the obvious risk of appeal and, ultimately, challenge in Strasbourg.

2.11   CONVENTION CLAIMS IN RELATION TO THE ACTS OF PRIVATE INDIVIDUALS: HORIZONTALITY

Although most of the provisions in the Human Rights Act 1998 focus on the acts or omissions of public authorities, the acts of private individuals do not fall outside its scope for three reasons. First, because the European Court and Commission have developed an elaborate doctrine of 'positive obligations' under the Convention according to which state authorities can be held liable, in certain circumstances, for not providing effective protection against the acts of private individuals. By analogy, where a public authority has failed to provide effective protection against the acts of private individuals in similar circumstances, section 7 will be triggered and proceedings may be brought against that authority (s. 7(1)(a)); alternatively the public authority's omission can be relied upon in other legal proceedings (s. 7(1)(b)).

The second reason why the acts of private individuals do not fall outside the scope of the Human Rights Act 1998 is that, as noted above, courts and tribunals are included within the definition of a 'public authority' under the Act. It follows that they will be acting unlawfully if they fail to develop the law — both statute law and the common law — in a way which is compatible with Convention rights, even where litigation is taking place between private individuals. Early examples are *Douglas* v *Hello!* (21 December 2000) and *Venables and Thompson* v *News Group Newspapers Ltd* (8 January 2001).

The Lord Chancellor recognised this in debate during the passage of the Bill through the House of Lords when he rejected an amendment to exclude courts and tribunals from the definition:

> We also believe that it is right as a matter of principle for the courts to have the duty of acting compatibly with the Convention not only in cases involving other public authorities but also in developing the common law in deciding cases between individuals. Why should they not? In preparing this Bill, we have taken the view that it is the other course, that of excluding Convention considerations altogether from cases

---

[27] House of Lords Committee Stage, 18 November 1997, Hansard, col. 514.

between individuals which would have to be justified. The courts already bring Convention considerations to bear and I have no doubt that they will continue to do so in developing the common law ... Clause 3 requires the courts to interpret legislation compatibly with the Convention rights and to the fullest extent possible in all cases coming before them.[28]

In other words, legislation must be read and given effect in a way which is compatible with Convention rights whoever is before the courts and the common law must be developed so as to be compatible with the Convention.

The third reason why the acts of private individuals do not fall outside the scope of the Human Rights Act 1998 is that s. 7(1)(b) provides that, in addition to proceedings against a public authority, Convention rights may be relied upon in 'any legal proceedings'. This includes proceedings brought by or at the instigation of a public authority but does not exclude proceedings between private individuals. However, in this respect, an unlawful act or omission of a public authority must be identified before s. 7(1)(b) comes into play by reason of the 'victim' requirement: Convention rights are not made directly enforceable against private individuals by this route.

2.12 THE RETROSPECTIVE EFFECT OF THE HUMAN RIGHTS ACT 1998

Proceedings against a public authority for breach of Convention rights can only be brought in relation to acts or omissions after 2 October 2000 (s. 22(4)). The same rule applies where individuals seek to rely on their Convention rights in other legal proceedings, save where proceedings are brought by or at the instigation of a public authority, in which case a breach of Convention rights can be relied upon whenever the breach took place (s. 22(4)). Criminal proceedings are proceedings brought by a public authority and therefore this special rule concerning the retrospective effect of the Human Rights Act 1998 applies to such proceedings and can be relied upon by defendants to challenge acts of omissions taking place before 2 October 2000.[29] In addition, it seems that the requirement to interpret legislation compatibly with the Convention applies *whenever* the action or conduct in question took place (*J. A. Pye* v *Graham* (6 February 2001, CA)).

---

[28] 24 November 1997, Hansard, col. 783.
[29] *R* v *DPP, ex parte Kebilene* [1999] 3 WLR 175.

Chapter Three

Articles of Specific Application in Criminal Proceedings

Keir Starmer

3.1 INTRODUCTION

All Convention rights are relevant to criminal proceedings. However, Article 3 (the prohibition of torture, inhuman and degrading treatment/punishment), Article 5 (the right to liberty), Article 6 (fair trial), Article 7 (the prohibition of retrospective criminal penalties), Article 8 (the right to privacy and family life) and Article 14 (the prohibition of discrimination) have specific application and warrant special attention.

3.2 ARTICLE 3

Article 3 provides that:

> No one shall be subjected to torture or to inhuman or degrading treatment or punishment.

It is one of the strongest rights under the Convention in the sense that it is unqualified[1] and is non-derogable. Since a violation of Article 3 is clearly a very serious matter, the European Court and Commission of Human Rights have insisted that treatment or punishment 'must attain a minimum level of severity'

---

[1] But see, Harris, O'Boyle and Warbrick, *Law of the European Convention on Human Rights*, 1st ed. (London: Butterworths, 1995), p. 56.

before Article 3 is breached.[2] The assessment of this minimum is relative; it depends on all the circumstances of the case, such as the duration of the treatment, its physical or mental effects and, in some cases, the sex, age and state of health of the victim.

In *Ireland* v *UK* (1978) 2 EHRR 25 the Court set out the following broad guidelines:

Torture	Deliberate inhuman treatment causing very serious and cruel suffering
Inhuman treatment	Treatment that causes intense physical and mental suffering
Degrading treatment	Treatment that arouses in the victim a feeling of fear, anguish and inferiority capable of humiliating and debasing the victim and possibly breaking his or her moral resistance

Note that (i) acts performed in private can be degrading; (ii) a custodial sentence could, in principle, amount to inhuman punishment,[3] but a finding to this effect is unlikely.

Both the Court and the Commission have recognised that the institutionalisation of certain practices can amount to degrading treatment contrary to Article 3. So, for example, in the *East African Asians* cases (1973) 3 EHRR 76 the Commission found a violation of Article 3 on the basis that the practice of refusing to allow British passport holders who had been expelled from Uganda, Tanzania and Kenya to take up residence in the UK amounted to institutionalised racism. This is possibly subject to the qualification introduced by the Court in *Abdulaziz, Cabales and Balkandali* v *UK* (1985) 7 EHRR 471 that degradation must be intentional to violate Article 3.

3.3   ARTICLE 5

Article 5 is concerned with the right to liberty and security of person. It provides that a state may legitimately detain someone, but only if the grounds for detention can be found in the list set out in Article 5(1). It also provides associated procedural rights to ensure speedy and effective judicial determination of the justification of detention. It is best treated as a two-limbed provision: (i) a test for the legality of detention and (ii) a set of procedural safeguards for detainees.

3.3.1   The legality of detention

So far as the legality of detention is concerned, the scheme of Article 5 is to set up a positive right to liberty and security with limited exceptions and an

---

[2] *Ireland* v *UK* (1978) 2 EHRR 25 at para. 62.
[3] See comments made by the Court in *Weeks* v *UK* (1987) 10 EHRR 293 at para. 47 and *Hussain* v *UK* (1996) 22 EHRR 1 at para. 53.

overriding requirement that any deprivation of liberty must be in accordance with a procedure prescribed by law. Thus Article 5(1) provides that:

> Everyone has the right to liberty and security of person. No one shall be deprived of his liberty save in the following cases and in accordance with a procedure prescribed by law:
>
> (a)   the lawful detention of a person after conviction by a competent court;
> (b)   the lawful arrest or detention of a person for non-compliance with the lawful order of a court or in order to secure fulfilment of any obligation prescribed by law;
> (c)   the lawful arrest or detention of a person effected for the purpose of bringing him before the competent legal authority on reasonable suspicion of having committed an offence or when it is reasonably considered necessary to prevent his committing an offence or fleeing after having done so;
> (d)   the detention of a minor by lawful order for the purpose of educational supervision or his lawful detention for the purpose of bringing him before the competent legal authority;
> (e)   the lawful detention of persons for the prevention of the spreading of infectious diseases, of persons of unsound mind, alcoholics or drug addicts or vagrants;
> (f)   the lawful arrest or detention of a person to prevent his effecting an unauthorised entry into the country or of a person against whom action is being taken with a view to deportation or extradition.

The exceptions provided for in Article 5(1)(a) to 5(1)(e) are to be narrowly construed and represent an exhaustive definition of the circumstances in which a person may be lawfully deprived of his liberty.[4]

Article 5(1)(a) provides for detention after conviction. However, so long as the detention is 'lawful' the fact that a conviction is later overturned will not affect the applicability of Article 5(1)(a).[5] And, for Article 5 purposes, detention after conviction covers confinement in a mental institution for treatment[6] and detention as an alternative to any original sentence.[7]

The first limb of Article 5(1)(b) authorises detention to effect the execution of an order of the court where there has been hindrance or obstruction. On this basis, detention may be justified to enable a blood test to be taken,[8] to enable an affidavit to be prepared,[9] a psychiatric opinion to be obtained[10] or to secure compliance

---

[4] *Winterwerp v Netherlands* (1979) 2 EHRR 387 at para. 37.
[5] *Krzycki v Germany* (1978) 13 DR 57.
[6] *X v UK* (1982) 4 EHRR 188.
[7] *Kotalla v Netherlands* (1978) 14 DR 238.
[8] *X v Austria* (1979) 18 DR 154.
[9] *X v Germany* (1971) 14 Yearbook 692.
[10] *X v Germany* (1975) 3 DR 92.

with an order to deliver up property[11] or pay a fine.[12] The second limb of Article 5(1)(b) is wider, but does not authorise detention to secure the performance of a general legal duty: the obligation must be specific and concrete. Hence a general obligation not to commit offences against public peace or state security cannot legitimise detention under Article 5(1)(b).[13] However, detention to facilitate questioning at ports and airports under anti-terrorism legislation might fall within Article 5(1)(b).[14]

Article 5(1)(c) authorises arrest on reasonable suspicion of having committed a criminal offence. The arrest must be for the purpose of bringing the person concerned before a 'competent legal authority' (e.g. a magistrates' court). The words 'reasonable suspicion' mean the existence of facts or information which would satisfy an objective observer that the person concerned may have committed the offence.[15] Reasons for arrest must be given and must be in 'simple, non-technical language'.[16]

The phrase 'in accordance with the procedure prescribed by law' refers to conformity with national law and procedure.[17] Nevertheless, it remains the function of the European Court and Commission of Human Rights to determine whether Article 5 has been violated, and these bodies therefore have the ultimate power to interpret and apply national law.[18] There is also a more general requirement under the Convention to respect a fair and proper procedure — that is, that 'any measure depriving a person of his liberty should issue from and be executed by an appropriate authority and should not be arbitrary'.[19] In *Van der Leer* v *Netherlands* (1990) 12 EHRR 567 the European Court found a violation of Article 5(1) where a judge failed to hear from a patient or her representative and gave no reason for not doing so.

3.3.2 Procedural safeguards for detainees

The procedural safeguards for detainees are set out in Article 5(2)–(5) which provide that:

(2) Everyone who is arrested shall be informed promptly, in a language which he understands, of the reasons for his arrest and of any charge against him.

(3) Everyone arrested or detained in accordance with the provisions of paragraph 1(c) of this Article shall be brought promptly before a judge or other officer

---

[11] *Shobiye* v *UK* (1976).

[12] *Airey* v *Ireland* (1977) 8 DR 42.

[13] *Lawless* v *Ireland* (1961) 1 EHRR 15.

[14] *McVeigh, O'Neill and Evans* v *UK* (1981) 25 DR 15.

[15] *Fox, Campbell and Hartley* v *UK* (1990) 13 EHRR 157

[16] Ibid.

[17] *Winterwerp* v *Netherlands* (1979) 2 EHRR 387.

[18] *Bozano* v *France* (1986) 9 EHRR 297, and *Van der Leer* v *Netherlands* (1990) 12 EHRR 567.

[19] *Winterwerp* v *Netherlands* (1979) 2 EHRR 387.

authorised by law to exercise judicial power and shall be entitled to trial within a reasonable period or to release pending trial. Release may be conditioned by guarantees to appear for trial.

(4) Everyone who is deprived of his liberty by arrest or detention shall be entitled to take proceedings by which the lawfulness of his detention shall be decided speedily by a court and his release ordered if a detention is not lawful.

(5) Everyone who has been the victim of arrest or detention in contravention of the provisions of this Article shall have an enforceable right to compensation.

Article 5(2) is dealt with at 10.3.2; and Article 5(3) is dealt with at 11.2 and 11.3.

3.3.3   Review of detention under Article 5(4)

The purpose of Article 5(4) is:

> ... to assure to persons who are arrested or detained the right to a judicial supervision of the lawfulness of the measure to which they are thereby subjected.

The scope of the supervision required under Article 5(4) varies with the context. A full review by a 'court' is needed where:

- the initial decision to detain was not taken by a court or tribunal;
- the grounds for detention may change over time: e.g. those detained on mental health grounds or prisoners serving the preventative part of their sentence.

For prisoners serving fixed term sentences, the judicial supervision of the lawfulness of detention required by Article 5(4) is incorporated in the decision of the trial court.[20]

For prisoners serving indeterminate sentences, separate Article 5(4) proceedings are required to determine release once the 'tariff' period has been served.[21] Where a court passes a sentence and imposes forfeiture or a fine with further detention in default, that second period (unlike the first) is subject to review under Article 5(4), depending as it does on solvency.[22]

The degree of scrutiny required under Article 5(4) also varies with the context; but unless the court can review compliance with domestic law and the general requirements of the ECHR, and examine soundness of the factual basis put forward in support of detention, Article 5(4) will be breached:

> ... it is clear that Article 5(4) does not guarantee a right to judicial review of such breadth as to empower the court, on all aspects of the case including questions of pure

---

[20] *De Wilde, Ooms and Versyp* v *Belgium* (1971) 1 EHRR 373, para. 76.
[21] *Thynne, Wilson and Gunnell* v *UK* (1990) 13 EHRR 666, paras 73 and 74.
[22] *Soumare* v *France* (24 August 1998).

expediency, to substitute its own discretion for that of the decision-making authority. The review should, however, be wide enough to bear on those conditions which are essential for the 'lawful' detention of a person according to Article 5(1).[23]

Any body tasked with determining the lawfulness of a detention must be independent of both the executive and the parties and follow a procedure which has:

> ... a judicial character and gives to the individual concerned guarantees, appropriate to the kind of deprivation of liberty in question, of [a] judicial procedure the forms of which may vary from one domain to another.[24]

It must have the power to take a legally binding decision to release the prisoner.[25]

The principle of 'equality of arms' applies under Article 5(4) and this implies that proceedings will be adversarial;[26] but the precise requirements will vary from case to case. However, where a detainee's character or attitude are in issue, he or she should be given an opportunity to participate fully in an oral hearing and be able to examine and cross-examine witnesses. This is an especially important safeguard in cases where prisoner misconduct is alleged and the facts are disputed.[27]

In addition, detainees are also entitled to full disclosure of any adverse material in Article 5(4) proceedings.[28] In criminal cases, this applies at an early stage and can require pre-bail disclosure: see 11.4.2.3.

Any review decision — up to and including the enforcement of remedies — must be made speedily. This means that:

- a detainee must have speedy access to a remedy;[29]
- once the remedy has been obtained it must be implemented quickly.[30]

3.3.4 Article 5(5) compensation

The right to compensation under Article 5(5) is distinct from and without prejudice to the power of the European Court to award just satisfaction under Article 41. Moreover, Article 5(5) gives a right to compensation; an *ex gratia* payment is insufficient.

---

[23] *Chahal v UK* (1996) 23 EHRR 413, at para. 127.
[24] *De Wilde, Ooms and Versyp v Belgium* (1971) 1 EHRR 373, at paras 76–8.
[25] *Hussain v UK* (1996) 22 EHRR 322, at para. 67.
[26] *Sanchez-Reisse v Switzerland* (1986) 9 EHRR 71.
[27] *Hussain v UK* (1996) 22 EHRR 1, at para. 59.
[28] *Weeks v UK* (1987) 10 EHRR 293, at para 66; *Thynne, Wilson and Gunnell v UK* (1990) 13 EHRR 666, at para. 80; *Woukam Moudefo v France* (1988) A 141-B, at paras 86–91; *Megyeri v Germany* (1992) 15 EHRR 584, at para. 23.
[29] *X v UK* (1982) 4 EHRR 188, at para. 138.
[30] *Sanchez-Reisse v Switzerland* (1986) 9 EHRR 71, at para. 55; see also *Roux v UK* (1986) 48 DR 263.

The fact that detention is lawful in domestic law does not affect the right to compensation under Article 5(5) if the detention is unlawful under the ECHR;[31] and any detention which is unlawful in domestic law is automatically unlawful under the ECHR.[32]

A rule that compensation is payable only on proof of damage is not contrary to Article 5(5);[33] but damage encompasses both pecuniary and non-pecuniary damage, including 'moral' damage such as distress, pain and suffering.[34]

Article 5(5) does not require the detainee to establish bad faith on the part of the authorities.[35] However, an error within jurisdiction does not necessarily give rise to a claim under Article 5(5).[36]

3.4   ARTICLE 6

Article 6 of the Convention guarantees the right to a fair and public hearing in all criminal cases. It provides that:

(1)   In the determination of his civil rights and obligations or of any criminal charge against him, everyone is entitled to a fair and public hearing within a reasonable time by an independent and impartial tribunal established by law. Judgment shall be pronounced publicly but the press and public may be excluded from all or part of the trial in the interests of morals, public order or national security in a democratic society, where the interests of juveniles or the protection of the private life of the parties so require, or to the extent strictly necessary in the opinion of the court in special circumstances where publicity would prejudice the interests of justice.

(2)   Everyone charged with a criminal offence shall be presumed innocent until proved guilty according to law.

(3)   Everyone charged with a criminal offence has the following minimum rights:

    (a)   to be informed promptly, in a language which he understands and in detail, of the nature and cause of the accusation against him;

    (b)   to have adequate time and facilities for the preparation of his defence;

    (c)   to defend himself in person or though legal assistance of his own choosing or, if he has not sufficient means to pay for legal assistance, to be given it free when the interests of justice so require;

    (d)   to examine or have examined witnesses against him and to obtain the attendance and examination of witnesses on his behalf under the same conditions as witnesses against him;

    (e)   to have the free assistance of an interpreter if he cannot understand or speak the language used in court.

---

[31] *Brogan and others* v *UK* (1988) 11 EHRR 117; *Fox, Campbell and Hartley* v *UK* (1990) 13 EHRR 157.

[32] *L* v *Sweden* (1988) 61 DR 62.

[33] *Wassink* v *Netherlands* (1990) A/185-A.

[34] *Huber* v *Austria* (1976) 6 DR 65, at para. 69.

[35] *Santa Cruz Ruiz* v *UK* (19 February 1999, ECtHR).

[36] *Benham* v *UK* (1996) 22 EHRR 293.

These provisions are the subject of detailed examination in chapters 12 to 19. In *Brown* v *Stott (Procurator Fiscal, Dunfermline)* [2001] 2 All ER 97, the Privy Council considered the nature of Article 6 and, in particular, the circumstances, if any, on which trial rights could be restricted. Lord Bingham observed that Article 6 had more in common with absolute rights, such as Articles 2 and 3, than qualified rights such as Articles 8, 9, 10 and 11: there being nothing to suggest that the fairness of the trial itself can be qualified, compromised or restricted in any way, whatever the circumstances and whatever the public interest in convicting the offender. If the trial as a whole is to be judged unfair, a conviction cannot stand (p. 105). However, Lord Bingham reasoned, while overall fairness cannot be compromised, the constituent rights compromised, whether expressly or implicitly, within Article 6 are not in themselves absolute. Limited qualification of these rights is acceptable if reasonably directed by national authorities towards a clear and proper public objective and if representating no greater qualification than the situation calls for (p. 115). See further at 14.1.

3.4.1   The meaning of criminal proceedings

In most cases the applicability of Article 6 will not be in issue: it clearly applies to ordinary criminal proceedings in magistrates' courts and the Crown Court, and to any appeal from those courts. The only question in cases is likely to be when Article 6 bites (in particular, whether fair trial guarantees apply at the police station prior to charge).

Where the position is less clear cut, the meaning of 'criminal charge' in Article 6 of the Convention will be important. In the leading case of *Engel and others* v *Netherlands* (1976) 1 EHRR 706 the Court made it clear that 'criminal charge' is an autonomous concept. In other words, the Strasbourg institutions will decide for themselves whether any given proceedings involve the determination of a 'criminal charge' within the meaning of Article 6; they will not be bound by the approach taken in domestic law. In particular, the Court has emphasised that there is nothing in the Convention to prevent decriminalisation, but this cannot, of itself, limit the operation of the fundamental guarantee of a fair trial in Article 6.[37]

For the Court and Commission, the question of whether proceedings involve the determination of a 'criminal charge' can be assessed by reference to three criteria: (i) the classification of the proceedings in domestic law, (ii) the nature of the offence or conduct in question, and (iii) the severity of any possible penalty.[38] The first criterion is not as important as the second and third,[39] unless the proceedings are classified as criminal in domestic law. If so, that classification is conclusive and Article 6 applies. In contrast, the fact that proceedings are classified as civil in domestic law is merely 'a starting point'.[40]

---

[37] *Öztürk* v *Germany* (1984) 6 EHRR 409.
[38] *Engel and others* v *Netherlands* (1976) 1 EHRR 706.
[39] *Öztürk* v *Germany* (1984) 6 EHRR 409, at para. 50.
[40] *Benham* v *UK* (1996) 22 EHRR 293.

3.5   ARTICLE 8

Article 8 provides that:

(1)   Everyone has the right to respect for his private and family life, his home and his correspondence.

(2)   There shall be no interference by a public authority with the exercise of this right except as is in accordance with the law and is necessary in a democratic society in the interests of national security, public safety or the economic well-being of the country, for the prevention of disorder or crime, for the protection of health or morals, or for the protection of the rights and freedoms of others.

The notion of 'private life' in Article 8 is a broad one and is not susceptible to exhaustive definition. It includes the idea of an 'inner circle' in which individuals may live their personal lives as they choose without interference from the state. On that basis, the European Court and Commission have reviewed cases involving the interception of communications, secret surveillance and the collection and retention of personal data, including medical records.

However, the Court has held that it would be too restrictive to limit Article 8 to the notion of an 'inner circle': it also covers the right to develop one's own personality and to create and foster relationships with others. And on the basis that most people develop relationships worthy of protection in their working lives, the Court has been unwilling to interpret Article 8 so as to exclude activities of a business or professional nature.

Private life also covers physical integrity. So, for example, the European Court and Commission have considered issues such as corporal punishment, physical abuse and medical treatment from an Article 8 perspective.

The primary duty of the state and public authorities under Article 8 is to refrain from interfering with an individual's right to respect for his or her private and family life, home and correspondence. However, the Court and Commission have extrapolated from the underlying principles of Article 8 an important secondary duty, namely a duty to take action to ensure that Article 8 rights are protected effectively.

Any interference with Article 8 rights must be justified. This means that:

- the interference in question must be 'prescribed by law';
- the interference must be legitimate — i.e. it must pursue one of the aims specifically listed in Article 8(2);
- the interference must be 'necessary in a democratic society': i.e. necessary and proportionate;
- the interference must not be discriminatory.

These requirements are dealt with in detail at 1.6.

3.6 ARTICLE 14

The prohibition of discrimination in Article 14 is framed in wide terms:

> The enjoyment of the rights and freedoms set forth in this Convention shall be secured without discrimination on any ground such as sex, race, colour, language, religion, political or other opinion, national or social origin, association with a national minority, property, birth or other status.

The use of the words 'such as' and 'other status' indicates that the categories of prohibited discrimination under the Convention are not closed.

Article 14 does not prohibit all kinds of distinction or differential treatment. The meaning of discrimination under Article 14 is a difference in treatment which has 'no reasonable and objective justification'. And such justification depends upon:

- whether a legitimate aim for the measure can be made out; and
- whether there is a reasonable relationship of proportionality between the means employed and that aim.

The reach of the prohibition of discrimination under Article 14 is limited to those rights embodied in the Convention and its Protocols. It can only be invoked in conjunction with one of the other Convention rights. And, in this sense, it is dependent upon those other rights.

However, a breach of Article 14 can be found even where there is no violation of a substantive right:

> While it is true that this guarantee has no independent existence in the sense that under the terms of Article 14 it relates solely to 'rights and freedoms set forth in the Convention', a measure which in itself is in conformity with the requirements of the Article enshrining the right or freedom in question may however infringe this Article when read in conjunction with Article 14 for the reason that it is of a discriminatory nature.[41]

While there can never be a breach of Article 14 considered in isolation, there may be a breach of Article 14 considered in conjunction with another Article of the Convention in cases where there would be no violation of that other Article taken alone.[42]

The test for the application of Article 14 is whether the facts in issue 'fall within the ambit' of one or more of the other Convention provisions.[43] This is fulfilled if the 'subject matter' falls within the scope of the Article in question.[44]

---

[41] *Belgian Linguistic Case* (1967) 1 EHRR 241, at para. 9.
[42] *Abdulaziz, Cabales and Balkandali v UK* (1985) 7 EHRR 471.
[43] *Rasmussen v Denmark* (1984) 7 EHRR 371.
[44] *X v Germany* (1976) 19 Yearbook 276.

Chapter Four

Convention Rights as Substantive Issues in Criminal Proceedings

Keir Starmer

4.1 INTRODUCTION

In broad terms, the Convention can be relied upon in criminal proceedings where the following issues arise:

(a) Certainty: i.e. where the definition or scope of a criminal offence is so vague and imprecise that it violates the principle of certainty inherent in the Convention and specifically required by Article 7.

(b) Retrospectivity: i.e. where the act or conduct penalised in criminal proceedings did not constitute a criminal offence at the time it was committed (the principle of non-retrospective application of the criminal law).

(c) Substantive challenges to the criminal law: i.e. where a criminal offence amounts to an unjustifiable interference with the exercise by the defendant of his or her Convention rights (for example, free speech).

(d) Compliance with the procedural requirements of Articles 5 and 6.

Each of these issues will be examined in turn, save for (d) which forms the subject matter of chapters 12 to 21.

4.2 CERTAINTY

Article 7 of the Convention provides that:

(1)   No one shall be held guilty of any criminal offence on account of any act or omission which did not constitute a criminal offence under the national or international law at the time when it was committed. Nor shall a heavier penalty be imposed than the one that was applicable at the time the criminal offence was committed.

(2)   This article shall not prejudice the trial and punishment of any person for any act or omission which, at the time when it was committed, was criminal according to the general principles of law recognised by civilised nations.

On its face, Article 7(1) deals simply with the principle that the criminal law should not be applied retrospectively. However, consistent with its short title in the Convention — no punishment without law — the Strasbourg institutions have interpreted this provision broadly. As the Court pointed out in *Kokkinakis* v *Greece* (1993) 17 EHRR 397 at para. 52:

> ... Article 7(1) of the Convention is not confined to prohibiting the retrospective application of the criminal law to an accused's disadvantage. It also embodies, more generally, the principle that only the law can define a crime and prescribe a penalty ... and the principle that the criminal law must not be extensively construed to an accused's detriment, for instance by analogy; it follows from this that an offence must be clearly defined in law. This condition is satisfied where the individual can know from the wording of the relevant provision and, if need be, with the assistance of the court's interpretation of it, what acts and omissions will make him liable.

This formulation of the principle of legality overlaps with the rule under Article 5 that deprivations of liberty be 'lawful' and with the more general rule that any restriction on the exercise of Convention rights under Articles 8 to 12 must be 'prescribed by law': a point emphasised by the Court in *SW and CR* v *UK* (1995) 21 EHRR 363 at para. 34/32:

> ... when speaking of 'law' Article 7 alludes to the very same concept as that to which the Convention refers elsewhere when using the term, a concept which comprises written as well as unwritten law and implies qualitative requirements, notably those of accessibility and foreseeability.

Thus in *Sunday Times* v *UK* (1979) 2 EHRR 245, the applicant newspaper challenged contempt of court proceedings on the basis that the uncertainty of the law violated Article 10 (freedom of speech) of the Convention; and in *Harman* v *UK* (1984) 38 DR 53 the applicant challenged the same provisions on the same basis, but under Article 7 of the Convention.[1]

However, absolute certainty is not required: reasonable certainty is enough. In the context of a challenge to a development in the common law removing the

---

[1] The case was declared admissible and was then settled by the UK Government.

immunity enjoyed by husbands from criminal liability for raping their wives,[2] the Court noted:

> However clearly drafted a legal provision may be, in any system of law, including criminal law, there is an inevitable element of judicial interpretation. There will always be a need for elucidation of doubtful points and for adaptation to changing circumstances. Indeed, in the United Kingdom, as in the other Convention States, the progressive development of the criminal law through judicial law-making is a well entrenched and necessary part of legal tradition. Article 7 cannot be read as outlawing the gradual clarification of the rules of criminal liability through judicial interpretation from case to case, provided that the development is consistent with the essence of the offence and could be reasonably foreseen.[3]

On the facts, the Court held that the decisions of the Court of Appeal and then the House of Lords did no more than continue a perceptible line of case law development dismantling the immunity of a husband from prosecution for rape upon his wife.[4]

An indication of the limits within which the common law must operate so as to conform with the principle of reasonable certainty was given by the Commission in *X Ltd and Y* v *UK* (1982) 28 DR 77. What Article 7 precludes is the extension of existing offences to cover facts which previously did not attract criminal liability:

> This implies that constituent elements of an offence such as e.g. the particular form of culpability required for its completion may not be essentially changed, at least not to the detriment of the accused, by the case law of the courts. (para. 9)

On the other hand, no objection can be taken where the courts merely clarify the existing elements of an offence and adapt it to new circumstances which can reasonably be brought under the original concept of the offence.

It is clear from the case law of the Court and Commission that the mere fact that legal advice may be needed to appreciate the precise definition or scope of a criminal offence will not necessarily take it outside the reasonable certainty test. So, for example, in *Cantoni* v *France* (15 November 1996) the Court concluded that, with legal advice, inconsistent case law on the meaning of 'medicinal product' could be clarified.

4.3   RETROSPECTIVITY

The principle of non-retrospectivity in Article 7 is reflected in domestic law where, in the absence of express words in a statute to the contrary, there is a

---

[2] Prior to July 1990, a husband had enjoyed immunity from criminal liability for raping his wife: *R* v *R* [1991] 4 All ER 481.
[3] *SW and CR* v *UK* (1995) 21 EHRR 363, para. 36/34.
[4] Ibid, para. 43/41.

presumption that the penal provisions in legislation are not intended to have retrospective effect.[5] The War Crimes Act 1991, which gives courts retroactive jurisdiction in relation to a number of offences committed in Germany or a place under German occupation during the Second World War, is protected from challenge under Article 7(1) by the qualification in Article 7(2):

> This article shall not prejudice the trial and punishment of any person for any act or omission which, at the time when it was committed, was criminal according to the general principles of law recognised by civilised nations.

The *travaux préparatoires* indicate that Article 7(2) was intended 'to make it clear that Article 7 does not affect laws which, under the very exceptional circumstances at the end of the Second World War, were passed to punish war crimes, treason and collaboration with the enemy, and does not aim at any legal or moral condemnation of those laws'.[6]

The retrospective imposition of heavier penalties — also prohibited by Article 7(1) — has caused greater difficulties. In *Welch* v *UK* (1995) 20 EHRR 247, the applicant was convicted of drug offences committed in 1986. In addition to a sentence of imprisonment, the trial judge imposed a confiscation order pursuant to the Drug Trafficking Offences Act 1986, the operative provisions of which came into force in January 1987. This, the applicant complained, constituted the imposition of a retrospective criminal penalty contrary to Article 7.

The Court took the view that the concept of a penalty in Article 7(1) is, like the notion of civil rights and obligations and criminal charge in Article 6(1), an autonomous Convention concept: to render the protection offered by Article 7 effective, the Court must remain free to go behind appearances and assess for itself whether a particular measure amounts in substance to a penalty. Factors relevant to this assessment are: whether the measure in question was imposed following conviction for a criminal offence; the nature and purpose of the measure in question; its characterisation under national law; the procedure involved in the making and implementation of the measure; and its severity (para. 28). Since the imposition of a confiscation order under the 1986 Act was conditional upon a conviction for one or more drug trafficking offences, and taking into account the fact that the 1986 Act was introduced to overcome the inadequacy of the existing powers of forfeiture, the Court concluded that there had been a violation of Article 7 in *Welch* v *UK*.

---

[5] *Waddington* v *Miah* [1974] 1 WLR 683.
[6] See: Harris, O'Boyle and Warbrick, *Law of the European Convention on Human Rights*, 1st ed. (London: Butterworths, 1995), p. 282.

The decision in *Taylor* v *UK* [1998] EHRLR 90 went the other way. There the applicant was convicted in 1994 of drug trafficking between 1990 and 1993. He was imprisoned and a confiscation order made in relation to trafficking dating back to 1974. The Commission distinguished *Welch* v *UK* on the basis that the applicant, when committing offences between 1990 and 1993, was aware of the possibility that a confiscation order could be made because the 1986 Drug Trafficking Offences Act 1986 had come into force by then. On that basis the complaint was declared inadmissible.

4.4 SUBSTANTIVE CHALLENGES TO THE CRIMINAL LAW

Subject to Article 7 and the procedural requirements of Articles 5 and 6, Convention states are free, in principle, to apply the criminal law to acts which are not carried out in the normal exercise of one of the rights protected under the Convention. This proposition was first advanced by the Court in the context of military disciplinary proceedings in *Engel and others* v *Netherlands* (1976) 1 EHRR 647 and affirmed in the context of ordinary criminal proceedings in *Salabiaku* v *France* (1988) 13 EHRR 379 at para. 27. On that basis, the criminalisation and punishment of drug trafficking is unlikely to raise any substantive Convention issue.

The position is different, however, where criminal offences overlap with Convention rights; particularly those contained in Articles 8 to 11. In such cases, the Strasbourg institutions will require any interference with a Convention right to be 'necessary in a democratic society' in pursuit of a legitimate aim. The tension between sexual activity classified as criminal in Convention states and the Convention protected right of privacy provides a classic example.

In *Norris* v *Ireland* (1988) 13 EHRR 186 the Court held that maintaining in force legislation prohibiting homosexual acts committed in private between consenting adult men constituted an interference with the applicant's right to respect for his private life under Article 8.[7] On the question of whether such legislation was 'necessary in a democratic society', the Court noted that the authorities had refrained from enforcing the law in respect of private homosexual acts between consenting adult males. There was no evidence that this had been injurious to moral standards in Ireland or that there had been any demand for stricter enforcement of the law. In light of this, the Court took the view that the Irish Government could not maintain that there was a 'pressing social need' to make such acts criminal offences. Although persons who regarded homosexuality as immoral might be offended by private homosexual acts, this could not on its own warrant the application of penal sanctions when only consenting adults were involved. The Court therefore found that there had been a breach of Article 8.

---

[7] Following its judgment in *Dudgeon* v *UK* (1981) 4 EHRR 149.

A like result followed in *Sutherland* v *UK* [1998] EHRLR 117 where the applicant complained that fixing the minimum age for lawful homosexual activities at 18, rather than 16 (the minimum age for heterosexual activities), violated his right to respect for his private life and was discriminatory. The Commission agreed. It noted that the body of medical opinion supported the proposition that sexual orientation in both sexes was fixed at 16 and that men aged 16–21 were not in need of special protection from homosexual 'recruitment'. In its opinion the argument advanced by the Government — that 'society's claimed entitlement to indicate disapproval of homosexual conduct and its preference for a heterosexual lifestyle' justified the measures in question — did not constitute either an objective or a reasonable justification for an inequality of treatment under the criminal law between homosexuals and heterosexuals.

In *Laskey* v *UK* (1997) 24 EHRR 39 the applicants complained that their prosecution and convictions for assault and wounding in the course of consensual, sado-masochistic activities between adults was in breach of Article 8. However, the Court accepted the Government's assertion that a state is entitled to punish acts of violence and that the criminal law can legitimately be used to deter certain forms of behaviour on public health and moral grounds. It held (at para. 43) that:

> ... one of the roles which the state is unquestionably entitled to undertake is to seek to regulate, through the operation of the criminal law, activities which involve the infliction of physical harm. This is so whether the activities in question occur in the course of sexual conduct or otherwise.

In deciding whether to prosecute, the state was entitled to have regard not only to the actual seriousness of the harm caused, but also to the potential for harm inherent in the acts in question (at para. 46).

How these Convention principles translate into domestic law is not altogether clear. But it seems, in addition to the s. 3, HRA 1998 requirement to interpret all legislation compatibly with the Convention rights, that s. 6 could be invoked. A court convicting and sentencing a defendant in breach of his Convention rights would be acting unlawfully under s. 6(1), unless protected by s. 6(2).

Equally, it seems that s. 7 could be invoked. Introducing s. 7 of the HRA 1998, both the Lord Chancellor and the Home Secretary indicated that Parliament intended, among other things, that under s. 7 individuals should be able to raise their Convention rights as a defence in criminal proceedings (see Hansard HL, 3 November 1997, col. 1232 (Lord Chancellor) and Hansard HC, 16 February 1998, col. 780 (Home Secretary)). Obviously, this could only apply where the offence in question restricted a Convention protected activity, such as free speech.

Chapter Five

Surveillance: General Principles and the Police Act 1997

Quincy Whitaker

5.1 SURVEILLANCE: GENERAL PRINCIPLES

Surveillance by the police (or any other intelligence gathering agency) can take a number of forms, including telephone tapping, the interception of communications, the use of covert listening devices and the use of visual surveillance equipment. Most of these activities 'interfere' with the right to privacy protected by Article 8 of the European Convention on Human Rights. That, of itself, does not mean that such activities are prohibited under the Convention: the prevention of crime and the protection of the rights of others are legitimate grounds for interfering with Article 8 rights.

However, it does mean that all forms of covert surveillance must be justified in accordance with Article 8(2) of the Convention, i.e.:

- The activity in question must be 'prescribed by law'. This means that the applicable legal rules must be accessible (unpublished internal guidelines are not sufficient) and formulated with sufficient precision to enable citizens to foresee — if need be with appropriate advice — the consequences of their actions.
- The activity in question must be necessary and proportionate. This means that surveillance should be restricted to that which is strictly necessary to achieve the required objective. What is legitimate for the prevention and detection of serious crime may not be legitimate for less serious crime. And, broadly speaking, intrusive surveillance should not be used where less intrusive measures are capable of achieving the same or similar results.

- There must be proper methods of accountability over both the authorisation and the use of police surveillance and other information gathering activities.
- There must be remedies for those whose privacy has been wrongly invaded.

These requirements have been developed over a long series of cases before the European Court of Human Rights and it is clear that the applicable standards are becoming gradually stricter (see, for example, *Amann* v *Switzerland* (2000) 30 EHRR 843).

In *Huvig* v *France* (1990) 12 EHRR 528, where a judge authorised a senior police officer to tap the applicant's business and private telephone lines and the resultant information was then used against him in criminal proceedings for attempted armed robbery and abetting a murder, the Court found a breach of Article 8 for a combination of the following reasons:

(a) The categories of people liable to have their telephones tapped was not defined.
(b) The categories of offence for which telephone tapping could be authorised was not defined.
(c) There were no limits on the duration of telephone tapping.
(d) No rules existed about disclosure of records created in the course of telephone tapping, in particular, disclosure to the defence.
(e) No rules existed to govern the destruction of information obtained by telephone tapping, in particular where proceedings against a suspect were not pursued and/or he or she was acquitted on criminal charges.

Moreover, the European Court recognises that as technology advances it is increasingly easy for the police and other public authorities to abuse their powers of surveillance. Recently it has maintained that having clear rules covering the issues outlined in *Huvig* v *France* is only the starting point. The rules must also establish how, in practice, they are to be carried into effect.

In *Kopp* v *Switzerland* (1998) 27 EHRR 91 the applicant was a lawyer whose telephone communications were intercepted even though he himself was not a suspect but because he was a 'third party' with whom it was believed those suspected would be in contact. The Swiss court ordered that 13 telephone lines be monitored, including the applicant's private and professional lines. Although the order expressly mentioned, in accordance with Swiss law on legal professional privilege, that 'the lawyer's conversations [were] not to be taken into account', the Court found a breach of Article 8 because the law did not make it clear how legal professional privilege was to be protected in practice.

The Court's view was that, since telephone tapping (and other forms of communication interception) constitutes a 'serious interference' with private life, particularly in light of increasingly sophisticated technology, it must be based on 'law' that is particularly precise. It is essential to have clear, detailed rules on the subject. Although Swiss law provided a number of safeguards, including the provision intended to protect legal professional privilege, the Court discerned:

> ... a contradiction between the clear text of legislation which protects legal professional privilege when a lawyer is being monitored as a third party and the practice followed in the present case. Even though the case law has established the principle ... that legal professional privilege covers only the relationship between a lawyer and his clients, the law does not clearly state how, under what conditions and by whom the distinction is to be drawn between matters specifically connected with a lawyer's work under instructions from a party to proceedings and those relating to activity other than that of counsel.

In this regard, the Court found it 'astonishing' that the task of distinguishing between privileged and non-privileged matters should be left, under Swiss law, to an official of the Post Office's legal department, without supervision by an independent judge. On that basis it found that Swiss law did not indicate with sufficient clarity the scope and manner of exercise of the power to intercept telephone conversations.

In the UK, establishing a legal framework for the exercise of surveillance powers has been a slow process. Sucessive governments adopted a piecemeal approach to a series of adverse decisions in Strasbourg. The Interception of Communications Act 1985 was passed as a result of the decision in *Malone* v *UK* (1984) 7 EHRR 14, the Police Act 1997 was passed when it became clear that the UK would lose the case of *Govell* v *UK* (App. No. 27237/95, 14 January 1998)[1] and the Regulation of Investigatory Powers Act 2000 is, at least in part, a reaction to the decision in *Halford* v *UK* (1997) 24 EHRR 523.

However, the legislative scheme for surveillance is now comprehensive. Surveillance which involves covert entry upon or interference with property or wireless telegraphy is covered by Part III of the Police Act[2] and is considered in this chapter. All other forms of covert surveillance are covered by the Regulation of Investigatory Powers Act 2000 and are discussed in chapters 6, 7 and 8.

5.2   THE SCHEME OF THE POLICE ACT 1997

Part III of the Police Act 1997 is designed to create a system of control and authorisation for intrusive surveillance techniques which would otherwise

---

[1] See also *Khan* v *UK* (App. No. 35394/97, 12 May 2000).

[2] Part III was brought into force on 22 February 1999 (Police Act 1997 (Commencement No. 6) Order 1999 (SI 1999/3240).

involve some form of unlawful conduct on the part of the police. So, for example, s. 92 provides that no entry on or interference with property or with wireless telegraphy shall be unlawful if it is authorised under the 1997 Act. However, surveillance methods not in themselves unlawful, e.g., the use of long-range microphones or telescopic lenses, were not made subject to the requirements of the 1997 Act and were not put on a statutory footing until the Regulation of Investigatory Powers Act 2000 came into force.[3]

For surveillance involving entry on or interference with property or with wireless telegraphy, the government initially sought only to formalise the existing system of authorisation by chief officers, set out in the Home Office Guidelines criticised by the European Court of Human Rights in *Govell* v *UK* and *Khan* v *UK*. However, this met with widespread opposition and eventually a substantial amendment was adopted.[4]

As a result, under the 1997 Act, prior authorisation is required where the property concerned is a dwelling or hotel bedroom or where the action is likely to result in any person acquiring knowledge of material protected by legal professional privilege, confidential personal information or confidential journalistic material.[5] In all other situations the matter is determined by an 'authorising officer' (a Chief Constable or equivalent)[6] who may authorise intrusive police action where he is satisfied the action is necessary because 'it is likely to be of substantial value in the prevention or detection of serious crime, and that what the action seeks to achieve cannot reasonably be achieved by other means' (s. 93(2)). Whether Part III of the 1997 Act complies with Article 8 has never been conclusively determined.

5.3 THE REQUIREMENTS OF NECESSITY AND PROPORTIONALITY

During the Debate Stage a Labour amendment was tabled to replace the requirement of 'substantial value' in s. 93(2) of the Police Act 1997 with

---

[3] See chapter 6.

[4] Parliamentary opposition to the Government's original proposals (HL Bill 10 of 1996–7: the amended Bill that went to the House of Commons was HL Bill 88 of 1996–7), whereby authorisation was to be provided by the Chief Constable alone, comprised a coalition of Liberals, cross-benchers and a number of Law Lords.

[5] See s. 97. The scheme for protected material follows the Police and Criminal Evidence Act (PACE) 1984, ss. 9–14 although under the 1984 Act an application for a search warrant involving protected material is made to a circuit judge who can hear evidence on oath where there are disputed questions of fact involved. The Commissioner by contrast under the 1997 Act can only hear the police version of events. There is no provision for hearing evidence and the matter is to be determined by hearing representations alone.

[6] Section 93(5). In the case of the RUC and the Metropolitan Police the functions may be performed by the Deputy Chief Constable and Assistant Commissioner respectively.

'necessary'. This would mirror the test under Article 8. However, the amendment was withdrawn on the basis of an assurance that 'proportionality' would be addressed in the Code of Practice issued under s. 101. Clause 2.3 of the Code of Practice[7] provides:

> A person giving authorisation should first satisfy him/herself that the degree of intrusion into the privacy of those affected by the surveillance is commensurate with the seriousness of the offence. This is especially the case where the subject of the surveillance might reasonably assume a high degree of privacy, for instance in their homes or where there are special sensitivities ...

This goes some way to fulfilling the requirement of proportionality.

The definition of 'serious crime' in the 1997 Act mirrors that in the Interception of Communications Act 1985, s. 10(3) and the Intelligence Services Act 1994, s. 5(3B). It provides that conduct will amount to 'serious crime' where an offence involves 'the use of violence, results in substantial financial gain, or is conduct by a large number of persons in pursuit of a common purpose' or where a person with no previous convictions could reasonably be expected to be sentenced to three years or more (s. 93(4)). Without the Code of Practice, this definition may have breached Article 8 of the Convention on grounds of proportionality. It was pointed out in the Debate Stage by Lord Browne-Wilkinson that the definition was wide enough to encompass most organised groups of protesters and that minor offences such as obstruction of a police officer or criminal damage could become 'serious crime' simply because a large number of persons were acting together.[8]

It is also possible that, as originally drafted, the 1997 Act would not have complied with Article 8, due to the lack of independence in the mechanism for regulating intrusive surveillance powers.[9] Safeguards against abuse are vital under Article 8. Although nothing in the Convention requires that authorisation for surveillance be given by a judicial officer, the European Court has held that, in principle, supervisory control should be exercised by such an officer. Other safeguards may suffice provided they are independent and vested with sufficient powers to exercise an effective and continuous control.[10] The fact that, as finally enacted, commissioners under the 1997 Act must be senior High Court judges at least fulfils this requirement.

Moreover, the system of independent Commissioners and Tribunals established under the Security Service Act 1989 and the Intelligence Services Act 1994 has

---

[7] In force 22 February 1999, *Police Act 1997 (Authorisation of Action in Respect of Property) (Code of Practice) Order 1998* (SI 1998/3240).

[8] House of Lords, 11 November 1996, Second Reading, Hansard, cols 811–12.

[9] See *Govell* v *UK* [1999] EHRLR 101, regarding the Police Complaints Authority and its inadequacy as an effective remedy.

[10] *Klass and others* v *Germany* (1978) 2 EHRR 214 at para. 67.

been found sufficient to discharge the United Kingdom's Convention responsibilities.[11] Nonetheless, it remains to be seen whether the regime of authorisation under the 1997 Act is compliant with Article 8 in all other respects. Notably, the Act does not require prior authorisation in all circumstances. In cases of urgency,[12] or where the owner of premises consents (even though it is not his or her privacy that is being intruded upon), no prior authorisation is needed.

5.4 PROTECTED MATERIAL

Like the Police and Criminal Evidence Act 1984, the Police Act 1997 has a special regime for intrusive surveillance touching on protected material (albeit not with such extensive protection as set out in PACE). However, the procedural safeguards are less extensive. Under PACE an application for a search warrant involving protected material is made on notice to a circuit judge who can hear evidence on oath if there are disputed questions of fact. Under the Police Act 1997, by contrast, the Commissioner only hears the grounds and circumstances advanced by the agency seeking authorisation. There is no provision for hearing evidence and the matter is determined by representations alone.

Protected material falls into three categories: legally privileged information, confidential information and journalistic material. All three are treated in the same way.

5.4.1 Legally privileged information

Legal privilege is defined in s. 98 in broadly the same terms as it is under PACE (s. 10) and the common law exceptions (concerning unauthorised possession and the furtherance of a criminal purpose)[13] to the otherwise absolute nature of privilege[14] are similarly preserved. Thus prior authorisation to bug a solicitor's office is not required where the authorising officer believes that the lawyer/client relationship is being abused for a criminal purpose. This creates the potential for abuse and it is difficult to see why the Commissioner should not, at least, determine whether the exception applies. Strasbourg jurisprudence makes clear

---

[11] *Esbester* v *United Kingdom* (1994) 18 EHRR CD 72.

[12] Section 97(3). In such cases surveillance may be carried out on the authority of the authorising officer alone.

[13] *R* v *Cox and Railton* (1884) 14 QBD 153. Communication to facilitate or guide a client in the commission of a criminal offence is not privileged but this is to be distinguished from advice warning of the risk of committing an offence arising from a particular course of action: *Butler* v *Board of Trade* [1971] Ch 680.

[14] The absolute nature of privilege was emphasised in *R* v *Derby Magistrates' Court, ex parte B* [1996] 1 AC 487 where the House of Lords held that the court had no power to order production of a privileged document at all in the absence of waiver by the client.

that compliance with Article 6 requires protection for confidential legal communications. Drawing on the UN Rules for the Treatment of Prisoners annexed to a Council of Europe resolution, the Court has read confidentiality of legal communications into Article 6 and has held that eavesdropping on such communications violates one of the basic requirements of a fair trial in a democratic society.[15]

5.4.2   Confidential information

The second category of protected material under the Police Act 1997 is confidential personal information. Material falling within this category is narrower than under the common law.[16] That is because the 1997 Act only classifies material as confidential if it fulfils the three requirements laid down in s. 99: that it was acquired in the course of a business, trade or profession; that it relates to the physical or mental health of the individual or to spiritual assistance or counselling they have received; and that it was acquired subject to an express or implied undertaking to hold it in confidence or subject to a statutory restriction on disclosure. Thus prior authorisation will be required if the police intend to conduct intrusive surveillance upon the premises of a doctor, counsellor or priest[17] but not in relation to other areas protected by the general law of confidence, such as credit status, commercial and financial information or personal diaries.

5.4.3   Confidential journalistic material

The third protected area concerns confidential journalistic material. The relevant section, s. 100, protects material received in confidence and held for the purposes of journalism, by requiring the prior authorisation of the independent Commissioner. However, the material must be in the possession of the person who acquired or created it for the purposes of journalism if it is to be protected. Thus material deposited by a journalist with a third party will not be covered by the section. Additional protection may be provided through the requirement of authorisation where access is sought to 'office premises' (s. 97(2)(a)(ii)).

---

[15] *S* v *Switzerland* (1991) 14 EHRR 670.

[16] At common law the tort of breach of confidence protects any information that is held or obtained subject to a duty of confidentiality. For the requirements to mount an action for breach of confidence see *Malone* v *Metropolitan Police Commissioner (No. 2)* [1979] Ch 344.

[17] In addition to the inclusion of 'spiritual counselling or assistance' in the statutory definition (defined in the Code as conversations with a minister of religion falling short of the sacramental confession), an undertaking was given that the police and other agencies to which Part III applies will not use surveillance measures in circumstances covered by the seal of confession (Code of Practice, para. 2.4 and Standing Committee F, 11 March 1997, Fifth Sitting, Hansard, cols 137 and 160.

As far as the European Convention is concerned, protection of journalistic sources has long been recognised as one of the essential elements of a free press and thus of democracy itself.[18] The Contempt of Court Act 1981 was enacted following the finding of the European Court that the existing English law was too wide to satisfy the requirements of Article 10 of the Convention.[19] However, even that Act has subsequently been found to have been applied in circumstances which violated the Convention.

In *Goodwin* v *UK* (1996) 22 EHRR 123 the European Court unanimously held that there was a violation of Article 10 on the grounds of proportionality when a journalist was ordered to disclose his sources in relation to confidential commercial information which had been passed to him by an employee of the company to which the information related. The Court found that much of the justification for the order was covered by an injunction against publication (which had not been breached) and the residual interests of the company in ordering disclosure (such as terminating the employment of the source) were outweighed by the 'vital public interest in the protection of the applicant journalist's sources', such protection considered to be 'one of the basic conditions for press freedom' (paras 45 and 39).

Despite these strong statements of principle, the original Bill for the Police Act 1997 contained no special protection for journalists' material. It was pointed out during the Debate Stage that placing listening devices in journalists' offices would enable the police to circumvent the protection provided by the Contempt of Court Act 1981 for confidential sources. As a result, journalistic material was included within s. 97 requiring prior independent authorisation for surveillance. However, in comparison with PACE, which also provides a special regime to protect such material, the protection afforded by the regime under the 1997 Act is considerably weaker.

Some differences, such as the requirement of notice so that the person with custody of the material can be heard on the issue, are inevitable because of the covert nature of the police operation, but others are more difficult to justify. The definition of 'serious crime' (see above at 5.3) covers offences that fall short of the threshold access requirement under PACE of reasonable grounds to believe the commission of a 'serious arrestable offence'.[20] On the existing definition, 'serious crime' under the 1997 Act could exist where the offence did not even amount to an arrestable offence.[21] Use of the 1997 Act in circumstances where the

---

[18] See e.g. *Goodwin* v *UK* (1996) 22 EHRR 123 at para. 39.

[19] *Sunday Times* v *UK* (1979) 2 EHRR 245.

[20] The special procedure for protected material is set out in sch. 1 to PACE. The first set of access conditions relate to serious arrestable offences. However, the second set of conditions applies where a warrant could previously have been issued and does not require that the offence is a serious arrestable one as such. Nearly all applications have been made under the first set; see Zander, *The Police and Criminal Evidence Act 1984*, 3rd ed. (London: Sweet & Maxwell, 1995), p. 29.

[21] I.e. an offence for which a person could be sentenced to five or more years in prison, or where the statute specifically provides; s. 24, PACE.

police could not have obtained access to information under PACE may be difficult to justify under the Human Rights Act 1998.

Journalism itself is not defined in either the Police Act 1997 or PACE. It appears to cover all forms of publication, which may cause difficulties in relation to the Internet. It remains to be seen where the line is drawn between a journalist and a person posting material on the Web.

Chapter Six

The Interception of Communications

Quincy Whitaker

6.1 INTRODUCTION AND BACKGROUND

The Regulation of Investigatory Powers Act (RIPA) 2000 governs the interception of communications. It replaces the Interception of Communications Act (IOCA) 1985, which followed the adverse ruling of the European Court of Human Rights in *Malone* v *UK* (1984) 7 EHRR 14.[1] It put most, but not all, interception of communications on a statutory footing.

The IOCA 1985 made it an offence to intercept any post or telecommunication being transmitted on a public system, save where the interception was carried out under the authority of a warrant issued by the Home Secretary or where either party to the communication consented. The product of any such (lawful) intercepts could not, however, be relied upon as evidence in court (s. 9). This scheme was held to comply with the requirements of legality in the case of *Christie* v *UK* (1993) 78-A DR 119. But it had a number of failings. Most significantly, it only covered interceptions of 'public' telecommunication systems and this led to a further adverse ruling in *Halford* v *UK* (1997) 24 EHRR 523,[2] because the applicant, the Assistant Chief Constable of Merseyside, had a tap put on her office telephone line, which, being an internal and therefore private line, was not covered by the provisions of the IOCA 1985. Thereafter, new legislation was inevitable.

---

[1] *The Times*, 6 March 1985, described the Bill as an act of 'dumb insolence' in which the minimum action possible was taken to comply with the letter of rulings under an international agreement.

[2] The intercept was installed in order to collect evidence to be used against Ms Halford, the most senior woman police officer in the UK at the time, at the forthcoming hearing of her claim for sexual discrimination. The claim was thereafter settled with an agreement that Ms Halford would take early retirement receiving a pension and a six-figure lump sum payment.

6.2   THE REGULATION OF INVESTIGATORY POWERS ACT 2000 — AN INTRODUCTION

Significant changes to the IOCA 1985 were first proposed in the consultation paper, *Interception of Communications in the UK* (Cm. 4368), published in June 1999. The RIPA 2000 incorporates most of the changes proposed in that paper and, the Government asserts, goes beyond what is strictly required for human rights purposes. It is also intended to provide for the changed nature of communications since 1985 and to implement Article 5 of Council Directive 97/66.[3]
    In publishing the Bill, the Home Secretary, Jack Straw, said:

> The Human Rights Act and rapid change in technology are the twin drivers of the new Bill. None of the law enforcement activities are new ... what is new is that for the first time the use of these techniques will be properly regulated by law, and externally supervised, not least to ensure that law enforcement operations are consistent with the duties imposed on public authorities by the European Convention on Human Rights.[4]

Part I of Chapter I of the RIPA 2000 repeals the IOCA 1985 and replaces it with a similar scheme which generally prohibits interception of post and telecommunications, subject to certain exceptions. However, it also covers interception of communications by private telecommunication systems. There are similar (but not identical) provisions as under the IOCA preventing information gained from interceptions being used as evidence.

6.3   INTERCEPTIONS

Section 1(1) of the RIPA 2000 creates a criminal offence[5] where a person 'intentionally and without lawful authority [intercepts], at any place in the UK, any communication in the course of its transmission by means of a public postal

---

[3] Article 5 of the European Telecommunications Data Protection Directive (97/66/EC) deals with confidentiality of communications prior to its expected implementation date of October 2000. The Home Secretary issued guidelines to cover the situation prior to the RIPA 2000 coming into force whereby he suggested that employers rely on the notion of 'implied consent' through warning employees or customers that their calls could be monitored and thereby defeating any 'expectation of privacy' (Home Office Circular 15/1999, *Interception of non-public telecommunications networks*).

[4] Home Office Press release, *Regulation of Investigatory Powers Bill published today*, 10 February 2000.

[5] The maximum penalty on summary conviction is the statutory maximum fine (currently £5,000); and two years or an (unlimited) fine, or both, upon conviction on indictment (s. 1(7)). By s. 1(8), the consent of the Director of Public Prosecutions is required to institute any proceedings.

service or public telecommunication system'. A postal service is defined as any postal service which is offered or provided to, or to a substantial section of, the public in any one or more parts of the UK (s. 2(1)). It is unclear whether the DX system falls within this definition. It does seem clear, however, that the definition does not cover internal office mail. 'Public telecommunication system' is similarly defined in terms of provision to the public. Hence, it is irrelevant that the service is provided by a private company.

Section 1(2) extends the legislation to cover 'private telecommunication systems' in order to comply with the *Halford* judgment. A criminal offence is created where a person 'intentionally and without lawful authority ... intercepts any communication in the course of its transmission by means of a private telecommunication system', subject to the exceptions or subject to it being conducted by a person 'who has a right to control the operation or the use of the system' and where there is 'implied or express consent' (s. 1(6)(a), (b)).

Private telecommunication systems are essentially defined in the negative as any system which is not public but is 'directly or indirectly' attached to a public system. An office network linked to a public system by a private exchange internal system would fall within the definition, but a self-standing system, such as a secure office intranet for instance, would not.[6]

However, only civil, rather than criminal, liability will be incurred where a person intercepts a private system which he or she has the right to control or where he or she is acting pursuant to the permission of such a person (s. 1(3)). Examples (provided by the Government) are where an individual in a household uses a second handset to monitor a telephone call and where a large company in the financial sector routinely records calls from the public in order to retain a record of such transactions.[7] The RIPA 2000 provides that the civil tort is actionable at the suit of either the sender, recipient or intended recipient of the intercepted communication. So where an employee believes that his or her employer has unlawfully intercepted a telephone conversation with a third party, either the third party or the employee may sue the employer.[8]

'Telecommunication system' is defined widely as any system which exists for the 'purpose of facilitating the transmission of communications by any means involving the use of electrical or electro-magnetic energy' (s. 2(1)). For these purposes this is to be taken to include 'any time when the means by which the communication is being, or has been, transmitted is used for storing it in a manner that enables the intended recipient to collect it or otherwise have access to it' (s. 2(7)). Thus the definition is intended to be wide

---

[6] See Explanatory Notes, Regulation of Investigatory Powers Bill, 27 April 2000.
[7] Ibid, para. 25.
[8] Section 1(3) and see Explanatory Notes (above at footnote 8), para. 21.

enough to include communications from a mobile telephone,[9] a portable telephone (i.e. where the base unit is connected to a land line) and e-mail, Internet and pager messages.[10]

6.3.1 'Lawful authority'

An intercept will not give rise to criminal or civil liability if it is done with 'lawful authority', defined in s. 1(5). Lawful authority includes interception under a warrant and also:

(a) where there are reasonable grounds for believing that both the sender and the recipient consents (s. 3(1));

(b) where one party consents and surveillance has been authorised under Part II of the RIPA 2000 (s. 3(2)); known as 'participant monitoring';

(c) where the interception is by the provider of a postal service for the provision of that service or the enforcement of any enactment of that service (s. 3(3)), e.g., opening a letter to determine the return address; and/or where the intercept occurs for the purposes of s. 5 of the Wireless Telegraphy Act 1949;[11]

(d) where the interception is carried out for the purpose of obtaining information about the communications of a person who is believed to be outside the UK and relates to the use of a public telecommunications system provided to persons in such a country, and the provider of the service is required by the law of the relevant country to carry out or facilitate the interception (s. 4(1));

(e) where the interception is authorised by regulations made by the Secretary of State in relation to business communications (s. 4(2));

(f) where the interception is carried out in the exercise of powers conferred under s. 47 of the Prison Act 1952[12] or similar legislation in Scotland and Northern Ireland, or in relation to high security psychiatric hospitals

---

[9] On the reasoning of *R* v *Ahmed* [1995] Crim LR 246, where the Court of Appeal held that 'the interception of a communication takes place when, and at the place where, the electrical impulse or signal which is passing along the telephone line is intercepted in fact', it is arguable that mobile phones fell outside the ambit of the IOCA 1985 although the view of the Home Office was that such communications did indeed fall within the purview of the statute.

[10] These three were only covered by the previous regime to the extent that they were carried on a public system.

[11] Concerned with misleading messages and interception and disclosure of wireless telegraphy messages (s. 3(4) and (5)).

[12] Section 47 is the general power for the Secretary of State to make rules. Standing Order 5B(34) provides that all calls using cardphones may be monitored and stopped on the same grounds that a letter may be stopped. Standing Order 5G(2B) prohibits any calls to the media which are intended for publication or broadcast. A challenge to this blanket ban by a prisoner was declared inadmissible by the European Commission on the grounds it was 'manifestly ill-founded' as the authorities could not otherwise exercise effective control (*Bamber* v *UK* [1994] COD 562).

pursuant to any direction given under s. 17 of the National Health Services Act 1977 (s. 4(4), (5));

(g) where the interception is conducted in relation to stored communications pursuant to a statutory power that is exercised for the purpose of obtaining information or taking possession of documentation (s. 1(5)(c)), e.g., an order from a circuit judge under sch. 1 to PACE.

Subject to certain exceptions, s. 17 of the RIPA 2000 prohibits evidence, questioning or assertion in (or for the purposes of, or in connection with) legal proceedings likely to reveal the existence or absence of a warrant.[13] The exceptions are set out in s. 18. In particular, s. 18(4) allows the disclosure of the contents of a communication if the interception was lawful without the need for a warrant by virtue of ss. 1(5)(c), (3) or (4). This means that interception carried out in those circumstances may be evidential. In addition, s. 18(7) allows the disclosure of the fact and contents of an interception to a person conducting a criminal prosecution. It is intended to allow the intercepting agency to give the prosecutor access to any intercept material which has not been destroyed so that he can discharge his duty to act fairly. Disclosure can also be made to a judge in exceptional circumstances (s. 18(8)). The judge can then direct the prosecution to make such admissions of fact as he or she thinks essential in the interests of justice (s. 18(9)). However, any admission must not tend to suggest that an interception has taken place (s. 18(10)). Different rules apply in relation to lawful interceptions in another country (*R* v *P* (2000) *The Times*, 19 December; *R* v *X, Y and Z* (2000) *The Times*, 23 May).

6.4 CONSENT

As noted above, an intercept will have 'lawful authority' where one party consents and surveillance has been authorised under Part II of the RIPA 2000. However, this distinction between consensual and non-consensual intercepts does not sit happily with some Convention case law. In a recent case, the European Court held that, as a matter of principle, Article 8 protects people not telephone lines. Otherwise, it reasoned, the situation could develop whereby:

> a very large number of people are deprived of the protection of the law, namely all those who have conversations on a telephone line other then their own. That would in practice render the protective machinery largely devoid of substance.[14]

---

[13] See *Interception of Communications in the UK*, response of the CBA/Bar Council Working Party. See also, *JUSTICE, Response to Consultation Paper*, para. 4.1 and the comments by W. G. Carmichael, member of Interception Communications tribunal. Cf. *An Analysis of Responses To The Government Consultation Paper* (Cm. 4368), ch. 8.

[14] *Lambert* v *France* [1999] EHRLR 123 at para. 38.

Similarly, in Canada, where the Canadian Criminal Code required a warrant for electronic surveillance generally but not where the informer was wired up to record conversations with a suspect, the Supreme Court held that there had been a violation of the defendant's right to privacy. Delivering the judgment of the Court, La Forest J stated:

> I am unable to see any logic to this distinction between third party electronic surveillance and participant surveillance ... the assessment whether the surreptitious recording entrenches on a reasonable expectation of privacy must depend on whether the person whose words were recorded spoke in circumstances in which it would be reasonable for that person to expect that his or her words would only be heard by the person he or she was addressing.[15]

6.5   MONITORING FOR BUSINESS PURPOSES

Under the RIPA 2000 the Secretary of State may by regulations authorise any conduct which reasonably appears to him to constitute a legitimate practice reasonably required for business purposes.[16] In relation to such interceptions the Government's view is that, provided employees are told that their calls may be listened to, no issues under Article 8 arise as the employees are presumed to have impliedly consented to such a course.[17]

However, the European Court has made clear that there is 'no reason of principle why this understanding of the notion of private life should be taken to exclude activities of a professional nature'.[18] Mere 'consent' may not, therefore, prevent the application of Article 8. In its response to the consultation paper to the Bill, *JUSTICE* argued that, in order to comply with the requirements of proportionality and necessity, and any meaningful notion of implied consent, employers would have to provide guidance to employees about the circumstances in which monitoring might occur, why it is necessary and what use will be made of the information.[19]

---

[15] *R* v *Duarte* [1990] 53 CCC (3d) 1. Section 184.2 of the Canadian Criminal Code now requires judicial authorisation for the interception of a private communication even where a party consents.

[16] Article 5 of Directive 97/66/EC (the Telecommunications Data Protection Directive) exempts from its prohibition on interception 'any legally authorised recording of communications in the course of lawful business practice for the purpose of providing evidence of a commercial transaction or of any other business communication'. The Government is, at the time of writing, engaged in a consultation process on draft lawful business practice regulations. Details can be obtained from the DTI website at http://www.dti.gov.uk/cii/regulation.html

[17] See the guidance issued by the Home Secretary intended to cover the situation prior to the RIPA 2000 coming into force: Home Office Circular 15/1999, *Interception of non-public telecommunications networks*.

[18] *Niemietz* v *Germany* (1992) 16 EHRR 97.

[19] *JUSTICE's Response to the Government Consultation Paper, 'Interception of Communications in the United Kingdom'*, para. 1.7.

Where it applies, the Data Protection Act 1998, sch. 1, para. 1, requires that data users explain to both customer and employee what use can be made of their data where it would not be obvious to them. OFTEL licensing regulations already require that efforts are made to ensure that parties whose conversation is being recorded are made aware of the fact.

6.6 THE WARRANT PROCEDURE

6.6.1 Authority to issue warrant

Despite representations to the contrary,[20] the Government was 'not persuaded'[21] of the need to depart from the pre-existing procedure whereby intercept warrants are authorised by the Secretary of State. As with the previous regime under the IOCA 1985, warrants are issued by the Secretary of State upon application by a restricted group of people.[22] In cases of urgency or for the purposes of providing assistance under an international mutual legal assistance agreement, a warrant of limited duration can be authorised by a senior civil servant; however, in the former case the Secretary of State must have expressly authorised the issue of the warrant in that particular case (s. 7(2)). The relevant Code of Practice details the information which must be provided when a warrant is applied for.[23]

The position of the European Court of Human Rights is that 'it is in principle desirable to entrust supervisory control to a judge'[24] and judicial oversight is the operative principle in a number of other countries including Canada, the USA, New Zealand and most European Union member states. Indeed the principle of judicial oversight was accepted in the warrant regime of the Police Act 1997. The

---

[20] See e.g. *Under Surveillance, Covert Policing and Human Rights Standards, JUSTICE* 1998. Liberty and the Data Protection Commissioner also supported judicial authorisation, see *The Regulation of Investigatory Powers Bill*, House of Commons Library Research Paper 00/25, 3 March 2000.

[21] Home Office Consultation Paper, *Interception of Communications in the United Kingdom*, Cm. 4368, June 1999.

[22] Section 6, RIPA 2000 lists the class of people who can apply for a warrant, who are generally all of Chief Constable rank, although Chief Constables in England and Wales (other than the Commissioner of the Metropolitan Police) are required to apply to the Director of the National Criminal Intelligence Service who in turn applies to the Secretary of State. Only organisations with a recording centre are permitted to apply for a warrant and this is located at NCIS in relation to forces in England and Wales.

[23] Interception of Communications and Accessing Communications Data, Code of Practice, para. 5.2.

[24] *Klass and others* v *Germany* (1978) 2 EHRR 214 at para. 56. See also *Huvig* v *France* (1990) 12 EHRR 528 at para. 33, 'The Court does not in any way minimise the value of the safeguards, in particular the need for a decision by an investigating judge, who is an independent judicial authority.'

number of applications has been rising steadily[25] and Her Majesty's Inspectorate of Constabulary recently stated 'we should move away from the notion that applications for warrants are a rare event'.[26] Increasingly it is impractical for the Home Secretary to exercise any effective scrutiny over their content and this breakdown of accountability can deprive citizens of effective protection against abuse in this area of far-reaching state surveillance.

Her Majesty's Chief Inspector of Constabulary has queried, 'If intrusive surveillance can be authorised by a commissioner, why not the interception of communications?'[27] The sole answer provided by the Government was that since it would still be necessary for the Home Secretary to issue warrants on the grounds of a threat to national security there would be an undesirable parallel authorisation scheme.[28] However, such schemes operate effectively in other countries such as Australia and a parallel regime already exists in the UK in relation to intrusive surveillance under Part III of the Police Act 1997 and the Intelligence Services Act 1994.

6.6.2   Grounds on which warrants are issued

The grounds on which a warrant can be issued have been drafted to comply with Article 8. Under s. 5 of the RIPA 2000, the Secretary of State must not issue an interception warrant unless he believes that interception is necessary for one of the stated reasons (national security, prevention or detection of serious crime, safeguarding the economic well-being of the UK or to give effect to any international mutual assistance agreement) and proportionate to the end sought to be achieved. One of the matters which must specifically be taken into account is whether the information to be obtained under the warrant could reasonably have been obtained by other means. However, it is arguable that this test is too weak and that there should exist a positive obligation on the part of the investigating authorities to show that other methods have failed, or are bound to fail, as is the case under sch. 1 to PACE where access is sought to confidential or other sensitive material.

Neither 'national security' nor 'economic well-being' are defined under the RIPA 2000 and both are capable of subjective interpretation. Liberty has argued that 'if activity is so great a menace to society as to justify interference with fundamental rights of the citizen, one would expect it to be prohibited by the

---

[25] The increase according to an IOCA Commissioner is largely attributable to smaller police forces recognising the potential of such intercepts in the fight against crime; *Annual Report of the Interception of Communications Commissioner for 1996*, June 1997, Cm. 3678, chapter 56, para. 10.

[26] Consultation Paper on the Interception of Communications in the United Kingdom: HMIC, *Observations on the proposed legislation.*

[27] Ibid.

[28] Home Office Consultation Paper, *supra*, ch. 7.

criminal law, with the definitional certainty that attracts' but its proposal that the 'prevention or detection of serious crime' be the sole criterion for which intercepts be authorised was rejected by the Government.[29] The economic well-being ground is currently limited to information concerning people outside the British Isles and although this restriction was criticised by a member of the Interception of Communications Tribunal,[30] presumably the fraudulent activities of the City trader that he feared might adversely affect sterling would fall within the definition of serious crime. 'Serious crime' bears the same definition[31] as it does under the Police Act 1997 and therefore the same issues with regard to Article 8 compatibility arise:[32] see above at 5.3.

6.6.3 Exemption for privileged material

Issues connected with legal privilege are dealt with in the Codes of Practice (s. 6 of the draft Code) which still remain in draft form at the time of writing.[33] The Government chose not to follow the preferable approach of setting such matters out in the legislation itself, as is the case with ss. 98–100 of the Police Act 1997.

6.6.4 Contents of warrants

The new statutory regime requires that the warrant specify either the person or the premises to be intercepted (s. 8(1), RIPA 2000). In a change from the previous scheme, one warrant can authorise interception of all premises relating to the named person. The warrant must be accompanied by one or more schedules setting out the addresses, telephone numbers, apparatus or other factors that are to be used in identifying communications to or from the relevant person or premises (s. 8(2)). These requirements, however, do not apply to certain interceptions where the Secretary of State has used the certification procedure under s. 8(4) (see below at 6.6.5, s. 8(3)–(5) and s. 15).

JUSTICE has recommended that the Secretary of State should have the power to add conditions to warrants to satisfy the proportionality requirement in Article 8. Such conditions are commonplace in most Commonwealth countries. For example, data published in Canada shows that the vast majority (95 per cent) of

---

[29] See Liberty Second Reading Briefing, *supra*.

[30] See comments by W. G. Carmichael on the Consultation Paper, 21 July 1999, available at http://www.homeoffice.gov.uk

[31] Serious crime is an offence for which a person aged 21 years or over with no previous convictions could reasonably be expected to be sentenced to three years or more, or where the conduct involves the use of violence, results in substantial financial gain or is conduct by a large number of persons in pursuit of a common purpose; s. 81(2) and (3), RIPA 2000.

[32] See the Liberty Second Reading briefing, *Regulation of Investigatory Powers Bill*, 28 February 2000, for criticism of the serious crime definition, in particular the 'common purpose' rule.

[33] The expected implementation date is Spring 2001, but see *JUSTICE*'s response for a detailed critique of the Draft's provisions in this area — www.justice.org.uk.

authorisations for electronic surveillance have conditions attached and this power is considered to account for the low rate of refusal for warrant applications among Canadian judges.[34] Certainly the more specific and limited the interference is the more likely it is to satisfy the proportionality test.

6.6.5 Certificated warrants and external communications

The RIPA 2000 retains the notion of certified warrants, which disapply some of the safeguards in relation to certain categories of interception. Most controversially, s. 8(4) disapplies the requirements to describe either the person or the premises in the warrant where the interception is of 'external communications' and the Secretary of State has issued a certificate providing a description of the intercepted material and certifying that examination of the material is necessary in the interests of national security, for the prevention/detection of serious crime or for the purpose of safeguarding the economic well-being of the United Kingdom.

'External communications' are defined in s. 20 as 'a communication sent or received outside the British Islands'. If the intercepted line or 'trunk' is an undersea cable or microwave beam which physically leaves the UK most of the traffic will come within the definition of 'external'. But some internal communications may also be caught. Communications that are sent and received in the UK may travel outside the UK for part of their journey (very common with Internet providers). The Government frankly admitted during the passage of the Bill that in such circumstances 'there is no way of filtering that out without intercepting the whole link, including the internal link. Even after interception, it may not be practically possible to guarantee to filter out all internal messages. Messages may well be split into separate parts which are sent by separate routes.'[35]

Nonetheless it was the stated intention of the Government that certificated warrants should be 'aimed at external communications' and protection was to be provided first through the certificate itself, which allows anything not within its terms to be intercepted but not to be 'read, looked at or listened to by any person'. It is not clear exactly how the exercise of identifying material within the terms of the certificate is to be undertaken without first reading it unless it is anticipated that this can all be done electronically.

In addition, s. 16 of the RIPA 2000 provides for 'extra safeguards in the case of certificated warrants' governing the selection of material to be read, looked at or listened to which should not be referable to an individual known for the time being to be in the British Isles, subject to certain exceptions. This clause

---

[34] *JUSTICE, Response to the Consultation Paper*, para. 3.9.
[35] 12 July 2000, Hansard, col. 323.

(described by one member of the House of Lords as 'hideously complicated'),[36] was the subject of various unsuccessful attempts during the debate to restrict the extent of the exceptions. The most controversial exception provides the Secretary of State with the power to certify that communications intercepted pursuant to a certificated warrant (limited to a three-month period) are searched by reference to an individual in the UK where it is necessary in the interests of national security, for the prevention or detection of serious crime or for the purpose of safeguarding the economic well-being of the UK. It has been argued that these definitions are wide enough to permit indiscriminate searches in the UK in relation to, for example, the activities of the anti-capitalist demonstrations in the City and football hooligans, as such activities certainly affect the economic well-being of the UK.[37] However, presumably in such circumstances the restriction in s. 5(5) would be operative: that section prohibits a warrant from being considered necessary on the grounds of safeguarding the economic well-being of the UK unless the information relates to the acts or intentions of a person outside the UK. This procedure is intended to cover the situation where for instance a foreign criminal or spy is plotting abroad but also has someone working on his behalf, sending solely internal communications. In such a situation intercepts of the internal and external communications would be covered by the certificated warrant where the Secretary of State has certified that the exception applies.

This procedure replaces 'overlapping warrants', a term coined by Lord Lloyd in his capacity as Interception Commissioner under the Interception of Communications Act 1985 when he sanctioned the non-statutory practice of an ordinary warrant being issued in tandem with a certificated warrant so as to intercept both internal and external communications on broader grounds than the statutory restriction of anti-terrorism. The legality of this practice was questioned during the debate in the House of Lords, where one opposition peer raised the question of how the targeted names or addresses required for an ordinary warrant are to be obtained without an unlawfully broad trawl.[38] However, the Government is of the view that the need for dual purpose warrants will continue to arise, and this is the reason for the inclusion of the modified procedure in the RIPA 2000, in circumstances where an ordinary warrant 'cannot be put into effect in any other way, for example, when a person in the United Kingdom chooses, perhaps in an attempt to avoid interception, to use a foreign internet service provider'.[39] This implies that where a target is using a foreign ISP, it cannot be served with an interception warrant but the target's communications (inside the UK) can still be picked up by GCHQ bulk trawling. Internal e-mails sent by the target within the UK would still be internal and therefore outside the scope of a certificated warrant

---

[36] Lord Cope of Berkley, ibid, col. 321.

[37] Lord Lucas, ibid, col 321.

[38] Ibid, col. 319.

[39] Letter from Lord Bassam of Brighton to Lord Phillips of Sudbury, quoted in ibid, col. 319.

unless the Secretary of State were to certify that the exception applied, in which case under the RIPA 2000 both situations are covered by a single certificated warrant.

6.6.6   Duration, cancellation and modification of warrants

The duration of a warrant is extended under the RIPA 2000 to three months from the two months specified under the IOCA 1985 and there appears to be no discretion for the Secretary of State to issue warrants for a lesser period.[40] Indeed the Interception of Communications Commissioner criticised the practice at the Foreign and Commonwealth Office of issuing warrants for less than the statutory period. He was of the view that the IOCA 1985 did not permit such flexibility and the only option was for the Minister to cancel the warrant once the grounds for it no longer applied, as he is statutorily obliged to do.[41] However, there seems to be no good reason for this restriction and proportionality suggests that interference with a person's private life be limited to a minimum. The Secretary of State can renew a warrant for six months while the warrant is still valid provided it is accompanied by a statement stating that the renewal is necessary on statutory grounds (s. 9(3)(b), RIPA 2000). Under s. 10 the Secretary of State may modify the provisions of a warrant or a certificate under s. 8(4).

6.7   DUTIES FOR COMMUNICATION SERVICE PROVIDERS

Under s. 11 of the RIPA 2000 new duties are imposed on Communication Service Providers (CSPs) whereby they are required to do everything reasonably required of them to give assistance to the police to effect an interception in accordance with a warrant. Under s. 12 the Secretary of State may require the installation of a reasonable permanent intercept capability by persons who provide a public postal or telecommunications system.

The details of how a reasonable intercept capability is to be determined, and the vexed question of who is to pay for the technology, are still subject to negotiation between the Government and the CSPs although the Government did bow to opposition pressure and create an independent Technical Advisory Board to advise the Secretary of State (s. 13). The figure of £20 million was cited in the debate as the level of the Government's contribution although there appeared to be no firm estimate of the likely cost overall of installing the capability.[42]

The Government further stated during the debate that it did not expect to make any requirement to provide a permanent intercept capability to service

---

[40] Section 9(6)(c). The period is five days with respect to a warrant issued under the hand of a senior official under s. 7(2)(a) (s. 9(6)(a); see above at 6.6.1.).

[41] *Interception of Communications Act 1985: Report of the Commissioner for 1998*, June 1999, Cm. 4364 at pp. 9, 10.

[42] 19 July 2000, Hansard, cols 1025–7.

providers that deal only with the financial services industry.[43] There is also provision for grants for the costs of installing and maintaining an intercept capability to be met from public funds (s. 14). A criminal offence is created where a person knowingly fails to comply with this duty and he or she is rendered liable to two years' imprisonment or a fine, or both, upon conviction on indictment (s. 11(7)). The duty is enforceable at the behest of the Secretary of State in civil proceedings for an injunction or for specific performance of a statutory duty (s. 11(8)).

6.8 METERING

Metering concerns the collection and retention of information about the use made of telephones rather than the content of the conversation. It includes details of the person making the call, details of the recipient of the call, and the date, time and duration of calls. 'Dynamic metering' enables the police to receive information while the call is taking place, such information being used particularly in relation to mobile phones. This practice was not covered by the IOCA 1985 but instead was governed by the Telecommunications Act 1984, s. 45 and the Data Protection Act 1998, s. 29, which contain a 'permissive' regime facilitating access to data where the relevant operators agreed: whether this was compliant with Article 8 is open to question.[44]

6.9 ACQUISITION AND DISCLOSURE OF COMMUNICATIONS DATA

Chapter II of Part I of the Regulation of Investigatory Powers Act 2000 (not in force at the time of writing) creates a framework to regulate access to communications data by investigating bodies. Section 21(4) lists various matters that are included in the definition of 'communications data', including the subscriber's details, the names, addresses and numbers of those contacted and websites visited. Data in relation to a postal item is defined as 'anything written on the outside of the item' which it seems would include a recorded delivery barcode and presumably the records to which the code relates.[45] The Act replaces

---

[43] Ibid, col. 1024.

[44] Section 29 of the Data Protection Act 1998 (s. 28 of the 1984 Act) permits telephone companies to release personal data where they are satisfied that not to do so would be likely to prejudice crime detection/prevention or the prosecution/apprehension of offenders or tax assessment/collection. It is difficult for companies to make any realistic assessment as to whether the strict criterion of prejudice has been met. The Data Protection Registrar in her Response to the Government Consultation Paper stated that s. 29 'does not provide a satisfactory basis for large scale disclosure'; Dep 99/1773, para. 8.1, also available at http://www.homeoffice.gov.uk/oicd/iocresp.htm

[45] The view of the Government Minister, Lord Bassam, in reply to a specific question on this point, was 'I suppose that the answer must be yes but I shall ponder it', 12 July 2000, Hansard, col. 264.

the permissive provision for disclosure by the holder of such data with a requirement to comply with a properly authorised request.[46]

The regime permits disclosure on broader grounds than under the warrant procedure, on the underlying assumption that metering represents a lesser intrusion on a person's privacy than actual interception of the communication. The additional grounds of disclosure include (s. 22(2)):

- preventing crime or disorder (with no requirement of seriousness);
- public safety;
- protection of public health;
- collecting any tax or levy payable to a government department;
- preventing or mitigating any damage to a person's mental or physical health; or
- any other ground that is specified in an order made by the Secretary of State.

These are potentially very wide grounds, particularly in the light of the catch-all provision for additional purposes to be added, and all uses will have to be strictly scrutinised to ensure they are legitimate for Article 8 purposes. In particular, the collection of taxes or other government levies is not a ground set out in Article 8(2) of the Convention and so, unless the activity falls under one of the other heads (such as the prevention or detection of crime), it may not amount to a justifiable interference with Article 8 rights.

In an effort to comply with Article 8, the RIPA 2000 enshrines the twin concepts of proportionality and necessity, which must be satisfied before the 'designated person' can require disclosure (ss. 22(5), 23(8)). The authorisation procedure is at a lesser level than is required for interception of communications. The designated person is defined as an individual holding such office in a relevant public authority (NCIS, NCS, Customs and Excise, any of the intelligence services, the Inland Revenue) as may be specified in an order made by the Secretary of State (s. 25(1)).

The regulations designating the level at which such authorisation may be made are likely to be published when this part of the RIPA 2000 is brought into force; however, it is likely to be at the same level as required for authorising covert surveillance under Part II, namely at the rank of Superintendent or above. Once again the Act provides the Secretary of State with an unlimited power[47] to add other additional public authorities which will be able to authorise disclosure. It is not clear that this process of self-authorisation within an agency will suffice for all purposes under Article 8. In the case of *Kopp* v *Switzerland* (1998) 27 EHRR 91

---

[46] Section 22(4) and (6). The duty is enforceable by civil proceedings or in an action for specific performance of a statutory duty under s. 22(8).

[47] Subject only to the affirmative resolution procedure.

(see further above at 5.1) the Court found a violation of the Convention where Swiss law left the task of distinguishing between privileged and non-privileged matters to an official of the Post Office's legal department, without supervision by an independent judge.

It is debatable whether the Government's underlying assumption that the provision of such data inherently involves a lesser intrusion on a person's privacy is correct.[48] The European Court made it clear in *Malone v UK* (1984) 7 EHRR 14 that Article 8 was relevant even to a print-out of a list of numbers called (essentially the limited nature of the data available in 1984). The broad nature of the category of people able to authorise disclosure of data, coupled with the extensive grounds for such authorisation, provide the potential for intrusive activities to take place on a widespread scale without sufficient independent scrutiny. Metering technology has undergone rapid change in recent years, rendering it more effective and intrusive, and this has increased calls for communications data to be subject to the same regime as interceptions, as is the case in America and Canada where judicial authorisation is required for both.[49]

The Data Protection Registrar recommended that the grounds for wishing to obtain communications data should be subject to prior external scrutiny, preferably by a judge or at least an independent person or body.[50] The RIPA 2000 does not provide for judicial scrutiny but the operation of the communications data regime will be included in the remit of the new Interception Commissioner appointed under s. 56.

In contrast to the intercepted material obtained under Chapter I of the 2000 Act, there is no restriction on the use that can be made of communications data.

6.10   ACCOUNTABILITY

6.10.1   The Commissioner

It was originally proposed that two new offices of Commissioner be created under Part IV of the RIPA 2000 to deal with the interception of communications and covert investigations, adding to the five already existing,[51] whose remits are expanded to cover activities under the Act (ss. 59, 61 and 62). However, following the tabling of an Opposition amendment that enjoyed both Conservative and Liberal Democrat support, the Government agreed to some rationalisa-

---

[48] See Liberty's Second Reading Brief on the RIPA Bill for a view that this assumption is misconceived and a recommendation that the sole ground be for the prevention or detection of serious crime as that organisation recommended in relation to the interception.

[49] See *JUSTICE's Response to the Government Consultation Paper*, para. 6.

[50] Data Protection Registrar's Response, para. 8.2.

[51] Intelligence Services Commissioner, Security Service Commissioner, Chief Surveillance Commissioner, Investigatory Powers Commissioner for Northern Ireland.

tion.[52] However, the distinct roles of each Commissioner are maintained because in the Government's view an amalgamation of their functions would 'risk obscuring the lines of accountability and compromising their expertise'.[53]

Thus the Interception Commissioner will oversee the use of interception of communication powers. The use of other surveillance methods under the Act will be overseen by the Intelligence Services Commissioner (who has been amalgamated with the Security Service Commissioner) in the case of MI6, MI5, GCHQ and MOD;[54] and by the Surveillance Commissioner (appointed under the Police Act 1997) in the case of the police etc., Customs and Excise and other authorities given powers under the Act. The initial proposal to create a Covert Investigations Commissioner was shelved and this role was brought within the office of the Surveillance Commissioners.

This goes some way towards giving effect to the view of the Chief Surveillance Commissioner, Sir Andrew Leggatt, who suggested during the consultation process that the work of agencies using intercepts against serious crime would be greatly simplified if they could make all their applications through one office. He also suggested bringing the Interception of Communications Commissioner within the purview of the Surveillance Commissioners in order to rationalise anomalies such as the responsibility assigned to him under the Police Act 1997, s. 93, for oversight of wireless telegraphy.[55]

The Interception of Communications Commissioner[56] must be a person who has held high judicial office, and his role is to oversee the exercise of the powers of the Secretary of State in authorising warrants for intercepts and the extent to which the Secretary of State has fulfilled the statutory duties imposed on him (s. 57). A statutory duty is imposed on a category of people to co-operate with the Commissioner and he or she is required to report any contraventions of the Act to the Prime Minister (s. 58(1), (2)). The Government proposal initially lacked any statutory provision for the Commissioner to be equipped with staff; however, following Opposition criticism, staff are provided through the secretariat. Provision is made for Commissioners to authorise that any of their functions be carried out by their staff. The Government refused, however, to be drawn on the extent of the delegation that was to be permitted, stressing that it was a matter for the Commissioners to determine.[57]

---

[52] House of Commons, 8 May 2000, Hansard, col. 532.

[53] Ibid.

[54] Both functions were in any event previously entrusted to the same person. It was announced on 12 April 2000 that Simon Brown LJ had been appointed to both posts.

[55] See *Response on behalf of Office of Surveillance Commissioners to Consultation Paper on Interception of Communications in the United Kingdom*, 13 August 1999.

[56] Lord Nolan of Brasted was the Commissioner from 1994 to 2000. On 17 May 2000 it was announced that he would be succeeded by Swinton-Thomas LJ. The appointment is for three years which was renewed in Lord Nolan's case following the resignation of his predecessor Bingham LJ after two years in the post.

[57] House of Commons, 8 May 2000, Hansard, col. 534.

The Act requires the Commissioner to publish a report on the carrying out of his functions once a year. This report is to be laid before Parliament, subject to the Prime Minister excluding matters in the public interest. Where this exclusion power is exercised, a statement made by the Prime Minister to that effect must accompany the report (s. 58(4)–(6)). The Commissioner's sanction is limited to this reporting mechanism: he has no power to quash a warrant if it has not been authorised or the circumstances no longer apply, unlike the Surveillance Commissioner in the discharge of his functions under the Police Act 1997. This illustrates the unjustified anomalies and lack of accountability which are a persistent feature of the legislation in this area.

The adequacy of the reporting procedure under the similar regime under the IOCA 1985 in fulfilling any aspiration of transparency has been questioned.[58] Clearly the effectiveness of such a measure relies on the comprehensiveness of the information that is placed in the public domain, and yet the information currently provided can provide a misleading picture. Only Home Office and Scottish Office warrant figures are made public (excluding e.g. those of the Foreign Office and Northern Ireland Office) and the Commissioner himself has repeatedly stated that even these figures can fail to convey the reality, since one warrant can cover an entire organisation, and the figures do not reveal the extent of interception that does not require a warrant (such as participant monitoring). The lack of detail required in the UK compares unfavourably with the procedure in other countries, such as Australia, New Zealand and the United States[59] where the law requires a breakdown of the information, including the number of applications refused, the average duration of warrants, the categories of serious crime involved and statistics on the effectiveness and cost of the operations.[60] An example of the comparative quality of the information available in the UK is to be found in relation to the number of warrants provided under the counter-subversion head. In his report for 1995, Lord Nolan stated that 'the amount of warrants issued under [this] head remains very small'; in his reports for 1996 and 1997 he stated that no warrants were in existence under this head, whereas his report for 1999 is silent on the issue for the first time in three years: the inference to be drawn is perhaps obvious.[61] From his 1998 report it can be seen that there was an increase of over 50 per cent in the number of warrants issued in England and Wales since 1996; this 'substantial increase' is apparently due to what is obliquely referred to as 'an increase in the interception facilities available'.[62] It is not possible to identify whether this is due to the interception of e-mail traffic for instance or a

---

[58] *JUSTICE, Response to Consultation Paper*, paras 5.8 to 5.10.

[59] See e.g. the US annual federal wiretap report which provides information on all these issues together with a 236-page annex containing a breakdown per warrant. Available at http://www.uscourts. gov/wiretap98/contents.html

[60] See *Under Surveillance, Covert Policing and Human Rights, JUSTICE*, 1998, pp. 22, 23.

[61] See *Statewatch* May–August 1999 (vol. 9 no. 3), September 1999.

[62] Report of the Commissioner for 1998, Interception of Communications Act, Cm. 4364.

straightforward increase in the number of individuals or organisations whose telephones are being tapped.

6.10.2   The tribunal

In addition to the reporting function of the Commissioner, the other method of accountability is the creation of a tribunal under s. 65 of the RIPA 2000. This tribunal amalgamates the previously existing separate tribunals established under the Security Service Act 1989, the IOCA 1985, the Intelligence Services Act 1994 and the Police Act 1997.

The jurisdiction of the new tribunal is as follows:

(a)   as the sole forum to determine proceedings brought under s. 7 of the Human Rights Act 1998 involving the intelligence services or any use of investigatory powers under the RIPA 2000 or any other entry on or interference with property or interference with wireless telegraphy;

(b)   to determine any complaints received by a person who believes he or she has been subject to investigatory powers under the Act or other entry on property etc. by the intelligence services in 'challengeable circumstances' (s. 65(7));

(c)   to determine any reference by a person that he has suffered detriment by virtue of the prohibition imposed by s. 17, RIPA 2000 in civil proceedings on any matter;

(d)   to determine such other proceedings as may be allocated by order of the Secretary of State.

The complaints jurisdictions under the Security Services Act 1989, the Intelligence Services Act 1994 and the Police Act 1997 are abolished. Members of the tribunal must hold or have held high judicial office and have had ten years' experience as a practitioner and are appointed for a renewable five-year period. The President of the tribunal must hold or have held high judicial office and he is required to designate at least one member as having special responsibility for matters involving the intelligence services (sch. 3, para. 1(1)–(3)).

When a complaint concerning surveillance activity governed by the Act is made to the tribunal, it must investigate whether the person against whom the complaint is made has engaged in any such conduct, investigate the authority (if any) for the action and determine the complaint by reference to judicial review principles (s. 67(2)). On determining any complaint the tribunal has the power to make any award of compensation or other order that it sees fit. This includes quashing the warrant or ordering the destruction of any information which has been obtained under the warrant (s. 67(7)).

In terms of providing an effective remedy for the purposes of Article 13 of the ECHR, the tribunal procedure was considered adequate by the Commission in the cases of *Esbester* v *UK* (1994) 18 EHRR CD 72, *Harman and Hewitt* v *UK* (1989) 67 DR 88 (although this case did lead to MI5, MI6 and GCHQ being placed on a statutory footing) and *Christie* v *UK* (1993) 78-A DR 119. These decisions were relied upon by the Government as a reason for not introducing any significant change to the procedure under the RIPA 2000[63] although it did note that the fact that the IOCA Tribunal has never upheld a complaint was 'a matter of concern for many respondents [to the consultation exercise]'.[64] The Government, however, did not consider the effect of the later cases of *Chahal* v *UK* (1996) 23 EHRR 413, *Tinnelly* v *UK* (1998) 27 EHRR 249 and *Smith and Grady* v *UK* (2000) 29 EHRR 493 in assessing whether the limitation of the function of the tribunal to a judicial review jurisdiction does ensure compatibility with Article 13.

Although judicial review can in some cases provide a sufficient basis for scrutiny under the Convention,[65] in the case of *Chahal*, the European Court found that judicial review did not provide an effective remedy in relation to deportations that were ordered on the grounds of national security. The Government argued that the remedy was as effective as it could be given the need to rely on secret sources of information. The European Court disagreed. It held that there was a violation of Article 13 as 'the notion of an effective remedy under Article 13 requires independent scrutiny of the claim that there exist substantial grounds for fearing a risk of treatment contrary to Article 3' (1997) 23 EHRR 413 at paras 150 and 151. This decision was however in the context of a potential Article 3 violation and recognised the importance that the Court attached to the prohibition on treatment which violates the Article.

Following the decision in *Chahal*, procedures were adopted under the Special Immigration Appeals Commission Act 1997 whereby where it is sought to deport a person on the grounds of national security, a special advocate is appointed to represent the interests of the potential deportee and rules require that the applicant be given a summary of the submissions and evidence. It has been suggested that this would be a more suitable model for the new tribunal[66] but, far from adopting this procedure, the rule-making power under s. 69(4) includes a power for the Secretary of State to make rules for the tribunal to hear any proceedings without the person bringing them having been given full particulars of the reasons for any conduct that is the subject of the complaint.

The rule-making power covers all aspects of the tribunal's procedure, including the power to make rules concerning matters of evidence, the mode and burden of

---

[63] See the Government Consultation Paper.
[64] Analysis of Responses to Government Consultation Paper, ch. 9.
[65] See for instance *Vilvarajah* v *UK* (1991) 14 EHRR 248 and *Soering* v *UK* (1989) 11 EHRR 439.
[66] See *JUSTICE's Response to the Consultation Paper*, para. 5.3.

proof, legal representation and the disposal of complaints which are considered to be frivolous and vexatious. Normally the rules must be approved by a resolution of both Houses of Parliament but the Act provides that where such rules are first made, they are to be made under the 40-day procedure[67] which ensures that the tribunal is operational as soon as the substantive provisions in the Act are brought into force.

6.10.3   Other aspects of accountability

The RIPA 2000 does not provide for a notification procedure whereby subjects are notified following completion of the surveillance activity, which inevitably impacts on the effectiveness of any accountability structure. A further difficulty arises under RIPA in that a strict interpretation requires that the person bringing the proceedings identify which agency is effecting the interception. This could present a serious hurdle to a person in securing effective examination of a complaint.

The Act provides one further limb of protection against abuse through the creation of a duty of confidentiality. This duty is imposed on a defined category of people (police, civil servants, postal and telecommunications workers) and an offence of unauthorised disclosure of any details relating to the warrant or the contents of the intercepted material is created by s. 19. A person is liable to five years' imprisonment or a fine, or both, on conviction on indictment. There is a special defence where the disclosure is made in circumstances of legal professional privilege (s. 19(6), (7)).

6.11   INTERCEPTION OF COMMUNICATIONS IN PRISONS

Interception of communications between prisoners and their legal advisers by the prison authorities may breach Article 8 for the reasons set out above (see 5.4.1). The requirement that any interference be 'prescribed by law' means that the relevant regulations must be accessible and foreseeable. In *Petra* v *Romania* (23 September 1998, ECtHR) the European Court held that Article 8 was breached where prison regulations governing the interception of prisoners' communications were unpublished. Further the Court held that regulations permitting the authorities to retain any material 'unsuited to the process of rehabilitating a prisoner' were too vague for compliance with Article 8. In the past the former practice in the UK of opening all prisoners' correspondence was held to violate Article 8 on the grounds of proportionality because the lesser measure of opening only such letters reasonably considered to contain prohibited material would suffice.[68]

---

[67] Section 69(9)–(11). The 40-day procedure validates instruments for 40 days unless before the end of the period they are approved by a resolution of both Houses of Parliament.
[68] *Campbell* v *UK* (1992) 15 EHRR 137.

Chapter Seven

Surveillance and Covert Human Intelligence Sources under the Regulation of Investigatory Powers Act 2000

Quincy Whitaker

7.1 INTRODUCTION

Part II of the Regulation of Investigatory Powers Act 2000[1] is intended to place covert surveillance on a statutory footing in the areas not already covered by Part III of the Police Act 1997 (i.e., where there is no physical interference with or entry on property by the police; see above at 5.2) or the Intelligence Services Act 1994 (similarly where such action is taken by the Intelligence Services). The Government implicitly acknowledged during the passage of the Bill that a non-statutory basis for covert policing would breach the HRA 1998 (Hansard HC, Vol. 345, col. 677). Unlike the regime in relation to the interception of communications, however, the RIPA 2000 does not create a duty on public authorities to obtain authorisation for surveillance and no specific criminal or civil offence is created if surveillance occurs without such authorisation. The explanatory notes accompanying the Act make it clear that any unauthorised interference by a public authority with an individual's Article 8 rights would be unlawful by virtue of s. 6, HRA 1998 (para. 180). The only remedy for a breach of the provisions of the RIPA 2000 in such circumstances would be for the

---

[1] In force 25 September 2000; SI 2000/2543. See further, Jennings, A. and Friedman, D., 'The Future of Covert Policing: Will it Rest in Peace?' [2000] 8 Archbold News 6, 9 Archbold News 6.

affected person to take proceedings under s. 7 of the Human Rights Act 1998 or to have the material declared inadmissible in evidence which may lack a sufficient deterrent effect given the potential for abuse.

The RIPA 2000 covers the use of intrusive techniques by the police, the National Criminal Intelligence Service (NCIS), the National Crime Squad (NCS), Customs and Excise, MI5, MI6 and Government Communications Headquarters (GCHQ). As with Part I of the RIPA 2000, however, the Secretary of State has (by s. 30(5)) an unfettered power to add to this list of agencies (see above at 6.9). In relation to directed (non-intrusive) surveillance, a surprisingly extensive list of Government departments are permitted to authorise such activity, including the Ministry of Agriculture, Fisheries and Food, the Department of Social Security, the Inland Revenue, the Department of Environment, Transport and the Regions, the Department of Health, the Department of Trade and Industry, the Environment Agency, the Financial Services Authority, the Personal Investment Authority, the Food Standards Agency, the Board for Agricultural Produce, the Post Office and all local authorities. Health authorities and NHS trusts can authorise directed surveillance, but not the use of Covert Human Intelligence Sources (see below). In addition, as with Part I of the 2000 Act, the Secretary of State has the power (subject to the affirmative resolution procedure) to add to this list of agencies (currently 36 in number).[2]

7.2   THE SCHEME OF THE RIPA 2000

Part II of the RIPA 2000 creates a two-tier system of authorisation. Greater protections exist in respect of intrusive surveillance than directed surveillance or the use of covert human intelligence sources. It is difficult to understand why it was not thought appropriate to have the same level of protection for the use of covert human intelligence sources as for the use of intrusive surveillance. It is certainly open to question whether the protections which exist in respect of covert human intelligence sources meet the concern expressed by the European Court in *Texeira de Castro* v *Portugal* (1998) 28 EHRR 101. The European Court said that the use of undercover officers must be restricted and safeguards put in place. Section 26 defines these three types of activity:

(a)   *Directed surveillance*: where covert but not intrusive surveillance is undertaken for the purposes of a specific investigation and is likely to reveal private information (including details of a person's private or family life; s. 26(10)), unless it is in circumstances where it would not be reasonably practicable for authorisation to be sought (i.e where the action

---

[2] See the Regulation of Investigatory Powers (Prescription of Offices, Ranks and Positions) Order 2000, SI 2000/2417.

is an immediate response to events; s. 26(2)). Surveillance is defined as 'covert' 'if and only if, it is carried out in a manner that is calculated to ensure that persons who are subject to the surveillance are unaware that it is taking place' (s. 26(9)).

(b) *Intrusive surveillance*: covert surveillance carried out in relation to anything taking place on residential premises or in any private vehicle. The surveillance may be carried out either by a person or by a device. Where the device is outside the premises, it must be capable of providing information of the same quality and detail as might be expected from an internally placed device in order to qualify as intrusive (s. 26(5)) and tracking devices are expressly excluded from consideration as such (s. 26(4), (5)). Equipment used to detect the presence of a television receiver is also excluded from the definition of directed and intrusive surveillance (s. 26(6)). The fact that the criterion under subsection 5 to determine whether the surveillance is intrusive is the recording capability of the device rather than the degree of intrusion may prove problematic in the future.

(c) *Covert human intelligence sources*: A person who establishes or maintains a personal or other relationship with a person for the covert purpose of using such a relationship to obtain information or to provide access to any information to another person, or covertly discloses information obtained by the use of such a relationship (s. 26(7)–(9)).

These definitions have been the subject of some criticism. The Data Protection Commissioner suggested that the definition of intrusive surveillance should be widened to include 'any premises or location where the individual has a legitimate expectation of privacy, for example a doctor's surgery or an MP's private office'.[3] She also suggested that the requirement that the information obtained from external devices be of similar quality to that obtained from an internal one in order to count as intrusive surveillance was unjustified as 'the fact that a picture from a long lens camera might not be quite as clear as from a camera placed in a room does not necessarily make the infringement of privacy any the less'.[4] One can in any event see practical problems in terms of making such an assessment in advance. The Commissioner made the further point that the approach taken under the RIPA 2000 differs from the approach under the Data Protection Act 1998 with regard to when an activity is to be regarded as covert. The approach of the latter is to define matters as covert not based on the intention of those conducting the

---

[3] *Response of the Data Protection Commissioner to the Government's Regulation of Investigatory Powers Bill*, a briefing for Parliamentarians, March 2000, para. 10. The title was changed to Commissioner from Registrar by the Data Protection Act 1998. See also *Niemietz* v *Germany* (1992) 16 EHRR 97.

[4] Ibid, para. 11.

surveillance but according to whether or not the person under surveillance is actually aware.[5]

The Government has made clear that the practice of 'participant monitoring' (where undercover officers and police informers record their telephone conversations in order to obtain evidence against a suspect thereby circumventing the need for a warrant under Part I) is to come within the weaker controls of 'directed surveillance'.[6] However, such surveillance could be highly intrusive and thus breach Article 8.

The attempt to draw a line between 'directed' and 'intrusive' surveillance may bring the operation of the RIPA 2000 into conflict with the requirements of Article 8 as some directed surveillance may nonetheless be considered sufficiently intrusive to warrant greater protection from misuse than is currently provided for under the RIPA 2000 (see below at 7.4). The position could become further confused by the exercise of the power in s. 47 whereby the Secretary of State can by order deem that any 'directed' surveillance be considered intrusive for the purposes of the RIPA 2000.

7.3   GROUNDS ON WHICH AUTHORISATION MAY BE GRANTED

7.3.1   Directed surveillance

The grounds on which directed surveillance and the use of covert intelligence sources may be authorised are wider than those on which a warrant for the interception of communications may be granted. Under s. 28, directed surveillance is not to be authorised unless it is believed to be necessary for one of the grounds set out in the section and it is considered proportionate to the end sought to be achieved. In addition to the familiar grounds of national security, for the purpose of directing or preventing crime or disorder (there is no requirement of seriousness) and in the interests of the economic well-being of the United Kingdom, such surveillance can also be authorised in the interests of public safety, for the purposes of protecting public health, for the purpose of assessing or collecting any tax or levy due to any government department or for any other purpose which the Secretary of State may order (s. 28(3)). The grounds of authorisation in relation to tax or for any purpose for which the Secretary of State may order are not explicitly set out in Article 8(2). The latter ground is one of troubling breadth. As with the permissible grounds for obtaining communications data under Part I, if these grounds cannot be brought within the legitimate objects of Article 8(2), the resulting surveillance may fall foul of the Convention (see above at 6.9).

Much of the detailed guidance as to what matters are of particular relevance are to be found in the Codes of Practice, which remain in draft form at the time of

---

[5] Ibid, para. 12.
[6] *Regulation of Investigatory Powers Bill Explanatory Notes*, para. 179.

writing.[7] Nonetheless, certain areas have been highlighted as of particular relevance. The issue of collateral intrusion on the privacy of others should be given particular consideration, especially where there are special sensitivities (such as premises used by lawyers, or for medical or professional therapy).[8]

Special rules apply in relation to particular types of information, for which it is 'recommended' that authorisation be at the level of Chief Constable (or Assistant Chief Constable in urgent cases):[9]

- *Confidential Material*: matters subject to legal professional privilege, confidential journalistic material ('material acquired or created for the purposes of journalism and held subject to an undertaking to hold it in confidence') and confidential personal information (information held in confidence relating to physical or mental health or spiritual counselling). Any application for authorisation should include an assessment of how likely it is that confidential material will be acquired. Where it is possible that a substantial proportion of the material acquired could be confidential, applications should only be granted in exceptional and compelling circumstances with full regard to the proportionality issues raised.[10] There are general principles which apply in relation to limitations on retention, and dissemination.[11]
- *Seal of Confession*: an undertaking has been given by the police, the National Criminal Intelligence Service and the National Crime Squad not to mount operations covered by the seal of confession. Nevertheless, the draft Codes permit such operations and where it is believed that the surveillance will intrude on spiritual counselling, serious consideration should be given to discussing the matter with the senior representative of the relevant religion, the view of whom will be included in the request for authorisation.[12]

The requirement in the draft Code of Practice on Covert Surveillance that the confidential material must amount to a substantial proportion of the material acquired before authorisation is withheld (except in legal circumstances) may lead to problems under the Convention. Confidentiality of communications between lawyer and client has been held to be one of the 'basic requirements of the right to a fair trial'.[13] In *Kopp* v *Switzerland* (1998) 27 EHRR 91, the European

---

[7] It is anticipated that the final Codes will be implemented in Spring 2001 following the conclusion of the public consultation process — see www.homeoffice.gov.uk for responses to the consultation exercise. These Codes replace the Codes of Practice under the Police Act 1997.

[8] Draft Code of Practice on Covert Surveillance, para. 2.3.

[9] Ibid, para. 3.13.

[10] Ibid, para. 2.10.

[11] Ibid, para. 2.11.

[12] Ibid, para. 2.8.

[13] *S* v *Switzerland* (1992) 14 EHRR 202 at para. 48.

Court stressed that the law must make it clear how professional privilege is to be protected in practice. It also severely criticised the practice of internal executive authorisation without recourse to an independent judge. Arguably, therefore, the self-authorisation (intra-agency) under the RIPA 2000 may not be sufficient for the purposes of Articles 6 and 8.

7.3.1.1   Procedure

There are detailed provisions as to what information should be included in the application for authorisation (including why the surveillance is considered to be proportionate, the extent of collateral intrusion, etc.).[14] Authorisations must be given in writing, unless the case is urgent in which case a statement of the authorising officer must be recorded as soon as is reasonably practicable. The Code of Practice recommends that authorising officers should not be responsible for authorising their own activities.[15] The level of independence of the authorisation is relevant to issues of proportionality and it is difficult to see how an officer authorising his or her own surveillance activities could satisfy Convention requirements. Written authorisations cease to have effect after three months, although they may be renewed repeatedly for additional three-month periods (except in relation to the security or intelligence services where the measure may be renewed for a six-month period) (para. 3.21). Urgent authorisations cease to have effect after 72 hours (para. 3.22).

A single authorisation may combine two or more different authorisations under Part II of the RIPA 2000, or an authorisation under Part II and an authorisation under Part III of the Police Act 1997, or a warrant for intrusive surveillance under Part II and a warrant under s. 5 of the Intelligence Services Act 1994.

7.3.2   Covert human intelligence sources

The use of informants and undercover police officers has been one of the most controversial areas of covert policing. Informants and undercover officers are now subsumed within the unattractively entitled generic term 'covert human intelligence sources'. The draft Code of Practice purports to provide guidance on the use and conduct of covert human intelligence sources. However, the Code rather surprisingly provides no guidance as to the permissible limits of the activities of such individuals. The Code simply states that covert human intelligence sources must operate 'within the limits recognised by law' (para. 2.4). Such advice barely merits the term 'guidance'. It is profoundly unsatisfactory that the Code does not reflect the classic statement of the permissible limits of conduct in such cases by Lord Bingham CJ in *Nottingham City Council* v *Amin* [2000] 1 Cr App R 426 at 431. Lord Bingham CJ said that domestic courts:

---

[14] Draft Code of Practice on Covert Surveillance, para. 3.18.
[15] Ibid, para. 3.10.

recognised as deeply offensive to ordinary notions of fairness if a defendant were to be convicted and punished for committing a crime which he had only committed because he had been incited, instigated, persuaded, pressurised and wheedled into committing it by a law enforcement officer. On the other hand, it has been recognised that law enforcement agencies have a general duty to the public to enforce the law and it has been regarded as unobjectionable if a law enforcement officer gives a defendant an opportunity to break the law, of which the defendant freely takes advantage, in circumstances where it appears that the defendant would have behaved in exactly the same way if the opportunity had been offered by anyone else.

This position can be contrasted with the detailed guidance in the 1969 Home Office guidelines and the ACPO Codes of Practice.

The use of covert human intelligence sources is subject to necessity and proportionality and can be authorised on the same grounds as directed surveillance (s. 29). There are statutory arrangements that are required to be in place when a source is so used: there must at all times be an office holder who is responsible for the day-to-day dealing with the source and for the source's security and welfare; there must be another officer holder who oversees the use made of the source; there must be a person who at all times is responsible for maintaining a record of the use made of the source (indicating any matters as may be specified in regulations made by the Secretary of State); and records revealing the source's identity will not in general be disclosed (s. 29(5)).

There are no geographical limitations on the use of human intelligence sources. The process of 'cultivating a source' (defined as covertly making a judgment as to their likely value and determining the best way of proposing that they become a source)[16] may itself involve infringing the privacy of the potential source, in which case authorisation will be required as with any other directed surveillance (para. 2.11). Where undercover officers represent themselves to be members of another public authority, authorisation as covert human intelligence is not needed unless the officer is acting as a source.[17]

The authorising officer should not grant an authorisation unless he or she is satisfied that there are arrangements in place for ensuring at all times that there is a person with responsibility for maintaining a record of the use made of the source. The matters that are required to be recorded are fully set out in the draft Code of Practice.[18] The Code of Practice suggests that authorisations should be drawn in broad terms to reflect a source's task, and not so narrowly drawn as to require a fresh authorisation each time a handler tasks his source.[19]

A risk assessment relating to the security and welfare of a source should be undertaken by an authorising officer, including an assessment of the likely

---

[16] Draft Code of Practice on the Use of Covert Human Intelligence Sources, para. 2.9.
[17] Ibid, para. 2.2.1.
[18] Ibid, paras 3.12–3.14.
[19] Ibid, para. 3.3.

consequences if the role of the source becomes known to the target. Issues relating to the source's rights under Articles 8 and 3, and possibly Article 2, may arise if the source is harmed.

In addition to the provisions in relation to confidential material, discussed above, higher authorisation is considered 'appropriate' for the following groups:

- *Vulnerable Groups*: for example, the mentally impaired (Code 2-28). Authorisation should be at Assistant Chief Constable level. The use of the mentally impaired as informants was prohibited under the ACPO Codes (Code 3, para. 1-12.1).
- *Juveniles*: the use of juveniles as a source is governed by the Regulation of Investigatory Powers (Juveniles) Order 2000 (SI 2000/2793)[20] which provides that authorisation should be at Assistant Chief Constable level. The Order provides that no authorisation can be granted to use a source under 16 to give information against his or her parents. In other cases, authorisations are not to be granted unless: a risk assessment has been undertaken covering the physical dangers and psychological aspects to their deployment; the officer is satisfied that any risks identified are properly explained; and particular consideration has been given to whether the juvenile is to be tasked to obtain information from a relative or guardian. In addition, the authorising officer must be satisfied that there will at all times be a person responsible for ensuring that an appropriate adult will be present for all the meetings. (See also Code 2-29–31.)

7.3.2.1   Undercover officers

Undercover law enforcement officers are permitted to act covertly in order to:

- infiltrate an existing criminal or terrorist conspiracy;
- arrest a suspected criminal or criminals;
- counter a threat to national security;
- counter a significant threat to public order;
- counter a significant threat to public safety;
- counter a threat to the economic well-being of the United Kingdom (para. 2.18).

Members of foreign law enforcement or other agencies or sources of those agencies may be authorised to be deployed in the UK in support of domestic and international investigations (para. 2.19).

---

[20] In force, 6 November 2000.

7.3.2.2   Technical equipment

Importantly, when such human intelligence sources are themselves carrying surveillance equipment (covert tapes or cameras), the draft Code of Practice provides that its use shall only be considered as intrusive if it is intended that the equipment remains on the premises after the source has left (i.e., that the visit is really a pretext for installing the device).[21] Thus, under the less exacting requirements of self-authorisation, the equivalent highly intrusive behaviour (e.g., recording and filming in a person's home) can be lawfully carried out. One of the anomalies of the fragmented legislative approach in this area is that to install a bug inside or outside the property will require judicial authorisation under the Police Act 1997 or the RIPA 2000, yet to send a person to a property carrying a recording device requires only Superintendent level authorisation. It is difficult to see how this distinction can be justified under Article 8, although it follows the same principle in Part I of RIPA concerning interception of communications, namely that where one party consents to the interception, it is to be considered directed surveillance for the purposes of RIPA.

7.3.2.3   Participating informants — conduct which may be authorised

The RIPA 2000 states that conduct under Part II will be lawful 'for all purposes if the authorisation confers an entitlement to engage in that conduct' (s. 27(1)). This is intended to provide a lawful basis for activity previously lacking statutory regulation, rather than to confer immunity from otherwise illegal criminal activity by making such activity lawful 'for all purposes'. The authorisation does not confer an entitlement to commit criminal actions outside the provisions of the law, although the draft Code rather opaquely states that a 'source may infiltrate or be a party to the commission of criminal offences within the limits recognised by the law'. However, it does clearly state that a source acting beyond the limits of the law will be at risk of prosecution (para. 2.4).

7.3.3   Intrusive surveillance

The grounds on which intrusive surveillance may be authorised are limited to: national security, prevention/detection of serious crime or the interests of the economic well-being of the United Kingdom and subject to the requirements of necessity and proportionality, including a mandatory consideration of whether the informant could reasonably be obtained by other means (s. 32). These grounds are narrower than those in respect of directed surveillance and covert human intelligence sources.

---

[21] Draft Code of Practice on the Use of Covert Human Intelligence Sources, para. 2.34.

7.4   MANNER OF AUTHORISATION

7.4.1   Directed surveillance and the use of covert human intelligence

Under s. 30 of the RIPA 2000, the Secretary of State (and under s. 31, the First and deputy First Minister of Northern Ireland jointly in relation to non-exempt conduct in Northern Ireland) may designate by an order the office holders in the relevant public authority who are capable of authorising directed surveillance and the use of covert human intelligence sources. The current regulations specify Superintendent level within the police force and various grades of civil servant within the relevant government departments.[22] Like many of the detailed controls under Part II, the important question of at what level a person is to be designated to grant authorisations is left unspecified on the face of the Act. Where one agency is acting on behalf of another, it is expected that the tasking agency will obtain authorisation, except where the Seurity Services are acting with another law enforcement agency in the field of serious crime, in which case they should obtain their own authorisation.[23]

7.4.2   Intrusive surveillance

Part II of the Act employs a regime similar to that under Part III of the Police Act 1997 by introducing a hybrid system of self-authorisation coupled with external scrutiny by a Surveillance Commissioner prior to the authorisation taking effect (except in urgent cases).

Under s. 32, the power to authorise intrusive surveillance is given to the Secretary of State and listed 'senior authorising officers' who all hold the rank of Chief Constable or equivalent. However, where the application is from the police, the case is urgent and it is not reasonably practicable to obtain authorisation from a senior authoring officer, the authorisation may be granted by the deputies of each senior office holder (s. 34). Once a person has given (or cancelled) authorisation for the intrusive surveillance to take place, they must notify a Surveillance Commissioner as 'soon as is reasonably practicable' after the grant (or cancellation) of the authorisation specifying any such matters as the Secretary of State 'may by order prescribe' and complying with any arrangements made by the Chief Surveillance Commissioner as are for 'the time being in force' (s. 35). The authorisation does not take effect until the Surveillance Commissioner[24] grants prior approval, except in urgent cases when the authorisation does have effect but the relevant senior authorising officer must notify the Commissioner as soon as is reasonably practicable providing reasons for proceeding

---

[22] The Regulation of Investigatory Powers (Prescription of Offices, Ranks and Position) Order SI 2000/2417; in force 25 September 2000.
[23] See also the draft Covert Surveillance Code of Practice, para. 2.14.
[24] Appointed under the Police Act 1997.

(s. 36). The Commissioner may quash any authorisation if he believes that the relevant criteria have not been met (see above at 6.9) or there are no longer any grounds for believing the criteria have been met (s. 37). A relevant senior officer can appeal to the Chief Surveillance Commissioner against a refusal to approve an authorisation by an ordinary Surveillance Commissioner (s. 38).

7.5   EVIDENCE AND DISCLOSURE

There is no prohibition on the use of material obtained under Part II of the RIPA 2000 as evidence unlike material obtained under Part I. Where the evidence has been obtained in breach of Article 8, the issue will be whether the defendant's right to a fair trial has been violated in all the circumstances — see *Khan* v *UK* (App. No. 35394/97, 12 May 2000) and chapter 16. The Code of Practice makes it clear that material obtained under Part II is subject to normal disclosure obligations under the CPIA 1996. It is likely, however, that compliance with Articles 5 and 6 provides a more extensive obligation of disclosure than had been the pre-existing practice under the CPIA (see chapter 13).

7.6   SURVEILLANCE BY NON-STATE PARTIES

The practice whereby private investigators video claimants in personal injury actions in their homes in the hope of obtaining incriminating evidence may well involve an interference with privacy rights, but such actions would not be provided with a lawful basis under the RIPA 2000. The private investigator may not be a public authority for the purposes of a claim under the HRA 1998,[25] but it may be that the courts' duty to develop the common law in accordance with the HRA 1998 will lead to developments in the law of tort, making such conduct actionable. Investigators acting on behalf of NHS trusts and health authorities, on the other hand, risk incurring liability if they fail to obtain authorisation at the appropriate level for such activity.[26]

---

[25] As to the definition of 'public authority', see the HRA 1998, s. 6(3).
[26] Currently, Chief Executive and Senior Manager Level 4 respectively (SI 2000/2417).

Chapter Eight

The Investigation of Electronic Data

Quincy Whitaker

8.1 INTRODUCTION

Part III of the Regulation of Investigatory Powers Act 2000, which covers the investigations of electronic data (not in force at the time of writing but anticipated to come into force in late 2001), was the most controversial aspect of the Bill's passage through Parliament. The central provisions of Part III contain a power to issue notices requiring disclosure of encrypted material and the creation of an offence of failure to comply with such a notice. The justification for these provisions was that society would suffer if 'criminals are able to use such technology without law enforcement having corresponding powers of decryption' (DTI, Summary of Responses to 'Promoting Electronic Commerce' (Cm. 4477, 1999). Many respondents to the consultation process feared that government access to decryption keys would seriously undermine 'e-commerce and the integrity of service providers, as well as causing huge potential costs in global key revocation and change' (ibid, para. 20).

8.2 NOTICES REQUIRING DISCLOSURE

Section 49(2) and (3) provide that where a 'person with the appropriate permission' believes on reasonable grounds that 'a key to the protected information is in the possession of any person' and that a disclosure requirement is necessary in the interests of national security, for the prevention or detection of crime or in the interests of the economic well-being of the UK, or for securing the effective exercise by any public authority of any statutory power or duty, they may serve a notice requiring disclosure of the material. Before they issue the notice, however, they must be satisfied as to the proportionality of the requirement and that it is not reasonably practicable to obtain the information without giving a notice under this section (s. 49(2)(c), (d)). Section 49(3) may well lack the precise wording and the clear, detailed rules required in respect of such provisions. A statutory basis for such powers is insufficient by itself. The law must be both accessible and foreseeable: *Amann* v *Switzerland* (2000) 30 EHRR 843.

The notice must be given in writing specifying the nature of the protected information, the time by which it must be complied with, and set out the form and content of the disclosure that is required by it (s. 49(4)). The effect of a notice is that the person in possession of the information is entitled to use any key in his possession to obtain access to the information and he is required to make disclosure of the information in an intelligible form. The obligation can be complied with by providing the key itself (s. 50(2)). A direction can be given that the notice can *only* be complied with by provision of the key where a chief officer of police (or equivalent) believes that there are 'special circumstances of the case' which means that to direct otherwise would defeat the purpose of the disclosure requirement and also believes that such a direction is proportionate (s. 51).

The Act had initially been drafted to require disclosure of the key as the first resort but the Government bowed to early Opposition pressure in the Commons on this issue to make disclosure of the key the exception rather than the norm.[1] Nonetheless, it was stated during the debate in the House of Lords that the only other countries with similar legislation were Russia, India and Singapore.[2] It is not clear what would be considered to amount to 'special circumstances' for the purpose of this section. The two examples provided by the Government were: (a) to prove the correspondence between protected information in encrypted and intelligible form; and (b) highly urgent access to protected information.

It has been argued that it would have been preferable to have catered for this first example directly (by requiring the person providing the information in intelligible form to show that the latter is genuine) and that the second example is unrealistic and therefore specious.[3] Despite the significant shift in the emphasis of the legislation it is clear that concerns remain about the use of any power to disclose keys.

Section 49(9) attempts to protect the integrity of signature keys. As access to cryptographic products often permits access to signature keys, this intention will often be defeated. This is recognised in the Code of Practice (para. 8.10). As has been pointed out by Akdeniz, Taylor and Walker [2001] Crim LR 73 at 86, this 'failure to distinguish will undermine the use of digital signatures and hinder the development of e-commerce, conflicting with the intentions of the Electronic Communications Act 2000'.

---

[1] House of Commons, 8 May 2000, Hansard, cols 545–53.
[2] House of Lords, 13 July 2000, Hansard, col. 411.
[3] See Dr B.R. Gladman's annotated version of Part III, dated 4 July 2000, available at http://www.fipr.org/rip

8.3   OFFENCES

8.3.1   Failing to make the required disclosure

An offence of knowingly failing to make the required disclosure is created by
s. 53. Under s. 53(2) a presumption of continued possession arises once initial
possession has been proved unless the accused shows otherwise. However, a
person shall be taken not to be in possession of a key to protected information
if 'sufficient evidence of the fact is adduced to raise an issue with respect to it'
and the contrary has not been proved beyond reasonable doubt (s. 53(3)).
Sufficient evidence to 'raise an issue' does not require evidence that could satisfy
a tribunal on the balance of probabilities and once such an issue has been raised
the offence still requires the prosecution to prove the contrary beyond a
reasonable doubt.

It is a defence to show that it was not reasonably practicable to make the
disclosure within the stipulated time but that disclosure was made as soon as it
was reasonably practicable (s. 53(4)). On conviction on indictment a person is
liable to a fine or two years' imprisonment, or both, and six months' imprisonment
or a fine, or both, on summary conviction (s. 53(5)). Section 53(2) does not now
appear to breach the principles concerning reverse onus clauses set out in *R v DPP,
ex parte Kebilene* [2000] 2 AC 326, HL; *R v Benjafield and others* (2000) *The
Times*, 28 December, CA; *R v Lambert* [2001] 2 WLR 211, CA.

A finely balanced question arises as to whether the privilege against
self-incrimination can be invoked where the key is committed to memory and
disclosure might incriminate the individual concerned. The Government has
argued (Hansard HL, vol. 614, col. 472) that the key has an independent existence,
like bodily samples considered in *Saunders* v *UK* (1996) 23 EHRR 313 at para.
69 (see 9.2.3.5). It would be an odd result if a document was protected from use
in evidence merely because it was electronically encrypted and the key committed
to memory.

8.3.2   Tipping off

In addition to the offence of failing to comply with a notice there is a further
offence of tipping off. Section 54, which creates this offence, applies where the
s. 49 notice contains a provision requiring the person to whom it is given, and
everyone else who becomes aware of its contents, to keep the giving of the notice,
its contents and all steps done pursuant to it, a secret (s. 54(1)). A secrecy
provision can only be included with the consent of the person who granted
permission for the service of the notice and where the protected information has
or is about to come into the possession of the police, customs or the intelligence

services by means which it is reasonable to keep secret from any other person (s. 54(2), (3)). It is a defence for the accused to show that disclosure was effected solely by software designed to indicate when a key has ceased to be secure and the accused could not reasonably have taken steps (after being aware of the notice) to prevent the disclosure (s. 54(5)).

A specific defence is provided where disclosure is made by or to a client from their professional legal adviser in connection with advice about the effect of this part of the Act (s. 54(6)) and legal professional privilege is specifically protected.

Revocation is normally effected when there is a suspicion that a key has been lost or stolen. In such a case it would be reasonable to explain why the key is being revoked so that others can assess what impact it has on their own security. It is suggested that, when no reason is given for revocation, wily individuals will be aware of the authorities' interest precisely because no reasons have been given for the revocation. However, no offence would have been committed.[4]

Section 55 provides 'safeguards' through the imposition of a duty on Chief Constables, government Ministers etc. to ensure that there are systems in place making certain that the uses to which the disclosed key are used are reasonable and also concerned with security of the key, including making sure that the key is not retained beyond what is necessary to guarantee that the protected information is in intelligible form. Loss or damage suffered by anyone who either made the disclosure or to whom the information or key belongs[5] as a result of the breach of duty is actionable against the duty-holder (the Chief Constable etc.). In such circumstances the court is required to have regard to any opinion that has been given by the relevant Commissioner (s. 55(7)). A complaint may also be made to the tribunal (see above at 7.10.2) concerning the issue of s. 49 notices 'or any disclosure or use of the key to protected information', other than where the notice was issued on judicial authority (s. 65(5)(e)). The Act does not create criminal liability in respect of the unauthorised disclosure of a person's data. The Trade and Industry Committee felt that 'the proposed code of practice may prove to be toothless' and 'the impression is given by the legislation that infringements of the code of practice will go unpunished'.[6]

8.4 AUTHORISATION

There is a somewhat complicated structure set out in sch. 2 to the RIPA 2000 as to who is able to grant permission to issue a s. 49 notice. The answer varies

[4] See *Key Revocation, Government Access to Keys and Tipping off* at http://www.fipr.org/rip/BG_revoke.htm

[5] Section 54(6) defines information as belonging to someone where they have any right that would be infringed by disclosure. A key belongs to a person if the information belongs to them or they have any right that would be infringed by the disclosure.

[6] House of Commons Trade and Industry Committee, Fourteenth Report on the Draft Electronic Communications Bill (1999–2000, HC 862, para. 34). For the Government response, see Third Special Report of the Trade and Industry Committee (1999–2000, HC 199).

according to how the information that is protected by the key has come into the relevant authorities' possession and also according to which authority is concerned. The scheme of the schedule provides that permission is to be granted in writing by a circuit judge in England and Wales[7] subject to a number of exceptions. Effectively, however, the grant of permission by a judge will only be required where the s. 49 notice is to be granted by a non-investigative authority (i.e. an authority other than the police, Customs and Excise, the Armed Forces and any of the Intelligence services).

8.4.1   Data obtained under a warrant etc.

Schedule 2, para. 2, concerns data obtained under a warrant. This paragraph provides that where the information has come into the possession of any person through the exercise of a statutory power to inspect, search etc. documents, to intercept communications or under Part I, Chapter II (communications data) or Part II (surveillance and covert intelligence) which requires a warrant issued by the Secretary of State, or by a person holding judicial office, or by a Commissioner under Part III of the Police Act, no further permission is necessary if the warrant contains the appropriate permission or written permission has been granted since the warrant was issued. Where the statutory power is exercised pursuant to a warrant issued by the Secretary of State, only people holding office under the Crown, the police and Customs and Excise are capable of having permission to issue the notice. Where the information is obtained pursuant to a warrant issued by a person holding judicial office, only people entitled to exercise the power under the warrant can acquire permission. Where authorisations are granted by the Commissioner under Part III of the Police Act 1997, only the police and Customs and Excise will be capable of having permission. Section 94 of the Police Act 1997 (permitting other persons to grant authorisations in urgent cases) is deemed to apply to s. 49 notices — see above at 8.2.2.

8.4.2   Data obtained under a statute without a warrant

Schedule 2, para. 3 concerns data obtained by the intelligence services under statute but without a warrant in which case permission to issue a s. 49 notice can only be granted by the Secretary of State. Where the information was obtained pursuant to a statutory power exercised without a warrant by the police, customs or a member of the Armed Forces, then self-authorisation is permitted without the grant by a judge provided they are of sufficient seniority (para. 4). In the case of the police this is satisfied by an officer with rank of superintendent or above, in relation to Customs and Excise by a Commissioner (of Customs and Excise), or a rank to be designated by them, and in the case of the Armed Forces by an officer of the rank of lieutenant colonel or equivalent (para. 6).

---

[7] A sheriff in Scotland or a county court judge in Northern Ireland.

8.4.3 Data obtained without the exercise of statutory powers

Schedule 2, para. 5 covers the situation whereby information has lawfully come into the possession of the police, customs or the Intelligence services without the exercise of a statutory power. Again, self-authorisation is permitted provided that the officer is of sufficient rank as discussed above, or written permission has been granted by the Secretary of State in the case of the Intelligence services.

Chapter Nine

General Surveillance and the Collection and Retention of Personal Data

Quincy Whitaker

9.1 GENERAL SURVEILLANCE

Surveillance can take a number of forms. Highly targeted covert surveillance is dealt with in chapter 7. The focus in this chapter is on more general surveillance. The main distinction is between routine and generalised surveillance of public places, or places where the public generally have access, and one-off surveillance of a particular public event or demonstration. These two types of surveillance are governed by different legal regimes.

9.1.1 Closed-circuit television

The first type of general surveillance, i.e. routine and generalised surveillance, is usually overt, e.g., closed-circuit television (CCTV) cameras which are operated by local authorities or private companies. Such surveillance is not police led. The use of such systems has become widespread over the last decade, their popularity promoted by the police who view them not only as an effective deterrent against crime through its visibility, but also as a source of intelligence and evidence.[1] Although there are moves to regulate by statute the use of CCTV cameras in other European countries such as Spain, Denmark and France, the position in the UK is currently regulated by two voluntary codes of practice (one drawn up by the Local Government Information Unit[2] and the more recent code produced by the British

---

[1] See *Policing with Intelligence*, HMIC Thematic Inspection Report, 1997/8.
[2] *A Watching Brief — Code of Practice for CCTV*, LGIU, March 1996.

Standards Institute).[3] Adherence to the scheme is voluntary, there is no sanction for breach and the Government has no view as to which code is to be preferred; indeed it appears that the practice of some local authorities is to incorporate aspects of both codes.

The British Standards Institute's code of practice is intended to supplement the HRA 1998 and the Data Protection Act 1998 to which 'all closed circuit television schemes that receive, hold or process data about a known person are obliged to conform'.[4] It lays down broad guidance for the drawing up of internal procedures concerning the principles and management of the schemes. Such procedures should include a written policy statement stating the purpose and extent of any scheme, including ancillary public information uses such as traffic congestion reports and availability of car parking spaces being relayed to local radio stations. In relation to privacy and disclosure issues the code states that, 'cameras should not be used to infringe the individual's rights of privacy. Ideally privacy zones should be programmed into the system as required, in order to ensure that the interior of any private properties within the range of the scheme is not surveyed by the cameras.'

Requests from the police, statutory authorities and defence solicitors to view the data obtained from the CCTV system may be granted for the purpose of providing evidence in criminal or civil proceedings, for the prevention or reduction of crime and disorder, the investigation of crime and the identification of witnesses. Requests for disclosure from a third party not falling into the above category must meet a public interest test of disclosure and attention is specifically drawn to the data protection and legal requirements pertaining to local authorities, principally the Criminal Justice and Public Order Act 1994, s. 163(7).

Release to the media of data that is currently part of an investigation is governed by PACE and authority to release should first be sought from the investigating officer.[5] Subject access disclosure from a named subject is governed by the data protection regime (discussed below) which broadly provides for disclosure provided that a fee has been paid and sufficiently accurate information has been provided concerning the time and place (a specification of 30-minute slots for a given date and place is suggested).[6]

The House of Lords' Science and Technology Committee has called for the creation of a regulatory framework and tighter data protection controls[7] but there are no Government plans at the time of writing to replace the existing voluntary system. The Data Protection Act 1998 does, however, provide a degree of

---

[3] *Closed Circuit Television — management and operation — Code of Practice*, 99/703319.
[4] Ibid, para. 4.
[5] Ibid, para. 8.
[6] Ibid, para. 8.3.1.
[7] *Digital Images as Evidence*, Report of the Select Committee on Science and Technology, 3 February 1998, p. 29.

protection through the extension of its ambit to include the processing of image data by CCTV systems, but it was not drafted specifically with the sophisticated surveillance matching processes that are increasingly used by the police in mind. There are for instance a number of vehicle identification schemes (AVLR) already operating in London within the 'Ring of Steel' where 90 CCTV cameras are said to check over 100,000 vehicles a day, and at some football stadiums, cameras scan the crowd for matches on their digital pictorial database of known or alleged troublemakers. The NCIS holds details and pictures of at least 6,000 suspected hooligans which are transmitted using 'photo-phones' to all participating football grounds in the run up to international competitions.[8] The photographs for new driving licences and passports are expected to be held in a digital form thereby creating the potential for wide-ranging surveillance and digital matching when used in conjunction with CCTV cameras.

CCTV film may come within the ambit of Article 8, ECHR depending on the activity recorded and the location. CCTV coverage of the victim of an accident which was then sold to the media[9] would involve a greater interference with a person's privacy than a person being filmed walking through a shopping mall. CCTV coverage which was then retained by the police and placed on a database may raise further issues under Article 8. CCTV schemes operated by local authorities will clearly come within the definition of actions of a public authority for the purpose of the HRA 1998, but the situation may be less clear in relation to the actions of a private business.

The European Court's jurisprudence is not entirely consistent in this developing area but it appears that the purpose for which the image is taken is relevant. In *Friedl* v *Austria* (1995) A/305–B, Comm. Rep., the Commission rejected as inadmissible a complaint that photographs taken of people participating at a public demonstration breached Article 8. However, in the same year in *Murray* v *UK* (1994) 19 EHRR 193 the Court held that the photographing of a suspect at a police station without her consent was covered by Article 8, although the interference was found to be justified on the facts.

It may be possible to reconcile these decisions by reference to the purpose for which the photographs were being taken. A distinction can be drawn between those cases where pictures are taken of a specific identifiable suspect for the purposes of criminal proceedings and where people are photographed for more general purposes during a public demonstration. In *Friedl* there was no identification of particular people and the photographs were kept on a general administrative file rather than being entered into the data processing system.

---

[8] See e.g., *The Guardian*, 10 February 1996.

[9] See also the New Zealand case of *TVNZ Ltd* v *R* (1996) 2 NZLR 462 (HC), 465 where it was held that a police suspect had the right to have his privacy protected against media intrusion and in particular there were firm policy reasons connected with the administration of justice for preventing the publication of videotaped interviews with suspects.

Arguably if the purpose of the photographing was to create a database of protesters with a view to identifying participants, then the activity would need to be justified under Article 8 and Article 10. In *McVeigh, O'Neill and Evans* v *UK* (1981) 5 EHRR 71 the applicants were detained upon their arrival at Liverpool from Ireland under prevention of terrorism legislation then in force. While detained they were searched, questioned and their fingerprints and photographs were taken. The Commission accepted that the applicants' privacy has been interfered with but held that it could be justified under Article 8(2) as being necessary for the prevention of crime. The activities were 'prescribed by law' and taken to establish the applicants' identities and whether or not they were involved in terrorism. This conclusion was unsurprising in view of the fact that the Commission had already found the detention to be lawful; however, it is implicit in the Commission's reasoning that had measures gone beyond this purpose they would not have been justified.

While the intrusions into privacy of an individual which are possible are no doubt more extensive than the infringements of privacy which are possible in the case of a company, companies have a right to privacy that can be protected and which will be infringed by filming without consent: *R* v *Broadcasting Standards Commission, ex parte BBC* [2000] 3 WLR 1327, CA.

9.2   TAKING PHOTOGRAPHS, FINGERPRINTS, DNA AND OTHER SAMPLES AT THE POLICE STATION

Domestic law in this area is principally governed by the Police and Criminal Evidence Act 1984, and the Codes made under it.

9.2.1   Photographs

Although there is no provision in PACE itself concerning the photographing of suspects, Code D provides that, subject to a specified exception, no photograph may be taken without a suspect's consent, or that of his or her parent or guardian, if he or she is under 16 (Code D, paras 1.11 and 4.1). The exception is, however, drawn in such terms as effectively to negative this protection by providing that consent is not required where the taking of the photograph is authorised by an officer of at least the rank of superintendent, having reasonable grounds for suspecting the involvement of the person in a criminal offence and where there is identification evidence. Consent is not required where a person has been charged with or convicted of a recordable offence or where he is arrested at the same time as other people and a photograph is necessary to establish who, was arrested, where they were arrested and at what time (Code D, para. 4.2). Force may not be used in taking a photograph, however, and there is no power of arrest attached to the power to take photographs after a person has been convicted, so the power to take photographs will only apply where the person is in custody pursuant to another power (e.g., s. 27, PACE; see below: Code D, para. 4.3 and 4.2(iii)).

Photographing detainees in police custody without their knowledge or consent will interfere with privacy rights under Article 8, but can be justified in certain circumstances: *Murray* v *UK* (1994) 19 EHRR 193 at para. 86.

9.2.2   Fingerprints

Section 61, PACE provides that fingerprints may be taken without a person's consent where an officer of at least superintendent rank has reasonable grounds for suspecting the involvement of that person in a criminal offence and the fingerprints will tend to 'prove or disprove his involvement'. They can be taken without such authority where the person has previously been convicted of a recordable offence or told that he will be reported for one (s. 61(3)(b), (6)). Section 61(9) preserves the power of compulsory fingerprinting contained in immigration and terrorism legislation.

Under s. 27(3) the police are provided with a power to request someone to come to the police station to be fingerprinted, with a power of arrest for the purpose of taking fingerprints for a recordable offence. The power under s. 27, however, is only exercisable where the person has not at any time been in police detention, so it appears that, where a defendant has received a non-custodial penalty and declines a request to provide his fingerprints, there is no power to compel him to do so as there is no similar arrest power attaching to s. 61.[10]

9.2.3   Body samples

PACE distinguishes between intimate and non-intimate body samples. The former (save for urine) can only be taken with consent and only by a doctor or dentist whereas the latter can, in certain circumstances, be taken by a police officer without consent.

9.2.3.1   *Non-intimate samples*

Non-intimate samples are defined by s. 65 and the Code of Practice (Code D, para. 5.11) to include: a sample of hair (other than pubic hair), a sample taken from or under a nail, a swab taken from any part of a person's body including their mouth (but not any other orifice), saliva, and a footprint or similar impression of a person's body other than their hand. When s. 65 was amended and the Codes of Practice were revised in 1995,[11] in conjunction with the Criminal Justice and Public Order Act (CJPOA) 1994, mouth swabs were redefined from being classed as 'intimate samples' and thus requiring the suspect's consent, to 'non-intimate' where no such consent is needed (CJPOA 1994, s. 54(5)(b); Code D, para. 5.11). The range of

---

[10] Further powers in relation to the retention of fingerprints and other samples are, at the time of writing, before Parliament in the Criminal Justice and Police Bill, clauses 77–82 (Second Reading).

[11] In force 10 April 1995, Police and Criminal Evidence Act (Codes of Practice) (No. 3) Order 1995, SI 1995/450.

offences for which non-intimate samples can be taken was also greatly increased as the amended code permits the taking of non-intimate samples for any recordable offence rather than the previous criterion of 'serious arrestable offence' (s. 54(3)(b); para. 5.1) (going well beyond the recommendation of the Runciman Commission that sampling should be extended to burglary and assault).[12] Research, however, shows that non-intimate samples were taken from approximately 7 per cent of suspects in a custody record sample.[13]

The third extension effected by the amendments enabled officers to take samples from people who have been charged or informed that they will be reported for an offence and from persons convicted of a recordable offence (s. 63 and Code D, para. 5.5). A power backed up by an arrest sanction provides that such individuals can be required to provide a sample within one month of the relevant event on seven days' notice, although the police may direct a time at which the person must attend (PACE, s. 63A). This power extends sampling to those cases where DNA evidence has not been a relevant factor in determining guilt and permits samples to be taken from a large number of people in order to build up the DNA database. The Criminal Justice and Public Order Act 1994[14] clarified the existing power to subject samples to a 'speculative search' (see PACE, s. 65, i.e., checking fingerprints or samples against existing records) and inserted a new requirement that a person must be informed that intimate and non-intimate samples may be the subject of such a search where the sample has been taken at a police station from the person.[15]

9.2.3.2 DNA database

The operation of the national DNA database, which it is anticipated will hold up to five million records, is governed by Home Office Circular 16/95. This circular states that the database is an *intelligence* database only and it is not intended that the fact that a match was found during a speculative search will be used for prosecuting purposes. Where a match is found to a stain from an unsolved crime, a further body sample should be taken under PACE as it will be taken as part of an investigation into a different offence (that relating to the unsolved crime).

The results of the profiling process are held electronically as a digital record and are required to be stored in compliance with the Data Protection Act 1998. The Forensic Science Service (FFS) is the current custodian of the database but local police forces are free to choose which organisation they wish to carry out their profiling for them, subject to overall quality control by the FSS.

---

[12] See Steventon, B. 'Creating a DNA database', Journal of Criminal Law, November 1995, pp. 411–419.

[13] *In Police Custody: police powers and suspects rights under the revised PACE codes of practice*, HO Research Paper, p. 42.

[14] Section 56 added s. 63A to PACE; CJPOA 1994, sch. 10, para. 57 inserted s. 63(8A) and (8B) in PACE.

[15] CJPOA 1994, sch. 10, para. 57 inserting s. 62(7A) in PACE; CJPOA 1994, sch. 10, para. 58(a) adding s. 63(8B) to PACE.

The use of DNA profiles from destroyed samples to form a database for use for statistical purposes does not breach s. 64: *R* v *Willoughby* (1997) 1 Archbold News 2, CA.

9.2.3.3   Intimate samples

Intimate samples are defined as including dental impressions, samples of blood, semen or any other tissue fluid, urine, pubic hair and swabs taken from a person's body orifice other than his mouth (s. 65 and Code D, para. 5.11). The taking of such samples is permitted in relation to any recordable offence but the authorisation of an officer of at least the rank of superintendent or above and the consent of the suspect is required. If a person refuses to provide a sample they may be warned that this refusal may harm their defence if the case goes to trial (PACE, s. 62(10)). The previous provision, that such a refusal could amount to corroboration of other evidence, was repealed by the CJPOA 1994, sch. 11.

A research study undertaken by the Home Office showed that such samples were taken from only 40 out of 10,496 suspects (not including Road Traffic Act (RTA) 1988 samples), 23 suspects were given a 's. 62 warning' after which three suspects still refused to provide a sample.[16] Other powers are available in relation to road traffic matters such as the taking of blood and urine samples under RTA 1988, ss. 4 to 11.[17]

9.2.3.4   Testing for drugs: proposals

The Criminal Justice and Court Services Act 2000, along with other drug testing measures both before and after sentence, includes an amendment to PACE to provide the police with a power to test a person in police detention for specified Class A drugs.[18] The power is exercisable where a person has been charged with a 'trigger offence'[19] or where a person has been charged with a non-trigger offence if an officer the rank of inspector or above reasonably believes that the misuse of the specified drug caused or contributed to the offence. An offence of non-compliance with such a request without good cause is created under the Act, punishable by up to three months' imprisonment and/or a fine up to level 4 (currently £2,500) (s. 57(8)). Detainees must be notified that a refusal could render them liable for prosecution and must be informed of the grounds for the authorisation, and there is provision for detention for up to six hours after charge to enable a sample to be taken. Failure to comply with these procedural requirements may give rise to issues of compliance with Article 8 of the ECHR in relation to the sample, and Article 5 in relation to the prolonged detention.

---

[16] *In Police Custody: police powers and suspects rights under the revised PACE codes of practice*, HO Research Paper, p. 46.

[17] Further powers in relation to the taking and retention of samples are, at the time of writing, before Parliament in the Criminal Justice and Police Bill, clauses 77–82 (Second Reading).

[18] Section 57(1)-(4) inserting new s. 63B into PACE.

[19] Theft, robbery, burglary, taking a motor vehicle without authority, obtaining property by deception, going equipped for stealing and possession, production and supply of a Class A drug.

9.2.3.5   *Articles 6 and 8 ECHR and body samples*

While the collection of the above discussed samples clearly engages Article 8, such interferences are likely to be justified on the ground of prevention of crime, provided that domestic law has been complied with and the samples are in fact being used for that purpose. The measure must, however, also comply with the principle of proportionality in order to ensure compatibility with the Convention.

Retention of the samples and other personal data is discussed below at 9.3.

The European Court has held that the compulsory obtaining of samples does not breach the right against self-incrimination under Article 6. In the case of *Saunders* v *UK* (1996) 23 EHRR 313 at para. 69, the Court was of the view that the principle did not extend to:

> the use in criminal proceedings of material which may be obtained through the use of compulsory powers but which has an existence independent of the will of the suspect such as, inter alia, documents acquired pursuant to a warrant, breath, blood and urine samples and bodily tissues for the purpose of DNA testing.

The Court, however, did not consider the means by which such items may be collected and the attendant Article 8 issues.

See also *Brown* v *Stott (Procurator Fiscal, Dunfermline)* [2001] 2 All ER 97 where it was held that the compulsory requirement to state the name of the driver of a vehicle under the Road Traffic Act did not violate Article 6 (see chapter 17).

9.3   RETENTION AND DISCLOSURE

The issue of retention of personal data through samples or otherwise has to be considered separately from the collection of such material under the Convention. Under domestic law the Police and Criminal Evidence Act 1984 provides that where a person is acquitted of an offence, fingerprints and other samples taken from a person in connection with that investigation must be destroyed as soon as is reasonably practicable after the conclusion of the proceedings (s. 64(1), (2)). Copies made of the data must also be destroyed and if the material is held on computer, access must be made impossible. A person has the right to be present during the destruction, provided he or she so requests within five days of being cleared (s. 64(5), (6); CJA 1988, s. 149). Under Code D the same applies to photographs with the important difference that they need not be destroyed after a person has been acquitted where that person had previously been convicted of a recordable offence (para. 4.4).

The rules regarding destruction of fingerprint and body samples, however, do not apply to terrorism cases. Nor do they apply to samples where the destruction of the sample would involve the destruction of a sample where a conviction had been secured, for instance involving DNA samples of two co-defendants one of whom is acquitted and the other of whom is convicted. In such a case, however, it is specifically provided that the information derived from the sample cannot be used either in evidence against the person who was acquitted or for the purpose of any investigation of any offence (s. 64(3B), PACE, added by CJPOA 1994, s. 57(3)). In *Attorney-General's Reference (No. 3 of 1999)* [2001] 2 WLR 56, the House of Lords held, reversing the decision of the Court of Appeal, that evidence derived from the use of a sample for the purposes of an investigation is not inadmissible solely by reason of a breach of the prohibition in s. 64(3B)(b). In circumstances where this provision is breached, the question of whether any resulting evidence is admitted at trial is determined by the trial judge under s. 78 of PACE.

It is clear that the retention of such material involves an interference with Article 8 but this is likely to come within the exception in Article 8(2). In an early case the Commission accepted that 'the keeping of records including documents, photographs and fingerprints relating to criminal convictions of the past is necessary in a modern democratic society for the prevention of crime and therefore in the interests of public safety'[20] in a case concerning criminal records compiled in relation to a conviction that was eventually quashed on appeal. In *McVeigh, O'Neill and Evans* v *UK* (1981) 5 EHRR 71 at para. 230 (discussed above at 9.1.1) the court considered the position where no criminal proceedings were brought. On the facts of the case, where the records were kept for the purposes of preventing terrorism, the action was found to be justified as the records were kept for identification purposes only and were kept separate from criminal records. However, continued retention of the information once the legitimate purpose was no longer being served would implicitly infringe Article 8.

9.4   DATA PROTECTION REGIME — THE DATA PROTECTION ACT 1998

Like its predecessor the 1984 Act, the Data Protection Act (DPA) 1998[21] establishes a strict regulatory regime based on eight (modified) data protection principles:

(a)   Personal data must be processed fairly and lawfully and only if at least one of the specified conditions in sch. 2 is met and, in the case of sensitive personal data, one of the conditions in sch. 3 is also met. The relevant conditions include consent, that the processing is necessary for contractual purposes, necessary to protect the vital interests of the subject, necessary for the administration of justice or the exercise of any function conferred under an enactment or by a government department or other function in the public interest, or for the legitimate interests of third

---

[20] *X* v *Germany*, 9 Collection of Decisions 53.
[21] In force 1 March 2000. Introduced to implement EC Directive 95/46/EC (*the Data Protection Directive*). However, in the absence of the Act being amended to apply to Parliament itself it seems that the UK may be in default of its EU obligations.

parties. Sensitive personal data (e.g., that relating to a person's race or ethnic category, physical or mental health, sexual, religious or political life including trade union membership and the commission or alleged commission of an offence, or proceedings related to an offence committed or alleged to have been committed by the subject) must further satisfy one of the conditions of sch. 3, namely explicit consent, the processing is necessary in connection with employment, to protect the vital interests of the subject or another where consent has been unreasonably withheld, for the legitimate purposes of a non-profit-making body relating to those connected with its purpose, in connection with legal proceedings or the administration of justice, for medical purposes, or for the exercise of any function of a government department.

(b) Personal data must be obtained only for specified and lawful purposes and not be processed in any matter incompatible with those purposes. In general this requires that data controllers notify the Commissioner of the purposes for which the data is held and the categories of people to whom the data may be disclosed. This requirement is not satisfied by simply registering, as was the case under the 1984 Act, but contains an additional requirement of compatibility with the purpose of registration. The standard police registration adopted under the 1984 Act has been 'The prevention and detection of crime: apprehension and prosecution of offenders: protection of life and property: maintenance of law and order, and rendering assistance to the public in accordance with force policies and procedures.'

(c) Personal data must be adequate, relevant and not excessive in relation to those purposes.

(d) Personal data must be accurate and kept up to date; data is inaccurate if it is misleading as to any matter of fact.

(e) Personal data must not be kept longer than is necessary for the specified purpose.

(f) Personal data must be processed in accordance with the rights of the subject under the Act.

(g) Appropriate technical measures must be taken against unlawful processing or loss.

(h) Personal data must not be transferred to any area outside the EU which does not have equivalent data protection.

Individuals are entitled to be told of and have access to data held on them and data controllers must ensure that there are security measures in place to prevent unauthorised access.

The ambit of the legislation is extended to include certain manual files (Data Protection Act 1998, s. 1(1)) and provides tighter controls for processing 'sensitive data' (s. 2). The definition of 'processing' is now more wide-ranging and covers obtaining, holding or recording data or carrying out any operation on the information, such as transmitting or analysing it (s. 1(1)). This will cover all CCTV systems (see 9.1.1) provided they relate to personal data. Individual rights are enhanced by the creation of new express rights for an individual to be told who is processing data concerning them and why, and to be protected from such data being used in direct marketing.

The police are in theory as subject to the regime as any other data controller but the statutory exemption for law enforcement purposes in reality nullifies much of the protection offered by the scheme. This provision exempts the police from the requirement of complying with the 'fair and lawful' processing provisions (except in relation to sensitive personal data), with a subject access request for personal information from an individual, and with the restrictions on disclosure of personal information if to comply would be likely to prejudice the prevention or detection of crime or the apprehension or prosecution of offenders. There is no definition of 'likely to prejudice' in the Act and the Commissioner has taken the view that for these exemptions to apply 'there must be a substantial chance rather than a mere risk that in a particular case the purposes would be noticeably damaged'.[22]

In addition, the police have broad powers to exchange information with other law enforcement agencies. Under the Crime and Disorder Act 1998, local crime partnerships between public agencies are introduced 'to formulate and implement ... a strategy for the reduction of crime and disorder'. Section 115 provides that that any person can lawfully disclose information *for the purposes of the Act* to the police, local authorities, probation or health service; however, the exercise of the power remains subject to the data protection regime and the common law. Agencies are encouraged to share information where to do so would be in the public interest.

9.5   DISCLOSURE OF INFORMATION

9.5.1   Criminal records under Part V of the Police Act 1997

The disclosure of some information by the police to the public is required by statute, such as criminal record certificates under Part V of the Police Act 1997. Any person can make an application for a basic criminal conviction certificate provided they are the subject of the certificate and provide two proofs of identity and fingerprints in the case of doubt (ss. 112(1), 118(2)). The combined effect of the 1997 Act and the Rehabilitation of Offenders Act 1974 (s. 1(4)) is that such certificates will include any unspent conviction in the UK or elsewhere, any conditional or absolute discharge and any finding in criminal proceedings that a person has committed an offence (i.e., a finding by a jury that a defendant who is judged unfit to stand trial did the act or omission charged pursuant to s. 4A of the Criminal Procedure (Insanity) Act 1964).

---

[22] *The Data Protection Act 1998, An Introduction*, October 1998, ch. 4, para. 2.2.4.

Section 113 of the Police Act 1997[23] created a system of comprehensive certification for sensitive areas of employment involving vulnerable groups and those involved with the administration of justice. At the time of writing the Home Office is in the process of establishing the Criminal Records Bureau,[24] which will administer the applications for criminal record certificates or 'disclosures', as they are to be known. Such a certificate includes details of all past convictions, including spent ones but is only available to employers or organisations that would be entitled to ask an exempted question under the 1975 Order.[25] Despite powerful objections being made at the time of the Bill's passage through Parliament, cautions are included in the category of information which can be supplied to those entitled under the Order. Lord Lester of Herne Hill QC had argued that the inclusion potentially put Britain in breach of the prohibition on retrospective penalties under Article 7 of the Convention as many cautions were administered at a time when there was no warning or expectation that the admission of guilt, obtained without legal advice, would gain such wide circulation.[26]

Sections 115[27] and 116 provide for 'enhanced criminal certificates' which allow for the disclosure of information going beyond convictions and cautions. Such information may include acquittals, the results of ongoing and inconclusive police investigations and uncorroborated allegations from informants. However, the certificates are confined to those seeking appointment to positions of responsibility working with children or vulnerable adults, the most sensitive areas of licensing, and the appointment of the judiciary (s. 115(3)–(5)).[28] Unauthorised disclosure of such information may well raise issues under Article 6(2) of the Convention (the presumption of innocence). See by analogy *Minelli* v *Switzerland* (1983) 5 EHRR 554 where it was held that the refusal of a defendant's costs following an acquittal could lead to a breach of Article 6(2).

Article 8 may also be relevant to disclosure. In *Leander* v *Sweden* (1987) 9 EHRR 433, the Court held that disclosure of a police file to a prospective employer on the grounds of national security did not violate Article 8. However, the principles of proportionality require that each case be individually considered. A blanket policy of disclosure may be difficult to justify under Article 8.[29]

---

[23] As amended by the Protection of Children Act 1999, s. 8(1), and the Care Standards Act 2000, s. 90(1).

[24] Due to be operational in May 2001 — see www.crb.gov.uk for details of the Bureau's remit.

[25] Rehabilitation of Offenders Act (Exceptions) Order 1975 (SI 1975/1023).

[26] The Police Bill, HL Report, 20 January 1997, cols 524–6.

[27] As amended by the Protection of Children Act 1999, s. 8(2), and the Care Standards Act 2000, s. 90(2).

[28] Section 115(4)(a) gives the Secretary of State power to extend these categories.

[29] See comments of Lord Bingham CJ in *R* v *Chief Constable of North Wales, ex parte AB* [1997] 3 WLR 724, discussed below at 9.5.2 as *R* v *Chief Constable of North Wales, ex parte Thorpe* [1998] 3 WLR 57.

9.5.2   Disclosure to the public generally

In the absence of a particular statutory provision, wider disclosure to non-policing authorities, the press and members of the public must be justified as falling within one of the non-disclosure exemptions under the Data Protection Act 1998 (see principle (b) above at 9.4). In *Hellewell* v *Chief Constable of Derbyshire* [1995] 1 WLR 804 the claimant argued that the police practice of giving local shopkeepers photographs of known trouble-makers was unlawful. Laws J held that the police were justified in breaching the duty of confidentiality which they owed in relation to the photographs by taking reasonable action for the purpose of crime. The Court of Appeal examined the practice in the case of *R* v *Chief Constable of North Wales, ex parte Thorpe* [1998] 3 WLR 57 where the decision of the police to reveal the details and convictions of two convicted paedophiles to the owner of a caravan site was challenged. The Court of Appeal approved the disclosure but only where it can be shown there is a pressing need to do so. This, as was highlighted by *JUSTICE*,[30] is a lesser standard than the Council of Europe's Recommendation R (87) 15[31] (covering data protection in the police sector) which states that disclosure should only be permitted where there is clear legal obligation, or in exceptional circumstances where it is clearly in the subject's interests, or to prevent a serious and imminent danger.

In *R* v *Local Police Authority in the Midlands, ex parte LM* [2000] 1 FCR 736, it was held that the power to disclose information about non-conviction matters existed in a case where there was genuine and reasonable belief in the necessity to disclose for the protection of children. A blanket approach to disclosure was impermissible and disclosure should only be made where there was a pressing need and it was in the public interest to do so.

In *R (A)* v *Chief Constable of C and another* [2001] 1 WLR 461 (QBD, Turner J), the applicant applied for a job with a local authority which involved working with children. The police authority obtained information from another police authority concerning inappropriate behaviour by the applicant with children, which they passed on to the local authority. The allegations had not led to any criminal proceedings. It was held that, although the material was 'sensitive personal data' under s. 2 of the DPA 1998, it was exempted from the first data protection principle under Part I of sch. 1 to the Act because it was data being processed for the prevention and detection of crime or other exempted purposes under schs. 2 and 3, or because its processing was 'necessary for the exercise of any functions conferred on a constable by any rule of law' in accordance with para. 10 of Article 2 of the Data Processing (Processing of Sensitive Personal Data) Order 2000.

---

[30] *Under Surveillance*, p. 96.
[31] The Recommendation supplements the 1981 Council of Europe's data protection Convention. The UK is one of two signatory countries that have entered reservations in relation to some aspects of the instrument's operation.

9.6 ACCOUNTABILITY

The DPA 1998 introduced a new system of notification which requires relevant details of all data controllers, as well as details of security measures, to be provided to the Data Protection Commissioner. It is a strict liability criminal offence to process personal data without notification (subject to stated exemptions) to which one can be subject to an unlimited fine on conviction on indictment.

A range of other offences exists under the Act including unlawful obtaining of data, unlawful selling of personal data (including advertising), and unlawful disclosure by staff of the Registry or their agents. It is also an offence to require a person to obtain subject access, particularly in relation to employment, subject to an exception in the public interest. The 1998 Act provides that the public interest requirement is not satisfied on the grounds of the prevention or detection of crime as this ground is specifically covered under Part V of the Police Act 1997 (discussed above at 9.5.1). There is, however, a specific defence to a charge of unlawful obtaining where a person can show that the action was necessary to prevent or detect crime or was required or authorised by law.

The data protection regime is overseen by the Data Protection Commissioner (formerly Registrar) whose duties include the promotion of good practice amongst data controllers and promotion of observance of the provisions of the 1998 Act. Any person who believes themselves to be directly affected by the processing of any data can make a request for assessment to the Commissioner who is obliged to carry out such an assessment and must notify the requester of the result. The Commissioner, if satisfied that a person has breached the data protection principles, may issue enforcement notices against that person and it is an offence to fail to comply with such a notice.

Subject access, and the requirement that data be kept accurate and up to date, remains a crucial aspect to the scheme of accountability under the Act. Section 69 of the Freedom of Information Act 2000 extends the right of access to personal data under the 1998 Act to all data held by public authorities, including that contained in unstructured paper files, although very few other aspects of the data protection regime will apply to this category of data.[32] In addition to the rights of subject access, individuals have under the 1998 Act the right, in certain circumstances, to apply to Court for an order that the data controller rectify, block, erase or destroy inaccurate data and to obtain compensation for damage and associated distress suffered as a result of inaccurate data or breach of subject access right (s. 14).

The Freedom of Information Act 2000 also brings the existing office of the Data Protection Commissioner within a single office of Information

---

[32] See *The Freedom of Information Bill: Data Protection Issues*, House of Commons Research paper 99/99, 3 December 1999, for a detailed discussion of the interface between the two regimes.

Commissioner who will have oversight of both the freedom of information and data protection legislation (s. 18). The Data Protection Commissioner welcomed the coherence and integration that such a move would promote and noted the potential for institutional conflict that could arise, particularly in relation to requests for information from third parties involving privacy issues, were the two offices to remain separated.[33]

---

[33] Memorandum from Data Protection Registrar to the Public Accounts Committee, Third Report of 1998–1999, *Freedom of Information Bill*, Vol. II: HC 570-II of 1998–99, 16.8.99, memorandum 2, p. 18.

Chapter Ten

Stop and Search, Arrest and Detention
Quincy Whitaker

10.1 INTRODUCTION

Stop and search, arrest and detention raise issues under Article 5 of the ECHR. The general scheme of this Article is examined above at 3.3. In brief, it safeguards liberty such that any deprivation of liberty must be justified in Convention terms. For the purpose of this chapter, Article 5(1)(c) is the most important. It provides that an individual may be deprived of his or her liberty on reasonable suspicion that he or she has committed a criminal offence.

10.2 STOP AND SEARCH

The extent to which the exercise of ordinary stop and search powers complies with the requirements of the ECHR has yet to be conclusively determined, and will probably vary on a case-by-case basis. Some roadside searches may be sufficiently speedy not to raise Article 5 issues at all, but otherwise they will have to be justified under Article 5 (e.g., where a search involves a significant period of detention). As noted above, Article 5(1)(c) provides for detention on reasonable suspicion that an offence has been committed; however, the purpose of this provision is to bring the arrested person before a court. The only other relevant provision is Article 5(1)(b) which permits detention to 'secure the fulfilment of an obligation prescribed by law'. However, a wide interpretation of this provision has consistently been rejected by the European Court. What is required is a 'specific and concrete obligation' not a general obligation to obey the criminal law.[1]

---

[1] *Guzzardi* v *Italy* (1980) 3 EHRR 333, at para. 101.

Neither the European Court nor the Commission has specifically considered the PACE stop and search powers; but in *McVeigh, O'Neill and Evans* v *UK* (1981) 5 EHRR 71 the Commission considered police powers to order the applicants' detention pending 'examination' under the prevention of terrorism legislation. It found that the applicants' detention was justified in order to 'secure the fulfilment of an obligation prescribed by law'. Although the Commission accepted that usually a person must have had a prior opportunity to fulfil the obligation in question before Article 5(1)(b) applies, for a number of reasons specifically related to the terrorist context in which the legislation was operating, it found that there were circumstances of a 'pressing nature' which justified detention in order to secure compliance with the obligation to submit to a security check. It is questionable whether Article 5(1)(b) operates in the same way where such factors are not present: e.g. detention for routine searches.

Moreover, it may also be relevant to consider the application of Article 14. The Convention does not provide for a freestanding right not to be discriminated against, but Article 14 provides that the enjoyment of the rights and freedoms of the Convention are to be secured without 'discrimination on any ground such as sex, race, colour, language, religion, political or other opinion, national or social origin, association with a national minority, property, birth or other status'. It is not necessary to show that the right of enjoyment under an Article has actually been breached, it is sufficient to show that the conduct or activity in question is within the 'ambit' of the relevant Article.[2]

Evidence in the UK shows that the use of stop and search powers has increased ninefold since PACE was introduced[3] but that the exercise of such powers varies widely according to region and ethnic make-up.[4] Published figures for 1998/99[5] showed that there was an overall stop and search rate of 20 per 1,000 of the whole population but within this average there were rates of 5 per 1,000 in Essex at one end of the scale to 101 per 1,000 in Cleveland at the other. The figures also show

---

[2] See *Belgian Linguistic Case (No. 2)* (1968) 1 EHRR 252 at para. 9; also *Abdulaziz, Cabales and Balkandali* (1985) 7 EHRR 471.

[3] 1,050,700 in 1997/8, '*Operation of certain police powers under PACE*', Graham Wilkins and Chris Addicott, Home Office Crime and Criminal Justice Unit, issue 2/99, 22 January 1999.

[4] See *Statewatch*, vol. 8, nos 3 and 4, May–August 1998, p. 16.

[5] Under s. 95, Criminal Justice Act 1991 all people working within the criminal justice system and the police in particular have a duty to avoid discriminating against anyone on the grounds of race, sex or other improper grounds. The Home Secretary is obliged to publish information that he considers expedient to monitor this duty. In 1993 Her Majesty's Inspectorate of the Constabulary began collating figures and in March 1995 a more extensive system of ethnic monitoring was agreed whereby the officer is required to use his own judgement to 'grade' the person on a '4 point scale' as 'White, Black, Asian or Other'. The failure to have a further category to denote Irish origin has been criticised as they form the largest ethnic minority in Britain and there is increasing evidence that they suffer widespread discrimination. The inclusion of Irish under 'White' has a distorting effect on the statistics which may mask discrimination.

that relative to the population, people considered to have a black appearance (from the officer's perspective) are six times more likely to be stopped than someone considered to be white, with again wide regional variation. In Leicester, for instance, 19 white people per 1,000 of population and 190 black people per 1,000 were stopped in 1998/99, whereas Humberside is the sole police force to search more white people (in percentage terms) than black people (6 as opposed to 5 per 1,000). The pattern for Asians varied but the numbers stopped and searched again were consistently higher than for whites.[6]

The general power to stop and search is contained in s. 1 of PACE which gives the police power to search 'any person or vehicle' and 'anything which is in or on a vehicle for stolen and prohibited articles' and to detain a person or vehicle for the purpose of such a search.[7] The power is only exercisable upon reasonable grounds for suspecting the presence of stolen or prohibited articles[8] and any such item that is found may be seized (s. 1(3), (6)).

However, the Criminal Justice and Public Order Act (CJPOA) 1994 gives the police power to stop and search without reasonable suspicion providing a superintendent reasonably believes that incidents involving serious violence may occur in the locality (s. 60).[9] The CJPOA 1994 also enabled stop/searches of vehicles and occupants to be made in order to prevent acts of terrorism (s. 81 inserting s. 13A in the Prevention of Terrorism (Temporary Provisions) Act 1989) and the 1989 Act was also amended to provide for searches of pedestrians in order to prevent acts of terrorism.[10]

The Terrorism Act 2000 continues both these powers. Section 44 provides that authorisation for the use of the stop and search power (without any requirement of suspicion) may be given by an officer of at least Assistant Chief Constable level where he considers it 'expedient for preventing acts of terrorism'. The 2000 Act provides a similar power to prohibit or restrict the parking of vehicles in a road specified in the authorisation (s. 48) and failure to comply with either direction will amount to an offence (ss. 47 and 51).

Section 4 of PACE permits an officer of at least superintendent rank (unless it is an emergency) to authorise a road check where he has reasonable grounds for

---

[6] *Statistics on Race and the Criminal Justice System*, a Home Office publication under s. 95, Criminal Justice Act 1991, 1999 (available on the Home Office website: http://www.homeoffice.gov.uk/rds/index.htm)

[7] Section 1(2). Searches are also permitted under the Misuse of Drugs Act 1971, various poaching and wildlife conservation statutes, the Firearms Act 1968, the Aviation Security Act 1982, the Customs and Excise Management Act 1979 and the Sporting Events (Control of Alcohol etc.) Act 1985.

[8] 'Prohibited articles' are defined in PACE, s. 1(7).

[9] 7,970 were carried out under this provision in England and Wales in 1997/8 and 377 individuals were found to be carrying offensive weapons which resulted in 103 arrests for offensive weapons and 332 arrests for other reasons, *'Operation of certain police powers under PACE'* (fn. 3 above).

[10] Prevention of Terrorism (Additional Powers) Act 1996 inserting new s. 13B in the 1989 Act.

believing that a serious arrestable offence has been committed and for suspecting that a person who committed, was intending to commit, witnessed or is unlawfully at large in relation to, such an offence is in the locality in which vehicles would be stopped. Road checks which are not carried out under s. 4 continue to be legitimate under s. 163 of the Road Traffic Act 1988.[11]

10.2.1 Procedural safeguards

Section 2 of PACE contains various procedural safeguards regarding the exercise of all stop and search powers.[12] The officer must take reasonable steps to bring to the person's attention his name (or number in terrorism cases), the name of his police station, the object of the search and his grounds of authorisation (s. 2(3); Code A, para. 2.4). In *R v Fennelly* [1989] Crim LR 142, the prosecution was unable to establish that the defendant had been told why he had been stopped, searched and arrested in the street and the evidence produced by the search (jewellery) as well as evidence produced from a strip search at the police station (heroin) was excluded at trial.[13] The officer must also inform the person that they are entitled to a record and to which station they should apply, unless it appears that it is not practicable to make a record (s. 2(3)(d); Code A, para. 2.6, 2.7). If the vehicle is unattended a notice must be left with the vehicle detailing the above information but the safeguards only apply to searches and thus do not apply when the stop does not lead to a search (s. 2(6)). The duration of the search is limited to such time as is reasonably necessary (s. 2(8)) and the thoroughness of the search will depend upon what is suspected of being carried.

It is specifically stated, however, that no power short of arrest authorises a police officer to *require* a person to remove in public any item other than an outer coat, jacket or gloves (s. 2(9)(a)) so such searches would have to take place out of public view in, for instance, a police van although officers are permitted to request people 'voluntarily' to remove more than the statutory minimum (Code A, note 3A). Any search beyond the statutory minimum should not be conducted in the presence of a member of the opposite sex unless this is specifically requested (Code A, para. 3.5) (and see search upon arrest below at 10.3.3).

10.3 ARREST

Detention or arrest in order to bring a person before a competent court is an exception to the right to liberty specifically provided for in Article 5 of the ECHR.

---

[11] See *Lodwick v Saunders* [1985] 1 WLR 382.

[12] Except those conducted at airports, ports and similar places.

[13] See also the Canadian case of *R v Feeney* (1997) 2 SCR 13 holding that any search and seizure following an unlawful arrest will also violate a suspect's rights.

To come within this exception, however, various pre-conditions to detention must be satisfied: the arrest and detention must be 'lawful' and 'in accordance with a procedure prescribed by law' (i.e. domestic law must set out the procedure to be followed by those authorised to arrest and detain and the law must be followed in practice) and the arrest must be based on a Convention ground (see below). In each case the purpose must be to bring the person arrested before a competent judicial authority but the 'existence of such a purpose is to be considered independently of its achievement'[14] so release without charge will not necessarily breach Article 5.

The grounds for arrest under Article 5(1)(c) of the Convention are: the existence of reasonable suspicion that the person has committed an offence; when it is reasonably considered necessary to prevent a person committing an offence; and when it is reasonably considered necessary to prevent the person fleeing after having committed an offence. To a large extent the existing domestic law reflects these requirements through ss. 24 and 25 of PACE which provide for a power to arrest a person on reasonable suspicion of having committed an arrestable offence[15] and for all other offences where the 'general arrest conditions' have been satisfied.[16]

10.3.1   Reasonable suspicion

Reasonable suspicion under the Convention requires an objective basis and honest belief,[17] as it does under domestic law. All the decided cases against the UK have involved arrest on suspicion of committing terrorist offences and even though the European Court has noted that 'terrorist crime falls into a special category ... as the police are obliged to act with the utmost urgency',[18] they nonetheless held that the applicants' rights under Article 5(1)(c) were breached when the police relied simply on the basis of their previous terrorist convictions as forming the basis for reasonable suspicion.[19]

The terrorist context has also been significant in the European Court's analysis of the extent to which the authorities can rely on confidential information and

---

[14] *Brogan and others* v *UK* (1988) 11 EHRR 117 at para. 53.

[15] Section 24, principally offences for which the maximum sentence is five years or more.

[16] Section 25: where the name and address of the arrestee is unknown and cannot reasonably be discovered; where there are reasonable grounds for believing the arrest is necessary to prevent physical harm to the relevant person or another; causing loss or damage to property; committing an offence against public decency; or causing an unlawful obstruction of the highway.

[17] *Fox, Campbell and Hartley* v *UK* (1990) 13 EHRR 157.

[18] Ibid, para. 34.

[19] Ibid. The Court of Appeal has affirmed this principle, e.g., *James* v *Chief Constable of South Wales Police* (1991) *The Independent,* 29 April, CA.

anonymous sources. It is inherent in the Court's reasoning in the case of *Murray v UK* (1994) 19 EHRR 193 that the reliance on sources justified in that case would not necessarily survive challenge in a non-terrorist context.

In domestic law, reasonable grounds for suspicion can arise from information given by another officer, so long as they are — objectively speaking — reasonable. However, a simple order from a superior officer to arrest a particular individual may not amount to reasonable suspicion — see *O'Hara* v *Chief Constable of the RUC* [1997] AC 286 at 293C–294A, HL. The officer must reasonably suspect the existence of facts amounting to an arrestable offence of the kind that he has in mind. Otherwise, the constable cannot comply with his or her obligations under s. 28(3) of PACE by informing the suspect of the grounds of his arrest — see *Chapman* v *DPP* (1988) 89 Cr App R 190 (DC) at 197 (see below) and *Hough* v *Chief Constable of Staffordshire Police* (2001) *The Times*, 14 February: reliance on computer entry.

The European Court has also held, as is the case under domestic law, that the level of suspicion required for an arrest need not be sufficient to charge, although the length of the detention is relevant and longer periods of detention may require more by way of suspicion.[20]

10.3.2   Information to be given upon arrest

Article 5(2) of the Convention requires that the arrested person be informed promptly 'in a language he understands' of the reason for his arrest, i.e., he must be told in 'simple non-technical language … the essential legal and factual grounds for his arrest'.[21] Again the position under PACE is similar as a person is required to be informed of the reasons for his arrest as soon as is practicable, even if it is obvious (s. 28).

The purpose of Article 5(2) of the Convention is to allow a person to challenge the legality of their detention, therefore merely informing a person that they have been detained pursuant to the provisions of emergency legislation was held to be insufficient in the case of *Ireland* v *UK* (1978) 2 EHRR 25 at para. 198. Further reasoning is provided by Lord Simonds, in the leading English authority of *Christie* v *Leachinisky* [1947] AC 573 at 593, where he stated that one of the reasons a person is 'entitled to know what … are the facts which are said to constitute a crime on his part' is so that he may give more than an unconvincing bare denial. The suspect should therefore be informed of sufficient relevant details, such as where and when the offence occurred and any facts which are said to constitute the offence. In some cases, the factual basis will not be fulfilled by simply naming the offence. Where a police officer can reasonably be expected to obtain sufficient details before arresting the suspect, he should do so — see *R* v

---

[20] *Murray* v *UK* (1994) at para. 56.
[21] Ibid, at para. 40.

Telfer [1976] Crim LR 562 and *Murphy* v *Oxford* (15 February 1985, unreported) per Sir John Donaldsdon MR, where the plaintiff's claim for false imprisonment succeeded because he was merely told that he was 'wanted on suspicion of burglary in Newquay'.

The question of promptness will depend on the circumstances and the fact that reasons were not given until a few hours after arrest was held not to violate Article 5 when the arrest was for a terrorist offence.[22]

10.3.3   Search upon arrest

In domestic law the police have a power under s. 32 of PACE to search an arrested person other than at a police station. It provides the police with the power to search an arrested person for a weapon, or where there are grounds for believing he may present a danger to himself, or for anything that might be used to effect an escape or which might be evidence. In addition the police have the power to search the premises in which the person was arrested, whether or not they are occupied or controlled by him, but only for items for which a search is permissible and on reasonable grounds that such items exist (s. 32(1), (2)). Random automatic searching is therefore not lawful.[23]

10.4   DETENTION

10.4.1   Preventative detention

Article 5(1)(c) authorises detention to prevent the commission of an offence but any such detention will always be subject to strict scrutiny. It does not authorise preventive detention generally. In *Ireland* v *UK* (1978) 2 EHRR 25, a case concerning the internment and interrogation techniques deployed by the UK in Northern Ireland from 1971–75, the European Court held that internment 'simply for the preservation of the peace and the maintenance of order' without any belief in an offence having been committed, could not be brought within the terms of Article 5(1)(c).

10.4.2   Length of detention

Article 5(3) provides that anyone arrested on a criminal charge has a right to be brought promptly before a court: see 11.2.3.

---

[22] *Fox, Campbell and Hartley* v *UK* (1990) 13 EHRR 157.

[23] See e.g., *Brazil* v *Chief Constable of Surrey* (1984) 148 JP 22; *Mann-Cairns* v *Ministry of Defence, Legal Action*, September 1988, 21.

10.4.3   Domestic law

The Terrorism Act 2000 is intended to comply with the requirements of Article 5 without the need for derogation. Under the Act the power to authorise detention in excess of 48 hours has been handed from the Secretary of State to the courts, but the seven-day maximum has been retained.[24]

Under PACE an arrested person may be detained in police custody for up to 24 hours without charge unless further detention is authorised, the initial 12 hours by a superintendent but thereafter by a magistrate up to a maximum of 96 hours (although no single extension can exceed 36 hours) (ss. 41–3). The application for a warrant of further extension is made with both parties present and it must be supported by information from a police officer, a copy of which must have been supplied in advance to the detainee, who must also be physically present, as well as a lawyer if he or she wants one (s. 43(2), (3)). The test applied by the court is the same as that applied by the superintendent, namely that the detention is necessary to secure or preserve evidence relating to an offence for which the person has been arrested or to obtain such evidence by questioning him *and* that the investigation is being conducted expeditiously and diligently (s. 43(4)).

The custody officer plays a central role in the scheme under PACE in authorising the detention and thereafter taking responsibility for the detainee. He or she must be at least the rank of sergeant and should not have played any role in the investigation of the offence (s. 36). The custody officer is required to consider whether there is sufficient evidence to charge the person when they are first brought to the police station. If there is not sufficient evidence then he or she must release the person, either with or without bail, unless they have reasonable grounds for believing that that person's detention without being charged is necessary to secure or preserve evidence relating to an offence for which that person is under arrest or to obtain such evidence by questioning them (s. 37(1), (2)). The officer is required to maintain a record of the detention (the custody record) in accordance with the Codes of Practice and is specifically responsible for ensuring that detainees are treated in accordance with the provisions of the Act and Codes (s. 39(1)).

The grounds for detention must be reviewed by an officer (known as the review officer), of at least the rank of inspector who has not been involved in the investigation, not later than six hours after the detention was first authorised and at not less than nine hourly intervals thereafter (PACE, s. 40). Where a person has been detained after charge[25] the review is conducted by the custody officer who must be satisfied that the grounds for detention continue to exist.

---

[24] Schedule 8, s. 29. The grounds on which such an extension may be authorised are set out in sch. 8, s. 32.

[25] Section 46. Broadly a person detained after charge must be brought before a court 'as soon as is practicable' and in any event not later than the first court sitting after charge.

10.4.4   Conditions and treatment

Article 5 of the Convention does not cover the conditions and treatment of detainees. Such matters may, however, engage Article 8 and Article 3 if they reach a sufficient level of severity. The UK was found to have violated Article 3 through its use of 'five techniques' of interrogation[26] leading to sensory deprivation and disorientation practised on detainees in Northern Ireland (*Ireland v UK* (1978) 2 EHRR 25). The purpose of any ill-treatment is also relevant. Where ill-treatment is administered with the aim of obtaining admissions or information from the suspect, it is more likely to be torture, not inhuman and degrading treatment.[27]

In *Selmouni* v *France* (1999) 29 EHRR 403, the Court held that as the Convention was a 'living instrument', what was previously considered inhuman and degrading treatment might amount to torture in the future. The Court found that torture had been inflicted on the applicant through the following treatment in police custody: being dragged along by his hair, being made to run along a corridor with a policeman either side to trip him up, having an officer showing him his penis and saying, 'look, suck this' before urinating over him and then threatening him with a blowtorch and syringe. The ill-treatment was disputed but where the injuries were consistent with the medical evidence the Court relied on the principle that has been developed in a series of cases that 'where an individual is taken into police custody in good health but is found to be injured at the time of release, it is incumbent on the State to provide a plausible explanation as to the causing of the injury, failing which a clear issue arises under Article 3 of the Convention'.[28]

In *Tomasi* v *France* (1992) 15 EHRR 1, the European Court also found that the applicant had been subjected to inhuman and degrading treatment when he alleged that he had been repeatedly beaten and subjected to other ill-treatment during 40 hours of police detention. The medical evidence was not wholly consistent but did show that the applicant had been subjected to a number of blows of some intensity which in the opinion of the Court was sufficient to render the applicant's treatment in custody inhuman and degrading. In *Assenov and others* v *Bulgaria* (1998) 28 EHRR 652 the Court held that the infliction of injuries which amounted to a band-like haematoma 5cm x 1cm on the upper arm, 3 band-like haematoma 6cm x 1cm on the chest, a 4cm bruise on the left scapula, haematoma

---

[26] Wall standing, hooding, subjection to noise, deprivation of sleep and deprivation of food and drink. These techniques were discontinued by the UK in March 1972 upon the application being lodged and an undertaking not to reintroduce them was given by the Attorney General in front of the European Court in February 1977.

[27] *Aksoy* v *Turkey* (1996) 23 EHRR 553.

[28] Ibid, at para. 61. See also *Ribitsch* v *Austria* (1995) 21 EHRR 573 at para. 31.

2cm diameter on the back of the head and five grazes to the chest was sufficiently serious to amount to ill-treatment within the meaning of Article 3.

Where an individual raises an arguable claim of serious mistreatment by the police or other state agents the state is obliged to hold an effective official investigation which should be capable of leading to the identification and punishment of those responsible. In addition, the notion of an effective remedy entails effective access to the investigatory procedure and the payment of compensation where appropriate.[29]

Serious and systematic discrimination can violate Article 3. In *East African Asians* v *UK* (1973) 3 EHRR 76, the European Commission held that 'publicly to single out a group of persons for differential treatment on the basis of race might in certain circumstances constitute an affront to human dignity'.

In domestic law, Code of Practice C deals with the conditions and treatment of those subject to police detention and questioning. As well as detailing such matters as bedding and the provision of refreshment (para. 8), it also covers substantive matters such as the right not to be held incommunicado (para. 5) and the right to legal advice (para. 6).

10.4.5 Charge

Both Article 5(2) and Article 6(3)(a) of the Convention provide for information to be given to a detainee at an early stage. Article 5(2) requires that everyone who is arrested is to be informed promptly, in a language he understands, of the reason for his arrest and of any charge against him. As soon as criminal proceedings are initiated however, Article 6(3) further provides that 'anyone charged with a criminal offence be informed in a language which he understands and in detail, of the nature and cause of the accusation against him', which implies a greater level of information than is necessary to satisfy the requirements of Article 5. In *Brozicek* v *Italy* (1989) 12 EHRR 371 the Court held that the requirements of Article 6(3)(a) were satisfied by the accused being informed of the list of offences of which he had been accused, the place and date of those offences, extracts from the relevant criminal code and the victims' details where the charge involved resisting police, assault and wounding, although it may be that less specific charges require greater information. In *Pélissier* v *France* (1999) 30 EHRR 715, the Court held that Article 6(3)(a) afforded the defendant the right to be informed not only of the cause of the accusation in terms of the acts he is alleged to have committed and on what the accusation is based, but also of the legal characterisation given to those acts. The provision of detailed information in this respect was in the view of the Court 'an essential prerequisite for ensuring that proceedings were fair' (at para. 5.2).

---

[29] *Assenov* v *Bulgaria*, at para. 117. See also *Labita* v *Italy* (6 April 2000, ECtHR), at para. 131 and *Veznedaroglu* v *Turkey* (11 April 2000, ECtHR), at para. 34.

The domestic law in relation to the charging procedure is governed by para. 16 of Code C of PACE which requires that a detainee be provided with a written notice upon charge, detailing the particulars of the offence in simple terms but also the precise offence with which he is charged and details of the officer in the case.

Chapter Eleven

Bail

Michelle Strange

11.1 INTRODUCTION

When examining whether a defendant has had a fair trial under Article 6, the European Court will examine the whole of the proceedings, including the pre-trial stage. Accordingly, many pre-trial rights, such as the right to be informed of the nature and cause of the accusation, the right to be tried within a reasonable time, and the right to legal representation, are contained within Article 6 and are dealt with in chapter 16. The right to liberty, which in criminal proceedings includes the right to bail unless certain exceptions apply, is contained within Article 5, and forms the basis of this chapter. A degree of overlap between topics is inevitable, as the European Court often imports some aspects of Article 6 fairness into its interpretation of the rights under Article 5.

Similarities in the European Court's interpretation of Article 5 and the 'exceptions to the right to bail' under the Bail Act 1976[1] may tempt lawyers into concluding that domestic law does nothing to violate the Convention. This may, however, be too complacent: although most domestic law is capable of complying, it may in many cases need some reinterpretation and procedural changes before it does so fully.

The following changes may be necessary:

- courts may have to look more deeply into their grounds for refusing bail, and at the plausibility of any objections raised by the Crown;
- full reasons will need to be given for withholding bail;

---

[1] See below at para. 11.3.

- more bail applications may need to be entertained without what is currently deemed to be a change of circumstances;
- the defence may need to be given notice of the Crown's objections to bail and in more cases to be present at the hearing.

All of these matters are dealt with in some detail below, together with an analysis of some provisions which may offend the Convention.

11.2 THE FRAMEWORK OF ARTICLE 5

Article 5 sets out an exhaustive list of circumstances in which a state can detain an individual. The text which is most relevant to criminal defendants[2] is as follows:

> 1.   Everyone has the right to liberty and security of person. No one shall be deprived of his liberty save in the following cases and in accordance with a procedure prescribed by law:
>
> . . .
>
> (c)   The lawful arrest or detention of a person effected for the purpose of bringing him before a competent legal authority on reasonable suspicion of having committed an offence or when it is reasonably considered necessary to prevent his committing an offence or fleeing after having done so.
>
> . . .
>
> 3.   Everyone arrested or detained in accordance with the provisions of paragraph (1)(c) of this Article shall be brought promptly before a judge or other officer authorised by law to exercise judicial power and shall be entitled to trial within a reasonable time or to release pending trial. Release may be conditioned by guarantees to appear for trial.
> 4.   Everyone who is deprived of his liberty by arrest or detention shall be entitled to take proceedings by which the lawfulness of his detention shall be decided speedily by a court and his release ordered if the detention is not lawful.

The text of Article 5 has been subject to much analysis by the European Court, and various terms will be discussed below.

11.2.1 'Prescribed by law'

The European Court has said that the central purpose of Article 5 is to 'protect the individual from arbitrariness'.[3] The concept is important, and underpins much of

---

[2] Article 5(1)(a) will apply at the post-conviction stage: see chapter 18. Article 5(1)(e) can operate in addition to or instead of Article 5(1)(c) where the defendant is mentally ill: see chapter 20. Where the defendant is a child, Article 5(1)(d) may be engaged.

[3] *Lawless* v *Ireland (No. 3)* (1961) 1 EHRR 15, para. 14, *Winterwerp* v *Netherlands* (1979) 2 EHRR 387, para. 37, *X* v *UK* (1981) 4 EHRR 188, *Bozano* v *France* (1986) 9 EHRR 297, *Herczegfalvy* v *Austria* (1992) 15 EHRR 437, *Erkalo* v *Netherlands* (1999) 28 EHRR 509.

the reasoning in the case law relating to the right to liberty. The phrase 'prescribed by law' involves consideration of three overlapping areas:

(a)   the detention must comply with domestic law of the detaining state;
(b)   the legal framework authorising the detention must itself comply with the Convention.[4] Where the Court concludes that it does comply, it will allow domestic courts to interpret whether national law has been respected;[5]
(c)   the provisions justifying the detention must be sufficiently clear for an individual to be able to predict whether he or she is liable to be arrested and detained.[6]

11.2.2   'Reasonable suspicion'

There is limited guidance as to the meaning of 'reasonable suspicion'. The clearest statement appears in the case of *Fox, Campbell and Hartley* v *UK* (1990) 13 EHRR 157 at para. 32, where the European Court said that reasonable suspicion 'presupposes the existence of facts or information which would satisfy an objective observer that the person concerned may have committed the offence'. Honest belief in the absence of objective grounds would not suffice.

At the outset of any detention (i.e., arrest), there will be no breach of Article 5 where the only ground for detention is reasonable suspicion.[7] As time passes, this will not be enough, and continuation will need to be justified on other grounds. The other grounds must be 'relevant and sufficient',[8] and will be discussed below. It appears that there is little scope to argue that the Convention imposes a higher duty on the authorities than domestic law.[9]

11.2.3   The right to be brought promptly before a court

What constitutes a 'prompt' appearance in court will depend upon the facts of each case. In *Brincat* v *Italy* (1992) 16 EHRR 591 a period of four days from the time of arrest for blackmail was considered to be too long. In *Brogan and others* v *UK* (1988) 11 EHRR 117 the applicants were held for a variety of periods under the Prevention of Terrorism Act 1984, the shortest of which was four days. The Court upheld the applicants' claim that this was insufficiently prompt, which gave rise to a derogation being entered by the UK Government under Article 15(1) to

---

[4] *Assenov and others* v *Bulgaria* (1998) 28 EHRR 652.
[5] See for example, *Winterwerp* v *Netherlands*, above at fn. 3.
[6] See for example, *Steel and others* v *UK* (1998) 28 EHRR 603, *Baranowski* v *Poland* (28 March 2000).
[7] *Brogan and others* v *UK* (1988) 11 EHRR 117.
[8] *Letellier* v *France* (1991) 14 EHRR 83.
[9] See for example, *O'Hara* v *Chief Constable of the Royal Ulster Constabulary* [1997] AC 286, and PACE Code A: 1.7.

allow for longer periods of detention. A challenge to the validity of the derogation was unsuccessful.[10]

Domestic law provides for relatively short times between arrest and charge, except in alleged acts of terrorism. It is unlikely that the general framework of the Police and Criminal Evidence Act 1984 (PACE) offends Article 5.

11.2.4 Trial within a reasonable time

Article 5(3) entitles the criminal defendant to 'trial within a reasonable time or release pending trial'. These are not alternatives,[11] and a lengthy time for investigating an offence may be necessary where custody is not.[12] The requirement of trial within a reasonable time also appears in Article 6(1), but the requirements of Article 5 are more onerous, in view of the serious consequences to the individual and the presumption of innocence under Article 6(2).[13] The European Court has stressed the need for the authorities to show 'special diligence' when bringing criminal matters to trial. Time begins to run from the point where a person is 'charged' within the meaning of the Convention,[14] and ends when any domestic appeal has been determined.[15]

In practice, delays in bringing a case to trial in England will rarely engage Article 5(3). Successful cases in Strasbourg generally concern delays which would be far outside the norm here.[16] In *Ferrantelli and Santangelo v Italy* (1996) 23 EHRR 288 proceedings against the applicants had lasted over 16 years, and had begun when they were minors.

Under domestic law, a person who has had to wait years before being brought to trial can argue that the prosecution is an abuse of process, and domestic courts will decide whether any prejudice has resulted from the delay. For the defendant kept in custody pending trial, the Prosecution of Offences (Custody Time Limits) Regulations 1987 provide tight timetables for ensuring that the trial is heard within a reasonable time. Our courts have begun to apply these regulations as a punitive sanction against the Crown, and in the absence of a finding that the prosecution has acted with 'all due expedition', a defendant must be granted bail even if it could be argued that exceptions to the right to bail exist.[17]

Where there has been delay, the conduct of the applicant may be of relevance, but he or she will not be penalised for using all available avenues of objection or

---

[10] *Brannigan and McBride v UK* (1993) 17 EHRR 539.
[11] *Wemhoff v Germany* (1968) 1 EHRR 55.
[12] See for example, *Clooth v Belgium* (1991) 14 EHRR 717.
[13] *Abdoella v Netherlands* (1992) 20 EHRR 585.
[14] *Eckle v Germany* (1982) 5 EHRR 1. See also chapter 16.
[15] *B v Austria* (1990) 13 EHRR 20.
[16] See for example, *Pepe v Italy* (27 April 2000), where the applicant had waited for four years and two months before trial on charges of corruption, and *Gravslys v Lithuania* (10 October 2000), where the period was four years and eleven months.
[17] *R v Sheffield Crown Court, ex parte Headley* [2000] Crim LR 374.

appeal.[18] Both the Commission and the Court were unimpressed by the arguments of the French government in *Kemmache* v *France* (1991) 14 EHRR 520 that the applicant had contributed to the delay by appealing, as virtually all of his appeals had been successful. In that case the applicant had been reimprisoned on charges of counterfeiting and not questioned for two years. The entire proceedings lasted eight and a half years.

11.3   RELEASE ON BAIL

As the rights to trial within a reasonable time and to release pending trial are not in the alternative, Article 5(3) must be read as conferring a right to bail unless there are relevant or sufficient reasons for withholding it.[19] Even if grounds do exist, it will be a violation of Article 5(3) if bail is withheld even though the grounds for withholding it could be overcome by the attachment of conditions to bail.[20] Article 5 does not specifically sanction the imposition of conditions for any other purpose than to secure attendance for trial, but these are clearly permissible as a means to avoid custody: the European Court has upheld conditions to surrender travel documentation,[21] and a condition of residence[22] in addition to sureties and securities.[23]

The following are grounds capable of justifying the removal of a person's liberty before trial:

(a)   fear of absconding;
(b)   interference with the course of justice;
(c)   commission of further serious offences;
(d)   the preservation of public order;
(e)   the protection of the defendant.

It follows that reasonable suspicion alone does not justify a significant deprivation of liberty in the absence of other factors. Nor can the strength of the evidence alone justify detention, or the anticipation of a lengthy custodial sentence.[24]

---

[18] *Yagci and Sargin* v *Turkey* (1995) 20 EHRR 505.
[19] Under the UN International Covenant on Civil and Political Rights, Article 9(3), there is 'a general presumption [that] individuals awaiting trial should not be detained'. In New Zealand, the test under the Bill of Rights Act 1990 is of 'just cause'. In *Gillbanks* v *Police* [1994] 3 NZLR 61 it was held that the interference with the right to liberty should be 'proportionate' to the risks to be avoided.
[20] The court or police may act unlawfully where they effectively acquiesce in the detention of a defendant admitted to bail by another person: *Riera-Blume* v *Spain* (1999) 30 EHRR 632.
[21] *Stogmuller* v *Austria* (1969) 1 EHRR 155.
[22] *Schmid* v *Austria* (1985) 44 DR 195.
[23] UK law on this point is probably compliant with the Convention: s. 3, Bail Act 1976. Paragraph 8(1) of Part I of sch. 1 to the 1976 Act prohibits the imposition of conditions unless it is necessary to prevent the occurrence of the specified events.
[24] In New Zealand the courts have held that there must be some 'additional factor' requiring detention which cannot be dealt with by bail conditions: *B* v *Police* [2000] 1 NZLR 31.

In practice the first three grounds will be most widely used, and most likely to be upheld by the European Court. It will be noted that there is a great overlap with provisions of the Bail Act 1976 (sch. 1, Part I).

11.3.1 Fear of absconding

The Court has been surprisingly willing to substitute its own robust view for that of the domestic authorities, looking for real risks that the defendant will abscond before it will uphold detention on this ground alone.

Several principles have emerged. The fear of absconding may not be justified solely on the ground that a person faces a severe sentence, particularly if they have already served a significant portion of the likely sentence on remand.[25] The Court is unimpressed by a theoretical risk of absconding which is not borne out by the defendant's actual behaviour.[26] A realistic view of the defendant's circumstances and community ties is called for. In *Letellier* v *France* (1991) 14 EHRR 83 the Court thought there was no real risk of the applicant absconding, although she faced a likely custodial sentence for planning her husband's murder, because she had eight children in the jurisdiction and ran a garage which was her only source of income. In *Clooth* v *Belgium* (1991) 14 EHRR 717 the Court was similarly dismissive of an argument that the Belgian authorities had reason to fear that the applicant would abscond because extradition took place at an early stage in the proceedings.

11.3.2 Interference with the course of justice

Concern that a person will interfere with justice will need to be supported with good reasons, and Convention law would most likely reject this ground where a defendant been on bail in current[27] or past proceedings with no suggestion of interference. The Court has stressed that there should be something more than a nebulous fear raised by the authorities. Once the enquiry is complete, opportunities for interference lessen.[28] For example, it may be justified to withhold bail on this ground where a man is accused of assaulting his wife in the course of relationship breakdown, and cease to be justified once tempers have cooled and time has passed.

---

[25] *Wemhoff* v *Germany* (1968) 1 EHRR 55. The reasoning was particularly attractive in *Tomasi* v *France* (1992) 15 EHRR 1, where the applicant had spent five years and seven months on remand before being acquitted.

[26] *Stogmuller* v *Austria* (1969) 1 EHRR 155, where the applicant had a pilot's licence and access to an aeroplane, and was in breach of various undertakings to the court. In spite of this, he had repeatedly returned to the jurisdiction when given bail at an earlier stage in the proceedings.

[27] *Maznetter* v *Austria* (1969) 1 EHRR 198, repeated in *Kemmache* v *France* (1991) 14 EHRR 520, above at 11.2.4.

[28] See for example, *Kemmache* v *France* (1991) 14 EHRR 520.

11.3.3   Commission of further offences on bail

Both Convention and English law recognise this as a ground to justify detention,[29] but Convention law is more generous to the accused. Domestic law allows for a defendant to be remanded in custody where 'the court is satisfied that there are substantial grounds for believing that the defendant, if released on bail ... would ... commit an offence on bail'.[30] There is no requirement that the further offence be serious, or relevant to the matter in hand, and it is permissible under English law to remand in custody a defendant who is, say, a regular domestic burglar with a string of convictions, but is currently charged with assault. Such a remand in custody would probably offend Article 5.

Convention law looks for more of a nexus between the offence with which the defendant is currently charged, his or her history, and the plausibility of the state's fear of further offences. Fear may be justified where there are a number of earlier similar offences on the defendant's record,[31] but it is not permissible to infer a risk of further offences merely from the existence of a criminal record,[32] or from earlier offences of a dissimilar character. In *Clooth* v *Belgium* (1991) 14 EHRR 198 the applicant was charged with murder. The state relied upon two minor convictions and the applicant's psychiatric problems, arguing that the applicant had a propensity to commit further serious violent offences. The European Court was not persuaded by either argument.[33]

The feared offence on bail must be a serious one. In *Maznetter* v *Austria* (1969) 1 EHRR 198, the charges were of large scale fraud over a lengthy period. The European Court said that it was permissible to look at the seriousness of any possible offence when deciding if a person should be released. There is no guidance on what is a serious offence, and it could be argued in our jurisdiction that 'summary only' matters do not fit within the definition.

11.3.4   Preservation of public order

Bail can be refused under the Convention on the basis of feared public reaction to the crime or the defendant. The ground should be relied upon only 'in exceptional circumstances ... so far as domestic law recognises the notion ...', and only where is a factual basis capable of showing that release would *actually* disturb public order.[34]

---

[29] Section 38(1)(a)(iii), Police and Criminal Evidence Act 1984, para. 2 of Part 1 of sch. 1 to the Bail Act 1976.

[30] Bail Act 1976, sch. 1, Part I, para. 2.

[31] *Toth* v *Austria* (1991) 14 EHRR 551; see below at fn. 33.

[32] *Muller* v *France* (17 March 1997).

[33] It may have influenced the European Court that the applicant was remanded for over three years, after which the Belgian court confirmed that there was no case to answer. See *Toth* v *Austria* (1991) 14 EHRR 551, where the court said there should be a 'genuine risk of repetition'.

[34] See for example, *Letellier* v *France* (1991) 14 EHRR 83.

This is probably provided for by domestic law,[35] which provides that a custody officer may refuse bail if he has 'reasonable grounds for believing that the detention of the person arrested is necessary for his own protection', which would presumably cover a situation where the allegation against the defendant has excited so much public revulsion to put him or her at risk of attack by an unruly mob. We can find no examples of the ground ever being relied upon in isolation and, in practice, such cases may often justify detention on other grounds.

11.3.5 Defendant's own protection

Bail may be refused under the Convention to protect the accused. In *IA* v *France* (23 September 1998), the defendant was detained for five years, having been charged with murdering his wife. One of the grounds intermittently relied upon by the authorities was the fear that the wife's family would attack him. The European Court accepted that in exceptional circumstances this was a valid ground, although not made out on the present case.[36]

It is unclear whether the fear that a person would harm himself or herself would justify detention under Article 5(1)(c). There is some authority to suggest that the risk of self harm would not justify detention under this head,[37] but recent authority has suggested a wider approach by the Court where a person is vulnerable.[38]

As noted above at 11.3.4, English law provides for remands in custody to protect the accused. The provision is open-ended, and is capable of covering situations where it is feared the accused will commit suicide, or even where domestic circumstances put him or her at risk.

11.4 BAIL HEARINGS

11.4.1 Reasons

In *Tomasi* v *France* (1992) 15 EHRR 1 at para. 84 the European Court said:

[the national courts] must examine all the circumstances arguing for or against the existence of a genuine requirement of public interest justifying, with due regard to the presumption of innocence, a departure from the rule of respect for individual liberty and set them out in their decisions on the applications for release.

---

[35] PACE, s. 38(1)(a)(vi); Bail Act 1976, sch. 1, Part I, para. 3.
[36] There was little evidence of this apart from court decisions referring to 'frequently barbaric and unjust [Lebanese] conditions'. All of the wife's family resided outside the jurisdiction.
[37] *Riera Blume* v *Spain* (2000) 30 EHRR 632.
[38] See *Litwa* v *Poland* (4 April 2000).

Convention jurisprudence therefore demands more rigorous reasoning from the detaining party than is current general practice in our jurisdiction.[39] There is a tendency in domestic law to muddle up the existence of grounds and reasons, and it is important at the outset to distinguish between the two. *Grounds* for refusing bail (set out above at 11.3) are only capable of justifying deprivation of liberty. Thereafter, if a ground is made out, it is the quality of the *reasons* which determines if the grounds are relevant and sufficient.

In *Neumeister* v *Austria* (1968) 1 EHRR 91 at para. 5 the Court held that 'it is for the national judicial authorities to seek all the facts arguing for or against the existence of a genuine requirement of public interest justifying a departure from the rule of respect for individual liberty'. The reasons given by the detaining court will form the basis for the European Court to review compliance with Article 5, and the Court is insistent that those reasons should be concrete and not stereotyped, particularly where the ground relied upon is fear of flight by the defendant.[40] Reasons should be specific, and apply to the case in hand, and should address any counterarguments by the defence. Where no reasons have been given, the European Court is quick to infer that the rationale behind the decision was defective.[41]

The Court has also been willing to assess the quality of the evidence said to justify the accused's detention. In *Labita* v *Italy* (6 April 2000) at para. 157 it stressed that national authorities should be wary of basing an arrest or pre-trial detention on statements made by alleged accomplices who are assisting the prosecution. The position was considered recently in Scotland in the case of *Procurator Fiscal, Glasgow* v *Burn and McQuilken* 2000 JC 403, in which the High Court of Justiciary on appeal held:

> In future the Crown must provide sufficient general information relating to the particular case to allow the sheriff to consider the merits of their motion that the accused should be committed to prison and detained there for further examination. What will be required will depend on the facts of the particular case and for that reason we cannot lay down any hard-and-fast rule. We are satisfied, however, that it will not be necessary for the Crown to disclose operational details. On the other hand, where, for example, the Crown oppose bail on the ground of the risk that the accused would interfere with witnesses, the procurator fiscal depute should be in a position to explain the basis for that fear. The same would apply where opposition is based on a fear that the accused would interfere with a possible search of premises which the police wished to carry out. It

---

[39] See the Law Commission paper, *Bail and the Human Rights Act 1998, No. 157*, HMSO 1999, Part IV, pp. 43 ff, for a convincing argument that grounds and reasons are often blurred by magistrates' courts in this country, and that matters under the Bail Act 1976, sch. 1, Part I, para. 9 are often wrongly cited as grounds for witholding bail.

[40] See for example, *Clooth* v *Belgium* (1991) 14 EHRR 717, *Letellier* v *France* (1991) 14 EHRR 83, and *Yagci and Sargin* v *Turkey* (1995) 20 EHRR 505.

[41] See for example, *Tomasi* v *France* (1992) 15 EHRR 1 at para. 98.

follows also ... that where opposition to bail is based on some such ground and the relevant enquiry is completed before the date for further examination the Crown will wish to bring the matter back before the sheriff so he can, if so advised, order the accused's release from custody.

Domestic law requires the giving of reasons for the refusal of bail,[42] although in practice they are often not given in any meaningful sense. Crown court judges often say little more than that all arguments have been canvassed and bail is refused, and magistrates' courts commonly hand the defendant a form with the reasons for refusal ticked in standard boxes. Under the Convention neither is sufficient without further explanation.

11.4.2 Procedure at the bail hearing

The European Court has given little specific guidance as to which procedures are required to satisfy Article 5. The text of Article 5(3) provides that every person detained should 'be brought promptly before a judge or other officer authorised by law to exercise judicial power', and Article 5(4) provides that he or she is entitled 'to take proceedings by which the lawfulness of his [or her] detention shall be decided speedily by a court and his release ordered if the detention is not lawful'. Under domestic law there is considerable overlap in the two provisions, as the first review of detention is conducted by a court rather than another judicial officer. Any subsequent review of detention, including further bail applications in the magistrates' court and Crown Court will fall within Article 5(4).

Over the years the European Court has read a number of procedural safeguards into Article 5(4). In *De Wilde, Ooms and Versyp* v *Belgium* (1971) 1 EHRR 373 the court spoke of the need for 'guarantees of judicial procedure', or in other words the concept of fair trial rights contained within Article 6. It is not clear how extensive these rights are, and the authorities are contradictory. The European Court has held that not all Article 6 rights apply, but the guarantees of judicial procedure require that the hearing be adversarial[43] and that there be equality of arms. The applicant has a right to participate,[44] but it may be sufficient to do so through a lawyer.

The clearest statement of the principle in domestic law can be found in *R* v *Havering Justices, ex parte DPP* (2001) *The Times*, 7 February, in which Latham LJ said:

---

[42] See Bail Act 1976, s. 5(1), (3) and (4), s. 5A(2) inserted by CJPOA 1994, s. 27(4). There is similar authority at common law: for example, *R* v *Immigration Appeal Tribunal, ex parte Patel* [1996] Imm AR 161. See also *R* v *Crown Court at Canterbury, ex parte Howson-Ball* (19 November 2000) for the general duty to give reasons.

[43] *Lamy* v *Belgium* (1989) 11 EHRR 529. See also *R* v *Havering Justices, ex parte DPP* (2001) *The Times*, 7 February for domestic authority on point.

[44] *Winterwerp* v *Netherlands* (1979) 2 EHRR 387.

the Court has been prepared to borrow some of the general concepts of fairness in judicial proceedings from Article 6. But that does not mean that the process required for conformity with Article 5 must also be in conformity with Article 6. That would conflate the Convention's control over two separate sets of proceeding, which have different objects. Article 5 ... is concerned to ensure that the detention of an accused person before trial is only justified by proper consideration relating to the risks of absconding, and of interfering with witnesses, or the commission of other crimes. Article 6 is concerned with the process of determining the guilt or otherwise of a person who if found guilty would be subject to criminal penalties.

11.4.2.1   Presence of the defendant

English law does not entitle the defendant to be present at a bail application, although it is the practice in the magistrates' court to allow defendants to be present unless they consent to a remand in their absence.[45] Pre-trial Crown Court bail applications are generally heard in chambers with the defendant not being produced from custody. There appears to be no reason for this except administrative convenience, and this may be subject to challenge under the principles of open justice and the right of the defendant to participate effectively under Article 6.[46] Although there are rules mandating the prosecution to give written notice of its objections to bail and to serve a copy of this on the defence,[47] these are rarely followed, and it is common for defence lawyers to be met with new material at court, when it is impossible to take instructions from the defendant or counter the allegation.

The European Court has said that the judge determining bail 'must himself or herself hear the detained person before taking the appropriate decision,'[48] but this appears to mean the hearing of representations from the defendant or his or her lawyer, rather than hearing oral evidence. The Convention probably does not require the presence of a defendant at a hearing under Article 5(4), so long as he or she is represented and there is no risk of injustice from this.[49] If the proceedings are to be adversarial, then the defendant must know the nature of the prosecution objections to his or her release, and be given the opportunity to comment on it.[50]

It is arguable that the HRA 1998 requires the Crown to put the defence on detailed notice of their objections to bail, and any evidence in support of these, in advance of the hearing, to allow for the defence to meet the objections. This may

---

[45] Magistrates may proceed in the absence of a defendant if there is legal representation: s. 122, Magistrates' Courts Act 1980. See also *Baxter* v *Chief Constable of West Midlands* (1998) *The Independent*, 15 June.
[46] See for example, *Scarth* v *UK* [1999] EHRLR 332, where the hearing of arbitration hearings in private on the basis of administrative convenience was said to be in breach of Article 6. But see *Campbell and Fell* v *UK* (1984) 7 EHRR 164, above, where there are considerations of security.
[47] Crown Court Rules 1982 (SI 1982/1109), r. 19(3).
[48] *TW* v *Malta* (1999) 29 EHRR 185.
[49] *Sanchez-Reisse* v *Switzerland* (1986) 9 EHRR 71. See *TW* v *Malta* above at fn. 48.
[50] See *Toth* v *Austria* (1991) 14 EHRR 551 at para. 84.

be difficult to achieve in a system where bail applications are often listed for hearing at the Crown Court within 48 hours of notification.

If there is any dispute as to the matters relied upon, or any new materials raised in court, then the accused should be given a right to attend the hearing.[51] Given the vagaries and delays of the prison 'production order' system, it may have to become standard practice to have all applicants present at court.

11.4.2.2 Hearing of evidence

There is nothing in UK law to prevent the court hearing evidence at the bail application stage. It is, however, common practice in the UK for the prosecution to outline objections to bail in general terms without evidence being called, and without any documentary confirmation of the facts alleged. The duty to give reasons makes it necessary for the courts to enquire more deeply into possible grounds for refusal of bail, and to avoid making automatic or stereotyped judgments (see above at 11.4.1).

Where the evidence relied upon is unlikely to be in dispute, for example the defendant's previous convictions for failing to appear, or the contents of the documentary evidence in the case, it is unlikely that the calling of evidence could provide any further safeguards to the accused. Where the objections depend upon the subjective views of an officer in the case, however, the need to give a reasoned judgment may necessitate the court hearing some oral evidence, if the reasons later relied upon are to survive a successful challenge. This is not to say that the evidence must be called in its 'best' form — hearsay evidence is likely to be sufficient at this stage. In the domestic authority of *R v Havering Justices, ex parte DPP* (2001) *The Times*, 7 February, Latham LJ made the following observations on admissibility of evidence at the bail stage:

> I see nothing in either Article 5 itself, or in the authorities to which we have been referred, which suggest that, in itself, reliance on material other than the evidence which would be admissible at a criminal trial would be in breach of the protection required by Article 5. It is true that the European Court of Human Rights on occasions refers to the need for evidence, but that is used in contra-distinction to mere assertion. (para. 39 of the transcript)

The *Havering Justices* case was concerned with hearings after arrest for breach of bail under s. 7 of the Bail Act (see 11.5.2 below), but the comments are relevant to all bail applications where there is dispute of fact between the parties. A mere assertion of a ground to deny bail is unacceptable. This may hail significant changes in some cases. Where, for example, the Crown is maintaining that the defendant has a drug addiction, which needs to be funded by the commission of

---

[51] In *Havering Justices*, above, the Divisional Court placed some reliance on the fact that a defendant could give evidence if he wished to do so.

further offences, it may be necessary for the Crown to support these allegations with evidence from the officer in the case as to his or her grounds for believing that these contentions are reasonable.

When a witness is called, the defence must be given an opportunity to cross-examine. The defence may challenge any contention which may result in a denial of bail, and call the defendant to give evidence if necessary.

11.4.2.3   Disclosure at the pre-committal stage

For there to be equality of arms, the defence must have access to the prosecution material in order to challenge the grounds for detention at an early stage:[52] this was restated in *Nikolova* v *Bulgaria* (25 March 1999). How many documents this entails will vary from case to case, but it would appear to extend to material which undermines the prosecution case at a very early stage in the proceedings, before there is any requirement of disclosure under the Criminal Procedure and Investigations Act 1996. This is already the position in UK law, following the case of *R* v *DPP, ex parte Lee* [1999] 2 All ER 237. This was a lengthy murder enquiry, where the prosecution had material to undermine some of the evidence of their own witnesses which the defence wished to put before the court to strengthen their arguments at a bail application. The Divisional Court accepted that for an accused to make a properly prepared bail application at the pre-committal stage, some residual duty of disclosure had to attach to the Crown under the common law, although it added the *caveat* that any such disclosure was not to be seen as a return to the general duty of disclosure that existed before the current disclosure scheme came into force (see also *R* v *Bow Street Magistrates' Court, ex parte Finch and Bossino* (1999) 10 Archbold News 1, DC).

Where material has been seen by the court and/or prosecution and has been taken into account before bail is withheld, Article 5(4) is engaged. In *Garcia Alva* v *Germany* (13 February 2001) the European Court found a violation where material had not been shown to the defence for fear of prejudicing the investigation. The Court accepted that the prosecution's aims were legitimate, but held that they could not be proportionate or justified at the expense of substantial restrictions on the rights of the defence.

11.4.2.4   Repeated applications for bail

As UK law currently stands, there is no obligation on the part of magistrates to hear more than two bail applications in the absence of a finding that the defendant's circumstances have changed.[53] It is generally the case in more complicated matters which take some time between arrest and committal that a defendant can have his bail unreviewed by a court over a number of hearings.

---

[52] *Lamy* v *Belgium* (1989) 11 EHRR 529.
[53] Bail Act 1976, sch. 1, Part IIA, para. 2.

This is contrary to the approach under the Convention, and to the wording of Article 5(4), which gives the detainee a right to take proceedings for the speedy determination of the lawfulness of the detention. The European Court has suggested that 'the nature of detention on remand calls for short intervals; there is an assumption in the Convention that detention on remand is to be of strictly limited duration'.[54] In this case the Court suggested that monthly intervals between bail reviews was not unreasonable. The general principles of Article 5 require the authorities to examine repeatedly the justification for detention in the light of any delays and developments in the case. The Court has recognised that objections to bail may cease to be valid where there has been substantial delay in the investigation,[55] where a substantial portion of a custodial sentence has already been served,[56] and where the investigation is complete.[57] As the duty is on the authorities to detain the accused no longer than is strictly necessary, a condition that bail will only be considered where the accused makes an application has been held by the European Court to be in violation of Article 5(3).[58]

11.5 PROVISIONS IN UK LAW WHICH MAY VIOLATE THE CONVENTION

11.5.1 Bail Act 1976, sch. 1, Part I, para. 2A

This provision permits a court to refuse bail, save in exceptional circumstances, where the defendant is already on bail for an indictable offence at the time of arrest on other matters. The provision dispenses with the need for the court to make an assessment of the defendant's particular circumstances, such as character or community ties, under para. 9 of the Bail Act 1976.

Other provisions already permit the court to withhold bail when it has substantial grounds for believing that the defendant would commit an offence on bail (sch. 1, Part I, para. 2(b)), and a further arrest, particularly for a similar offence, would be a relevant consideration under that head. If para. 2A creates a separate ground for refusing bail, it is likely to violate the Convention, particularly the presumption of innocence under Article 6(2). It has all the hallmarks of the mechanical reasoning based on stereotypes which the European Court so dislikes, suggesting to the Court that further arrests on bail are a valid ground for refusing bail without further enquiry. The only way to read the provision compatibly with the Convention is to read the provision as creating a strong reason for refusal, albeit with the sanction of Parliament, and to assume that the other safeguards within the Bail Act 1976 still apply. Read in such a way

---

[54] *Bezicheri* v *Italy* (1989) 12 EHRR 210.
[55] For example *Clooth* v *Belgium* (1991) 14 EHRR 717.
[56] *Toth* v *Austria* (1991) 14 EHRR 551.
[57] *Kemmache* v *France* (1991) 14 EHRR 520.
[58] *Aquilina* v *Malta* (1999) 29 EHRR 185. See also the judgment of *Burn and McQuilkern* 2000 JC 403 at 11.4.1 above, where it was held that the Crown had a duty to bring the matter back to court for determination of bail, if enquiries were complete before the time allowed for an adjournment.

the provision adds nothing to the general body of law, and gives rise to the risk of unlawful decision-making. With this in mind the Law Commission has recommended that the provision is repealed.[59]

11.5.2 Where a defendant has been arrested for breach of bail under the Bail Act 1976

The Bail Act 1976 (sch. 1, Part I, para. 6) creates a further exception to the right to bail where a defendant previously on bail has been arrested under s. 7. Section 7 allows for an arrest in various circumstances, including where a constable has reasonable grounds to believe that a defendant will abscond or break a bail condition, or reasonable grounds for suspecting he or she has already broken a bail condition. In such circumstances the court may deem that one of the exceptions to the right to bail apply, whether or not it fits the facts of the case.[60]

This again smacks of automatic reasoning, particularly where the entry point for losing the right to bail is an arrest merely on reasonable suspicion or belief.[61] It is difficult to see what it adds to the law, especially as the Bail Act 1976, s. 7(5) envisages some enquiry into the facts by the court before deciding whether to grant bail after the alleged breach, and it may be that in practice justices continue to assume that the right to bail exists in the absence of good reasons to the contrary. In *R* v *Havering Justices, ex parte DPP* (see para. 11.4.2.2 above) the Divisional Court considered this issue, and said that, although the circumstances of an arrest or a finding under s. 7(5) were capable of providing good reason to deny bail, they could not form a ground in themselves. Accordingly, s. 7 does little beyond providing a mechanism for bringing a defendant back before the court, and deciding whether the conditions of bail have been breached.

A person arrested under s. 7 must be brought before a court within 24 hours or has an absolute right to bail.[62] Where magistrates do enquire into the circumstances of the alleged or threatened breach, there is domestic authority that the strict rules of evidence do not apply, and there is no power to adjourn the hearing.[63] This practice was challenged in the *Havering Justices* case, in which it was argued that the absence of a power to adjourn and the failure to adhere to the strict rules of evidence were in breach of Article 5, which requires that fair trial procedures under Article 6 be respected. The Divisional Court held that the procedure was

---

[59] *Bail and the Human Rights Act 1998*, para. 6.13. The Law Commission has also argued in favour of repealing sch. 1, Part I, para. 6.

[60] *R* v *Liverpool City Justices, ex parte DPP* [1993] QB 233.

[61] The position in Canada is that presumption in favour of bail is reversed only when the defendant is charged with a breach: s. 515(6)(a)(i), Canadian Criminal Code. Additional provisions reverse the presumption for defendants not normally resident in the country, and in certain drugs offences punishable with life imprisonment.

[62] *R* v *Governor of Glen Parrva Young Offender Institution, ex parte G (a minor)* [1998] 2 Cr App R 349.

[63] *R* v *Liverpool City Justices, ex parte DPP* [1993] QB 233.

compatible with Article 5. Latham LJ, giving the judgment of the court, said that Article 5 did not require that all Article 6 rights apply, and that it was acceptable for evidence to be presented in a form which would be inadmissible at trial. Regarding the absence of a power to adjourn, he said that the procedure was designed for emergencies, and there was no power to detain an individual for the adjourned proceedings. The procedure was intended to allow for the magistrate to 'come to an honest and rational opinion on the material put before him ... bear[ing] in mind the consequences to the defendant, namely the fact that he is at risk of losing his liberty in the context of the presumption of innocence' (para. 40 of the transcript). It is difficult to see how the authority works in all cases. What should the court do when a person is arrested in breach of bail and there is cogent evidence, for example an alibi or computer printout, which will not be available for three days? In such circumstances, it is difficult to see how the procedural requirements of Article 5(4) could be respected, however limited the scope of Article 6 at this stage. It appears on the current authority that all the defence can do at this stage is to give hearsay evidence of what the witnesses or documents are likely to prove, and impress upon the magistrates not to find a breach on this occasion, or to adjourn the matter for a limited period with the defendant remaining on bail. The position may be unsatisfactory in many cases.

11.5.3 Criminal Justice and Public Order Act 1994, s. 25

This section prohibits the grant of bail to a defendant who has previously been convicted of rape or homicide, and who is charged with another such offence, in the absence of exceptional circumstances. The section originally prohibited bail in all such cases, and was amended following applications to Strasbourg,[64] where the Commission held that the removal of the court's right to examine whether the defendant could have bail amounted to an arbitrary deprivation of liberty.

Whether the measure is now Convention compliant is open to debate. There is no definition of 'exceptional circumstances', but authorities on the interpretation of the same words in the context of automatic life sentences under the 'two strikes' rule[65] have shown a more open, purposive approach to the phrase. The Court of Appeal has held[66] that 'exceptional' should be given its ordinary meaning, with the court having regard to the intention of Parliament that life sentences should be the norm for those convicted of more than one serious offence. In *R* v *Offen* [2001] 2 All ER 154, it was read into Parliament's intention

---

[64] *BH* v *UK* (1997) 25 EHRR CD 136, *Caballero* v *UK* (2000) 30 EHRR 643.

[65] Crime (Sentences) Act 1997, s. 2(2) (now repealed and replaced by s. 109 of the Powers of Criminal Courts (Sentencing) Act 2000): the section reads 'unless ... there are exceptional circumstances relating to either of the offences or to the offender which justify its not doing so'. For a similar provision in New Zealand, see s. 318(3), Crimes Act.

[66] (In the context of automatic life sentences) *Attorney-General's Reference (No. 53 of 1998)*; *R* v *Sandford*; *R* v *Kelly* [2000] 1 QB 198; *R* v *Offen* (9 November 2000).

that it could not have meant that life sentences should be passed in the absence of an offender presenting an ongoing danger to the public.

Applying the same reasoning to bail, the courts would have to give effect to the intention of Parliament normally to withdraw bail for any person falling within the terms of the section, but the context of this would be an intention not to cause injustice, or contravene the Convention. If there is a genuine discretion vested in the court, and individual circumstances must still be considered, then the section can be strained to comply with the Convention. The mere fact that there is a 'reverse onus' on the accused, although harsh, may not be objectionable in Strasbourg,[67] so long as the authorities remain charged with the duty of justifying the remand in custody on grounds falling within Article 5(1)(c).

If, however, s. 25 provides the court with a justification for removing bail when there are no grounds for believing that any of the other exceptions to bail apply, there is likely to be a breach of Article 5. This is contrary to the most natural reading of the section, which appears to provide that bail will be *automatically* withdrawn unless the defence show highly unusual reasons why it should be granted. It follows that the section creates a great risk of unlawful decision-making, and is likely to need clarification or amendment to ensure this does not occur.[68]

---

[67] See *Salabiaku* v *France* (1988) 13 EHRR 379, dealt with at 13.15 and *R* v *DPP, ex parte Kebilene* [1999] 3 WLR 972 for a recent House of Lords analysis of 'mandatory' and 'discretionary' provisions.
[68] The Law Commission recommends amendment or further guidance on interpretation in *Bail and the Human Rights Act* (see above at fn. 58), chapter 9.

Chapter Twelve

The Right to Legal Representation
Michelle Strange

12.1 INTRODUCTION

The right to legal representation is central to safeguarding the defendant's rights to a fair trial, and to ensuring equality of arms under Article 6. Under Article 6(3)(c), everyone charged with a criminal offence has the right to:

> defend himself in person or through legal assistance of his own choosing or, if he has not sufficient means to pay for legal assistance, to be given it free when the interests of justice so require.

The provision should be read together with the defendant's right to have adequate time and facilities for the preparation of a defence under Article 6(1)(b), which is discussed below at 14.10.

12.2 THE SCOPE OF ARTICLE 6(3)(c)

The effect of Article 6(3)(c) is to grant a right to consult a lawyer from the point when Convention law recognises that a person is 'charged with a criminal offence'. This must be provided by the state (i) where he or she lacks the means to pay, and (ii) where the interests of justice require it.[1] A person who has the means to instruct a private lawyer has a greater degree of choice about which lawyer represents him or her in court. All of these issues have been considered by the Strasbourg bodies and will be discussed below.

---

[1] Cf. Article 14(3)(d), International Covenant on Civil and Political Rights, which is in similar terms.

The Court and Commission have also written into Article 6(3)(c) the right to have representation which is 'practical and effective'.[2] This includes the right to consult a lawyer privately (see below at 12.2.8.1), and the right to take advice that the lawyer gives,[3] within reasonable limits, as a means of ensuring the right to a fair trial under Article 6(1).

12.2.1   Criminal offences

It should be remembered that Convention law has autonomous concepts of what constitutes both criminal proceedings[4] and a criminal 'charge' (see at 14.2).

Thus in *Benham* v *UK* (1996) 22 EHRR 293, the Court held that proceedings to commit a person to prison for non-payment of the community charge were criminal notwithstanding the domestic classification as civil proceedings, and that persons defending such proceedings should have been entitled to legal aid, despite domestic authority to the contrary.[5] The Court was impressed by the fact that the proceedings involved considering arcane legal concepts, and could result in a custodial sentence.

12.2.2   Charge

Early cases suggested that 'charge' meant the point at which a person was informed that they would be prosecuted,[6] but the concept has since been developed. In *Eckle* v *Germany* (1982) 5 EHRR 1, the Court defined 'charge' as 'the official notification given to an individual by the competent authority of an allegation that he has committed a criminal offence', a wider definition which can include arrest. In *Imbrioscia* v *Switzerland* (1993) 17 EHRR 441, the Court found that the right to a lawyer could arise at the stage of police questioning, if the circumstances of the case demanded it for the defendant to have a fair trial. Accordingly, the right to a lawyer may in some circumstances crystallise at the point of arrest.[7]

UK law provides particularly good reasons for lawyers to be present at the pre-trial stage, which are largely recognised by the framework of the Police and Criminal Evidence Act 1984. The relationship between the rights to a lawyer and the later drawing of inferences was addressed by the European Court in *John Murray* v *UK* (1996) 22 EHRR 29. The case concerned Northern Irish provisions which were equivalent to the Criminal Justice and Public Order Act 1994, s. 34,[8]

---

[2] *Artico* v *Italy* (1980) 3 EHRR 1.
[3] *Condron* v *UK* (2000) 8 BHRC 290; see below at 19.8.2.
[4] See *Engel* v *Netherlands* (1976) 1 EHRR 706, *Benham* v *UK* (1996) 22 EHRR 293, and 14.2.
[5] *Ex parte Bold* (1996) *The Times*, 15 July.
[6] *G* v *UK* (1983) 35 DR 75.
[7] As it does under English law: PACE, s. 58. Access to a solicitor can be delayed in some circumstances with the authorisation of a senior officer.
[8] Criminal Evidence (Northern Ireland) Order 1988.

where a court is permitted to draw inferences from silence during questioning. The applicant had been arrested under the Prevention of Terrorism (Temporary Provisions) Act 1989, and was denied access to a lawyer for a lengthy period in which he was interviewed 12 times.

The Court held that the defendant should normally have access to a lawyer at the questioning stage. This is not an absolute right, but the failure to provide a lawyer may in the longer term give rise to an unfair hearing in breach of Article 6.[9] In *Murray*, the later drawing of inferences from silence in the absence of a lawyer was in breach of Article 6.

12.2.3 The right to represent oneself

Article 6(3)(c) gives each a defendant a right to represent himself or herself.[10] This right is not absolute. Those accused of sexual assault,[11] and unruly or unreasonable defendants, may have their rights curtailed to protect the rights of others.[12] Similarly, legal representation may be required where the proceedings are particularly complicated. In *Philis* v *Greece* (1990) 66 DR 260 the Commission did not find a requirement of legal representation before a higher court incompatible with Article 6(3)(c).

Where a defendant has waived his or her right to a lawyer, the Court should ensure that the waiver is unequivocal, and that he or she understands the nature of the charge faced.[13] Failure to appear does not constitute a waiver.[14] Whether the defendant is unrepresented through choice, or the unavailability of legal aid, the trial court may need to give him or her particular assistance to ensure fair trial.[15] The principle was recently set out in the Scottish case of *Bullock* v *HM Advocate* 1999 JC 260 where the High Court of Justiciary said:

---

[9] *Murray* v *UK* at para. 62. See also *Magee* v *UK* (2000) 8 BHRC 646, *Averill* v *UK* (2000) *The Times*, 20 June, on similar points. In the Scottish case of *Campbell* v *Her Majesty's Advocate* (21 September 1999), the High Court ruled that the denial of a solicitor for an identification parade where there is no complaint of its conduct does not violate Article 6(3)(c).

[10] As does domestic law: s. 2, Criminal Procedure (Lord Denman's) Act 1865.

[11] *Baegan* v *Netherlands* (1995) A/327-B, Commission.

[12] *Croissant* v *Germany* (1992) 16 EHRR 135. English law has made similar inroads into the right which, if fairly exercised, are unlikely to violate the Convention. See *R* v *Lyons* (1979) 68 Cr App R 104, and the Youth Justice and Criminal Evidence Act 1999, which permits the court to appoint special counsel to cross-examine the complainant in sex cases. Presumably any refusal by the accused will pass the burden of cross-examination on to the trial judge. See also *R* v *De Oliviera* [1997] Crim LR 600.

[13] In New Zealand the courts have held that any waiver will carry no weight unless the authorities establish that the accused understands the jeopardy he or she faces, and the nature of the prosecution evidence: *R* v *Lory (Ruling No. 4)* (3 September 1996). In Canada the unrepresented defendant who has waived rights to a lawyer must be reminded of the right should the nature of the investigation change: *R* v *Smith* (1989) 2 SCR 368.

[14] *Krombach* v *France* (13 February 2001, ECtHR), *R* v *Hayward and others* (31 January 2001, CA).

[15] *Artico* v *Italy* (1980) 3 EHRR 1. See also 15.8.2, where the unrepresented defendant is assisted by the magistrates' clerk.

> While it is no part of the Sheriff's function to act as defence counsel, he must ensure not merely that an unrepresented accused is given every opportunity, within reasonable limits, to bring out any points which he wishes to make, particularly in cross-examination, but also that no advantage is taken by the prosecutor, whether deliberately or unintentionally, of the fact that the accused is unrepresented.

In Scotland, the courts have considered that this role may in some circumstances involve giving serious consideration to a late application for legal aid where it becomes clear to the unrepresented defendant that he is out of his depth and would now like representation.[16]

It is not clear what the Convention approach would be to a situation where the unrepresented defendant conducts himself so badly that he is disrupting the proceedings or undermining the authority of the court. There is domestic case law sanctioning the withholding of the right to a closing speech by an unrepresented defendant. In *R* v *Morley* [1988] QB 601 the Court of Appeal upheld the right of a trial judge to exclude an unrepresented defendant from court at the time when he would have made his closing speech, on the basis that the court had no alternative but to exclude him. Although the European Court might lack some sympathy for the badly behaved defendant in these circumstances,[17] it may be that Article 6 requires another person to undertake this role on the defendant's behalf, whether it be the judge or special counsel, for a fair trial to be maintained.

12.2.4   Privately funded lawyers

The text of Article 6(3)(c) shows that the privately funded accused has the advantage over the legally assisted defendant, in that he or she may have a lawyer of choice. Under the Convention that choice should be respected where possible, but the right is not absolute, especially if the integrity of the lawyer of choice is in question. The Court can exclude a lawyer if he or she is in breach of ethics or professional codes, or shows disrespect to the court.[18]

The Court considered the matter in *Croissant* v *Germany* (1992) 16 EHRR 135. The applicant, who was a member of the Red Army Faction, objected to a lawyer imposed by the court on the ground that he was not of his choosing and was a member of the Social Democratic Party. The lawyer was the third member of the legal team, and the applicant had been permitted to choose the first two, who did not practise locally. The Court upheld the trial court's decision to impose a further lawyer, as the case was complicated, and the appointed lawyer was both appropriate and local.

---

[16] *Bullock* v *Her Majesty's Advocate* 1999 JC 260. See also *Venters* v *Her Majesty's Advocate* 1999 SLT 1345.

[17] See for example, *X* v *UK* (1980) 21 DR 126.

[18] *Ensslin and others* v *Germany* (1978) 14 DR 64, where the lawyers of choice were believed by the court to be criminally involved with the defendants.

12.2.5 Legal aid

The Convention provides that a defendant should be given free legal assistance when he or she lacks the means and where the interests of justice require it. The Court has set little guidance as to when it will be necessary to provide legal aid in the interests of justice, preferring to look at the facts of the particular case to see if the right to a fair trial has been breached. The Court has taken into account the complexity of the proceedings,[19] the capacity of the individual to represent himself or herself,[20] and the severity of any potential sentence.[21] Where further detention is a possible outcome of the hearing, Article 5(4) requires that a mentally ill person should have legal assistance whether or not they request it.

12.2.6 The quality of legal representation and advice provided by the state

The purpose of the right to legal representation and advice is to safeguard the defendant's fair trial rights, including equality of arms, cross-examination of witnesses, and effective preparation for trial. With this in mind the Court has said that rights guaranteed by the Convention must not be 'theoretical or illusory but rights that are practical and effective'.[22] Accordingly, Article 6(3)(c) may be breached by the mere nomination of a lawyer who is for some reason unable to represent the defendant properly. Where the authorities are aware of shortcomings, they may be required to intervene.[23] A failure to assign another lawyer after reasonable complaint by the defendant can engage Article 6.

It is not clear how poor the level of representation should be before the Convention will be breached. In *Kamasinski v Austria* (1989) 13 EHRR 36 the applicant's lawyer had not attended for a hearing, nor taken full instructions nor fully prepared himself for trial. The Court found that the domestic authorities could not be responsible for minor shortcomings by legally aided lawyers, saying:

> ... the conduct of the defence is essentially a matter between the defendant and his counsel, whether counsel be appointed under a legal aid scheme or be privately funded ... the competent authorities are required under Article 6(3)(c) to intervene only if a failure by legal aid counsel to provide effective representation is manifest or sufficiently brought to their attention in some other way.[24]

---

[19] *Hoang v France* (1993) 16 EHRR 53.

[20] *Granger v UK* (1990) 12 EHRR 469; *Quaranta v Switzerland* (1991) A/205.

[21] *Benham v UK* (1996) 22 EHRR 293.

[22] *Artico v Italy* (1981) 3 EHRR 1.

[23] *Quaranta v Switzerland* (1991) A/205. In England, it is possible to raise competence of counsel as a ground of appeal against conviction.

[24] *Kamasinski v Austria* at para. 65. On the facts of the case, there was evidence that the trial lawyer had taken many appropriate steps in the case. The Court appears to have been wary of setting a precedent for hearing unlimited numbers of complaints from dissatisfied convicted defendants.

A narrow approach was also taken by the Commission in *F* v *UK* (1992) 15 EHRR CD 32, a Scottish case where the defendant met counsel on the morning of his trial for attempted murder. The new counsel refused to apply for an adjournment and the case proceeded. The Commission found that the responsibility of the state was not engaged. The position may be different where it is clear that new counsel has not had time to prepare the defence.[25]

The defendant has no right to insist that the case be run in an unprofessional or unethical way,[26] but the state should have some regard to his or her views on the lawyer appointed. In *Croissant* v *Germany* (1992) 16 EHRR 135 at para. 29 the Court said that although the right of choice was not absolute:

> the national courts must certainly have regard to the defendant's wishes ... they can override those wishes when there are relevant and sufficient grounds for holding that this is necessary in the interests of justice.

12.2.7   Challenging domestic provision of legal aid

UK law has an unusually comprehensive system of free representation, and the criteria for the grant of legal aid in England are in similar general terms to the Convention[27] — they include the risk of a custodial sentence, considerable questions of law, lack of understanding of the proceedings by the accused, the need to interview or cross-examine witnesses, and consideration of whether it is in someone else's interest that the accused is represented. This will soon be subject to limitations,[28] and compatibility cannot be predicted at the time of writing because the regulations have not been published.

The UK has been held to be in violation of the Convention on a number of occasions. 'Weak spots' in our system appear to be the classification of proceedings as criminal/civil,[29] and a failure to review a refusal of legal aid if proceedings become more complex.[30]

12.2.8   The importance of a lawyer's advice

The European Court has held that for rights under Article 6(3)(c) to be effective, the accused must have (i) a right to consult his or her lawyer privately and (ii) to take account of the lawyer's advice when it is given.

---

[25] *Goddi* v *Italy* (1984) 6 EHRR 457, *Daud* v *Portugal* (1998) 30 EHRR 400.
[26] *X* v *UK* (1980) 21 DR 126.
[27] Legal Aid Act 1988, s. 21(2)(a).
[28] Access to Justice Act 1999.
[29] *Benham* v *UK* (1996) 22 EHRR 293.
[30] *Granger* v *UK* (1990) 12 EHRR 469. See also *Bullock* v *HM Advocate* 1999 JC 260.

12.2.8.1   *Confidentiality of lawyer/client communications*

Lawyer/client communications are protected by Article 6(3)(c) and Article 8. In general they must be private, confidential and not subjected to restrictions. In the case of *Schonenberger and Durmaz* v *Switzerland* (1988) 11 EHRR 202 the European Court rejected the Swiss Government's claim that it had intercepted a letter from a lawyer to his client advising him of his right to remain silent because the advice jeopardised the proper conduct of pending criminal proceedings.

The notion of privacy and confidentiality was developed by the Court in *S* v *Switzerland* (1991) 14 EHRR 670 where almost all communications between the applicant and his lawyer were monitored by the authorities. Although there is no guarantee of communications out of hearing of a third person, the Court held (para. 48) that:

> ... an accused's right to communicate with his advocate out of the hearing of a third person is one of the basic requirements of a fair trial in a democratic society and follows from Article 6(3)(c) of the Convention. If a lawyer were unable to confer with his client and receive confidential instructions from him without such surveillance, his assistance would lose much of its usefulness, whereas the Convention is intended to guarantee rights that are practical and effective.

This principle has significant implications for practices in the UK. It is commonplace for police stations and magistrates' courts to have no facilities for a person who has been arrested or is appearing at court to speak to a lawyer in private. This is not justified under Convention law, unless there is a real risk of collusion between a client and his or her lawyer.[31] Lack of resources or facilities will be unlikely to satisfy the European Court, which has recently held on other grounds that the administrative problems of a court will not justify breaches of the Convention.[32]

12.2.8.2   *The right to take the lawyer's advice*

This developing principle is currently subject to significant qualification. In the recent case of *Condron* v *UK* (2000) 8 BHRC 290, the applicants remained silent in police interviews on legal advice. Their solicitor gave evidence on a *voir dire* that he had given the advice after observing that both applicants were withdrawing from heroin. The trial judge nonetheless permitted the jury to draw

---

[31] *S* v *Switzerland* at para. 49. See also *Foxley* v *UK* (2000) *The Times*, 4 July where the Court stressed that interception of lawyer/client communications could be justified only in exceptional circumstances where there was a real risk of abuse.

[32] *Majaric* v *Slovenia* (8 February 2000) where the state sought to justify lengthy delays on the basis of its heavy workload. See also *Scarth* v *UK* (22 July 2000).

an inference of guilt as they thought fit, and the Court of Appeal ([1997] 1 Cr App R 185) upheld his ruling.

The European Court disagreed, saying that the trial judge should have limited what inference the jury could have drawn, telling them to draw inferences only if satisfied that the applicants remained silent because they had no answer, or none which would stand up to questioning. The European Court stressed that the fact that an accused is advised by his lawyer to maintain his silence should be given 'appropriate weight' by the domestic court, as there may be good reason why such advice may be given. It remains to be seen how this principle is further developed by the European Court, but it is open to the defence to argue, in the absence of evidence or suspicion of collusion, that the right to consult a lawyer under Article 6(3)(c) involves a right to take the advice given. In the recent case of *R v Betts* (9 February 2001) the Court of Appeal allowed an appeal where a jury had been invited to draw any inference they thought fit from silence, which could have arisen merely because of solicitors' advice.

In *Condron* the European Court was nonetheless unsympathetic to the argument that the provisions of the Criminal Justice and Public Order Act 1994, s. 34 were themselves in violation of Article 6(3)(c), in that they required an accused to reveal the details of confidential discussions with his or her lawyer or risk inferences being drawn from silence at the police interview stage. The European Court said:

> ... the fact that the applicants were subjected to cross-examination on the content of their solicitor's advice cannot be said to raise an issue of fairness under Article 6 of the Convention. They were under no compulsion to disclose the advice given, other than the indirect compulsion to avoid the reason for their silence remaining at the level of a bare explanation. The applicants chose to make the content of their solicitor's advice a live issue as part of their defence. For that reason they cannot complain that the scheme of section 34 of the 1994 Act is such as to override the confidentiality of their discussions with their solicitor.

The Court interpreted the notion of 'compulsion' very narrowly, and appears to have placed some reliance on the fact that the solicitor had been called by the defence to give evidence, suggesting a degree of positive choice to reveal the contents of the conversations between lawyer and client. It is not clear whether it would have reached the same conclusion if the defendants had refused to reveal the advice given, citing the privacy of lawyer/client communications as the reason.[33]

---

[33] There may be good reason for doing so when there is potentially prejudicial material in the privileged documents, particularly as domestic law provides for a waiver of privilege whether or not the solicitor is called to give evidence: *R v Bowden* [1999] 2 Cr App R 176. The defendant is 'compelled' in a real sense to reveal the conversations or have it held against him.

12.3 DEFENDANT'S COSTS

There is no right to costs under the Convention.[34] Where the question of costs arises after trial, the presumption of innocence requires that a judge should be slow to make adverse comment about the guilt of an acquitted defendant, even if this is on a technicality. In *Minelli* v *Switzerland* (1983) 5 EHRR 554 the European Court found a violation of Article 6(2) where a domestic court ordered the applicant to pay part of the prosecution costs, on the basis that he would 'very probably' have been convicted had the trial progressed.

The issue was revisited by the Court in *Rushiti* v *Austria* (21 March 2000), where an acquitted defendant was denied compensation on the basis that suspicion against him had not been dissipated. The Court held that the voicing of suspicion about guilt was incompatible with Article 6(2).

It is not clear whether domestic law as to costs will survive the latter ruling. Under Costs in Criminal Cases (General) Regulations 1986 (SI 1986/ 1335), and the *Practice Direction (Costs in Criminal Proceedings)* (1991) 93 Cr App R 89, it was permissible for costs to be refused to an acquitted defendant where (i) the defendant's own conduct brought suspicion on himself and had 'misled the prosecution into thinking that the case against him is stronger than it is' or (ii) 'where there [was] ample evidence to support a conviction but the defendant is acquitted on a technicality which has no merit'. The second ground has now been deleted [2000] 1 Cr App R 60, and there is recent authority that the court should give reasons and rely upon material to support any refusal under the first ground.[35] It remains to be seen whether ground (i) can be satisfied without offending Article 6(2).

---

[34] *Lutz* v *Germany* (1988) 10 EHRR 182.
[35] *Mooney* v *Cardiff Justices* (1999) *The Times*, 17 November.

Chapter Thirteen

Disclosure

Tim Owen QC

13.1 DISCLOSURE AND THE REQUIREMENTS OF THE CONVENTION

The Convention confers no express right to disclosure in criminal proceedings. However, the European Court and Commission have read such a right into the fair trial guarantees under Article 6(1) and the more specific requirement under Article 6(3)(b) that everyone charged with a criminal offence must 'have adequate time and facilities for the preparation of his defence'. In addition, as noted above at 11.4.2.3, Article 5(4) can require speedy access to documents where the defendant is being held in custody. In *R* v *Stratford Justices, ex parte Imbert* [1999] 2 Cr App R 276 Buxton LJ emphasised the context in which the issue of disclosure arose under the Convention, commenting that '[t]he Convention right to which the applicant [is] entitled is not an absolute right to pre-trial disclosure but a right to a fair trial'. But it may be that this point, while formally correct, is more semantic than substantive. In order to have a fair trial a defendant *does*, as we shall see, have an absolute Convention right to pre-trial disclosure of any and all material which may help him to prove his innocence

The question of disclosure was first considered in detail by the Commission in *Jespers* v *Belgium* (1981) 27 DR 61 in which the applicant complained that a 'special folder' held by the public prosecutor's department had not been properly disclosed to him in violation of Article 6(1) and 6(3)(b). The Commission began its analysis by observing the requirement of 'equality of arms' between the prosecution and the defence in a criminal prosecution. Noting the considerable resources and powers available to the investigating and prosecuting authorities, the Commission held that the equality of arms principle (which it read into both Article 6(1) and (3)) 'recognizes the right of the accused to have at his disposal, for the purposes of exonerating himself or of obtaining a reduction in his sentence, all relevant elements that have been or could be collected by the competent authorities' (para. 58).[1] It is implicit in the Commission's reasoning that equality of arms could be achieved in criminal proceedings only if the authorities were under a duty to gather evidence in favour of the accused as well as evidence against him, with the defence having access to all relevant material before trial.

The Commission emphasised that the 'facilities' which everyone charged with a criminal offence should enjoy under Article 6(3)(b) included '. . . the opportunity to acquaint himself, for the purposes of preparing his defence, with the results of investigations carried out throughout the proceedings' (para. 56). For the Commission this right was to be applied broadly. It mattered little by whom, and when, investigations had been ordered or under whose authority they were carried out (para. 56). And the duty to permit a defendant to have access to the results of investigations applied at all stages, not just in relation to preliminary investigations. Despite the qualification of the word 'facilities' in Article 6(3)(b) by the word 'adequate', the Commission in *Jespers* insisted that the accused must be provided with facilities 'which assist or may assist him in his defence' (para. 57). If the 'element' in question is a document, access to that document is a necessary 'facility' if 'it concerns acts of which the defendant is accused, the credibility of testimony etc.' (para. 58). And, in the Commission's view, where the applicant had been given no access at all to the 'special folder' in question, it was unrealistic, and unfair, to expect him to specify which documents he wished to see (para. 60).

The Commission's starting point was adopted by the European Court in *Edwards* v *UK* (1992) 15 EHRR 417. In that case, the applicant complained that Article 6(1) and 6(3)(d) had been violated because of the failure of the police at his trial for robbery and burglary to disclose: (a) the fact that one of the victims, who had made a statement that she thought she would be able to recognise her assailant, had failed to identify the applicant from a police photograph album; and (b) the existence of fingerprints which had been found at the scene of the crime. This non-disclosure, it was argued, denied the defence a fair opportunity to cross-examine police witnesses in violation of the principle of equality of arms. Recognising that the guarantees in Article 6(3) are specific aspects of the wider right to a fair trial under Article 6(1), the Court held that 'it is a requirement of fairness under Article 6(1), indeed one which is recognised under English law, that the prosecution authorities disclose to the defence all material evidence for or against the accused' (para. 36).[2] The Court approved the English common law

---

[1] The Commission adopted a broad approach to the duty of disclosure stating that 'it considers that if the element in question is a document, access to that document is a necessary "facility" if, as in the present case, it concerns acts of which the defendant is accused, the credibility of testimony, etc.'.

[2] See also the Court's endorsement of this approach in *Jasper* v *UK* (2000) 30 EHRR 441 at para. 51 and in *IJL, GMR & AKP* v *United Kingdom* ('the Guinness trial') (App. Nos 29522/95, 30056/96 and 30574/96, 19 September 2000) at para. 112.

rules governing disclosure as being in conformity with the spirit of Article 6 and concluded that there had been an obvious violation of both domestic law and Article 6 at the trial stage. In the end, however, it concluded that, looked at as a whole, the criminal proceedings did not give rise to a violation of Article 6 because the defect in the disclosure process had been cured before the appeal was heard. The appeal had afforded the accused an opportunity to know and challenge the previously undisclosed evidence, thus ensuring that the right to a fair trial was upheld. The Court of Appeal was able to assess the impact of the undisclosed evidence on the safety of the conviction.

The European Court re-examined the question of disclosure in *Bendenoun* v *France* (1994) 18 EHRR 54 a case involving very special facts. The applicant, a company director, was involved in three sets of proceedings — customs, tax and criminal proceedings — which all, more or less, progressed in parallel. In the customs proceedings, the applicant was given access to all documents. In the tax proceedings, in which he was challenging a supplementary tax assessment, he was denied access to a customs report, which the authorities refused to disclose. But in the criminal proceedings, the same report was available to his lawyer throughout the investigatory stages. The applicant complained to the European Court on the basis that the non-disclosure of the customs file in the tax proceedings violated the principle of equality of arms under Article 6 of the Convention.

The European Court considered that the tax proceedings involved 'criminal charges' within the meaning of Article 6(3)(b), but found no violation of the Convention. The Court noted that the authorities had disclosed all those documents from the file which had been relied upon in the proceedings and that the rest of the file had not been before the domestic court dealing with the tax matter. While the Court accepted that, in itself, this did not necessarily preclude the possibility that disclosure should be made, it held that it did put the applicant under an obligation to specify why he wanted further documents (para. 52).

The extent to which the Court's approach in *Bendenoun* qualifies the Commission's approach in *Jespers* is unclear. Clearly the Court came to its decision on the basis that, since the applicant was seeking documents not relied upon by the prosecution to prove its case, he had to specify, at least in outline, why he wanted them. However, the Court was undoubtedly influenced by the fact that, having already had access to the same documents in the file in the parallel criminal proceedings, the applicant was in a perfectly good position to do so. It may be that where a defendant has no way of knowing what further documents are held by the authorities, the broader approach favoured by the Commission should prevail, namely one which places no onus on the defence to justify an entitlement to access to relevant material in the possession of the prosecution authorities.

In some cases, disclosure to a defendant's lawyer may suffice for Article 6(3)(b) purposes. In *Kamasinski* v *Austria* (1989) 13 EHRR 36 the Court found no incompatibility between the Austrian Code of Criminal Procedure, which restricted the right to inspect and make copies of the court file to the defendant's lawyer, and the Convention. The Austrian Code made an exception for unrepresented defendants, The issue of limiting disclosure to unrepresented defendants arose in *Foucher v France* (1997) 25 EHRR 234 where the applicant and his father were charged with having used insulting and threatening words and behaviour towards public service employees. The applicant decided to conduct his own case, and sent his mother to the police court registry to consult the case file and procure copies of the relevant documents. This was refused to her on the ground that copies could not be issued to individuals. The applicant met with similar refusal when he went in person to the registry. At the hearing, both defendants argued that the proceedings were unlawful due to the denial of access to the case file and documents. The court of first instance accepted this submission, but it was overturned on appeal.

The European Court recognised that the principle in *Kamasinski* did not apply on the facts. It cited with approval the decision of the first-instance court that 'the defendants should have been allowed access to their case file in order to prepare their defence [as] the value of such access is sufficiently demonstrated by the use legal representatives make of it ...'. Since such access had been denied to the applicant, Article 6(3)(b) had been violated.

In *Hardiman v UK* [1996] EHRLR 425 the European Commission held that there was no duty to disclose a co-defendant's prison psychiatric reports prepared for the trial judge notwithstanding its potential relevance to the credibility of the testimony of the co-accused.[3] Given the practice of not referring to such reports unless a medical issue arose and bearing in mind that the co-defendant had not been cautioned before meeting the psychiatrist and did not have a solicitor present, the Commission found that non-disclosure was not unfair or arbitrary.[4]

In *Preston and another v UK* [1994] 2 AC 130 it came to light during the applicants' trial that their telephone conversations had been intercepted pursuant to a warrant issued under the Interception of Communications Act 1985. The applicants applied for disclosure of the records, but the Court of Appeal and House of Lords took the view that such disclosure would breach the terms of the 1985 Act. The European Commission rejected the applicants' complaints under Article 6 on the basis that they had failed to show how access to the records of their telephone conversations by the police prior to their arrest had any effect thereafter on the proceedings or in what respect the material was used to their detriment in preparing the prosecution case, other than to provide the prosecuting

---

[3] The applicant and the co-accused were jointly charged with murder and each ran a cut-throat defence. The applicant argued that access to his co-accused's prison psychiatric report would have enabled him to undermine the co-accused's incriminating evidence.

[4] The case really turns on its special facts and is to be seen as a decision which vindicates an accused's right to maintain legal privilege.

authorities with a starting point from which to gather admissible evidence against them.

A similar conclusion was reached in *Jasper* v *UK* (2000) 30 EHRR 441 in which the applicant alleged that his trial had been unfair because the product of a telephone intercept had been withheld from the defence without being placed before the trial judge for him to rule upon its disclosure. Noting that in fact there was no evidence that such material ever existed by the time of the trial, the European Court held that as under s. 9 of the 1985 Act both prosecution and defence were prohibited from adducing evidence which might tend to suggest that calls had been intercepted by state authorities, the principle of equality of arms was respected. Moreover, the applicant himself could have testified or called evidence from other sources as to the content of the phone calls in question had he chosen so to do.

From the above summary of the case law, it can be seen that the Strasbourg standards for a fair trial in the area of disclosure impose a positive and wide-ranging duty on the prosecuting authorities to enable an accused to respond effectively to the charges laid against him. Thus in *Jespers*, the Commission referred to the principle that an accused should have 'the opportunity to acquaint himself, *for the purposes of preparing his defence*, with the results of investigations carried on throughout the proceedings' (para. 56). This approach tends to suggest that an accused's Convention right to disclosure is not (and cannot be made to be) dependent on the defence revealing its case in outline or at all. Furthermore, the reference by the Commission in *Jespers* to the duty of disclosure extending to material to which the prosecution could gain access imports a potentially wide-ranging duty on the Crown to ensure or secure third party disclosure. Against this background we turn to consider the extent to which domestic law complies with Convention standards.

13.2   THE COMPATIBILITY OF THE CRIMINAL PROCEDURE AND INVESTIGATIONS ACT 1996 WITH CONVENTION PRINCIPLES

The much criticised disclosure regime introduced by the Criminal Procedure and Investigations Act (CPIA) 1996 was presented to Parliament as a scheme designed to secure efficiency and sound judicial administration of the criminal trial process by early identification of issues and as a way of eliminating unjustifiable defence tactics resulting in unmerited acquittals. A focused and timely two-stage disclosure exercise would mean that criminal trials could be conducted as cheaply and quickly as was consistent with justice. The Royal Commission's 1993 *Report on Criminal Justice* identified a number of problems with the former disclosure provisions, not least a lack of clarity in the role and responsibilities of the police as well as the oppressive burden of requiring the prosecution to disclose large quantities of material for no good purpose. It recommended a statutory scheme backed by a code of practice.

The clear purpose of the CPIA 1996 was to bring about a significant restriction of the prosecution's common law duty of disclosure as this had been developed in a series of decisions in the 1990s (beginning with *R* v *Ward* (1993) 96 Cr App R 1). In reality the CPIA 1996 scheme has attracted critical attention from all quarters not least because surveys have revealed grave failures on the part of the police and prosecutors in complying with the Act's procedures for the recording and preservation of all material collected in the course of an investigation and for primary and secondary disclosure.[5] The CPS Inspectorate's report highlighted examples where disclosure was shown to be grossly inadequate and pointed out that, far from easing the problems of prosecutors in relation to disclosure, the burden of compliance on the police and prosecuting authorities is now much greater than under the regime which existed before the decision in *R* v *Ward* (para. 13.7).

The CPIA 1996 regime provides for the first time a statutory framework for the disclosure of unused material and places duties upon prosecutors for deciding what to disclose at two different stages before the trial, applying two tests. Section 3 imposes a duty on the prosecutor to disclose automatically to the accused any prosecution material which has not been previously disclosed to the accused and which, in the prosecutor's opinion, might undermine the case for the prosecution against the accused.[6] This is known as primary disclosure.[7] Following receipt of the defence case statement (which must be served in Crown Court cases and may be served in a magistrates' court case) the prosecution must then disclose any prosecution material which has not previously been disclosed and which might reasonably be expected to assist the accused's defence as disclosed by the defence

---

[5] The CPS Inspectorate's *Report on the thematic review of the disclosure of unused material*, March 2000, began by stating that 'what is clear is that the CPIA is not at present working as Parliament intended; nor does its present operation command the confidence of criminal practitioners', para. 1.6. In November 2000 the Attorney-General issued Guidelines addressed to investigators, prosecutors and disclosure officers designed specifically to address the multiple criticisms which had been made of the practical operation of the CPIA disclosure regime. The commentary which accompanies the Guidelines states that 'there is an inter-relationship between the differing responsibilities of the participants in the trial process. Investigators and disclosure officers may not be able to do their job properly without advice from the prosecutor. Equally prosecutors cannot do their job properly without satisfactory recording and retention of material, followed by full revelation of the material. Again prosecutors may not be able to do their jobs properly without adequate defence statements. Prosecution advocates will not be able to make reliable disclosure decisions nor comply with their obligation to keep the need for further disclosure under continuing review if they have not been placed in a fully informed position by the investigator, disclosure officer and prosecutor.'

[6] The CPIA 1996 defines 'prosecution material' as material '(a) which is in the prosecutor's possession and came into his possession in connection with the case for the prosecution against the accused; or (b) which, in pursuance of a code operative under Part II he has inspected in connection with the case for the prosecution against the accused.' (s. 3 (2)).

[7] The primary disclosure duty applies in all cases where there is a plea of not guilty in the magistrates' court, a committal or transfer of a case for trial at the Crown Court or the preferment of a voluntary bill of indictment.

statement. This is known as secondary disclosure. The CPIA 1996 and the Code of Practice together place the police in the position of controlling the flow of unused material to the defence. Whereas the decision and ultimate responsibility for ensuring compliance with the primary and secondary disclosure obligations is that of the prosecutor, he makes the decision on the basis of information provided to him by the investigators of the offence. Apart from requiring the defence to reveal its hand in advance of the trial to trigger the secondary disclosure duty, the CPIA 1996 also provides for the making of comments and the drawing of adverse inferences where an accused gives evidence in terms which differ from the content of the defence statement.[8]

In considering the extent to which the CPIA 1996 regime is potentially in conflict with Convention principles, it should be recalled that in *R* v *Brown (Winston)* [1998] AC 367 Lord Hope commented on the continuity of principle between the common law rules governing disclosure and the principles of the CPIA 1996:

> If a defendant is to have a fair trial he must have adequate notice of the case which is to be made against him. Fairness also requires that the rules of natural justice must be observed. In this context, as Lord Taylor of Gosforth observed in *R* v *Keane*, the great principle is that of open justice. It would be contrary to that principle for the prosecution to withhold from the defendant material which might undermine their case or which might assist his defence. *These are the rules upon which sections 3 and 7 of the Act of 1996 have been based.* But they had already found their expression in decisions by the Courts.

These remarks echo those of Steyn LJ in the same case in the Court of Appeal. He said that 'the right of every accused to a fair trial is a basic or fundamental right and his right to fair disclosure is an inseparable part of his right to a fair trial' *R* v *Brown (Winston)* (1995) 1 Cr App R 191 at p. 198. This approach suggests that even before the Human Rights Act 1998 came into force, the CPIA 1996 should have been interpreted or applied in a way which ensured compliance with the requirements of Article 6. And indeed it is clear that regardless of the CPIA 1996's formal division of the disclosure process into two stages, the second being dependent on defence disclosure, many prosecutors take the view that they should disclose all relevant matter at the stage of primary disclosure with the defence statement being used as a safeguard to ensure that the disclosure process is kept under review. Some police forces and many prosecutors operate an informal, open-door policy in relation to unused material thereby, in effect, ignoring the strict formalities of the CPIA 1996. The CPS Inspectorate's report (see footnote 5) commented that the drivers for this approach were a recognition of the

---

[8] See chapter 17 for the compatibility of the drawing of adverse inferences by reference to the content of a defence case statement with the presumption of innocence contained in Article 6(2).

limitations on the disclosure decisions made by prosecutors because of their heavy dependence on schedules prepared by the disclosure officer of variable reliability and, secondly, a belief that the disclosure process required a greater degree of transparency. It is therefore important to distinguish the legislative provisions themselves from the reality on the ground when considering the compatibility of the disclosure regime with the requirements of the Convention. The contrast between strict legislative requirement and practice has become even more marked since the Attorney-General's Guidelines ('Disclosure in Criminal Proceedings') were issued in November 2000. With this in mind we consider below those aspects of the legislative regime which are capable of challenge on the basis that domestic law fails to secure compliance with Article 6.

13.2.1   The CPIA 1996 disclosure duty

As we have seen, the Article 6 duty of disclosure is a very broad one. It extends to all evidence or material obtained in the course of an investigation whether for, neutral or against the accused. As we have noted above, the common law duty of disclosure established in *R* v *Keane* [1994] 1 WLR 746 reflected the requirements of Article 6. It required the prosecution to disclose to the defence all unused material which passed the test of materiality, defined as being material which can be seen 'on a sensible appraisal by the prosecution (i) to be relevant or possibly relevant to an issue in the case (ii) to raise or possibly raise a new issue whose existence is not apparent from the evidence that the prosecution proposes to use or (iii) to hold a real (as opposed to a fanciful) prospect of providing a lead on evidence which goes to (i) and (ii)'.[9] Any material which fulfilled this criteria and which the prosecution did not wish to disclose because of its sensitivity had to be placed before the court for a ruling.

To the extent that the CPIA 1996 limits a prosecutor's duty of disclosure to material which may undermine the prosecution case or assist the defence, the domestic law duty is expressed in narrower terms than the Convention obligation. And of course the Act only imposes the secondary disclosure duty once a defence statement has been served. The linkage of the disclosure process to the new concept of a defence case statement is the provision of the CPIA 1996 most obviously incompatible with the requirements of Article 6. The Article 6 duty of disclosure is not dependent on disclosure of the defence case at all. As it happens, the current Director of Public Prosecutions is on record as saying that the Crown's duty to secure a fair trial is separate from any duty imposed on the defence to disclose its defence. In the light of this it seems unlikely that any Crown

---

[9] The Court of Appeal adopted the materiality test set out by Jowitt J in *R* v *Melvin and Dingle*. The Jowitt test is based on relevance not assistance. Thus under this test all relevant unused material should be disclosed to the defence save where an issue of public interest immunity arises.

prosecutor would seek to refuse to disclose relevant, disclosable material by reference to a failure to serve a defence statement.[10] Moreover a Crown prosecutor's duties under the CPIA 1996 cannot be separated from his wider common law duties. A Crown prosecutor is personally responsible for conducting prosecutions fairly, as a minister of justice assisting in the administration of justice, in accordance with the common law duty of the prosecutor. All Crown prosecutors are required to exercise individual and independent judgment, subject to the direction of the Director of Public Prosecutions and the superintendence of the Attorney General, in advising, reviewing and prosecuting cases in accordance with the provisions of the code for Crown prosecutors. With the coming into force of the Human Rights Act 1998, Crown prosecutors, as public authorities, must ensure that all decisions taken under the code in exercise of prosecutorial discretion are compatible with Article 6. The mere fact that the CPIA 1996 imposes a duty of disclosure in narrower terms than the Convention does not thereby prevent a prosecutor or disclosure officer from acting compatibly with the requirements of Article 6. A narrowly expressed statutory duty cannot oust a permissive general discretion retained by prosecutors in relation to disclosure decisions. A prosecutor will not be able to argue that the terms of primary legislation in the form of the CPIA 1996 make it impossible for him to act compatibly with the Convention thereby making a declaration of incompatibility the only available remedy on an application for judicial review or on appeal to the Court of Appeal following a conviction where it is alleged that the Crown failed to comply with its Article 6 disclosure obligation.

Furthermore, in applying the interpretative obligation in s. 3 of the Human Rights Act 1998 to the wording of s. 3 of the CPIA 1996 ('might undermine the case for the prosecution') it is highly likely that the courts will conclude that the primary disclosure obligation on the prosecuting authorities involves a return to the principles in *R* v *Keane*. The fact that Parliament may have intended the primary disclosure obligation to be narrower than the Keane definition is neither here nor there. The issue will be not what Parliament intended but whether it is possible to interpret s. 3 of the CPIA 1996 in a way which results in compliance with the Article 6 duty of disclosure (which, as stated above, is not dependent upon disclosure of the defence case). The CPIA 1996 regime, with its carrot and stick approach to disclosure, clearly indicated an intention to sanction the withholding of relevant material at the primary disclosure stage. But the inherent ambiguity of the words 'might undermine the case for the prosecution' affords ample scope for a construction which loads upon the prosecution a duty to give disclosure in accordance with the requirements of Article 6 regardless of the service of a defence statement. Without the need for any repeal or amendment of

---

[10] This approach is now arguably enshrined in para. 13 of the Attorney-General's Guidelines issued in November 2000.

the CPIA 1996 regime, the Human Rights Act 1998 will thus be likely to have the effect of restoring the pre-existing common law rules of disclosure (which were held in *Edwards* v *UK* (1992) 15 EHRR 417 to satisfy the requirements of Article 6) free from any pre-condition of service of a defence case statement.[11]

13.2.2 Third party disclosure

It is frequently the case that potentially relevant information is in the possession of a third party rather than the prosecution or the defence (for example banks or social services or hospital authorities).[12] Before turning to consider the impact of the Convention case law on the Crown's disclosure duty in relation to this category of material, we summarise the domestic law framework for securing defence access to third party material.

13.2.2.1 Domestic law

The Code of Practice (issued under the CPIA 1996, ss. 23 and 25) states at paragraph 3.5 that:

> if the officer in charge of an investigation believes that other persons may be in possession of material that may be relevant to the investigation ... he should ask the disclosure officer to inform them of the existence of the investigation and to invite them to retain the material in case they receive a request for its disclosure. The disclosure officer should inform the prosecutor that they may have such material.

Thus although an investigating officer is not obliged to make speculative enquiries of third parties in the hunt for potentially relevant material, he does have a duty to invite third parties to retain such material. Where material is actually inspected or obtained from a third party, then it becomes unused material within the terms of the Code of Practice and liable to be disclosed on that basis. If the disclosure officer or the investigating officer has viewed, but not obtained, the third party material, this becomes information which, according to the CPS Inspectorate's report, 'must be recorded to comply with paragraph 4.4 of the Code of Practice' (para. 8.25). The record made by the disclosure officer is unused material and

---

[11] Anticipating this development, the Attorney-General's Guidelines on Disclosure in Criminal Proceedings (November 2000) require prosecutors to 'do all they can to facilitate proper disclosure, as part of their general and personal professional responsibility to act fairly and impartially, in the interests of justice' (para. 13). Paragraph 21 states that 'if prosecutors are satisfied that a fair trial cannot take place because of a failure to disclose which cannot or will not be remedied, they must not continue with the case'.

[12] The concept of a third party does not of course include other departments of the state (including the National Crime Squad and the National Criminal Intelligence Service) and/or the security services. Thus documents in the possession of one or other state department or some other agency involved in an inter-agency consideration of a crime are to be regarded as being in the possession of the Crown as an indivisible entity: *R* v *Blackledge* [1996] 1 Cr App R 326 at p. 337. See now para. 29 of the Attorney-General's Guidelines on Disclosure in Criminal Proceedings (November 2000).

therefore should be listed, complete with a description of the material on the appropriate schedule, so that the prosecutor can decide whether the record should be disclosed to the defence under the requirements of the CPIA 1996.

Where material is retained by the third party and has not become subject to the terms of the Code of Practice, separate procedures for applying to the court for its disclosure are set out in s. 2 of the Criminal Procedure (Attendance of Witnesses) Act 1965 (as amended by s. 66 of the CPIA 1996). The purpose of the CPIA 1996 amendments was to promote an early resolution of the issue of third party disclosure. If the court decides that the material should be disclosed, it will order the third party to make disclosure. In the process, the court will also resolve any claim for public interest immunity asserted by the third party. This exercise will frequently involve a balancing of an accused's right to a fair trial with the third party's right to respect for private and family life. Where a third party witholds material and the Crown is aware of its existence, the Crown can and should apply itself for a summons for the production of the material if it forms the view that the material is a necessary aspect of its duty to secure a fair trial. This obligation is implicit in the provisions of para. 3.4 of the Code of Practice which states that 'in conducting an investigation, the investigator should pursue all reasonable lines of enquiry, whether these point towards or away from the suspect. What is reasonable in each case will depend on the particular circumstances.'[13]

13.2.2.2 *Convention law*

Convention case law appears to impose a very broad duty upon the prosecution to secure third party disclosure. Thus in *Jespers* v *Belgium* (1981) 27 DR 61 the Commission held that Article 6(3)(b) recognised an accused's right to have at his disposal 'all relevant elements that have been or could be collected by the competent authorities'. The logic of this approach is that the state is obliged to use its powers and greater resources to ensure that all relevant material is accessible to both prosecution and defence in a criminal trial.[14] The Commission's statement in *Jespers* may reflect the fact that most European legal systems are inquisitorial rather than adversarial but in principle this should make no difference. Thus, whenever the investigating and/or prosecuting authorities become aware, either independently or because they are alerted by the defence, that a third party may possess relevant material, compatibility with Article 6 would appear to require them to take action to secure access to it rather than simply leaving it to the defence to pursue the enquiry. This does not amount to the imposition of a general

---

[13] Paragraphs 30–33 of the Attorney-General's Guidelines now explicitly require the prosecution to take steps to secure disclosure from a third party in circumstances where the prosecutor forms the view that it is reasonable to seek production.

[14] This reflects the principle enunciated by Steyn LJ in *R* v *Brown (Winston)* [1995] 1 Cr App R 191 at p. 198 that 'in our system in which the police and prosecution control the investigatory process, an accused's right to fair disclosure is an inseparable part of his right to a fair trial'.

duty upon an unconnected party to proceedings to hand over what may often be sensitive, confidential material merely to satisfy a defendant's idle curiosity. It is simply a reflection of the Crown's overriding duty to do its utmost to ensure that a defendant receives a fair trial and that the principle of equality of arms is maintained.

13.2.3 Disclosure in summary proceedings

There is no legal duty on the prosecution to provide the defence with advance disclosure of the statements of any witnesses upon whom they intend to rely at the trial.[15] By contrast the CPIA 1996 requires the prosecutor to disclose unused material to the defence in all cases where there is a plea of not guilty in the magistrates' court (CPIA 1996, s. 1(1)(a)). At this stage, the prosecutor has to apply the primary disclosure test and must disclose all material in his possession or which he has inspected and considers might undermine the prosecution case. After receipt of primary disclosure, the defendant may, in magistrates' court cases, serve a defence statement on the prosecution (CPIA 1996, s. 6). Where a defence statement *is* served, the prosecutor must apply the secondary disclosure test and disclose any material not yet disclosed which might assist the defence case as disclosed by the defence statement. The position in relation to disclosure in the magistrates' court is thus highly unsatisfactory. Under the CPIA 1996, the defendant has the right to primary disclosure of material which might undermine the prosecution case but he is not entitled to see the witness statements of those who will give evidence against him. Moreover the right to secondary disclosure is made to depend upon service by the accused of a defence case statement setting out the matters on which he takes issue with the prosecution's witnesses and the reasons he takes issue with them (CPIA 1996, s. 5(6)). How can a defendant take advantage of this opportunity — in practice a fundamental protection against an unfair trial — if he has not been able to see the prosecution's evidence in the first place?

The argument that the terms of the CPIA 1996 and the requirments of Article 6 obliged a prosecutor to provide advance disclosure of prosecution witness statements in summary proceedings was roundly rejected by the Divisional Court in *R v Stratford Justices, ex parte Imbert* [1999] 2 Cr App R 276. But the Divisional Court's reasoning is controversial and likely to be overturned now that

---

[15] Magistrates' Courts (Advance Information) Rules, SI 1985/601; *R v Kingston-upon-Hull Justices, ex parte McCann* (1991) 155 JP 569 and *R v Stratford Justices, ex parte Imbert* [1999] 2 Cr App R 276. Chapter 13.2.3 concerning disclosure in summary proceedings must now be read subject to the Attorney-General's Guidelines on Disclosure in Criminal Proceedings (November 2000). Paragraph 43 of the Guidelines states that prosecutors 'should, in addition to complying with the obligations under the CPIA, provide to the defence all evidence upon which the Crown proposes to rely in a summary trial'. Only exceptionally may statements be withheld 'for the protection of witnesses or to avoid interference with the course of the trial'.

the Human Rights Act 1998 is fully in force. In particular Buxton LJ's reliance on the Strasbourg doctrine of the margin of appreciation in his analysis of the meaning and reach of Article 6 reveals a fundamentally wrong approach to the case law in Strasbourg on an accused's right to pre-trial disclosure. This led him to the conclusion that because the European Court looks at the domestic proceedings as a whole and may find that an earlier breach of Article 6 was cured by subsequent events on an appeal (as happened in *Edwards* v *UK* (1992) 15 EHRR 417), this means that Article 6 does not require full disclosure to the defence of all relevant evidence. He summed up the position by saying that:

> the approach of the Strasbourg court strongly warns that criminal proceedings must be assessed as a whole and stands strongly against the contention advanced in our case that failure to give disclosure at a particular stage of those proceedings must necessarily render them unfair.

Regardless of whether the decision of the Divisional Court was correct on the basis that it was then considering an application for judicial review at a time when the Human Rights Act 1998 was not in force, it seems clear that Buxton LJ's approach cannot possibly be a sure guide to the outcome of a similar application now that the 1998 Act is in force. The domestic court is now obliged to act compatibly with the disclosure obligations inherent in Article 6 and to take account of the Strasbourg case law on the prosecution's obligation to provide pre-trial disclosure. This, as we have seen, does impose a broad duty on the prosecution to disclose *all* evidence and material obtained in the course of an investigation whether for, neutral or against the defendant. Such a duty clearly encompasses the prosecution witness statements and, barring primary legislation which prevents the Crown from acting compatibly with Article 6, it seems clear that advance disclosure of witness statements will be required as a matter of law in summary proceedings from 2 October 2000.

13.2.4 Public interest immunity

Until the European Court of Human Rights decided the issue in the linked cases of *Rowe and Davis* v *UK* (2000) 30 EHRR 1 and *Jasper* v *UK* (2000) 30 EHRR 441, there had been several statements in the Strasbourg case law which suggested that the prosecution were required to disclose the whole of the evidence regardless of its sensitivity once a criminal prosecution had been commenced. The issue arose in *Edwards* v *UK* (1992) 15 EHRR 417 where the applicant complained that the police report into his case which led to its reference back to the Court of Appeal had not been disclosed to him. The applicant's lawyer's request for disclosure of the report was refused on the grounds of public interest immunity. The fact that his lawyer did not then apply to the Court of Appeal for an order that the report be disclosed was fatal in the judgment of the majority in the European Court. In their view (para. 38):

> It is no answer to the failure to make such an application that the Crown might have resisted by claiming public interest immunity since such a claim would have been for the Court to determine.

However, as Judge Pettiti (dissenting) pointed out, the European Court's silence in *Edwards* was not to be understood as approval of the principle of public interest immunity. He took the view that:

> ... once there are criminal proceedings and an indictment, the whole of the evidence, favourable or unfavourable to the defendant, must be communicated to the defence in order to be the subject of adversarial argument in accordance with Article 6 of the Convention.

On examination of the competing arguments for and against disclosure, Judge Pettiti decided that the report should not have been protected by any immunity, and should have been disclosed. He concluded by remarking that under the European Convention an old doctrine such as that of 'public interest' must be revised in accordance with Article 6.

Judge Pettiti's concerns about the basic compatibility of public interest immunity with the requirements of Article 6 were eventually rejected by the European Court in its judgments delivered in February 2000 in *Rowe and Davis* v *UK* and *Jasper* v *UK*. The cases raised fundamental challenges to the *ex parte* procedure for determining a claim to public interest immunity in criminal proceedings. This procedure had originally been a development of the common law by the Court of Appeal in *R* v *Davis, Johnson and Rowe* (1993) 97 Cr App R 110 but was later enshrined in statute by the provisions of the CPIA 1996 (at least in relation to the Crown Court).

By the narrowest of margins (the Court split 9:8), the European Court of Human Rights held that *ex parte* hearings to determine prosecution claims to public interest immunity do not violate Article 6(1).[16] The majority thus rejected the applicant's case that such hearings afford no safeguards against judicial bias or error and no opportunity to put arguments on behalf of the accused in violation of the equality of arms principle which underpins Article 6(1). The short answer to the question whether or not the existing public interest immunity procedure passes muster with Strasbourg is, therefore, 'yes, just about'.

The reasoning of the majority was that the entitlement to disclosure of relevant evidence is not an absolute right; that in some cases it may be necessary to

---

[16] *Jasper* v *UK* (2000) 30 EHRR 441 at paras 51–8.

withhold certain evidence from the defence so as to preserve or safeguard an important public interest; and that the English system placed a clear onus on the trial judge (who satisfies the Article 6(1) requirements of independence and impartiality) to consider and, thereafter, to monitor the issue of disclosure by reference to legal principles which satisfy the Court's case law for ensuring a fair trial. The Court was careful to emphasise the trial judge's ability to review any ruling in favour of non-disclosure in the light of the evidence and the issues as they emerge from day to day in the course of the trial. By contrast, the minority accepted the argument that the defence's inability to make any informed representations to the Court on the issue of non-disclosure was a violation of the principles of adversarial proceedings and equality of arms. They did not consider that the trial judge's duty to monitor the need for disclosure could remedy the unfairness created by the defence's absence from the *ex parte* proceedings. Nor did they feel that the proceedings before the Court of Appeal were adequate to remedy the defects at first instance as the defence faced the same obstacles to the making of informed representations.

The context in which the public interest immunity procedure came under attack in *Jasper* was one of continuing concern at the potential for injustice arising from non-disclosure in criminal trials. The Criminal Bar Association and Law Society survey published in 1999 reported serious failings in the system. One of the most frequent complaints cited by those who responded was that evidence which does not fall within any of the categories of public interest immunity was recorded in the prosecution file as being too sensitive to disclose to the defence and sometimes was not recorded in the file at all. Complaints that evidence which contradicts the prosecution case had been deliberately withheld from the defence were described as 'alarmingly frequent'.[17] Affidavit evidence before the European Court confirmed that non-disclosure of evidence by the prosecution is now the single most likely cause of miscarriages of justice in England and Wales. Concern was expressed that the system of *ex parte* public interest immunity hearings in particular has encouraged the police and prosecuting authorities to withhold relevant evidence from the defence.[18]

---

[17] See also *R v Jackson* (2000) *The Times*, 5 January where the Court of Appeal quashed a conviction after grossly inaccurate information had been given to a trial judge in the course of a public interest immunity hearing.

[18] For a graphic illustration of how the existing *ex parte* procedure can result in prosecuting counsel misleading the trial judge and both judge and prosecutor in turn misleading the defence without correction or independent scrutiny, see the ruling of Turner J in *R v Doran and others*. It is hard to see how such an unhappy sequence of events could have occurred if the special counsel procedure had been in place. Paragraph 42 of the Attorney-General's Guidelines on Disclosure in Criminal Proceedings states that 'prior to or at the [*ex parte*] hearing, the court must be provided with full and accurate information. The prosecution advocate must examine all material which is the subject matter of the application and make any necessary enquiries of the proseutor and/or investigator. The prosecutor (or representative) and/or investigator should attend such applications.'

It should be recalled that a public interest immunity hearing is not concerned with mere formalities. In what is frequently described as a balancing exercise (but which is more appropriately categorised as a ruling upon the status of a document or other material)[19] a judge is required to make an assessment of the relevance and weight of the hitherto undisclosed material and to predict whether, and to what extent, it might help the defence. By the time a public interest immunity application is made, the basic issue of relevance has been resolved in favour of disclosure but for the assertion of the public interest immunity claim. The judge's task is not to decide if evidence or material is relevant but rather *how* helpful it might be to the defence. Without any effective representations by or on behalf of the defence, the judge must speculate how the defence might conduct itself if the evidence were disclosed. An *ex parte* hearing involves no adversarial procedure for testing the merits of the prosecution's claim to public interest immunity. Plainly there will be cases where the disputed material provides no assistance to the defence and there are strong arguments in favour of secrecy. At the other extreme, there will be cases where the material obviously helps the defence and no question of a balancing exercise arises. But between those two extremes will be difficult cases. It is in these cases that informed representations on behalf of the defence may make a real difference to the judge's decision. The material before the judge may include an item of evidence which could throw a different light on some aspect of the case or which could affect the tactics of the defence or its approach to a particular witness. But since the defence lawyers are left in the dark, they are unable to identify any issue which would point to the existence of the evidence or ask for it to be produced.

These same procedural defects are reproduced on appeal with the defence unable to engage in adversarial debate about whether the evidence should be disclosed or the effect of the undisclosed evidence on the safety of the conviction — the very issue to be determined on appeal. Worse still from the defence point of view, the judges of the Court of Appeal may be exposed *ex parte* to material which is deeply prejudicial to the accused and then be required to empty their minds of it when deciding on the issue of safety. Before the European Court, the applicants in *Jasper* pointed out that the *ex parte* procedure involves a substantial incursion into the rights of the defence and that where any departure from the requirements of adversarial justice has been approved by the Court, stringent safeguards have been demanded to compensate for the handicap imposed on the defence. Most importantly, the Court has applied a test of strict necessity so that if a less intrusive measure may suffice, it should be applied (see *Van Mechelen and others* v *Netherlands* (1997) 25 EHRR 647 at para. 58). This is a test of strict

---

[19] See the analysis by Sir Richard Scott VC of the role of public interest immunity in the criminal trial process in his *Report of the Inquiry into the export of defence equipment and dual use goods in Iraq and related prosecutions*, section K, paras 6.12–6.14 and 6.18.

proportionality and reflects a narrow margin of appreciation in matters of procedural fairness (see also the approach of the Court in *Chahal* v *UK* (1996) 23 EHRR 413 and *Tinnelly* v *UK* (1998) 27 EHRR 249). The clear principle that emerges is that if it is possible to secure the legitimate objectives of the state in a manner which is less invasive of the rights of the defence, then it is a requirement of fairness in Article 6 that such a measure should be applied. Hence the argument in favour of a special counsel procedure akin to that which was introduced in asylum and discrimination cases raising national security issues following the UK Government's defeat in *Chahal* and *Tinnelly*.[20]

In its response to the applicants' arguments in favour of a special counsel procedure, the Government raised practical problems rather than matters of basic principle. First, it argued that the proposed procedure would be a significant inroad into the adversarial nature of criminal proceedings in England and Wales. But this was a strange argument to raise in the context of the current public interest immunity procedure which *itself* substantially undermines the basic principle of adversarial proceedings. Secondly, it was argued that special counsel would have to be appointed in several hundred cases a year. But this simply illustrates the scale of the problem. It is not an argument against securing a fair solution. Thirdly, it was said that the special counsel would have to be present throughout the trial. This is certainly wrong. In many cases, disclosure could be resolved well before the trial and if an issue arose during the course of the trial there is no reason why notice could not be given to the special counsel. The fourth and final objection was cost. But the Convention requires contracting states to organise their legal systems so that courts can comply with Article 6 and the issue of cost must always be weighed against the risk of miscarriages of justice with their own costs both human and financial.

Against this background, it is likely that any wide-ranging review of the criminal justice system (such as the one conducted by Lord Justice Auld's Review Committee) will revisit the issue which so recently divided opinion in Strasbourg. This is not because there is necessarily a strong likelihood of the European Court changing its mind in the near future in a different case. The Convention may be a 'living instrument' and the strict English doctrine of precedent does not operate in Strasbourg but the judges of the European Court do generally regard themselves as bound by earlier decisions absent compelling reasons for a shift in attitudes or a case which raises relevantly different facts. But the fact is that the European Court, like the Commission, was split down the middle on this important issue and there are obviously compelling reasons to re-examine the arguments in favour of the special counsel procedure which so nearly persuaded a majority of the Court in *Jasper*.

---

[20] See *SSHD* v *Shatiq Ur Rehman* (23 May 2000, unreported), for an analysis of the role of special counsel in the context of the Special Immigration Appeals Commission Act 1997.

13.2.5   How should the Court of Appeal resolve public interest immunity issues not raised at first instance?

A degree of uncertainty surrounds the procedural rules governing public interest immunity hearings in the Court of Appeal where the material in question has not been the subject of a ruling by the trial judge. As stated above (at 13.2.4), the *ex parte* procedure established in *R* v *Davis, Rowe and Johnson* (1993) 97 Cr App R 110 was a creation of the common law. The CPIA 1996 and the rules made thereunder (the *Crown Court (Criminal Procedure and Investigations Act 1996) Disclosure Rules 1997* SI 1997/698) abolished the common law procedure for *ex parte* hearings in the Crown Court and replaced it with a statutory scheme. But both the Act and the Rules are silent in relation to the Court of Appeal. The editor of *Archbold* has commented that 'in cases where the investigation began after April 1997, it was widely assumed that the intention behind the legislation was to abolish the whole of the common law so far as it related to the disclosure of material by the prosecutor to the defence' (para. 12–46). If the CPIA 1996 has had this effect, it is arguable that there is currently no legal basis for the *ex parte* procedure in the Court of Appeal.

If, however, the pre-existing common law regime did survive the enactment of the CPIA 1996 in so far as it applied to the Court of Appeal, the fact remains that to date there is no appellate authority which has satisfactorily addressed the question whether the common law procedure should be the same on appeal as at first instance. Neither in *R* v *Davis, Rowe and Johnson* nor in *R* v *Keane* [1994] 1 WLR 746 was argument heard on the question whether the Court of Appeal should have embarked on *ex parte* hearings. And both cases of course pre-date the CPIA 1996. In a brief and somewhat jejeune judgment, the Court of Appeal in the second appeal of *R* v *Davis, Rowe and Johnson* (2000) *The Times*, 24 April dismissed the appellants' argument that it would be a violation of Article 6 for the Court of Appeal to proceed *ex parte* to determine *de novo* claims for public interest immunity in circumstances where the trial judge had never had an opportunity to review the material. In the court's view there was no domestic authority which suggested that the procedure was unlawful and the judges did not seem to be concerned that the whole basis for the majority's conclusion in *Jasper* v *UK* (i.e., that the *ex parte* public interest immunity procedure was compliant with Article 6) was that the trial judge (i.e., not the Court of Appeal) could ensure that an accused's right to a fair trial was maintained. In these circumstances, it is desirable that this issue is finally resolved domestically by a judgment which addresses the arguments with some care.

In the light of the European Court's decision in *Rowe and Davis* v *UK* and *Jasper* v *UK* it is possible to summarise the position under the Convention where relevant evidence has not been disclosed to the defence in the following way:

(a) If the evidence is disclosed subsequent to conviction but prior to the consideration of the merits of the case by the Court of Appeal, there will be no breach of Article 6 because any defect at first instance will be remedied by an *inter partes* hearing before the Court of Appeal (*Edwards v UK*).

(b) If the trial judge carried out an *ex parte* hearing before or during the trial and scrupulously weighed the factors for and against disclosure with the benefit of a close knowledge of the case and subject to a continuing duty of review, there will be no violation of Article 6 (see *Jasper*).

(c) If however the trial judge did not conduct a proper public interest immunity hearing because the material was not disclosed or emerged subsequent to the conviction, there will be a breach of Article 6 which cannot be cured by the carrying out of an *ex parte* hearing before the Court of Appeal.

Thus in *Rowe and Davis* the European Court held that:

> the Court does not consider that this [*ex parte*] procedure before the Appeal Court was sufficient to remedy the unfairness caused at the trial by the absence of any scrutiny of the withheld information by the trial judge. Unlike the latter, who saw the witnesses give their tesimony and was fully versed in all the evidence and issues in the case, the judges in the Court of Appeal were dependent for their understanding of the possible relevance of the undisclosed material on transcripts of the Crown Court hearings and on the account of the issues given to them by prosecuting counsel. In addition the first instance judge would have been in a position to monitor the need for disclosure throughout the trial, assessing the importance of the undisclosed evidence at a stage when new issues were emerging, when it might have been possible through cross-examination seriously to undermine the credibility of key witnesses and when the defence case was still open to take a number of different directions or emphases. In contrast the Court of Appeal was obliged to carry out its appraisal *ex post facto* and may even, to a certain extent, have unconsciously been influenced by the jury's verdict of guilty into underestimating the significance of the undisclosed evidence.
>
> In conclusion therefore the prosecution's failure to lay the evidence in question before the trial judge and to permit him to rule on the question of disclosure deprived the applicants of a fair trial. (paras 65–66)

No doubt the prospect of having no choice but to quash a conviction and order a retrial whenever public interest immunity material emerges after conviction is an unpalatable one to both the prosecuting authorities and courts. But this seems an inevitable consequence of a procedure whose somewhat fragile integrity crucially depends on the role of the first instance judge in conducting a scrupulous and continuing review of the disclosure issue. Of course, the existence of the special counsel scheme both at first instance and on appeal would resolve this particular dilemma at a stroke.[21]

---

[21] It should be noted that the special counsel scheme is not without its strong critics amongst defence lawyers. The Bar Council together with the Criminal Bar Association invited views in early 2001 about the possibility of permitting defence counsel to participate in an '*ex parte*' PII hearing in the absence of the defendant but subject to an undertaking not to disclose what transpires. Such an approach would conflict with the views of both the Court of Appeal in *R v Davis, Rowe and Johnson* (1993) 97 Cr App R 110 and the House of Lords in *R v Preston* [1994] 2 AC 130 and would almost certainly require an amendment to the Bar Code of Conduct. In many cases, however, a defendant may be happy to permit his counsel to participate in an *ex parte* PII hearing subject to such an undertaking on the basis that it represents the least worst alternative to no representation at all.

Chapter Fourteen

Fair Trial

Anthony Jennings QC

14.1 INTRODUCTION TO THE FAIRNESS PRINCIPLE OF ARTICLE 6 OF THE ECHR

In the determination of criminal charges Article 6 of the ECHR is primarily concerned with securing procedural fairness. The object and purpose of Article 6 is 'to enshrine the fundamental principle of the rule of law'.[1] The right to a fair trial in a democratic society holds such a prominent place that a restrictive interpretation of Article 6 would be inconsistent with the object and purpose of the provision.[2] Article 6 is, therefore, to be given a broad interpretation. Article 6 will occupy a key position in the sphere of criminal law and march hand in hand with the discretionary powers to exclude evidence and the abuse of process doctrine.

As Lord Bingham has pointed out in *Brown* v *Stott (Procurator Fiscal, Dunfermline)* [2001] 2 All ER 97 (PC), there is nothing to suggest that the fairness of a trial may be 'qualified, compromised or restricted in any way, whatever the circumstances and whatever the public interest in convicting the offender. If the trial as a whole is judged to be unfair, a conviction cannot stand'. His Lordship added that, 'What a fair trial requires cannot, however, be the subject of a single, unvarying rule or collection of rules.' The constituent rights comprised, whether expressly or implicitly, within Article 6 'are not themselves absolute'. Limited qualification of these rights, added Lord Bingham, is acceptable 'if reasonably directed by national authorities towards a clear and proper public objective and if

---

[1] *Salabiaku* v *France* (1988) 13 EHRR 379.
[2] *Delcourt* v *Belgium* (1969) 1 EHRR 355; *Moreira Azevedo* v *Portugal* (1990) 13 EHRR 721.

representing no greater qualification than the situation calls for'. Although all of their lordships accepted that the general right to a fair trial was an absolute right, Lord Bingham appeared to imply that both explicit and implied rights could be qualified.

Lord Hope (and indeed Lord Steyn) did not appear to go as far as this when he said, 'Once the meaning of those rights [the minimum rights listed in Article 6(3)] has been determined, there is no room in their case for any implied modifications or restrictions.' Lord Hope added that only the rights that are not set out in absolute terms may be the subject of modification or restriction provided that is not incompatible with the 'absolute right to a fair trial'. As Lord Hope said, the European Court has read both implied rights and restrictions into Convention. There is a balance to be struck between the general interest of the community and the personal rights of the individual. But as Lord Bingham observed, once it has been established that the guarantee to a fair trial has been breached, 'it is never possible to justify such a breach by reference to the public interest or on any other ground.'

Lord Hope said that a three stage test was required in determining the question of incompatibility with Article 6:

(a) Is the right which is in question an absolute right, or is it a right which is open to modification or restriction because it is not absolute?

(b) If it is not absolute, does the modification or restriction which is contended for have a legitimate aim in the public interest?

(c) If so, is there a reasonable relationship of proportionality between the means employed and the aim sought to be realised?

Lord Hope explained that the answer to the question whether the right is or is not absolute is to be found by examining the terms of the Article in the light of the judgments of the European Court. The question whether a legitimate aim is being pursued enables account to be taken of the public interest in the rule of law. The principle of proportionality directs attention to the question whether a fair balance has been struck between the general interest of the community in the realistation of that aim and the protection of the fundamental rights of the individual.

In an article entitled 'The New Legal Landscape' [2000] 6 EHRLR 549 at 553, Lord Steyn argued that three considerations would constrain the application of the fair trial provisions. First, technical arguments have no place in Convention jurisprudence. Secondly, the fairness of the trial must be determined in the light of the proceedings as a whole. Thirdly, the existence of the tension between the public interest and the rights of the defendant must be taken into account.

The European Court has stated that absolute rights cannot be qualified.[3] Therefore any restrictions on the constituent element of Article 6 must be very

---

[3] *Chahal v UK* (1996) 23 EHRR 413. For a detailed discussion of the doctrine of inherent limitations and its potential impact under the HRA 1998, see Clayton and Tomlinson, *The Law of Human Rights* (Oxford University Press, 2000), pp. 315–19.

carefully scrutinised. If overall fairness is compromised, those restrictions will not be legitimate. Moreover, fair trial rights require 'a high degree of constitutional protection'.[4]

The central pillar of Article 6 is the principle of 'equality of arms'. This principle requires that the defendant in a criminal trial is not put at a substantial disadvantage compared with his opponent.[5] From this general principle flow a number of specific rights. The list of rights set out in Article 6(3) is not meant to be an exhaustive one but simply the guarantee of a number of minimum guarantees.[6] The relationship between Article 6(1) and Article 6(3) 'is that of the general to the particular' and so a breach of Article 6(1) could occur even in the absence of a breach of Article 6(3).[7] The generality of the right to a fair trial has permitted both the European Commission and the European Court to read further specific rights into Article 6. Although Strasbourg will permit considerable variation in rules and procedures between states, those domestic provisions must nonetheless produce fairness.

Considerably less latitude will now be given to this principle domestically because the effect of ss. 2, 3 and 6 of the Human Rights Act (HRA) 1998 is that domestic courts must apply Convention rights to any given situation as statutory rights.[8] Domestic courts will not simply be required to look at the question of fairness in the round but to address the question of the effect of breaches of individual rights because the effect of s. 6 of the HRA 1998 is that the court will be acting unlawfully if it does not act compatibly with a Convention right.

Lord Bingham pointed out in *Brown v Stott (Procurator Fiscal, Dunfermline)* that while a national court does not accord the margin of appreciation recognised by the European Court as a supra-national court, it will give weight to the decisions of a representative legislature and a democratic government within the discretionary area of judgment accorded to those bodies. The Convention is concerned with rights and freedoms which are of real importance in a modern democracy governed by the rule of law. It does not, Lord Bingham added, as is sometimes mistakenly thought, offer relief from 'The heart-ache and a thousand natural shocks That flesh is heir to' (*Hamlet*, Act 3, Scene I). Perhaps Lord Bingham had in mind that the Convention might offer relief from 'The oppressor's wrong ... the law's delay' (ibid).

14.1.1 The fairness principle and domestic law

The general concept of fairness encapsulated in Article 6 underpins domestic common law (*Woolmington v DPP* [1935] AC 462 at 481, HL; and the quickly

---

[4] *Libman v Attorney-General of Quebec* 3 BHRC 269 at 289.
[5] *Neumeister v Austria* (1968) 1 EHRR 91; *Delcourt v Belgium* (1969) 1 EHRR 355; *Dombo Beheer v Netherlands* (1993) 18 EHRR 213; *De Haes and Gijsels v Belgium* (1997) 25 EHRR 1.
[6] *Edwards v UK* (1992) 15 EHRR 417 at para. 33; *Foucher v France* (1997) 25 EHRR 234 at para. 30.
[7] *Jespers v Belgium* (1981) 27 DR 61 at para. 54.
[8] See the remarks of the Lord Chancellor, Lord Irvine of Lairg, during the Committee Stage of the Bill: HL, Hansard, vol. 583, cols 514–515; and during the Report Stage: vol. 584, cols 1270–1271

developing abuse of process doctrine) and a number of important statutes (ss. 34–38 of the Criminal Justice and Public Order Act 1994, s. 78, Police and Criminal Evidence Act 1984 (PACE)).

14.2 CRIMINAL CHARGES

14.2.1 'Criminal'

Article 6 is limited to circumstances in which there is a 'criminal charge'. This concept has been interpreted broadly and although the European Court will be guided by the classification applied by the relevant state, such a classification being the 'starting point',[9] it will also look at the nature of the offence, whether the offence applies to a specific group or is of general application[10] and the possible penalty.[11] This last factor is of particular importance.[12] Thus proceedings that are classified as regulatory or disciplinary may still fall within the definition of 'criminal charge'.[13] Court-martial proceedings,[14] prison disciplinary proceedings,[15] commitment to prison for non-payment of the community charge[16] and contempt proceedings[17] have all been held to fall within the concept of 'criminal charge'.

A procedure which permitted a driving licence to be withdrawn for up to 15 days in circumstances where a driver was suspected of being drunk did not involve a violation of Article 6.[18] Even though the procedure was a preventative one, there was no investigation and no finding of guilt; the impact of the measure was limited in scope and time and was not sufficiently substantial to amount to a 'criminal charge'. In a situation, however, where penalty points were added to a driver's licence in the context, and after the outcome, of a criminal prosecution, the criminal aspect of Article 6 was engaged.[19] Similarly, the detention of a suspect in the psychiatric ward of a prison following an arrest for assault did not involve the 'determination of a criminal charge' but the outcome of the proceedings was decisive for civil rights within Article 6(1).[20] Disqualification

---

[9] *Engel* v *Netherlands* (1976) 1 EHRR 647 at para. 82. See also *Georgiou and another (t/a Marios Chippery)* v *UK* [2001] STL 80.
[10] *Öztürk* v *Germany* (1984) 6 EHRR 409.
[11] Ibid. *Garafallou AEBE* v *Greece* (1999) 28 EHRR 344; *Lauko* v *Slovakia* [1999] EHRLR 105; *JJ* v *Netherlands* (1999) 28 EHRR 168.
[12] *Brown* v *UK* (1998) 28 EHRR CD 233.
[13] Ibid.
[14] *Findlay* v *UK* (1997) 24 EHRR 221; *Coyne* v *UK* (1997) *The Times*, 24 October; *Cable and others* v *UK* (1999) 30 EHRR 1032; *Hood* v *UK* (1999) 29 EHRR 365; *Moore and Gordon* v *UK* (1999) 29 EHRR 728; *Jordan* v *UK* (2000) *The Times*, 17 March.
[15] *Campbell and Fell* v *UK* (1984) 7 EHRR 165.
[16] *Benham* v *UK* (1996) 22 EHRR 293.
[17] *Harman* v *UK* (1984) 38 DR 53.
[18] *Escoubet* v *Belgium* (1999) 10 Archbold News 2.
[19] *Malige* v *France* (23 September 1998).
[20] *Aerts* v *Belgium* (1998) 29 EHRR 50.

proceedings under s. 6 of the Company Directors Disqualification Act 1986 did not involve the determination of a criminal charge as the proceedings were inherently regulatory and the penalty did not involve a fine or imprisonment but disqualification.[21]

In *Brown* v *Chief Constable of Avon and Somerset* [2000] 1 WLR 1382, Lord Bingham CJ said that an application for a sex offender order under s. 2 of the Crime and Disorder Act 1998 did not involve the determination of a criminal charge because there was no penalty arising from the imposition of the order itself (see also *R* v *Chief Constable of Avon and Somerset Constabulary* [2001] 1 All ER 562). Of course, there is a penalty in relation to a failure to comply with the order (s. 2(8)) and presumably such proceedings would come within the definition of criminal charge. The same approach will apply to anti-social behaviour orders under section 1 of that Act[22] and banning orders under s. 1 of the Football (Disorder) Act 2000.

Proceedings in which a defendant may be bound over to keep the peace[23] or to be of good behaviour[24] involve the determination of a criminal charge.

14.2.2 'Charge'

'Charge' has been given an autonomous Convention meaning and has been defined as the 'official notification given to the individual by the competent authority of an allegation that he has committed a criminal offence'.[25] Such an allegation may be implied.[26] In criminal proceedings a charge will normally arise at the point of arrest[27] or upon formal notification of an intention to prosecute. It may well be that persons who attend a police station voluntarily for the purposes of an interview will be covered by the definition of charge.[28] A charge does not, however, arise at the point at which hearsay allegations are made to the police.[29]

14.3   AN INDEPENDENT AND IMPARTIAL COURT

Article 6(1) guarantees the right to a fair and public hearing by an 'independent and impartial tribunal established by law'. Independence in this context means

---

[21] *DC, HS and AD* v *UK* [2000] BCC 710. See also *Wilson* v *UK* (1998) 26 EHRR CD 195.

[22] *R* v *Manchester Crown Court, ex parte McCann* (1 March 2001, CA). The offence of failing to comply with the order arises under s. 1(10).

[23] *Steel and others* v *UK* (1998) 28 EHRR 603.

[24] *Hashman and Harrap* (1999) 30 EHRR 241.

[25] *Deweer* v *Belgium* (1980) 2 EHRR 439 at para. 46. See also *Reinhardt and Slimane-Kaid* v *France* (1998) 28 EHRR 59; *Serves* v *France* (1997) 28 EHRR 265.

[26] *Foti* v *Italy* (1982) 5 EHRR 313.

[27] *X* v *UK* (1979) 17 DR 122.

[28] For a view to this effect see, Clayton and Tomlinson, *The Law of Human Rights* (Oxford: Oxford University Press, 2000), para. 11.182. Such persons in police stations should be treated 'with no less consideration' than those in police detention: Code of Practice C:1A, 3.15, 3.16. See Archbold (2001) 15–268.

[29] *R* v *HM Advocate* (2000) *The Times*, 14 April, JC.

independent of both the executive and the respective parties.[30] In order to establish whether a tribunal is 'independent' for the purposes of Article 6(1), regard must be had, *inter alia*, to the manner of appointment of its members and their term of office, the existence of safeguards against outside pressures and the question of whether the tribunal presents an appearance of independence.[31]

As to the condition of impartiality, there are two tests to be applied: the first consists in attempting to determine the personal conviction of a particular judge in a given case and the second in ascertaining whether the judge offered guarantees sufficient to exclude any legitimate doubt in this respect.[32] In deciding whether there is a legitimate reason to fear that a particular court lacks independence or impartiality, the standpoint of the accused is important without being decisive; what is decisive is whether his doubts are objectively justified.[33]

Thus the relevant test involves both subjective impartiality, which will require proof of actual bias,[34] and objective impartiality, which is more concerned with the appearance of bias.[35]

Pre-trial involvement with the defendant which is limited to case supervision will not involve a breach of Article 6(1) but any decision which involves something approaching a determination of the merits of the case may breach the Convention right.[36] The European Commission in *Brown* v *UK* (1986) 8 EHRR 272 held that a judge who sat in determination of a leave to appeal hearing was not biased because he had previously granted an injunction against the defendant. This decision needs to be contrasted with the decision of the European Court in *Castillo Algar* v *Spain* (2000) 30 EHRR 827, where a similar situation was held to have involved a breach of Article 6(1).

Any direct involvement in the passage of legislation, or of executive rules, is likely to be sufficient to cast doubt on the judicial impartiality of a person who later had to adjudicate upon that legislation or executive rules.[37] Such a situation raises potential problems for Members of Parliament who sit as Recorders in the Crown Court and who will have to make rulings on legislation in respect of which they had an involvement in the legislative passage of the Act. Similar problems arose in respect of the now abolished part-time judicial post of Assistant Recorder. In Scotland it had been held that similar part-time posts where renewal

---

[30] *Ringeissen* v *Austria* (1971) 1 EHRR 455.
[31] *Incal* v *Turkey* (1998) 29 EHRR 449. See also, *Le Compte, Van Leuven and De Meyere* v *Belgium* (1981) 4 EHRR 1; *Piersack* v *Belgium* (1982) 5 EHRR 169; *Delcourt* v *Belgium* (1969) 1 EHRR 355; *Campbell and Fell* v *UK* (1984) 7 EHRR 165; *Bryan* v *UK* (1995) 21 EHRR 342; *Gautrin* v *France* (1998) 28 EHRR 196; *Castillo Algar* v *Spain* (2000) 30 EHRR 827.
[32] *Incal*, at para. 65. See also *Gautrin* v *France* (1998) 28 EHRR 196.
[33] *Incal*, at para. 71.
[34] *Hauschildt* v *Denmark* (1990) 12 EHRR 266.
[35] *Delcourt* v *Belgium* (1969) 1 EHRR 355.
[36] *Hauschildt* v *Denmark* (1989) 12 EHRR 266; *Ferrantelli and Santangelo* v *Italy* (1996) 23 EHRR 288.
[37] *McGonnell* v *UK* (2000) 30 EHRR 289.

of the position was both possible and expected, but was at the discretion of the executive, meant that there was not independence but dependency. A judge could be influenced, consciously or unconsciously, by his hopes and fears about his possible treatment by the executive.[38] Recorders are not susceptible to challenge as they occupy part-time but permanent judicial posts.

Judges are entitled to criticise legal developments, but they cannot with impunity publish either criticism or praise of such a nature or in such language as to give rise to a legitimate apprehension that, when called upon in the course of their judicial duties to apply that particular branch of the law, they would not be able to do so impartially.[39] In the instant case the judge had written an article highly critical of the European Convention and its incorporation into domestic law. The judge had described the incorporation of the Convention into domestic law as, 'A field day for crackpots, a pain in the neck for judges and a goldmine for lawyers.' This case can be contrasted with the situation domestically where a judge had expressed the view before a trial that the right to silence was a charter for the dishonest and never helped the innocent.[40] The court held that the judge did not have to disqualify himself even though the right to silence was an issue in the case. It is submitted that a different conclusion would now occur under the HRA 1998.

A judge's summing-up to a jury must be 'balanced, fair and accurate'.[41]

14.3.1   The independent and impartial court and domestic law

The test of bias in domestic law was the 'real danger' test and this test applied equally to judges, jurors and magistrates.[42] A judge who is a party to the cause or has a relevant interest in the subject matter should be automatically disqualified[43] unless the relevant interest is so small as being incapable of influence.[44] The first step is to ascertain whether the judge knew of the matter it is alleged will undermine his impartiality. If the judge did not know of the matter in question, the danger of bias is dispelled. If a judge becomes aware of any matter that might give rise to a fear of bias then disclosure should be made to the parties.[45] As to the effect of the HRA 1998 on the bias test, see 14.4.1.

---

[38] *Starrs v Procurator Fiscal, Linlithgow* (2000) 8 BHRC 1, JC.
[39] *Hoekstra v HM Advocate* [2000] UKHRR 578, JC.
[40] *R v Browne* (1997) *The Times*, 23 August, CA.
[41] *X v UK* (1973) 45 CD 1.
[42] *R v Gough* [1993] AC 646.
[43] *R v Bow Street Metropolitan Stipendiary Magistrate, ex parte Pinochet Ugarte (No. 2)* [1999] 2 WLR 272, HL.
[44] *Locabail (UK) Ltd v Bayfield Properties; Locabail (UK) Ltd v Waldorf Investment Corporation; Timmins v Gormley; Williams v HM Inspector of Taxes; R v Bristol Betting, Gaming and Licensing Committee, ex parte O'Callaghan* [2000] QB 451, CA.
[45] Ibid.

There is also a requirement in domestic law that any summing-up by a judge to a jury is to be fair and balanced.[46]

14.4　JURY BIAS

The need for impartiality applies equally to juries. Bias in the jury room raises discrete and difficult problems for domestic law. There is obviously a strong presumption that all tribunals are free of bias.[47] An allegation of bias must be investigated unless it is 'manifestly devoid of merit'.[48] Links between a juror and prosecution witnesses will not necessarily lead to a finding of bias.[49] In *Gregory v UK* (1997) 25 EHRR 577, a note was sent by a jury in retirement saying, 'Jury showing racial overtones. One member to be excused.' The jury was warned by the judge in relation to the question of potential bias. The European Court found no breach of Article 6(1) largely because of the judge's warning but also because the defence at the trial had not asked for the jury to be discharged.

Gregory was distinguished in *Sander v UK* (2000) 8 BHRC 279 where a juror trying two Asian defendants complained in writing about at least two jurors making racist remarks and jokes and expressing the concern that the defendants would be convicted because of their race. After the judge raised the matter with the jury a note was received signed by all of the jury (including the juror who had complained) refuting the allegations. A separate note was received from a juror admitting making racist jokes but denying that the remarks were serious or that he was a racist. The European Court found that there was insufficient evidence of subjective bias but there was sufficient evidence of objective bias. The fact that the joint note contradicted the earlier note and that one juror admitted racism meant that something may have been fundamentally wrong in the jury room. The judge's direction was not going to change racist views overnight and could not dispel the reasonable impression of partiality.

14.4.1　Jury bias and domestic law

The 'real danger' test for bias also applied to jurors. As Sedley LJ has pointed out,[50] the 'real danger' test may have to be revisited in light of the Human Rights Act 1998 because it involves a higher threshold than under the Convention. This may mean, for example, that the trial of a black defendant in a racially sensitive

---

[46] *R v Marr* (1990) 90 Cr App R 154; *R v Berrada* (1990) 91 Cr App R 131; *R v Wood* [1996] 1 Cr App R 207.
[47] *Piersack v Belgium* (1982) 5 EHRR 169; *Thommann v Switzerland* (1997) 24 EHRR 553.
[48] *Remli v France* (1996) 22 EHRR 253 at para. 48.
[49] *Pullar v UK* (1996) 22 EHRR 391.
[50] *Hampshire County Council v Gillingham* (5 April 2000, unreported). See also, *Locabail*, above at fn. 44.

case by an all-white jury may involve the appearance of bias.[51] In *Re Medicaments and Related Classes of Goods (No. 2)* (2001) *The Times*, 2 February (DC), Lord Phillips MR extensively reviewed both domestic and Convention jurisprudence concerning the bias test. Lord Phillips MR accepted that the term 'apparent bias' had not been used domestically with great precision and recognised that 'a modest adjustment of the test in *Gough* is called for'. His Lordship said that a court must first ascertain all the circumstances that have a bearing on the suggestion of bias. It must then be asked whether those circumstances 'would lead a fair-minded and informed observer to conclude that there was a real possibility, or a real danger, the two being the same, that the tribunal was biased'. Lord Phillips MR went on to say that the material circumstances will include any explanation of the tribunal under review as to their knowledge or appreciation of those circumstances. Where the explanation is accepted by the applicant for review it can be treated as accurate. Where it is not accepted, his Lordship added, it becomes one further matter to be considered from the viewpoint of the fair-minded observer. The court does not have to rule on whether the explanation should be accepted or rejected. Rather, Lord Phillips MR added, it has to decide whether or not the fair-minded observer would consider that there was a real danger of bias notwithstanding the explanation advanced. This re-stated test should now ensure that the test for bias in domestic law is compliant with Convention jurisprudence.

Another potential problem in domestic law for investigating complaints of jury bias is s. 8 of the Contempt of Court Act 1981. This section prevents investigations into the deliberations of juries. In *R v Young (S)* [1995] 2 Cr App R 379, jurors staying at a hotel in the course of their retirement used a ouija board in an attempt to contact the deceased in order to establish who killed him. Contact was apparently made and the defendant named as the guilty party. The Court of Appeal said that s. 8 was drawn in the widest terms and permitted 'no exceptions' (per Lord Taylor CJ at p. 382). The Court of Appeal was only able to make inquiries because the conduct complained of had not occurred in the course of deliberations.

But what if the problems in *Young* had occurred in the course of the deliberations of the jury? In *R v Anthony Martin* (25 September 2000, unreported) the Court of Appeal adopted the sensible device of permitting a questionnaire to be put to the jury in relation to allegations of intimidation but emphasising that in responding to the questionnaire the jury must not reveal their deliberations. In *Gregory v UK* (1997) 25 EHRR 577 the European Court described the bar on inquiring into jury deliberations as a 'crucial and legitimate feature' but the Court

---

[51] In *R v Ford* (1989) 89 Cr App R 278, the Court of Appeal was highly critical of the practice in some racially sensitive cases of judges taking positive steps to try to achieve some ethnic minority representation on the jury panel. Ironically, in the instant case the police officer was of mixed race and the all-white jury acquitted the defendant of the more serious charge. The Royal Commission (1993, Cm. 2263) recommended (at paras 62–64) that both the prosecution and defence in an appropriate case should be able to apply for representation by an ethnic minority on the jury.

was not addressing the question of the compatibility of s. 8 with Article 6 in circumstances where the statute might frustrate the investigation of a genuine complaint which, if true, as in *Young*, would mean that the defendant had clearly not received a fair trial. It has been held that at common law the Court of Appeal was powerless to inquire into an allegation that a verdict was decided by lot[52] or where the majority of a jury had been ready to acquit until the foreman read out a list of the defendant's previous convictions.[53] It is submitted that s. 8 cannot be read compatibly with Article 6. The use of the questionnaires in *Martin* may circumvent a legal, head-on collision between s. 8 and Article 6 and avoid the need for a certificate of incompatibility under section 4 of the HRA 1998. However, it is not difficult to foresee circumstances where it would be impossible for a juror to reveal details of bias without at the same time revealing details of deliberations. One solution would be to use s. 2 of the HRA 1998 to read the word 'deliberations' narrowly. Although the court in *Young* at p. 383 adopted the dictionary definition of the word as including 'consideration with a view to a decision', 'weighing in the mind', 'careful consideration', 'discussions of reasons for and against' and 'debate', it could be argued that such a consideration is an examination of legitimate and proper issues in the case. The exhibition of bias is thus extrinsic to a consideration of the issues in the case and falls outside the definition of 'deliberations'.

14.5   THE RIGHT TO A PUBLIC HEARING

Article 6(1) provides that 'everyone is entitled to a ... public hearing within a reasonable time' from which the press and public are not excluded. This right is not unqualified and exceptions include the interests of morals, public order, national security and the welfare of juveniles. Prison disciplinary hearings may be held in private.[54] In *T and V v UK* (1999) 30 EHRR 121,[55] the European Court noted that there might be a conflict between the right to a public hearing and the rights of children on trial. Such a trial must have modified procedures in order to ensure compliance with the Convention. The Convention does not, however, prevent the trial of an 11-year-old.[56]

14.5.1   The right to a public hearing and domestic law

There is at common law a general presumption of hearings in public[57] but there are a number of procedures which permit hearings in camera. Generally, the

---

[52] *Straker v Graham* (1839) 4 M & W 721.
[53] *R v Thompson* (1962) 46 Cr App R 72. See also, *Ellis v Deheer* [1922] 2 KB 113; *R v Miah and Akhbar* [1997] 2 Cr App R 12.
[54] *Campbell and Fell v UK* (1984) 7 EHRR 272; *Gautrin v France* (1999) 28 EHRR 196.
[55] See the commentary by Andrew Ashworth at [2000] Crim LR 287.
[56] *R v C (a minor)* (2000) *The Times*, 5 July, CA.
[57] *Scott v Scott* [1913] AC 417.

determining feature justifying a court sitting in camera is the interests of justice.[58] One practice that may be susceptible to challenge is the automatic hearing of bail applications in chambers in the Crown Court.[59] The rules governing such applications do not prohibit public hearings but simply provide for a discretion for such applications to be heard in chambers. In *Jasper v UK* (2000) 30 EHRR 441 the *ex parte* procedure for disclosure applications laid down in *R v Davis, Johnson and Rowe* (1993) 97 Cr App R 110[60] survived a challenge at the European Court by nine votes to eight. The Court rejected the argument that the 'special counsel' system in immigration appeals[61] was required in criminal cases. As Professor Andrew Ashworth points out in his commentary in the Criminal Law Review ([2000] at p. 287), the narrowness of the majority decision and the 'formulaic' nature of the majority judgment mean that this subject will inevitably be reopened under the HRA 1998.

As a result of *T and V*, a *Practice Direction*[62] was issued in relation to the trials of children and youths and one of the features of the direction is the ability to restrict attendance at the trial. The *Practice Direction* also states that the norm should be separate trials for juveniles charged jointly with adults. As has been pointed out,[63] the only reason that the juvenile appears in the Crown Court is because the magistrates' court has determined that it is in the interests of justice for them to be tried together.[64] The Crown Court has no power to remit the juvenile to the youth court[65] and so legislative change would appear inevitable.

14.6   THE RIGHT TO PARTICIPATE EFFECTIVELY

It flows from the notion of a fair trial that a person should generally be entitled to be present at the trial hearing.[66] Effective steps must be taken to ensure the exercise of this right.[67] The right is not without exception[68] and the right may be

---

[58] See *Att-Gen v Leveller Magazine Ltd and others* [1979] AC 440. Applications to sit in camera are governed by the Crown Court Rules 1982, rule 24A(1) (Archbold (2001) 4–7). Such applications may include pre-trial applications: *Ex parte Guardian Newspapers Ltd* [1999] 1 Cr App R 284.

[59] Crown Court Rules 1982, rule 27(1), 2(a). Bail applications in the magistrates' court are normally heard in open court. The Law Commission has recognised that the position as to whether bail applications in the Crown Court need to be in open court is 'not exactly clear': *Bail and the Human Rights Act* (CP 157), para. 11.25.

[60] See also *Rowe and Davis v UK* (2000) 30 EHRR 1.

[61] See *Chahal v UK* (1996) 23 EHRR 413.

[62] *Practice Direction* (Crown Court: Trial of children and young persons) [2000] 1 Cr App R 483.

[63] James Richardson, *Criminal Law Week*, 00/7/5.

[64] Magistrates' Courts Act 1980, s. 24(1)(b).

[65] Where the trial would be in private.

[66] *Ekbatani v Sweden* (1988) 13 EHRR 504. The position is the same at common law: *R v Preston* [1994] 2 AC 130, HL.

[67] *Goddi v Italy* (1984) 6 EHRR 457.

[68] *Ensslin and others v Germany* (1978) 14 DR 64.

waived.[69] The right must be an effective one and the procedures in place must provide for effective participation.[70] Article 5 generally requires the presence of the accused at any oral hearing for bail.[71]

14.6.1 Effective participation and domestic law

It is generally desirable that a defendant is present at his trial.[72] A defendant may appear at a pre-trial hearing via a video link if he has been remanded into custody.[73] It is the practice in the Crown Court and High Court that the defendant is not produced for a bail application in chambers and he could only attend if the court gave leave.[74] Such a practice is likely to constitute a breach of Article 6 and some courts have tried to meet this problem by setting up a pilot scheme video link between the defendant in prison and the court.

14.7 THE RIGHT TO A HEARING WITHIN A REASONABLE TIME

Article 6(1) guarantees the right to a hearing within a reasonable time. Time runs from the moment of charge and continues until the conclusion of any appeal. The right is a free-standing one and there is no need to show prejudice to the defendant.[75] In determining what period of delay is reasonable the problems of the state will provide no excuse[76] but delay on the part of a third party may be a relevant consideration.[77] A failure to comply with set time limits will not inevitably involve a breach of Article 6(1).[78] The court will look at the circumstances of the case including complexity and the behaviour of the defendant.[79] Nevertheless, there is no obligation on the defendant to co-operate with the authorities[80] and what is at stake for the defendant is a relevant consideration.[81] 'Special diligence' is required to ensure that minors are brought to trial within a reasonable time.[82] These principles apply to delay before sentencing.[83]

---

[69] *Colozza* v *Italy* (1985) 7 EHRR 516.
[70] *T and V* v *UK* (1999) 30 EHRR 121.
[71] *Keus* v *Netherlands* (1990) 13 EHRR 700; *Farmakopoulos* v *Belgium* (1992) 16 EHRR 187.
[72] *R* v *Lee Kun* [1916] 1 KB 337.
[73] Crime and Disorder Act 1998, s. 57.
[74] Crown Court Rules 1982, rule 19(5).
[75] *Crummock (Scotland) Ltd* v *HM Advocate* (2000) *The Times*, 9 May, JC.
[76] *Garafallou AEBE* v *Greece* (1999) 28 EHRR 344.
[77] *Procurator Fiscal, Fort William* v *McLean and another* [2000] UKHRR 598 (JC).
[78] *G* v *Italy* (1992) A/228–F.
[79] *Selmouni* v *France* (1999) 29 EHRR 403. See also *Howarth* v *UK* [2000] 9 BHRC 253.
[80] *Zana* v *Turkey* (1997) 27 EHRR 566.
[81] *FE* v *France* (1998) 27 EHRR 667.
[82] *Assenov and others* v *Bulgaria* (1998) 28 EHRR 652 at 712.
[83] *Howarth* v *UK* [2000] 9 BHRC 253.

14.7.1   Right to a hearing within a reasonable time and domestic law

Certain time limits have been laid down concerning the period from first appearance in the magistrates' court and committal (70 days),[84] from first appearance in the magistrates' court and the opening day of the trial (56 days) and between committal for trial and arraignment (112 days). These time limits can be extended subject to the satisfaction of certain criteria (1985 Act, s. 22(3)) but the scales are weighted against such an extension.[85] Apart from a refusal to extend custody time limits, a court has an inherent jurisdiction to stay a prosecution as an abuse of the process of the court because of delay.[86] Unlike the position in Convention law, however, a defendant must show prejudice caused by the delay.[87] If the courts permit a delay of 300 days from a defendant's first appearance without regarding such delay as an abuse of process, then such a decision will render the provisions mere window dressing.[88]

There are conflicting authorities on the effect of a breach of Article 6 because of delay. In *R v Court Martial Administration Officer, ex parte Jordan* [2000] COD 106, the Divisional Court said that such a breach of Article 6(1) did not prevent a fair trial from taking place. This is not a permissible approach under the HRA 1998 because of the effect of section 6 which makes any breach of a Convention right unlawful. The approach of the Privy Council in *Darmalingum v The State* [2000] 2 Cr App R 445,[89] was to regard an analogous right to Article 6 in Mauritian law as freestanding and a breach of which should normally involve a termination of the proceedings. Lord Steyn pointed out that the importance of the right was greater when the right was enshrined in law. As he put it, at p. 451, 'The stamp of constitutionality was an indication of the higher normative force which was attached to the relevant rights.'[90] *Darmalingum* was considered by a differently constituted Board in *Flowers v The Queen* [2000] 1 WLR 2396. The Board did not, as the Board had in *Darmalingum*, regard the right to a fair trial, within a reasonable time and before an independent and impartial tribunal as three independent rights but three elements of one embracing form of protection. The Board, relying heavily on the judgment of Powell J in *Barker v Wingo*, 407 US 514 (1972) also took into account the strength of the evidence against the appellant and the seriousness of the offence. As to the latter factor, as James

---

[84] Prosecution of Offences Act 1985, s. 22; Prosecution of Offences (Custody Time Limits) Regulations 1987, SI 1987/698.

[85] *R v Manchester Crown Court (Minshull St), ex parte S* (23 August 1999, unreported).

[86] *R v Telford Justices, ex parte Badhan* [1991] 2 QB 78.

[87] *Attorney-General's Reference (No. 1 of 1990)* [1992] QB 630.

[88] *R (on the application of the DPP) v Croydon Youth Court* (14 December, unreported, DC) and the commentary thereon by James Richardson in *Criminal Law Week*, 01/4/1.

[89] See the commentary by James Richardson in *Criminal Law Week* 28/2/00. Historically delay has been treated as a mitigating feature: *R v Derby Crown Court, ex parte Brooks* (1985) 80 Cr App R 164 at 169.

[90] See also *Mohammed v The State* [1999] 2 AC 111 at 123, PC.

Richardson has pointed out in his trenchant commentary to *Flowers* (*Criminal Law Week* 00/43/2), 'It is in the case of the most heinous crimes that there is the need for the greatest vigilance.' There Lordships also required proof of actual prejudice to the appellant which, as has been pointed out above, is not a requirement in Convention jurisprudence. The Board in *Flowers* appears to be upholding convictions on public interest grounds. If this is to become the approach domestically, then, as James Richardson observes, 'the incorporation of Article 6 will have had little effect on the criminal process.' Domestic courts, it is submitted, will have to apply the right to a speedy trial irrespective of direct prejudice to the accused. The HRA 1998 means that the failure to comply with a defendant's Convention right itself involves prejudice because the state has acted unlawfully towards him.

14.8   TRIAL *IN ABSENTIA*

Trial *in absentia* does not violate the Convention provided the protections discussed above are in place. If the defendant's absence was for good reason then he may be entitled to a rehearing.[91] The absence of the defendant must not deprive him of the right to be legally represented at the hearing.[92] In *Belziuk* v *Poland* (1998) 30 EHRR 614, the European Court pointed out that this right may be weaker in appellate proceedings.

14.8.1   Trial *in absentia* and domestic law

In the UK, a defendant who absconds may be tried in his absence.[93] A defendant who absconds during his trial may also be tried in his absence but his legal representative may continue to represent his interests.[94] A trial may take place[95] or continue[96] in the absence of an unruly defendant. The discretion to continue in the absence of a defendant who is ill should be exercised sparingly.[97]

14.9   INFORMATION AS TO THE ACCUSATION

Article 6(3)(a) provides that a person charged with a criminal offence be 'informed promptly, in a language which he understands and in detail, of the nature and cause of the accusation against him'. The words 'in detail' do not mean

[91] *Colozza* v *Italy* (1985) 7 EHRR 516.
[92] *Poitrimol* v *France* (1993) 18 EHRR 130; *Geyseghem* v *Belgium* [1999] EHRLR 337.
[93] *R* v *Jones (No. 2)* (1972) 56 Cr App R 413. See also *R* v *Jones (Jerome)* (2001) *The Telegraph*, 6 February; *R* v *Hayward and others* (2001) *The Independent*, 8 February.
[94] *R* v *Shaw* (1980) 70 Cr App R 313.
[95] *R* v *Browne* (1980) 70 JP 472.
[96] *R* v *Berry* (1897) 104 LTJ 110.
[97] *R* v *Howson* (1982) 74 Cr App R 172; *R* v *Pearson and others* (1998) *The Independent*, 25 February.

that the prosecution has to disclose evidence. Notification of the offences and the details of where and when they were allegedly committed will suffice.[98] The equality of arms principle also imposes an obligation on the prosecution to disclose any material in their possession, or to which they could gain access, which may assist the accused in exonerating himself.[99]

14.9.1   Information as to the accusation and domestic law

The disclosure scheme under the Criminal Procedure and Investigations Act 1996 and potential conflicts with Convention law are set out in detail in chapter 13 of this work.

14.10   ADEQUATE TIME AND FACILITIES

Article 6(3)(b) provides that a person charged with a criminal offence must be provided with adequate time and facilities for the preparation of his defence. The adequacy of the time permitted will partly depend upon the complexity of the case.[100] This principle requires that a defence lawyer must be instructed in sufficient time to properly prepare the case.[101] Currently the emphasis is on the appearance of unfairness rather than proof of the existence of actual unfairness.[102] The requirement to provide adequate time and facilities is a positive one designed to ensure parity between the parties.[103]

14.11   LEGAL AID

Article 6(3)(c) guarantees the right to legal aid in 'criminal proceedings'.[104] There are two restrictions to this right: (a) the accused must lack 'sufficient means' to pay for legal assistance; (b) the interests of justice must require legal aid to be granted. In respect of the latter restriction, the complexity of the case is a relevant factor.[105] Moreover, an unrepresented defendant must be able to present his case adequately without legal assistance[106] and complex questions of law will be a relevant consideration.[107] If the deprivation of liberty is involved the interests of justice call for legal representation.[108]

---

[98] *Brozicek* v *Italy* (1989) 12 EHRR 371.
[99] *Jespers* v *Belgium* (1981) 27 DR 61.
[100] *Albert and Le Compte* v *Belgium* (1983) 5 EHRR 533; *Can* v *Austria* (1985) 8 EHRR 121.
[101] *Goddi* v *Italy* (1984) 6 EHRR 457.
[102] *Artico* v *Italy* (1980) 3 EHRR 1.
[103] *Pataki and Dunshirn* v *Austria* (1963) 6 YB 714.
[104] This latter expression must be interpreted in accordance with the Convention jurisprudence on the definition of 'criminal charge'.
[105] *Benham* v *UK* (1996) 22 EHRR 293.
[106] *Granger* v *UK* (1990) 12 EHRR 469.
[107] *Hoang* v *France* (1993) 16 EHRR 53.
[108] *Benham* v *UK* (see above at fn. 101). This decision led to the amendment of the Legal Advice and Assistance (Scope) Regulations 1989 (SI 1989/550) by the Legal Advice and Assistance (Scope) (Amendment) Regulations 1997 (SI 1997/997). See also *Perks and others* v *UK* (1999) 30 EHRR 33.

Any determination in respect of the granting of legal aid must be capable of review.[109] There is, moreover, no requirement to prove actual prejudice in respect of a refusal to grant legal aid.[110]

A system of legal aid involving fixed payments to the accused's legal representative did not *per se* involve a breach of Article 6. Whilst such a system gave rise to a potential conflict of interest (the less work done the greater the payment), no actual prejudice had been demonstrated.[111]

14.11.1   Legal aid and domestic law

The grant of legal aid is governed by the Legal Aid Act 1988 which, consistent with Article 6(3), provides free advice and assistance on the basis of means. The Access to Justice Act 1999 repeals the 1988 Act and provides, from a date to be appointed, for the setting up of a Criminal Defence Service[112] to ensure that individuals involved in criminal investigations or criminal proceedings have access to such advice and assistance as the interests of justice require (sch. 3, para. 5(4)). Section 15 attempts to give effect to the right to legal assistance of the defendant's choosing whilst at the same time providing for the making of regulations to qualify that right but those regulations cannot insist that only a person employed by the Community Legal Service may be selected (s. 15(4)). The criteria for granting representation are set out in a schedule to the Act (sch. 3, para. 5) and include a consideration of the interests of justice.

The 1999 Act rather deftly combines the extension of the right to legal representation with a restriction on the choice of legal representative. The extent to which this may breach Article 6(3)(c) can only be assessed when the regulations are published. Where an individual is represented in any court other than the magistrates' court, such a person may be ordered to pay some or all of the legal costs involved (s. 17(2), subject to any rules made under s. 17(3)).

14.12   LEGAL REPRESENTATION

Legal representation must be 'practical and effective'.[113] Article 6(3)(c) speaks of assistance and not nomination. The state is not responsible for every shortcoming of a lawyer appointed under the legal aid scheme but it should intervene if there has been a manifest failure to provide effective representation.[114] This obligation

[109] *Granger* v *UK* (1990) 12 EHRR 469.
[110] *Artico* v *Italy* (1980) 3 EHRR 1.
[111] *Procurator Fiscal, Fort William* v *McLean and another* [2000] UKHRR 598, JC.
[112] Section 12. The Act received the Royal Assent on 27 July 1999.
[113] *Artico* v *Italy* (1990) 12 EHRR 469.
[114] *Kamasinki* v *Austria* (1991) 13 EHRR 36. See also *F* v *UK* (1992) 15 EHRR CD 32; *Daud* v *Portugal* (1998) 30 EHRR 400.

will undoubtedly increase in respect of legal representatives provided under the UK's new Criminal Defence Service because of the closer links with the state.

Generally the equality of arms principle requires the state to ensure that the obligations of the legal representative are fulfilled.[115]

If any inequality of arms is brought about by disreputable behaviour by the defendant, then he only has himself to blame.[116]

The right to a legal representative of the defendant's choice is not unfettered. The wishes of the defendant can be overridden where there are 'relevant and sufficient grounds' for so doing.[117] A more generous test in relation to privately paying defendants may give rise to problems under Article 14 (the prohibition on discrimination). The right to defend oneself is also not absolute.[118]

14.12.1   Legal representation and domestic law

Domestic law includes the concept of the right to be represented by counsel of one's choice[119] but such a choice must be reasonably practicable. The overriding criterion is the interests of justice.[120]

A defendant has a right to represent himself[121] but a judge has a discretion to refuse such an application.[122]

There are certain restrictions on unrepresented defendants cross-examining in particular cases.[123] If the court concludes that it is in the interests of justice for such an accused to be legally represented (whatever the wishes of the accused), then it may so order.[124] This is consistent with Convention case law.[125]

14.13   THE RIGHT TO CONFRONT PROSECUTION WITNESSES

Article 6(3)(d) guarantees an accused the right to examine or have examined witnesses against him, and to obtain the attendance and examination of witnesses on his behalf under the same conditions as witnesses against him. This right is not absolute but such restrictions that exist must not destroy the essence of the right.[126] The accused has a right to confront a witness whose attendance has been excused

---

[115] *Goddi* v *Italy* (1984) 6 EHRR 457.

[116] *X* v *UK* (1980) 21 DR 126.

[117] *Croissant* v *Germany* (1992) 16 EHRR 135 at para. 29.

[118] *Phillis* v *Greece* (1990) 66 DR 260; *Croissant* v *Germany*.

[119] *R* v *De Oliviera* [1997] Crim LR 600; *R* v *Kingston* (1948) 32 Cr App R 183.

[120] *R* v *Mills* [1997] 2 Cr App R 206.

[121] *R* v *Woodward* (1944) 29 Cr App R 159.

[122] *R* v *Lyons* (1979) 68 Cr App R 104.

[123] Criminal Justice Act 1988, s. 34A; Youth Justice and Criminal Evidence Act 1999, ss. 34–36 (as from 4 September 2000 (Youth Justice and Criminal Evidence Act 1999 (Commencement No. 4) Order 2000 (SI 2000/2091)).

[124] *Youth Justice and Criminal Evidence Act 1999*, s. 38. The commencement date is as in fn. 123.

[125] *Croissant* v *Germany* (1992) 16 EHRR 135.

[126] *Brandstetter* v *Austria* (1991) 15 EHRR 378.

although evidence from abroad may be admissible.[127] The admission of hearsay will be looked at in the context of the fairness of the proceedings as a whole.[128]

14.13.1 The right to confront prosecution witnesses in domestic law

A number of statutory provisions permit certain categories of witness to give evidence anonymously: victims of sexual offences (Sexual Offences (Amendment) Act 1976, s. 4, Sexual Offences (Amendment) Act 1992, ss. 1–4); children and young persons (Youth Justice and Criminal Evidence Act 1999, s. 45). At common law the court retains a discretion to allow a witness to give evidence anonymously in appropriate cases, for example, blackmail (*R v Socialist Worker, ex parte Attorney-General* [1975] QB 637 (DC). In *R v Taylor (G)* (1994) *The Times*, 17 August, the Court of Appeal set out some of the relevant factors to be taken into account in the rare and exceptional decision to permit a witness to conceal his identity entirely from the accused. Such factors are not rules of law (*Al-Fawwaz v Governor of Brixton Prison and another* (2000) *The Times*, 22 December (DC)).

Statements of prosecution witnesses may be read to the jury under the provisions of ss. 23, 25 and 26 of the Criminal Justice Act 1988. These provisions cover witnesses who are dead or unfit to attend, witnesses who are outside the United Kingdom and it is not reasonably practicable to secure their attendance, and where all reasonable steps have been taken to find the witness but he or she cannot be found (s. 23). The Act sets out the principles to be followed by the court (s. 25) and the additional considerations in respect of statements in documents prepared for criminal proceedings (s. 26). Prior to the introduction of the HRA 1998, it has been held that these statutory provisions do not breach Article 6(3)(d) (*R v Gokal* [1997] 2 Cr App R 266 (CA)).

14.14 INTERPRETERS AND TRANSLATIONS

Article 6(3)(e) guarantees the defendant the right 'to have the free assistance of an interpreter if he cannot understand or speak the language used in court'. This right is unqualified but it must be clear that the defendant has genuine difficulty in understanding or speaking the language used in court.[129] This right applies irrespective of the defendant's means. It is wrong in principle to impose the cost of an interpreter on a convicted defendant.[130]

The right under Article 6(3)(e) applies to the translation of prosecution material. The criterion is what is necessary to secure a fair trial.[131]

---

[127] *X v Germany* (1987) 10 EHRR 521; *S v Germany* (1983) 39 DR 43.
[128] *Kostovski v Netherlands* (1989) 12 EHRR 434.
[129] *Luedicke, Belkacem and Koc v Germany* (1978) 2 EHRR 149.
[130] Ibid; *Öztürk v Germany* (1984) 6 EHRR 409.
[131] *Luedicke* (see above at fn. 129); *Brozicek v Italy* (1989) 12 EHRR 371.

This principle appeared to be diluted in *Kamasinski* v *Austria* (1989) 13 EHRR 36 where the European Court held that this right did not apply to the translation of all documents. This situation has, however, only occurred where someone on the defence team could interpret the relevant documents.[132]

14.14.1   Interpreters etc. and domestic law

A defendant must be able to comprehend fully the criminal proceedings to which he is a party and this involves the right to have an interpreter.[133] Although the services of an interpreter are normally provided free of charge, the court has a discretion to order a defendant to pay such costs.[134] Such an order would clearly breach Article 6(3)(e).[135]

14.15   THE BURDEN OF PROOF

Article 6(2) enshrines the presumption of innocence and thereby ensures that the burden of proof in criminal trials falls on the prosecution.[136] As Lord Bingham has pointed out in *Brown* v *Stott (Procurator Fiscal, Dunfermline)* [2001] 2 All ER 97 (PC) this right appears on its face to be an absolute requirement. There are, however, two exceptions to this rule: (a) the burden may fall on a defendant in seeking to establish a specific defence;[137] (b) rules containing presumptions of law or fact against a defendant do not necessarily infringe Article 6(2).[138] As the Court pointed out in *Salabiaku* v *France* (1988) 13 EHRR 379, presumptions of fact or law must be confined within reasonable limits and take into account the importance of what is at stake and maintain the rights of the defence (at para. 28).

It is unclear from the decision in *Salabiaku* as to the extent to which the European Court was upholding strict liability offences. It seems clear that strict liability offences which leave no defence would breach the Convention.

14.15.1   Burden of proof and domestic law

In *R* v *DPP, ex parte Kebilene* [1999] 3 WLR 972, the House of Lords considered Article 6(2). Lord Hope said (at p. 990) that the principle contained in Article 6(2) was 'wholly consistent' with the common law of England and Scotland. Lord Hope pointed out the difference between the 'evidential burden' placed on an accused and a 'persuasive burden'. The latter burden reverses the burden of proof. Statutory presumptions which place an evidential burden on an accused are not incompatible with Article 6(2).

---

[132] *Hayward* v *Sweden* (App. No. 14106/88, 6 December 1991).
[133] *R* v *Iqbal Begum* 93 Cr App R 96; *Kunnath* v *The State* (1994) 98 Cr App R 455, PC.
[134] *Practice Direction (Crime Costs)* [1991] 1 WLR 498.
[135] See, *Luedicke* (above at fn. 129) at para. 40.
[136] *Barberà, Messegué and Jabardo* v *Spain* (1988) 11 EHRR 360 at para. 77.
[137] *Lingens* v *Austria* (1981) 26 DR 171.
[138] *Salabiaku* v *France* (1988) 13 EHRR 379.

His Lordship then outlined three species of persuasive burden. First, there is the mandatory presumption of guilt as to an essential element of the offence and this presumption is inconsistent with the presumption of innocence. Secondly, there is the presumption of guilt as to an essential element of the offence which is discretionary. This presumption may be inconsistent with the presumption of innocence. Thirdly, there are reverse onus clauses which relate to an exemption or proviso which the accused must establish if he wishes to avoid conviction but which is not an essential element of the offence. These provisions may also violate the presumption of innocence, depending on the circumstances. Provisions which prima facie breach the presumption of innocence do not inevitably lead to a conclusion that Article 6(2) has been violated.

In order to determine where the appropriate balance lies the court should ask three questions: (i) what does the prosecution have to prove in order to transfer the onus to the defence? (ii) what is the burden on the accused — does it relate to something which is difficult for him to prove or is it something within his knowledge? (iii) what is the nature of the threat faced by society which the provision is designed to combat? In *R v Lambert and others* [2000] UKHRR 864, Lord Woolf CJ, applying *Kebilene*, said that where an accused was required to disprove an essential element of the offence it will be difficult to justify the provision.

14.16   THE STANDARD OF PROOF

Although it is not specifically set out in the Convention the standard of proof beyond a reasonable doubt appears to flow from the presumption of innocence.[139]

14.17   REASONS

Article 6(1) requires domestic courts to give reasons for their decisions.[140] Detailed reasons are not required for every decision and the extent of the obligation will generally depend on the importance of the relevant decision.[141] There is no requirement for a jury to give reasons for its verdict[142] but it appears likely that magistrates will be required to give a reasoned judgment.[143]

---

[139] *Austria v Italy* (1963) 6 Yearbook 740; *Barberà, Messegué and Jabardo v Spain* (1988) 11 EHRR 360.

[140] *Van de Hurk v Netherlands* (1994) 18 EHRR 481; *Hiro Balani v Spain* (1995) 19 EHRR 566.

[141] *Ruiz Torija v Spain* (1994) 19 EHRR 553; *Georgiades v Greece* (1997) 24 EHRR 606; *Helle v Finland* (1997) 26 EHRR 159.

[142] *Saric v Denmark* (App. No. 31913/96).

[143] This proposition flows from the Strasbourg case law on the giving of reasons in bail cases: *Letellier v France* (1991) 14 EHRR 83; *Sargin v Turkey* (1995) 20 EHRR 505. For the role of the court clerk, see *Practice Direction (Justices: Clerk to Court)* (2000), *The Times*, 11 October.

14.17.1   Reasons and domestic law

There is no general obligation to give a reasoned ruling in criminal proceedings but as *Archbold* points out,[144] such a practice would be of great assistance. In *Stefan* v *General Medical Council* [2000] HRLR 1, the Privy Council referred to the 'possible reappraisal of the whole position [concerning the giving of reasons] which the passing of the Human Rights Act 1998 may bring about', and added that the provisions of Article 6 'will require closer attention to be paid to the duty to give reasons, at least in relation to those cases where a person's civil rights and obligations are being determined'. In *Pullum* v *CPS* [2000] COD 206, the Divisional Court said that the minimum a defendant was entitled to by way of reasons was a clear statement as to the issues that had to be resolved and the basis upon which they had been resolved. See also *Cedeno* v *Logan* [2001] 1 WLR 96.

Magistrates are now advised to give reasons for their decisions (*Practice Direction (Justices: Clerks to Court)* [2001] 1 WLR 1886).

14.18   COSTS IN CRIMINAL CASES

There is no general right to costs or expenses under the Convention.[145] Where, however, a costs decision amounts to a determination of guilt then the presumption of innocence will be engaged. Much will depend upon the terms of any order. Where a court made a costs order because, had the case progressed to trial, the applicant would 'very probably' have been convicted, Article 6 was breached.[146] Where a defendant has been acquitted costs should normally be awarded and the court should not express suspicions in respect of the defendant's guilt.[147]

14.18.1   Costs in criminal cases and domestic law

The award of costs in criminal cases is governed by the *Practice Direction (Costs in Criminal Proceedings)* (1991) 93 Cr App R 89.[148] A defendant's costs order should normally be made in respect of an acquitted defendant unless 'there are positive reasons for not doing so'. Examples of such reasons are (*Practice Direction*, para. 2.2): (a) the defendant's own conduct has brought suspicion on himself and has misled the prosecution into thinking that the case against him is stronger than it is; (b) there is ample evidence to support a conviction but the defendant is acquitted on a technicality which has no merit. If costs are refused under 2.2(a) there must be material to support such a determination.[149] The

---

[144] (2001) 15–440.
[145] *Lutz* v *Germany* (1987) 10 EHRR 182.
[146] *Minelli* v *Switzerland* (1983) 5 EHRR 554.
[147] *Sekanina* v *Austria* (1993) 17 EHRR 221.
[148] This power is derived from the Prosecution of Offences Act 1985, s. 16.
[149] *Mooney* v *Cardiff JJ* (1999) *The Times*, 17 November.

Practice Direction (Costs in Criminal Proceedings (No. 2)) [2000] 1 Cr App R 60, amends the earlier *Practice Direction* by deleting paragraph 2.2(b). The remaining single ground for refusing costs is probably compliant with the Convention provided it is not applied in a way that implies guilt on the part of the acquitted defendant.

14.19 DOUBLE JEOPARDY

The rule against double jeopardy is contained in Article 4 of Protocol 7 of the Convention. Protocol 7 was not brought into effect by the Human Rights Act 1998, although the Government has indicated an intention to sign, ratify and incorporate the provision. The rule indicates that no one should be tried or punished again for the same offence in respect of which he has already been acquitted or convicted. Article 4(2) permits domestic law to allow a case to be reopened if there is 'evidence or new or newly discovered facts, or if there has been a fundamental defect in the previous proceedings, which could effect the outcome of the case'.

There are conflicting decisions at Strasbourg as to whether the rule against double jeopardy is inherent in Article 6.[150] The prohibition in Article 4 is concerned with trying a defendant for two offences which are 'based on the same conduct' (*Gradinger* v *Austria* (1985) A/328-C).[151] In *Oliviera* v *Switzerland* (1999) 28 EHRR 289, the European Court appeared to suggest that the test was narrower than the one stated in *Gradinger* by permitting separate offences arising from a single criminal act. This appears to suggest that the same offence meant the same offence in law. Indeed, in a dissenting judgment in *Oliviera* (at p. 303), Judge Repik describes the two decisions as 'wholly conflicting'.

14.19.1 Double jeopardy and domestic law

A defendant may not be tried for a crime in respect of which he has previously been convicted or acquitted, or in respect of which he could, on some previous indictment, have been lawfully convicted.[152] The fresh evidence exception in Article 4(2) has no parallel in English law. There is, however, a limited parallel to the 'fundamental defect' exception in the 'tainted acquittals' provisions.[153]

Domestic law undoubtedly provides greater protection for an accused than the European Convention. The incorporation of Protocol 7 will not affect domestic law as Article 4 would only apply once a domestic law provided a similar

---

[150] *X* v *Austria* (1970) 35 CD 151; *S* v *Germany* (1983) 39 DR 43.
[151] See the article on double jeopardy by Ian Dennis at [2000] Crim LR 933.
[152] *Connelly* v *DPP* [1964] AC 1254, HL.
[153] The Criminal Procedure and Investigations Act 1996, ss. 54–6.

provision. The Law Commission[154] has recommended the retention of the double jeopardy rule but recommended that it should be extended for an offence founded on the same or substantially the same facts and the rule and any exceptions should be in a statutory form. The Commission recommends an exception for certain cases based on new evidence.[155] The case should be one leading to a sentence of three years or more, the new evidence should substantially strengthen the prosecution case and the evidence as a whole would lead to the conclusion that a jury would very probably or certainly convict. The Law Commission has invited views on which of the latter thresholds is to be preferred. The new evidence should not have been available at the original trial if the prosecution had acted with due diligence. The overarching criterion must be the interests of justice.

In an analogous field the House of Lords held, in *R* v *Z* [2000] 3 WLR 117, that the double jeopardy rule did not prevent the prosecution calling relevant evidence from cases in respect of which the defendant had been acquitted. The double jeopardy principle was not involved because the defendant was not being prosecuted in respect of the earlier allegations. The House of Lords did not consider the European Convention and so did not consider the effect of Article 6. Nonetheless, the argument of the House of Lords doubtless would have been that Z's presumption of innocence in respect of the offence with which he was tried remained intact and as he was not on trial for the earlier offences, the presumption of innocence did not arise. This position flows from the fact that the presumption of innocence in Article 6(2) is concerned with an offence with which the accused has been charged.

---

[154] Consultation Paper No. 156.
[155] This recommendation is partly inspired by recommendation 38 of the 'Macpherson Report' (*The Stephen Lawrence Inquiry* (1999), Cm. 4262–I).

Chapter Fifteen

Criminal Proceedings before the Magistrates' Court

Michelle Strange

15.1   INTRODUCTION

The HRA 1998 has already had a significant impact in the magistrates' courts, both during trials and at the interlocutory stage. The system in the magistrates' courts, where lay justices make rulings on both fact and law assisted by a legally trained clerk, is unique to UK law and needs careful reassessment in the light of the Convention. In summary, the following areas are likely to develop:

- the giving of reasons;
- the granting of legal aid;
- the granting of search warrants;
- provision of facilities for legal advice;
- consideration of applications for bail;
- disclosure;
- the requirement that the tribunal be independent or impartial;
- the role of the court clerk;
- *voir dire* in the magistrates' courts.

These issues are discussed in detail below.

15.2   REASONS

Many decisions are made in the magistrates' court without any full reasons being given to the parties. In hearings where bail is refused, for example, it has been commonplace in many magistrates' courts to hand the defendant a standard form in which one or more grounds for refusal are ticked. Although the practice has in theory changed, old habits may linger in some areas.[1] The European Court has often stressed the importance of the need for reasons, and has on occasion assumed, in the absence of reasons being given, that no valid ones exist.[2] Under the HRA 1998 it is incumbent upon justices to give reasoned decisions whenever a ruling is sought on a significant issue in the case, most notably on issues of bail, submissions of no case to answer, and when a defendant is found guilty after a trial. The Divisional Court has, however, held[3] that full reasons need not be given when magistrates decide to commit a defendant to the Crown Court for sentence, as there is ample opportunity in the subsequent proceedings to make representations on the appropriate level of sentence (see also *Cedeno* v *Logan* [2001] 1 WLR 96).

Because of the need for reasons, a note should be taken of proceedings, at least by the clerk of the court.[4] It is not clear to what extent the court clerk should be permitted to assist in the drawing up of reasons in a case. The role of the clerk is subject to revision on a number of grounds,[5] and an attempt by the clerk to assist the justices in drawing up reasons in private may be subject to challenge. The Judicial Studies Board recommends that justices draft their reasons alone, and the clerk checks them thereafter. It further recommends that, if the clerk's legal advice is required, it be given in open court.

15.3 LEGAL AID

Under Article 6(3)(c) the criminal defendant has a right to legal advice (i) when he lacks the means to pay for it and (ii) where the interests of justice require it to be granted. The provisions have been discussed in detail elsewhere in this book,[6] but have particular relevance for magistrates, as they determine many applications for legal aid. The Strasbourg bodies have held that interpretation of the phrase 'interests of justice' includes consideration of the complexity of the case, the ability of the defendant to represent himself, and the gravity of any possible

---

[1] See 11.4.1 above.

[2] See for example *Tomasi* v *France* (1992) 15 EHRR 1 at para. 84, *Hiro Balani* v *Spain* (1994) 19 EHRR 566 at para. 27, *Hadjianastassiou* v *Greece* (1992) 16 EHRR 219 at para. 33.

[3] *R* (on the application of Jermyn) v *Wirral Magistrates Court* (20 October 2000, unreported). For a domestic decision in a civil context, see *Stefan* v *General Medical Council* [1999] 1 WLR 1293 at p. 1299.

[4] There is currently no statutory obligation for a court clerk to take notes of evidence in a summary trial, but in practice court clerks do so. There is an obligation to take a note of reasons for withholding bail, or the evidence on a committal for sentence. Although poor notes may not themselves be the subject of challenge, the failure to record reasons may result in problems in a higher court.

[5] See 15.8 below.

[6] See chapter 12

sentence. When there is a risk of a custodial sentence, legal aid should be granted.[7] There is a continuing duty to review a refusal of legal aid if proceedings become more complex.[8]

Broadly speaking, the test for eligibility of legal aid[9] is in accordance with the 'interests of justice' test contained within Article 6(3)(c), but there will be areas where magistrates will need to take into account the Convention and grant legal aid. Provisions classified as civil under domestic proceedings may nonetheless be held to be criminal under the Convention.

15.4   FACILITIES FOR LEGAL ADVICE

Many magistrates' courts now have facilities for lawyers to take instructions from their clients in privacy, but they are not always available. Where a defendant is in custody, it is not uncommon for a lawyer to meet a client through the bars of the cell door with a number of other defendants and prison officers listening in. The courts are aware that the position is likely to be unacceptable under the Convention, and needs serous consideration.

Communications between lawyers and clients are protected by Article 8 (privacy and family rights) and Article 6(3)(c), and should be read together with Article 6(3)(b), which gives the criminal defendant the right 'to have adequate time and facilities for the preparation of his defence'.

The European Court has said that lawyer/client communications should be private, confidential and not subject to restrictions. Although there is no decision from the European Court which specifically deals with facilities at court, it is clear that the right to confidentiality is taken seriously in Strasbourg. In *S v Switzerland* (1991) 14 EHRR 667 the Court held that '... an accused's right to communicate with his advocate out of the hearing of a third person is one of the basic requirements of a fair trial ...'[10]

Although many hearings in the magistrates' court take place long before the trial, it is often necessary for lawyers to take instructions from defendants on matters such as bail, new evidence, and the potential for a guilty plea. On a bail application, the European Court has held that the defendant's right under Article 5(4) to 'take proceedings by which the lawfulness of his detention shall be decided ...' includes a number of fair trial rights under Article 6,[11] including the

---

[7] *Benham* v *UK* (1996) 22 EHRR 293.

[8] *Granger* v *UK* (1990) 12 EHRR 469. See also the Scottish case of *Bullock* v *HM Advocate* 1999 JC 260.

[9] The 'statutory criteria' under the Legal Aid Act 1988.

[10] See *R* v *Piper* (1995) 3 NZLR 540, for a New Zealand authority that a telephone call between a suspect and his solicitor, which could be overheard by police was an infringement of his right to lawyer/client confidentiality.

[11] *De Wilde, Ooms and Versyp* v *Belgium* (1971) EHRR 373.

right to participate,[12] that the hearing be adversarial[13] and that there be equality of arms. It is difficult to see how these rights can be respected if there is no opportunity for the defendant to give instructions to his lawyer in private, and it is submitted that failure to afford private consultation rooms may in some cases result in an unlawful decision to remand the defendant in custody, or an unfair trial.

On a non-contentious interlocutory hearing where the lawyer has previously taken instructions from the defendant, or where the case will be adjourned for him to do so, the lack of facilities may have little bearing on the fairness of the trial. Where, the lawyer has not met the defendant before, or needs to take full instructions on new material or canvass a guilty plea where there has been no other opportunity to do so, lack of confidential access to the defendant may have serious implications on the outcome of the case. It is submitted that in such a situation lawyers should be quick to require that facilities are available, and seek an adjournment or release on bail until they are provided.

15.5   SEARCH WARRANTS AND WARRANTS TO ENTER PROPERTY

Magistrates' courts are often asked to grant search warrants to enter property,[14] thereby affecting the Convention rights of the suspect and any other occupiers of the property. The home is protected by Article 8 and Article 1 of Protocol 1 (the right to property). Article 8(2) allows for interference with this right:

> in accordance with the law and [where it] is necessary in a democratic society in the interests of national security, public safety or the economic well-being of the country, for the prevention of disorder or crime, for the protection of health or morals, or for the protection of the rights and freedoms of others.

All of these exceptions can apply to criminal proceedings. Article 1 of Protocol 1 allows interference with the right to peaceful enjoyment of possessions 'in the public interest and subject to the conditions provided for by law and by the general principles of international law'. This has been held to require a balance between 'the demands of the general interest of the community and the requirements of the protection of the individual's fundamental rights'.[15]

Any search warrant should be granted 'in accordance with the law'; decisions of the European Court on other areas[16] make it clear that this includes a requirement that the powers should not be exercised in an arbitrary fashion. In

---

[12] *Winterwerp* v *Netherlands* (1979) 2 EHRR 387.
[13] *Lamy* v *Belgium* (1989) 11 EHRR 529.
[14] For example under s. 8, PACE 1984.
[15] *Sporrong and Lonnroth* v *Sweden* (1982) 5 EHRR 35.
[16] See for example, *Winterwerp* v *Netherlands* (1979) 2 EHRR 387.

practice, it will be necessary for magistrates to enquire whether it is necessary for the application to be heard *ex parte*.[17] The court should also enquire into the nature and strength of the 'reasonable grounds' of the police officer before issuing a search warrant, and not issue a search warrant merely because the police require it. An attempt to found 'reasonable grounds' because of membership of a particular group may engage Article 14 (freedom from discrimination.)

This is not to say that the strict rules of evidence will apply at the warrant stage — it is no doubt permissible for reasonable grounds to be founded on evidence which will not be admissible at trial[18] — but magistrates will need to provide a proper independent scrutiny of police activities to avoid violating the Convention. With this in mind, it would be advisable for any magistrate granting a search warrant to make a note of his or her reasons for doing so.

This was considered in the Scottish case of *Birse* v *HM Advocate* 2000 SLT 869, where the magistrate had no recollection or record of his reasons for granting a warrant. The Scottish court nonetheless found no breach of Article 8 in the issuing of a search warrant for drugs, because the magistrate said it was his invariable practice to ask questions during the application, and the officer said that he had told him that local residents had smelt unusual smells emanating from the applicant's home on weekend evenings. The court said that this was sufficient to show he had satisfied himself of the grounds for the search, but this type of *ex post facto* reasoning might not satisfy the Strasbourg Court.[19]

15.6 BAIL

Under Article 5, the defendant has a right to liberty unless one of the exceptions under Article 5(3) applies. Under Article 5(4) the incarcerated defendant has a right to 'take proceedings by which the lawfulness of his detention shall be decided speedily by a court'. The HRA 1998 is likely to bring about significant change in both the practice and procedure at bail applications in the magistrates' courts. This has been discussed in detail in chapter 11. The important areas are:

(a)   more bail applications will need to be entertained, even if there is no 'change of circumstances' currently recognised under domestic law;[20]

(b)   the authorities will need to provide more comprehensive reasons and material to support any objection to bail;[21]

---

[17] In cases where it is thought that a person is keeping stolen goods, it probably will be. If, however, the application is to enter to disconnect electricity or gas supplies, an *ex parte* application would rarely be justified.

[18] *Windisch* v *Austria* (1990) 13 EHRR 574.

[19] In Canada, the courts have held that the warrant procedure should be meaningful, and the person granting the warrant must 'assess the evidence and consider whether the interests of the state clearly outweigh those of the individual': *R* v *Collins* (1987) 1 SCR 265.

[20] See 11.4.2.4.

[21] See 11.4.1.

(c)   full reasons will need to be given for any refusal to grant bail;[22]

(d)   in situations where there is a real dispute as to the grounds for refusing bail, the court may be obliged to hear evidence from one party or both of the parties. It is not clear how strict the rules of evidence will be.[23]

15.7   TRIAL BY AN INDEPENDENT AND IMPARTIAL TRIBUNAL

Article 6(1) guarantees the defendant the right to an independent and impartial tribunal.[24] As in domestic law, the concept embodies both subjective and objective impartiality.[25] Where actual bias is alleged, the European Court will presume good faith unless the contrary is proved.[26] In cases of objective bias, the European Court has looked for 'ascertainable facts which may raise doubts as to [the court's] impartiality',[27] and has stressed that 'any judge in respect of whom there is a legitimate reason to fear a lack of impartiality must withdraw'.[28] Appearances of impartiality are taken very seriously by the European Court.[29]

In *Castillo Algar* v *Spain* (2000) 30 EHRR 827 two members of a military trial court had sat on an earlier hearing and determined that there was a case to answer against the applicant. No point was taken about impartiality at the trial, but it was raised on appeal. The European Court found that the failure to raise the point at the trial hearing was not a bar to bringing proceedings under the Convention, as it was raised in the domestic courts. In the circumstances of the case, which included an unfortunately worded ruling that there was evidence 'to allow ... the conclusion that an offence had been committed', there had been a violation under Article 6(1).[30]

It is difficult to predict how the European Court would approach the practice in England, whereby it is common for magistrates to encounter a frequent offender on many occasions in their local court. Domestic law appears similar in principle to the case law under the Convention.[31] Under both, it would in most circumstances be unacceptable for a magistrate to hear a trial of a defendant whom he had previously found guilty. At the other end of the scale, the European

---

[22] Ibid.

[23] See 11.4.2.2.

[24] See chapter 14, especially at 14.3.

[25] *Piersack* v *Belgium* (1982) 5 EHRR 169.

[26] *Hauschildt* v *Denmark* (1989) 12 EHRR 266.

[27] Ibid at para. 47.

[28] *Castillo Algar* v *Spain* (28 October 1998), at para. 45.

[29] See for example *Daktaras* v *Lithuania* (10 October 2000).

[30] In domestic law, magistrates who sat on a trial would be disqualified from sitting on an appeal hearing in the Crown Court.

[31] See for example *R* v *Altrincham Justices, ex parte Pennington* [1975] QB 549, where the Divisional Court held that a magistrate should take the initiative of drawing to the attention of the parties any reason why there should be an objection to him or her sitting. See also *R* v *Bow Street Metropolitan Stipendiary Magistrate, ex parte Pinochet Ugarte (No. 2)* [1999] 2 WLR 272 (HL).

Court has held that the mere fact that a magistrate has previously dealt with a defendant does not necessarily breach Article 6(1);[32] but there are many shades in between. Where a magistrate has previously been party to a decision to refuse bail, and has expressed any views on the case itself, the decisions in *Algar* and *Hauschildt*[33] suggest that if a magistrate sat on a trial in these circumstances it would be open to challenge. The same may be true in a successive bail application if the magistrate has expressed strong views about the case.

For discussion of the position where a magistrate determines the admissibility of evidence under s. 78, Police and Criminal Evidence Act 1984, see below at 15.10.

15.8   ROLE OF THE COURT CLERK

The European Court has has interpreted the concept of an independent and impartial tribunal widely, to include the role of any non-parties who may have a say in the outcome of proceedings.[34] Equality of arms requires that the defence should have an opportunity to hear and make representations upon any advice given to the court. This is the case even if the advice is on the law alone. In *JJ* v *Netherlands* (1999) 28 EHRR 168 the Procurator General sent a written advice on the law to the Supreme Court, which the defence had no right to see under domestic law. The European Court held (para. 42) that although the opinion '[was] objective and reasoned in law, the opinion [was] nevertheless intended to advise and accordingly influence the Supreme Court'. Accordingly, there had been a breach of Article 6(1) because the defence had not been permitted to comment upon it. The principle was restated in the recent case of *Krcmar* v *Czech Republic* (3 March 2000)[35] in which the Court said (para. 40):

> the concept of a fair hearing also implies the right to adversarial proceedings, according to which the parties must have the opportunity not only to make known any evidence needed for their claims to succeed, but also to have knowledge of and comment on, all evidence adduced or observations filed, with a view to influencing the courts' decision.

This has significant implications for the role of the justices' clerk. Lawyers who regularly appear in the magistrates' courts will have seen the clerk retiring with the bench, or being asked to assist the magistrates in their deliberations in private. Some of these practices were already outlawed by little-observed domestic

---

[32] *Brown* v *UK* (1986) 8 EHRR 272.
[33] See above at fn 26.
[34] See for example, *Delcourt* v *Belgium* (1969) 1 EHRR 355, *Ruiz-Mateos* v *Spain* (1993) 16 EHRR 505, *Van Orshoven* v *Belgium* (1997) 26 EHRR 55.
[35] The case concerned proceedings for restitution in relation to the applicant's companies which had been nationalised in 1945.

Practice Directions,[36] and there is domestic authority that justices should make clear in open court why they are requesting the clerk to join them.[37] The position is now governed by *Practice Direction (Justices: Clerk to Courts)* (2000) *The Times,* 11 October. This requires advice to be given in open court, but allows provisional advice to be given in private, so long as it is repeated in open court. This course had already been recommended to court clerks by the Judicial Studies Board and *Stone's Justices' Manual.*[38]

Although the justices' clerk system is not exactly the same in Scotland, the point was addressed directly in the Scottish case of *Procurator Fiscal, Kirkcaldy* v *Kelly* (18 August 2000, High Court of Justiciary), where the appellant argued that the giving of legal advice in private was contrary to Article 6. The Court of Appeal held (at para. 18) that communications between the clerk and the justices did not form part of the trial, and sought to distinguish *Delcourt* v *Belgium* (1969) 1 EHRR 355 and *Borgers* v *Belgium* (1991) 15 EHRR 92, on the basis that these cases involved private submissions in which the court was urged to follow a particular course, whilst the clerk's advice on the law had no such purpose. The Court of Appeal was impressed by the fact that magistrates need not follow the advice of the clerk.[39] The case does not follow the spirit of Convention jurisprudence, and it appears from the judgment that the Scottish court was not referred to *JJ* v *Netherlands.* The point remains open, and the judgment in *Kelly* would be unlikely to find favour in Strasbourg. The position of the clerk in England will be considered by the European Court in the near future.[40]

15.8.1   Independence of the executive

For a tribunal to be independent and impartial, the court must be independent of the executive.[41] Under the Justices Clerks Rules 1999[42] the court clerk may exercise judicial functions in many interlocutory hearings,[43] including extending and varying bail, committing the case to the Crown Court under section 6(2), Magistrates' Courts Act 1980, and issuing warrants for arrest. The status of these powers, and the general role of the clerk, raises issues under Article 6, and it is not clear whether the clerk is sufficiently independent of the executive, despite a

---

[36] These can be found at [1953] 2 All ER 1306; [1954] 1 All ER 230; [1981] 2 All ER 831.

[37] *R* v *Eccles Justices, ex parte Fitzpatrick* (1989) 89 Cr App R 324.

[38] *Stone's Justices' Manual 2000* (London: Butterworths), para. 1-32.

[39] Although in England they should generally do so, and a judgment may be subject to challenge if they do not: *Jones* v *Nicks* [1977] RTR 72.

[40] *Mort* v *UK* (case pending).

[41] *Piersack* v *Belgium* (1982) 5 EHRR 169; *Campbell and Fell* v *UK* (1980) 1 EHRR 355.

[42] SI 1999/2784; following s. 49, Crime and Disorder Act 1998.

[43] See the Justices Rules 1999.

statutory provision attempting to ensure independence.[44] The Lord Chancellor's department has recently published a consultation paper to explore how the administrative and judicial roles of the court clerk could be separated.[45]

A similar point was considered in *Procurator Fiscal, Kirkcaldy* v *Kelly*, where the Court of Appeal considered whether the clerk of the district court was performing a judicial function, and if so, whether he had the necessary security of tenure to qualify as an independent or impartial tribunal. The court rejected an argument that the role was judicial, and that the court clerk was part of the tribunal. The Solicitor General conceded that, if the clerk did exercise a judicial function, the necessary security of tenure would be absent, and the clerk would be insufficiently independent of the executive. There are reasons for arguing that this case is wrongly decided,[46] and has limited domestic application, especially in the light of the expressly judicial powers granted to the justices' clerk in England.

15.8.2   Unrepresented defendants

Where a defendant is unrepresented, the European court has held[47] that the trial court may need to assist him in presenting his case in order to ensure that the defendant has a fair trial. In family proceedings in the magistrates' court, this requirement is set out in statute,[48] and there is case law to suggest that this role should be undertaken by the clerk.[49] As the European Court has stressed the continuing duty of the court to monitor whether it is in the interests of justice that legal aid be granted,[50] it may be necessary to revisit the question of legal aid where an unrepresented defendant is struggling to present or comprehend the case.

Where the hearing is to determine whether a fine defaulter has the means to pay, it is permissible on domestic authority for the clerk to question the defaulter: in *R* v *Corby Justices, ex parte Mort* (1998) 162 JP 310 the Divisional Court said the practice did not result in unfairness unless the clerk 'were to assume an adversarial or partisan role in the conduct of any proceedings'. The case is currently awaiting judgment in the European Court, and may give rise to a change in the law.

---

[44] Section 89, Access to Justice Act 1999. See also the Scottish case of *Starrs and Chalmers* v *Procurator Fiscal, Linlithgow (Ruxton)* 2000 SLT 42.

[45] 'Future Role of Justices' Clerk: A Strategic Steer', January 2000, www.open.gov.uk/lcd. The paper makes no reference to the Convention.

[46] See above at 15.8.

[47] *Artico* v *Italy* (1980) 3 EHRR 1.

[48] Magistrates' Courts Act 1980, s. 73.

[49] *Simms* v *Moor* [1970] 2 QB 327; *Marjoram* v *Marjoram* [1955] 2 All ER 1.

[50] *Granger* v *UK* (1990) 12 EHRR 469; *Hoang* v *France* (1993) 16 EHRR 53.

15.9 DISCLOSURE

This topic has been discussed in detail in chapter 13. The European Court has held that Article 6(1) requires that the prosecution discloses 'all material evidence for or against the defence'.[51] This includes both advance disclosure of the prosecution case and of relevant 'unused material'.[52]

15.9.1 Advance disclosure in the magistrates' court

Domestic law provides that the accused has a right to advance disclosure of the prosecution case where the matter is triable 'either way' or only on indictment, but provides no such right where the defendant is charged with an offence triable only by magistrates.[53] In many areas advance disclosure is given as a matter of course, and where it is not, the prosecution will permit the defendant or his representative to see the material prior to the trial. This was not the case in *R* v *Stratford Justices, ex parte Imbert* [1999] 2 Cr App R 276, where the defendant faced a charge of threatening behaviour under s. 4, Public Order Act 1986. The prosecution refused to make advance disclosure of witness statements and the High Court was asked to judicially review the magistrates' refusal to stay proceedings as an abuse of process. The court specifically considered the compatibility of the provisions with the defendant's right to a fair trial under Article 6,[54] and came to the view that there was no breach. The court asked itself whether the proceedings as a whole had been adversely affected by the non-disclosure, and concluded that they had not been, as it remained possible to prevent unfairness by adjournments for the defendant to confer with his lawyer, or to proof witnesses.

Notwithstanding the ruling, the advance disclosure provisions are capable of leading to breaches of Article 6, and the *ad hoc* approach of Collins J would be likely to offend Article 6(3)(b) (right to adequate time and facilities to prepare defence) unless many hearings were adjourned or aborted to allow for further enquiries or the tracing of witnesses. With this in mind the CPS now generally gives advance disclosure in summary proceedings.

15.9.2 Unused material

The disclosure of unused material is governed by the Criminal Procedure and Investigations Act (CPIA) 1996, which is discussed in detail in chapter 13. The scheme works with some adaptations in the magistrates' courts, where there is no

---

[51] *Edwards* v *UK* (1992) 15 EHRR 417.
[52] *Jasper* v *UK; Fitt* v *UK* (2000) 30 EHRR 441.
[53] Magistrates' Courts (Advance Information) Rules 1985, r. 2.
[54] Which the court itself recognised as obiter.

obligation to provide a defence case statement. Sections 3 and 7 of the CPIA 1996 set out different tests for disclosure at the primary and secondary disclosure stages. At primary disclosure, prior to the service of any defence case statement, material must be disclosed which 'in the prosecutor's opinion might undermine the case for the prosecution against the accused'. It is only after the service of any case statement that the prosecutor must disclose material which 'might be reasonably expected to assist the accused's defence as disclosed by the defence statement given under s. 5 or 6' (s. 7). If these two tests are substantively different, and it is possible to envisage information which satisfies the s. 7 but not the s. 3 test, the provisions sit uncomfortably with Article 6. It may be that the only way to avoid breach of the Convention is to give a very wide interpretation to the words 'might undermine' in s. 3, effectively reinstating the common law position after *R* v *Ward* [1993] 1 WLR 619, and forcing the Crown to disclose anything which might be relevant.

15.9.3 Public interest immunity

Under the Convention, the right to disclosure is not absolute, and it will in some circumstances be legitimate to withhold evidence from the defence in order to protect the rights of others or safeguard the public interest.[55] Only such measures which are strictly necessary are permissible, and there must be sufficient counterbalances to safeguard the rights of the defence. The balancing exercise should be decided by a court and not the prosecution.

Public interest immunity claims in the magistrates' courts are very rare, but there are rules providing for *ex parte* applications by the prosecution.[56] There is no European Court authority relating to public interest immunity in the magistrates' court, but the issue may raise significant problems. A system in which lay justices can see potentially damning inadmissible evidence, and withhold it from the defence before going on to try the case on the facts, is likely to be the subject of challenge under Article 6(1). It may be that a special procedure will need to be devised for dealing with claims of public interest immunity in the magistrates' court.

15.10 *VOIR DIRE*

In summary trials, the defendant has no right to demand that a question of admissibility be determined as a preliminary issue.[57] This in itself is unlikely to

---

[55] *Rowe and Davis* v *UK* (2000) 30 EHRR 1; *Jasper* v *UK*; *Fitt* v *UK* (2000) 30 EHRR 441.
[56] Magistrates' Courts (Criminal Procedure and Investigations Act 1996) (Disclosure) Rules 1997: SI 1997/703, rr. 2(3)–(5), 3(3) and 5(8).
[57] *Vel* v *Owen* [1987] Crim LR 49, *Halawa* v *Federation Against Copyright Theft* [1995] 1 Cr App R 21.

violate the Convention — the European Court will look at the proceedings as a whole with regard to fairness. So far, domestic courts have rejected the argument that magistrates who have decided issues of admissibility cannot fairly continue with the case,[58] but the matter may need reconsideration in the light of Article 6. It is arguable that a lay tribunal which has ruled a confession inadmissible under s. 76 may not satisfy the bias test, especially if the ruling was by a majority.[59]

15.11   TRIAL *IN ABSENTIA*

Under the Convention trial *in absentia* may be permitted where the authorities have given the defendant clear notice of the hearing,[60] where the interests of justice require,[61] or where the defendant has clearly waived his or her right to be present.[62] The fact that a defendant is not present does not mean that he or she has waived his or her right to representation, and the lawyer must be permitted to attend trial.[63]

In the magistrates' court the position is governed by ss. 11 to 14, Magistrates' Courts Act 1980. A summary trial may be heard in the defendant's absence where it is proved that a summons was served in reasonable time for the trial, and there is a bar to passing a sentence of imprisonment. There is a right to have the matter reheard if it subsequently emerges that the accused was unaware of proceedings (s. 14). Domestic law is unlikely to violate the Convention,[64] so long as magistrates enquire fully into the facts and exercise their discretion to proceed fairly and judicially.

15.12   HANDCUFFS AND CLOSED DOCKS

Many magistrates' courts have poor security arrangements, and it is relatively common for the prison authorities to make an application for a defendant who faces a very serious charge to be heard in handcuffs. This raises several issues under Article 6: the handcuffing may constitute cruel and inhuman treatment under Article 3, and may undermine the right to a fair trial under Article 6(1) and

---

[58] *R v Sang* [1980] AC 402.
[59] The point is, however, open whether such a breach could be 'cured' at a subsequent appeal hearing *de novo* in the Crown Court before a judge.
[60] *Colozza v Italy* (1985) 7 EHRR 516.
[61] *Ensslin and others v Germany* (1979) 14 DR 64.
[62] *Poitrimol v France* (1993) 18 EHRR 130.
[63] *Geysegham v Belgium* [1999] EHRLR 337.
[64] See *R v Bolton Justices, ex parte Merna* [1991] Crim LR 848. For recent decisions on trial *in absentia*, see *Krombach v France* (13 February 2001, ECtHR); *R v Hayward and others* (31 January 2001, CA).

(2). Under European law, as in domestic law,[65] there is a duty to enquire into the need for handcuffs, and to look for a less restrictive alternative. Where the reason for handcuffing is prison policy, or lack of court facilities, and the hearing involves determination of a significant issue in the case, it is possible to argue a violation of the Convention.[66]

---

[65] *R* v *Vratsides* [1998] Crim LR 251, *R* v *Mullen* [2000] Archbold News Issue 6, p. 2.
[66] See *Raninen* v *Finland* (1997) 26 EHRR 563 at para. 56. The European Court left open the question of whether the handcuffing could be a breach of Article 3 when it involved 'public exposure [or] exceeding what was necessary in the circumstances'.

Chapter Sixteen

Evidence

Michelle Strange

In the past, most courts have assumed that domestic rules of evidence comply with Article 6,[1] and it appears that they remain reluctant to find violations in domestic law.[2] In theory, the wide powers vested in the trial judge, which include the power to stop any case where a fair trial would not be possible, and a general discretion to exclude any evidence which ought not to be admitted in the interests of justice, comply with Article 6(1). Specific provisions such as s. 78, Police and Criminal Evidence 1984 and ss. 23 to 26, Criminal Justice Act 1988 are generally compatible and there is little by way of statutory provision which can be said in itself to be in violation. In practice, however, there remains case law which is questionable.

The areas that may give rise to argument are:

- where the prosecution case is likely to be made up either wholly or mainly of the hearsay evidence of absent witnesses;
- where prosecution witnesses refuse to give evidence at all or wish to do so anonymously;

---

[1] See for example, *R v Gokal* [1997] 2 Cr App R 266, *R v Thomas* [1998] Crim LR 887, *R v DPP, ex parte Kebilene* [1999] 3 WLR 972.

[2] See for example, *R v Perry* (2000) *The Times*, 28 April, where the Court of Appeal criticised counsel for taking points under the Convention in a case involving video identification evidence which had been obtained outside any statutory framework. The Court of Appeal made the surprising observation that the Convention had been drafted to prevent more serious abuses of human rights, and any attempt by lawyers to 'jump on a bandwagon' would be likely to bring the Human Rights Act into disrepute.

- where evidence has been obtained unlawfully or by means of entrapment;
- where the Crown attempts to rely on the hearsay evidence of an available witness under the provisions of s. 68, Criminal Procedure and Investigations Act 1996.

These issues will be discussed in detail below. Other important topics, including the burden and standard of proof and the presumption of innocence, are dealt with in chapter 14.

16.1 THE APPROACH OF THE EUROPEAN COURT TO EVIDENCE

The Convention itself contains little specific reference to the rules of evidence in criminal proceedings. Most evidential issues will involve consideration of the presumption of innocence in Article 6(2), or of Article 6(3)(d), which gives each criminal defendant:

> the right to examine or have examined witnesses against him and to obtain the attendance and examination of witnesses on his behalf under the same conditions as witnesses against him.

The need to apply the Convention to a number of very different legal systems has made the European Court unsurprisingly reluctant to involve itself in the application of the rules of evidence at a domestic level. Instead, the Court tends to look at whether the application of such rules interferes with the accused's right to a fair trial under Article 6(1), using Article 6(2) and (3)(d) as factors to be considered. The position was recently restated in *Khan* v *UK* (2000) *The Times*, 23 May, where the Court said (at para. 34):

> it is not the role of the Court to determine, as a matter of principle, whether particular types of evidence — for example, unlawfully obtained evidence — may be admissible or, indeed, whether the applicant was guilty or not. The question which must be answered is whether the proceedings as a whole, including the way in which the evidence was obtained, were fair. This involves an examination of the unlawfulness in question and, where violation of another Convention right is concerned, the nature of the violation found.

It is nonetheless difficult to predict the extent to which the European Court will be willing to pass comment on matters of evidence. Where the application of domestic rules of evidence has produced a patently unfair result, the Court and the Commission have been willing to substitute their own views for that of the domestic authorities. In *Ferrantelli and Santangelo* v *Italy* (1996) 23 EHRR 288 the Commission expressed its disapproval of a conviction in which the domestic court had relied on tenuous circumstantial evidence,[3] explaining why this was not permissible, and in *Condron* v *UK* (2000) 30 EHRR 1 the Court criticised the trial judge for giving insufficient weight to a lawyer's advice. In other cases, however, decisions at a domestic level which would cause alarm in the UK have raised no comment. In *Unterpertinger* v *Austria* (1986) 13 EHRR 175 (where the trial was found to have been unfair on other grounds) the Court quoted, but did not pass any comment upon, the domestic court's specific reliance upon the applicant's previous convictions as evidence of his general propensity for violence.

16.2   INTERPRETATION OF ARTICLE 6(3)(d)

The text of Article 6(3)(d) appears to guarantee each criminal defendant the right to require all evidence to be presented orally, and to confront all witnesses by way of cross-examination. The case law makes clear that these rights are subject to qualification, and will be balanced against the rights of others. The European Court has derived a number of general principles, which can be stated as follows:

- evidence should in principle be produced in the presence of the accused at a public hearing.[4] In most cases the accused should be physically present, but in some cases the presence of a lawyer[5] will be sufficient;
- the hearing of witnesses should be adversarial;[6]
- the accused should be given adequate and proper opportunity to challenge and question a witness against him or her, either at the time the witness was making the statement or at some later stage in the proceedings;[6]
- in certain circumstances there may be limited infringements of the above rights, where it is necessary to achieve fairness between the prosecution and defence, or to safeguard the rights of witnesses. It may be permissible to admit hearsay evidence or protect the identity of witnesses, but only where it is necessary, at the minimum level, and where it remains possible for the accused to have a fair trial;
- the concept of a witness is autonomous to Convention law, and includes any person whose evidence is taken into account by the court.[6]

---

[3] The domestic court had referred to the fact that the applicants had been involved in buying oxygen cylinders later used in an arson attack, and that their alibis were not convincing.

[4] *Barberà, Messegué and Jabardo* v *Spain* (1988) 11 EHRR 360. The decision that there had been a violation of Article 6 was on a majority of 9:8. See also *Windisch* v *Austria* (1990) 13 EHRR 281, at para. 23.

[5] See for example, *X* v *Denmark* (1982) 27 DR 50, *Doorson* v *Netherlands* (1996) 22 EHRR 330. Cf. the position in s. 122, Magistrates' Courts Act 1980, where a party is not deemed to be absent when he or she is represented by a lawyer.

[6] *Kostovski* v *Netherlands* (1989) 12 EHRR 434 at para. 41.

16.3   THE RIGHT TO CROSS-EXAMINE WITNESSES AT TRIAL

There is nothing within the Convention to provide the defendant with an absolute right to cross-examine a witness personally or through his or her lawyer,[7] although the principle of equality of arms means that this should generally be the case. Article 6(3)(d) gives the defendant the right 'to examine or have examined witnesses against him' — the wording is designed to cover both the common law systems, where the witnesses are directly questioned by the parties, and several continental systems where questions are put on the parties' behalf by the judge. Accordingly, the European Court will be less concerned by who conducts the questioning of the witness than by the substance of the questions put, so long as the defence are able to participate in the process fully.[8]

It is clear from the authorities that, where a witness is not available to give live evidence at trial, the defendant's rights may not be infringed if there has been an opportunity to cross-examine the witness at an earlier stage. It is therefore unlikely that objection could be raised to the various English provisions allowing for questions to be put to a witness prior to the trial,[9] unless their use has resulted in incurable unfairness to the accused.

16.4   HEARSAY EVIDENCE

There is nothing in the Convention to prohibit a court relying on hearsay evidence — many continental legal systems have no rule against it. The Strasbourg bodies are nonetheless wary of hearsay evidence, recognising that where disputed hearsay is taken into account by a court, there will be some limitation on the rights of the accused. They have repeatedly observed that hearsay evidence is inferior to evidence in a live form,[10] and will look for the reasons given for the need to rely upon it, weighing this against the factors available to preserve the rights of the defence. In *Van Mechelen and others* v *Netherlands* (1997) 25 EHRR 647, the Court made it clear that the balance should be generally in favour of the defence, saying that the measures should be 'strictly necessary ... if a less restrictive measure can suffice then that measure should be applied' (at para. 58).

---

[7] Cf. the position under Article 6(3)(c), at 12.2.3, and *Croissant* v *Germany* (1992) 16 EHRR 135. English law makes similar provision under the Youth Justice and Criminal Evidence Act 1999.

[8] For authorities where the Strasbourg bodies have found the applicant to have had a fair trial although the defence have not been able to question witnesses, see *Bricmont* v *Belgium* (1989) 12 EHRR 217; *Artner* v *Austria* (1992) Series A, No. 242; *Liefveld* v *Netherlands* (1995) 15 EHRR 597.

[9] See for example, s. 3, Criminal Justice (International Co-operation) Act 1990 (evidence of foreign witnesses); ss. 42 and 43, Children and Young Persons Act 1933 (taking of depositions of young person's evidence by magistrates); s. 28, Youth Justice and Criminal Evidence Act 1999 (pre-recorded cross-examination for use at trial).

[10] See for example, *Trivedi* v *UK* (1977) 89 DR 136, in which the Commission placed some reliance on the trial judge's warning to the jury that they should attach less weight to statements not tested by cross-examination.

The European Court has expressed disquiet about cases where all or most of the prosecution case is made up of hearsay evidence. In *Unterpertinger* v *Austria* (1986) 13 EHRR 175[11] the applicant was convicted of assault upon his ex-wife and stepdaughter, in which their evidence formed almost all of the the prosecution case. The witnesses exercised their right under Austrian law to refuse to attend court, and the evidence was read at trial, whereupon the applicant was convicted. The European Court found that the rule providing that family members were not compellable witnesses, and the provision that their evidence could be read, were not in themselves in violation of Article 6(1) or (3)(d).[12] In the particular case, however, there had been a breach of the Convention, as the applicant's rights had not been sufficiently protected. There was other evidence, but the conviction had been based 'mainly' on the women's evidence, and there were particularly good reasons why the court may have benefited from hearing cross-examination of the witnesses.[13] Accordingly, the Court found that the proceedings as a whole had been unfair to the applicant.

Unterpertinger was distinguished in the later case of *Asch* v *Austria* (1991) 15 EHRR 597, where the same domestic provision was used to admit written evidence of assault from the applicant's co-habitee. The European Court was influenced by the fact that there was other evidence against the applicant, and did not find a violation of Article 6(3)(d). The Court suggested that there would only be a violation where the hearsay evidence was the 'sole' rather than main evidence in the case. This watering down of the test in *Unterpertinger* has not been followed in subsequent cases on related areas.[14] Although there are no comparable provisions in English law,[15] it appears from the case law that convictions based solely or mainly on hearsay evidence are unlikely to find favour in Strasbourg.

16.5   SPECIFIC SITUATIONS

The following paragraphs will discuss how the European Court has applied the above principles in particular situations where the prosecution have relied upon hearsay evidence of missing witnesses at trial.

---

[11] The applicant succeeded on the substantive application.
[12] The Court recognised that family members were entitled to avoid the 'moral dilemma' of giving evidence for the prosecution.
[13] It is worth mentioning the facts of the case, which were peculiarly unfair to the applicant. His defence was that his wife had attacked him. He made the first complaint to the police, and had injuries which his wife accepted causing with a paper-knife, although she said that she had acted in self-defence. Both of the prosecution witnesses had originally been questioned by the police.
[14] *Doorson* v *Netherlands* (1996) 22 EHRR 330; *Van Mechelen and others* v *Netherlands* (1997) 25 EHRR 647.
[15] For the position in English law about non-compellable witnesses, see s. 80, 1984. The evidence of a non-compellable witness cannot be relied upon in hearsay form unless the general requirements of s. 23, Criminal Justice Act 1988 are made out.

16.5.1 Where a witness is ill or dead

Where witnesses are seriously ill or have died, the reliance upon hearsay evidence may be acceptable, but only where there is no available alternative which is less restrictive, and where the accused remains able to have a fair trial.

16.5.1.1 Death

In *Ferrantelli and Santangelo* v *Italy* (1996) 23 EHRR 288, on a charge of murder, the court relied upon written evidence of an accomplice who had died in suspicious circumstances prior to the trial. There was other corroborative evidence, including full confessions from the applicants which they had later retracted. The European Court found in favour of the applicants on other grounds (see above at 16.1), but rejected the applicant's claim that it had been unfair to admit the written evidence, as the authorities could not be held responsible for the death, and that this factor had not in itself rendered the trial unfair.[16]

16.5.1.2 Illness

Where a witness is seriously ill, the European Court will look at the available alternatives. In *Bricmont* v *Belgium* (1989) 12 EHRR 217 the Prince of Belgium had been excused from giving evidence on grounds of ill health. The Court found that there had been a breach of Article 6, observing:

> In the circumstances of the case, the exercise of the rights of the defence — an essential part of the right to a fair trial — required in principle that the applicants should have an opportunity to challenge any aspect of the complainant's account during a confrontation or an examination, either in public or, if necessary, at his home.

In *Trivedi* v *UK* [1997] EHRLR 521 where the applicant, a doctor, was convicted of false accounting, the main witness was an elderly patient, who had deteriorated to a point that he would never be able to give evidence. The statements were read at trial under ss. 23 and 26 of the Criminal Justice Act 1988. The Commission said there had been no violation as the trial judge had conducted a thorough inquiry before admitting the evidence, and the jury had been directed to give less weight to the statements because they were hearsay. The Commission placed some reliance on the fact that there was considerable corroborative evidence.

A similar approach was taken in *MK* v *Austria* (1997) 24 EHRR CD 59. The applicant was charged with unlawful sex with a young boy, and wished him to give evidence to cross-examine him on the issue of consent.[17] The domestic court

---

[16] The trial court in that case was aware that the dead witness had changed his account on more than one occasion.

[17] In Austrian law, as in the UK, the consent of a minor does not provide a defence to the charge.

refused, on the basis that the boy was in psychiatric care and the giving of evidence would cause further damage to his mental health.[18] The domestic court heard evidence from a court appointed psychiatrist, who interviewed him on the court's behalf, and who gave hearsay evidence of the boy's account. Significantly, the defence did not object to this course of action, ask to be present at the interview, or attempt to instruct its own expert to assess the boy. The Commission upheld the course, stressing that the rights of victims should also be protected, and that the defence had an opportunity to cross-examine the psychiatrist.[19]

16.5.1.3 Death or illness of a witness: summary

It follows that where a witness has died or is too ill to give evidence, the European Court will be sympathetic to the needs of the prosecution to present their evidence without bringing the witness to court. Where witnesses are ill, however, the case law needs to be considered in the light of advances in technology, which may allow for cross-examination via live video links, if necessary in the witnesses' home or in hospital. Courts should be advised to make full enquiry of available alternatives, and to proceed to read evidence only if there are no other realistic ways of hearing it. Provisions already exist in domestic law in this regard.[20]

16.5.2   Where a witness has disappeared

The European Court has performed similar balancing exercises in cases where witnesses have disappeared or absconded. In *Artner* v *Austria* (1992) Series A, No. 342 the key witness had already been examined by the presiding judge, but not the defence, and was untraceable at trial. The Court found, by a majority,[21] that there had been no violation of the Convention, placing some reliance on the existence of other evidence and the failure by the accused to confront the witness at the pre-trial stage. In *Delta* v *France* (1990) 16 EHRR 574 the applicant was convicted of robbery on the evidence of two witnesses who failed to appear at trial despite attempts to secure their appearance by the prosecution, where there was no other significant evidence in the case. There had been no efforts made by the trial court to secure the witnesses' attendance. The Court found a breach of Article 6(3)(d).

---

[18] For a similar (although rarely used) provision in domestic law, see s. 42, Children and Young Persons Act 1933.

[19] A similar situation arose in the Scottish case of *Her Majesty's Advocate* v *Nulty* 2000 SLT 528, where the Court of Appeal found that there were adequate safeguards for the defendant although he had been prevented from cross-examining a mentally unfit teenage complainant in a rape case, as the judge had directed the jury about the need for corroboration of the complainant's account.

[20] Section 16(2)(b), Youth Justice and Criminal Evidence Act 1999 provides for 'special measures' to be adopted by the court at trial where a witness is disabled or ill, where the court is satisfied that these would improve or maximise the quality of the evidence. These include use of screens, evidence by live link, in private, cross-examination through an intermediary, and the use of video recorded evidence: see ss. 23–29.

[21] Of 5:4. The Commission had reached similar conclusions on a majority of 9:7.

In *Doorson* v *Netherlands* (1996) 22 EHRR 330 the court had done all it could to bring the witness to court, but he absconded before his evidence was heard. The European Court found that, in the circumstances, it was permissible for the trial court to have regard to his witness statement to police.

16.5.3   Where a witness is in fear

In some circumstances, there may be justification for relying on the written statements of witnesses who are too afraid to attend court at all.[22] Again the rights of those witnesses will be balanced against possible prejudice to the defendant, and the evidence should only be admitted in this manner if there is no less restrictive alternative, for example screens, video testimony, or a measure of anonymity. In *Windisch* v *Austria* (1990) 13 EHRR 281 the European Court found a violation of Article 6(3)(d) where the applicant's conviction was based mainly on the hearsay evidence of two witnesses who were too afraid to testify. The safeguard offered at trial to cross-examine the police officers who had taken the statements was insufficient to safeguard the defence rights (at para. 41).

The European Court appeared to adopt a less generous approach to the defence in *Doorson* v *Netherlands* (1996) 22 EHRR 330 which involved allegations of drug dealing. The evidence of two witnesses was given in hearsay form at trial, because they feared reprisals.[23] There was no suggestion that the applicant had threatened them, but the European Court said it was well known that drug dealers frequently resorted to threats or violence.[24]

16.5.4   Reassessing domestic law on hearsay in the light of the Convention

In England, there are several statutory frameworks which allow contested hearsay evidence to be admitted in evidence. The most likely source of complaint for defendants is s. 23 of the Criminal Justice Act 1988, which provides that a statement of an absent witness may be read under two broad headings: where the witness is too frightened to testify (s. 23(3)(b)), or where the witness is absent because it is impracticable to secure attendance by reason of illness or death, residence overseas, or because the witness is untraceable (s. 23(2)(a)–(c)). Sections 25 and 26 govern the exercise of the trial judge's discretion to exclude otherwise admissible hearsay evidence in the interests of justice. Under s. 26, statements prepared for the purposes of criminal proceedings are not to be admitted without leave, which is not to be given unless the court is of the view

---

[22] See also 'Anonymous witnesses' below at 16.6.2.

[23] Other evidence was given to the examining magistrate in the presence of defence counsel: see below at 16.6.2.

[24] For a similar, domestic authority, see *R* v *Fairfax* [1995] Crim LR 949. In *R* v *Rutherford* [1998] Crim LR 490, the Court of Appeal applied the same principles where there was no other significant evidence against the defence.

that the statement ought to be admitted in the interests of justice. All other first-hand hearsay may be put in evidence, subject to the other party's right to object and the court's power under s. 25 to exclude the evidence in the interests of justice. These factors, which include having regard to the importance of the evidence (s. 25(2)(b), (c)) in the proceedings, and the risk of unfairness to the accused (s. 25(2)(d)) are, in theory, broadly in keeping with the European Court's ruling in *Van Mechelen and others* v *Netherlands* (1997) 25 EHRR 647.[25]

In order to lay the foundations of an application under s. 23 of the Criminal Justice Act 1988, the prosecution must prove or have an admission that the section applies to the criminal standard of proof. When the evidence has been admitted, it will be necessary to give warnings to the jury that there has been no opportunity for the defence to cross-examine the witness, although there is no standard direction to be given, and no requirement that the judge directs the jury about the weight to be given. Once the evidence is led, the defence has a right to adduce evidence as to the credibility of the maker of the statement, and of any other inconsistent accounts (sch. 2, para. 1(a) and (c)).

In the light of the European Court's approach to hearsay evidence, it is unlikely that the provisions of s. 23 will violate the Convention,[26] so long as there is other evidence against the accused, there is no less restrictive alternative, and sufficient safeguards are in place to protect the rights of the defence. It should be noted that there is no Convention authority on domestic provisions to read the evidence of a witness when it is impracticable to secure his or her attendance, but it is likely that the European Court would conduct a similar exercising in balancing the needs of the parties.[27]

16.5.4.1   Where hearsay is the sole or main evidence in the case
Convention authorities suggest that less weight should be given to hearsay,[28] and repeated statements by the Strasbourg bodies that there should be other

---

[25] See below at 16.6.2. It is however arguable that the words of s. 25(b), that the court should have regard 'to the extent to which the statement appears to supply evidence which would otherwise not be readily available', may make it more likely that the evidence will be admitted the less corroborative evidence there is. See also *R* v *Patel* (1993) 97 Cr App R 291; *R* v *Batt and Batt* [1995] Crim LR 240.

[26] The Court of Appeal specifically considered, in *R* v *Thomas* [1998] Crim LR 887, whether s. 23(3)(b) (witness in fear) was in keeping with Article 6(3)(d). In the trial of the appellants for supplying drugs, the evidence of a witness who had himself been convicted of related offences was read to the jury. He alleged that he was in fear because of an earlier unrelated punishment beating from the appellants. The Court of Appeal dismissed the appeal, giving amongst their reasons the fact that there had been other live evidence in the case, that the appellants had been able to tell the jury about the conviction of the witness and mitigation of his sentence, and he had given evidence at a contested committal hearing at an earlier stage in the proceedings.

[27] As in *X* v *Austria* (1973) 43 CD 50 where the Commission held that Article 6(3)(d) was satisfied when a witness was examined outside the jurisdiction and the defence had a right to put supplementary questions.

[28] See for example, *Trivedi* v *UK* [1997] EHRLR 521 above at 16.5.1.2.

corroborative evidence reinforce the notion that hearsay is by its nature inferior to live evidence with cross-examination. This is not always respected by domestic law. Where the trial judge has ruled the evidence admissible under s. 23, and there is no criticism of the judge failing to exclude that evidence in the interests of justice, the Court of Appeal has tended to treat the hearsay evidence as being on a par with live evidence. The result is case law which is questionable in the light of the Convention.

In *R* v *Dragic* [1996] 2 Cr App R 232[29] the appellant was convicted of burglary on disputed identification evidence of a witness who was later too ill to testify. There was no scientific evidence to link the appellant to the crime. The trial judge admitted the evidence under ss. 23 and 26 of the Criminal Justice Act 1988, and the defendant was convicted. Dismissing the appeal, the Court of Appeal accepted that the evidence was crucial to the Crown's case, but relied on the fact that the appellant had been able to call alibi evidence. Lord Taylor CJ in his judgment said (at p. 239) that 'the fact that there is no ability to cross-examine, that the witness who is absent is the only evidence against the accused, and that his evidence is identification evidence is not sufficient to render the admission of written evidence from that witness contrary to the interests of justice or unfair to the defendant, *per se*'. The same principle was more widely stated in *R* v *Setz Dempsey* (1994) 98 Cr App R 23, where the Court of Appeal said that using the Criminal Justice Act 1988 would be acceptable if the statement read was tendered as the only evidence of a fact.

There are signs that the Court of Appeal is retreating from this approach. In *R* v *McCoy* (2000) Archbold News 6, p. 2, it allowed an appeal where hearsay evidence had formed the main evidence against the appellant, because the judge had given the jury insufficient warning to attach less weight to the evidence in the absence of cross-examination. There are good arguments that this approach is more in keeping with the European Court's rulings in this area and should be followed in subsequent cases.

16.5.4.2   Section 68, Criminal Procedure and Investigations Act 1996
Under s. 68 and sch. 2, paras 1 and 2 of the 1996 Act, where a written statement has been admitted in evidence at committal proceedings, it may be read as evidence at trial without further proof, subject to the right of the defence to object. Further provisions allow for depositions of reluctant witnesses[30] to be given in evidence at trial. The court can override any objection if it considers that the evidence should be admitted in the interests of justice (sch. 2, paras 1(4) and 2(4)).

---

[29] See also *R* v *Scott* (1989) 89 Cr App R 153, *R* v *Cole* (1990) 90 Cr App R 478, *R* v *Price* [1991] Crim LR 707 and *R* v *Moore* [1992] Crim LR 882. For a domestic authority going the other way see *R* v *French* (1993) 97 Cr App R 421.

[30] See s. 97A, Magistrates' Courts Act 1980. There is no requirement to be present when the deposition is taken.

The Act provides no guidance as to the principles to be applied by the trial judge when deciding whether to admit the evidence.[31] The section has astonishingly wide potential for trials of 'either way' offences. At the time of writing there is no evidence of widespread use of these powers by UK courts, but it is submitted that if they are used to admit disputed hearsay evidence they will be subject to challenge under Article 6.[32]

16.6   PROTECTION OF THE RIGHTS OF WITNESSES AND VICTIMS

Convention law recognises that the rights of the defence may sometimes be circumscribed by the need to respect the rights of victims and witnesses. In *Doorson* v *Netherlands* (1996) 22 EHRR 330 the European Court said that although Article 6 contained no express provision about witnesses (at para. 70):

> their life, liberty or security of person may be at stake, as may interests coming generally within the ambit of Article 8 of the Convention. Such interests of witnesses and victims are in principle protected by other, substantive provisions of the Convention, which imply that contracting states should organise their criminal proceedings in such a way that those interests are not unjustifiably imperilled. Against this background, principles of fair trial also require that in appropriate cases the interests of the defence are balanced against those of witnesses or victims called upon to testify.

16.6.1   Screens

The use of screens has been sanctioned by the Commission. In *X* v *UK* (1993) 15 EHRR CD 113, the witnesses could be seen by the judge and defence counsel, and could be heard by everyone in court. Their evidence did not involve identifying the applicant, and the Commission did not find a breach of Article 6(3)(d).

Domestic case law on the use of screens makes it relatively commonplace for screens to be used where the witnesses are children, and less likely where the witnesses are adults.[33] New provisions under s. 23, Youth Justice and Criminal Evidence Act 1999 provide a statutory framework for the use of screens, but there are no clear guidelines as to when the use of screens is appropriate, and the case law is presumably still valid. It is unlikely that Convention law adds anything to domestic provisions.

---

[31] Although it was indicated at the debate stage in the House of Lords that the then Government expected that the courts would use the provisions narrowly, and look to s. 26, Criminal Justice Act 1988 for guidance: HL, Hansard, vol. 573, col. 952.

[32] The Law Commission recommended repeal of paras 1(4) and 2(4) in *Evidence in Criminal Proceedings: Hearsay and Related Topics* (1997) Law Com. No. 245: the report raised concerns about compatibility with the Convention.

[33] See Archbold (2001), paras 8-67 and 8-551.

16.6.2 Anonymous witnesses

The use of anonymous witnesses is not in principle incompatible with the Convention (in domestic law, see *R* v *Bedfordshire Coroner, ex parte Local Sunday Newspapers Ltd* 164 JPN 370). In *Van Mechelen and others* v *Netherlands* (1997) 25 EHRR 647, the European Court recognised that anonymity may be justified where life, liberty or security of witnesses may be at stake, but stressed that adequate safeguards must exist so that the interests of the defence are balanced against those of the witnesses. In *Windisch* v *Austria* (1990) 13 EHRR 281 the European Court observed that whilst the authorities can justify relying on the evidence of anonymous informants in the course of an investigation:

> ... the subsequent use of their statements by the trial court to found a conviction is another matter. The right to a fair administration of justice holds so prominent a place in a democratic society that it cannot be justified.

The Strasbourg bodies have had regard to the following factors in deciding whether the evidence of anonymous witnesses has undermined the fairness of the trial:

(a) the importance of the evidence against the accused;
(b) the reality of the fears of the witnesses;[34]
(c) the opportunities that the court and the defence have had to observe the demeanour of the witness under questioning;
(d) the safeguards offered to the defence.[35]

The European Court has been reluctant to find that there has been a fair trial where the conviction rests wholly or mainly on the evidence of anonymous witnesses, and where there has been inadequate opportunity for the defence to observe or question fully the witness giving evidence. In *Kostovski* v *Netherlands* (1989) 12 EHRR 434 one of the witnesses had not even been seen by the trial court, and the defence had no knowledge of who they were. The European Court was not reassured by statements from the examining magistrates that the witness had displayed caution in giving his evidence, nor by the fact that the defence had been able to present limited written questions to the witness. The European Court found the procedure irreconcilable with the guarantees of fair trial. The court took into account that the applicant's conviction was based 'to a decisive extent' on the anonymous statements.

Following the judgment in *Kostovski*, the Dutch authorities adopted a more detailed procedure for admitting anonymous evidence, which included a detailed

---

[34] *Doorson* v *Netherlands* (1996) 22 EHRR 330, *Van Mechelen and others* v *Netherlands* (1997) 25 EHRR 647, *Kostovski* v *Netherlands* (1989) 12 EHRR 434.
[35] See also *Ludi* v *Switzerland* (1992) 15 EHRR 173.

report from the judge receiving the evidence as to his perception of the reliability of the witness. In *Van Mechelen and others* v *Netherlands* (1997) 25 EHRR 647,[36] the defence were connected to the witnesses via a sound link, but were unable to see them give evidence or ask a number of significant questions.[37] The Commission found no violation of Article 6, but the Court disagreed, holding unanimously that the procedure violated Article 6(1) and 6(3)(d).

Van Mechelen concerned four applicants who were suspected by the authorities to be members of a criminal gang responsible for a series of robberies and manslaughter. No fewer than 11 police officers gave evidence anonymously, with the state citing the officers' fear of reprisals and operational needs as a justification. There was some other evidence in the case. The European Court was unimpressed by the need for police officers to give evidence anonymously, in all but the most exceptional cases, observing that it is in the nature of a police officer's duties to give evidence in open court. It said that particular caution should be exercised, because of the links between police officers and the state.[38] In the circumstances the reasons given were insufficient, particularly when a civilian witness had given evidence in the proceedings without being offered protection, and had not been threatened.[39]

The European Court was persuaded by better counterbalancing in the case of *Doorson* v *Netherlands* (1996) 22 EHRR 330.[40] There the witnesses, who were all drug addicts, were known to the applicant, who was accused of drug dealing. The Court agreed that the fear of reprisals was justified, in the light of previous threats and violence during similar operations. The Court was satisfied that the procedure, in which the witnesses were questioned by an investigating magistrate in the presence of defence counsel, was fair. Counsel was permitted (through the magistrate) to ask any questions in the interests of the defence, except those which might lead to the disclosure of the identity of the witness.[41] The European Court noted that the defence were able to cast some doubt on the reliability of the evidence because the witnesses were known to be drug addicts.

---

[36] See also *Liefveld* v *Netherlands* (1995) 18 EHRR CD 103, where the Commission found that there was no breach of Article 6(3)(d) where the statement of an informer was read to the court, and the identity of an undercover police officer was kept secret. The Commission was heavily influenced by the fact that the evidence complained about formed a relatively small part of the prosecution case.

[37] Including questions as to where an identification witness was standing at the time of the identification, or whether he wore glasses.

[38] The Court was even less impressed by the state's reasoning in *Ludi*, above at fn. 35, where the evidence of an undercover police officer that the applicant knew by sight was read to the court to preserve the operational needs of the police.

[39] Cf. the current state of authority under s. 23, CJA 1988, where the fear need only be a genuine one, but need not relate to the accused or any action taken by him or on his behalf: *R* v *Fairfax* [1995] Crim LR 949; *R* v *Rutherford* [1998] Crim LR 490.

[40] The Commission also found no violation of Article 6, with no fewer than 13 people joining the dissenting opinion in favour of a violation.

[41] The dissenting members of the Commission did not agree, pointing out that the witnesses had identified the applicant solely from a photograph shown by police, without ever confronting the applicant.

16.7 HOSTILE WITNESSES

The position of hostile witnesses was considered by the Commission in *X* v *Germany* (1980) 17 DR 231. The applicant was charged with supplying heroin to two witnesses, who had provided statements to the police in support of the prosecution case. There was other corroborative evidence. At trial both denied that they had received the drugs from the accused, and said that their statements were untrue. The Commission found no unfairness in the court relying upon the original statements, 'as long as the use of such evidence is not in the circumstances unfair'. In the circumstances, the defence had cross-examined both witnesses at trial, and there had been oral evidence from both civilian and police witnesses. Accordingly, the Convention provides less protection than domestic law, which outlaws the use of the original statement where the witness continues to deny that it is true.[42]

16.8 ENTRAPMENT AND *AGENTS PROVOCATEURS*

Intrusive police surveillance will generally engage Article 8, and is the subject of full discussion in chapter 6 of this book. It also raises issues under Article 6, where the defendant alleges that he has been encouraged or trapped into committing a criminal offence by agents of the prosecuting authority.

In *Teixeira de Castro* v *Portugal* (1998) 28 EHRR 101 the applicant was convicted on the evidence of two undercover police officers who had visited his home to buy heroin. He had none in the house, and the officers took him to the home of a third party, where the applicant bought the drugs on their behalf. The applicant argued that he had been denied a fair trial, as he had been incited by police officers to commit a crime he would otherwise not have committed. The European Court agreed, observing (para. 87):

> The use of undercover agents must be restricted and safeguards put in place even in cases concerning the fight against drug-trafficking. Whilst the rise in organised crime undoubtedly requires that appropriate measures be taken, the right to a fair administration of justice nevertheless holds such a prominent place that it cannot be sacrificed for the sake of expedience . . . the public interest cannot justify the use of evidence obtained as a result of police incitement.

The Court did not set out a definitive test of what constituted incitement, but it does appear to have accepted the state's argument that a distinction can be drawn between (i) *agents provocateurs* — where the police officer's action creates a criminal intent which was previously absent; and (ii) cases where the offender

---

[42] See *R* v *Golder* (1960) 45 Cr App R 5; *R* v *Governor of Pentonville Prison, ex parte Alves* [1993] AC 284.

'had already been predisposed to commit the offence' (para. 32).[43] In the particular case it took into account the fact that the applicant was not part of an ongoing police operation, was of good character and hitherto unknown to police, and that the circumstances of the offence itself suggested that the applicant had to go beyond his normal activities to buy further drugs at the house of a third party.

The issue was considered by the Divisonal Court in *Nottingham City Council* v *Amin* [2000] 1 WLR 1071. In that case the respondent, a taxi driver, was prosecuted for plying for hire when he picked up two plain clothes officers in an area where he had no licence. His hire light was not on at the time that the officers hailed him, but he stopped nonetheless. In the judgment of the court, Lord Bingham said that there was, in both the European and the domestic case law, a distinction to be drawn between cases where (a) the defendant is 'pressurized or wheedled' into committing the offence (at p. 1077) and (b) where the defendant is given an opportunity to break the law and freely takes it, as he would if offered it by somebody else.[44] The judgment assumes that domestic case law is in keeping with the Convention, but Lord Bingham's categories may not be in keeping with *Texeira de Castro*. In that case, the European Court did not suggest that incitement involved any degree of coercion and it could be argued that the applicant's activity fell within Lord Bingham's second category.[45] The Court of Appeal has been similarly reluctant to extend categories of entrapment in domestic law, in the recent authority of *R* v *Shannon* (also known as *Alford*) (14 September 2000) where an appeal was dismissed on grounds that the appellant 'had had ample opportunity for second thoughts'. It remains to be seen whether English law satisfies the Convention.

16.9   EXCLUSION OF EVIDENCE

Exclusion of evidence will by its nature involve consideration of the facts of the case and the exercise of judicial discretion and, as discussed above, the European Court is generally less concerned with issues of admissibility and weight of evidence than whether the proceedings were unfair as a whole.[46]

It is nonetheless possible to distil some principles from the Court's approach:

- where a confession has been obtained as a result of maltreatment, it should not be used as part of the prosecution case;

---

[43] Canadian law recognises a similar distinction between agents who observe and those who 'actively elicit' crime: *R* v *Herbert* (1990) 2 SCR 151 at para. 108. For New Zealand authorities see *R* v *Szeto* (1998) 30 September (CA, 240198).

[44] See *R* v *Smurthwaite* [1994] 1 All ER 818; *R* v *Williams and O'Hare* (1994) 98 Cr App R 209; *London Borough of Ealing* v *Woolworths plc* [1995] Crim LR 58.

[45] Not least that the applicant had on arrest been in possession of more drugs than those requested by the officers.

[46] See for example, *Khan* v *UK* at 16.1 above.

- with evidence obtained by other unlawful means, or by breach of another Article of the Convention, the illegality may be a foundation for arguing that there has been a breach of Article 6, but is not determinative of it. The Court will look to the fairness of the proceedings as a whole (*Khan* v *UK*).

16.9.1 Ill-treatment

Under the Convention, the use of evidence which has been obtained by maltreatment will engage both Articles 3 and 6. Treatment which passes the Article 3 yardstick should always be excluded for the trial proceedings to be fair.[47] The Commission has said that that where a confession is made when an accused has been denied the right to a lawyer, it would require very close scrutiny,[48] and an allegation of ill-treatment with supporting evidence may trigger a duty on the part of a court to investigate under Article 3.[49]

What constitutes ill-treatment is subject to the 'living instrument principle'. Recent authority has suggested that the vulnerability of a person in custody may make relatively minor injuries capable of falling within Article 3.[50] In *Tekin* v *Turkey* (9 June 1998) the European Court said that in principle unnecessary physical force will infringe Article 3 when a person is in custody. In *Selmouni* v *France* (1999) 29 EHRR 403 the European Court said (at para. 101):

> the Convention is a 'living instrument' which must be interpreted in the light of present-day conditions ... the Court considers that certain acts which were classified in the past as 'inhuman and degrading treatment' as opposed to 'torture' could be classified differently in future. It takes the view that the increasingly high standard being required in the area of the protection of human rights and fundamental liberties correspondingly and inevitably requires greater firmness in assessing breaches of the fundamental values of democratic societies.[51]

16.9.2 Other illegality

Other forms of illegality by the state provide a foundation for arguing a breach of Article 6. The European Court will consider a number of factors before determining whether the illegal activity affects the fairness of the trial process — the importance of the evidence, whether it was obtained in bad faith, and whether the activity is illegal in the sense of being against the law or merely because it is not subject to a statutory framework. The more serious the infringement of the

---

[47] *Austria* v *Italy* (1963) 6 Yearbook 740.
[48] *G* v *UK* (1984) 35 DR 75. See also *Barberà, Messegué and Jabardo* v *Spain* (1988) 11 EHRR 360.
[49] *Veznedaroglu* v *Turkey* (11 April 2000).
[50] *Assenov and others* v *Bulgaria* (1998) 28 EHRR 652.
[51] The maltreatment included officers urinating over the applicant, and threatening him with a blowlamp and syringe.

law, the more likely it is that the evidence will taint the trial as a whole, and be in breach of Article 6.[52]

In *Schenk* v *Switzerland* (1988) 11 EHRR 84 the applicant was convicted of arranging his wife's murder. The informant, posing as a hit man, produced taped evidence of the applicant's conduct, which had been obtained in breach of Swiss law. Under Swiss law there is a right to privacy, and intrusive surveillance must be ordered by an investigating judge. The European Court found that although there had been a breach of Article 8, a breach of Article 6 did not automatically follow. It took into account the fact that it had been open to the applicant to challenge the unlawfulness or authenticity of the recordings in court, and that the evidence was not the only evidence upon which the conviction was based. In the circumstances, it found no violation of Article 6.

In *Khan* v *UK* the evidence was almost entirely based on telephone recordings which had been obtained without the benefit of a legal framework.[53] The European Court found a breach of Article 8, but in the circumstances[54] found no breach of Article 6, stating:

> The central question in the present case is whether the proceedings as a whole were fair. With specific reference to the admission of the contested tape recording, the Court notes that, as in the *Schenk* case, the applicant had ample opportunity to challenge both the authenticity and the use of the recording. He did not challenge its authenticity, but challenged its use at the *voir dire* and again before the Court of Appeal and the House of Lords. The Court notes that at each level of jurisdiction the domestic courts assessed the effect of the admission of the evidence on the fairness of the trial by reference to section 78, Police and Criminal Evidence Act 1984, and the courts discussed, amongst other matters, the non-statutory basis for the surveillance. The fact that the applicant was at each step unsuccessful makes no difference.

It should be noted that the European Court paid great regard to the fact that the applicant's incriminating conversations were voluntary, and there existed no right of privacy under English law. The illegality was technical, in that it related to the absence of a statutory framework alone (at para. 36). Under the HRA 1998, and Article 8, a right of privacy now exists in English law, and it remains open for lawyers to argue that future illegality of this type is capable of undermining the fair trial process.

---

[52] Cf. the position in Canada, where the Canadian Charter outlaws reliance on illegal acts which would bring the administration of justice into disrepute: s. 24(3), and in South Africa, where a 'conscious and deliberate violation' of rights will lead to evidence being inadmissible: *State* v *Motloutsi* (1996) 1 SACR 78.

[53] Such recordings are now placed on a statutory footing by the Police Act 1997, and the Regulation of Investigatory Powers Act 2000, see above at chapters 5 and 6.

[54] The applicant had not challenged the authenticity of the tapes, and had pleaded guilty when the evidence was admitted.

The Commission has taken a similarly robust view of voluntarily made statements obtained by ruses or undercover officers. In *X* v *Germany* (1989) 11 EHRR 84 the applicant was taped in the cell confessing to his co-defendant by an Italian undercover officer posing as a remand prisoner who spoke no German. The Commission held that there was no breach of Article 6, because the applicant spoke freely of his criminal intent in the presence of a third party. Domestic law has reached similar conclusions,[55] but, of course, the trial judge is required to examine the effect of such evidence on the fairness of the proceedings under s. 78, PACE.

16.10 ACCOMPLICE EVIDENCE

There is nothing in the Convention to prevent the authorities from relying on the evidence of an accomplice in a criminal trial,[56] or to prevent the trial court hearing of the guilty plea of a co-accused in the same proceedings.[57] Safeguards must nonetheless exist for the protection of the accused, with the minimum requirement being the right of the accused to cross-examine the witness effectively. Evidence of an accomplice should always be approached with caution,[58] and in the case of *Baragiola* v *Switzerland* (1993) 75 DR 76 the Commission said that the Courts should adopt a 'critical approach' when assessing the evidence of accomplices who may, in giving evidence, benefit by way of a reduction in sentence.

The arguments in favour of caution are stronger where a witness has been granted immunity from prosecution. In *X* v *UK* (1976) 7 DR 115 the witness was a 'supergrass' who had such immunity. The Commission accepted that Article 6 was engaged, but on the facts of the case held that the rights of the accused had been sufficiently safeguarded. Accordingly, the Commission was of the view that the applicant had had a fair hearing. The Commission took into account the fact that both the jury and the defence had been aware of the terms of the agreement between the witness and the Crown, that the applicant's counsel did not object to the procedure, and that the applicant had called no evidence. The fact that the jury had acquitted the applicant on one count was clearly a relevant factor.

16.11 EVIDENCE FOR THE DEFENCE

Equality of arms demands equal treatment of prosecution and defence witnesses. This does not necessarily mean that there will be a breach of Article 6 for any

---

[55] See for example, *R* v *Bailey and Smith* (1993) 97 Cr App R 365; and the approach of the House of Lords in *R* v *Khan* [1997] AC 558.
[56] *App. No. 1599/62* v *Austria*.
[57] *MH* v *UK* [1997] EHRLR 279.
[58] See for example, *Labita* v *Italy* (6 April 2000), where the European Court said that the authorities should be slow to base an arrest or pre-trial detention on accomplice evidence.

failure to hear every witness the defence wish to call.[59] It is generally within the ambit of the domestic courts to decide whether a witness is necessary or relevant, although the European Court observed in *Bricmont* v *Belgium* (1989) 12 EHRR 217 that exceptional circumstances might lead the Court to find a violation of Article 6.

It is not clear what those 'exceptional circumstances' will be, but the case law suggests that any refusal to call or secure the attendance of important defence witnesses should be exercised with great care. In *Unterpertinger* v *Austria* (1986) 13 EHRR 175 the European Court was critical of the domestic court's refusal to allow the applicant to call evidence to undermine the credibility of witnesses whose evidence had been read.[60]

A more extensive review was undertaken by the Court in *Vidal* v *Belgium* (22 April 1992), where the applicant complained of a breach of Article 6 where the court refused to compel an important but reluctant witness to give evidence on his behalf. The European Court agreed that he had had an unfair trial, and observed that although it generally exercised no review on the relevance of evidence, 'the complete silence of the judgment . . . on the point in question is not consistent with the concept of a fair trial . . .' (at para. 34).

---

[59] *Engel* v *Netherlands* (1976) 1 EHRR 647 at para. 89; *Bricmont* v *Belgium* (1989) 12 EHRR 217 at para. 89.
[60] In England a specific provision exists to allow the defence to call such evidence under sch. 2, Criminal Justice Act 1988.

Chapter Seventeen

Self-incrimination and the Right to Silence

Anthony Jennings QC

17.1   INTRODUCTION

The presumption of innocence, guaranteed by Article 6(2), gives rise to two closely related but discrete rights: the right against self-incrimination and the right to silence. Lord Bingham described the relationship between these rights as that of 'first cousin once removed'. [1] Both the privilege against self-incrimination and right to silence are not specifically set out in the European Convention but the European Court has been prepared to read in to Article 6 the right of a defendant 'to remain silent and not to contribute to incriminate himself'.[2] Such rights lie at the heart of the notion of a fair trial under Article 6[3] and contribute towards the avoidance of miscarriages of justice.

In *R* v *Director of Serious Fraud Office, ex parte Smith* [1993] AC 1 at p. 30, Lord Mustill described the right to silence as arousing 'strong but unfocused feelings'. Lord Mustill went on to say that the right to silence does not denote a single right but rather refers to a 'disparate group of immunities, which differ in nature, origin, incidence and importance' (at p. 30). His Lordship identified general immunities not to answer questions or to incriminate oneself and also specific immunities not to be compelled to answer questions (including after charge), give evidence or have adverse comment made in respect of the exercise of these immunities (at pp. 30, 31). Each of these immunities is concerned with

---

[1] 'Silence is Golden — or is it?', in *The Business of Judging*, p. 285.
[2] *Funke* v *France* (1993) 16 EHRR 297 at para. 44.
[3] *Condron* v *UK* (2000) 8 BHRC 290 at para. 56.

protecting citizens against the abuse of power but they are not different ways of expressing the same principle. Lord Mustill added that it is therefore necessary to look at the motives that have caused these immunities to become embedded in English law to understand their importance.

In *Brown* v *Procurator Fiscal, Dunfermline* [2000] UKHRR 239 at p. 247, Lord Justice General Rodger pointed out that the European jurisprudence on these rights was not extensive and it is not always easy to discover the scope of these rights from the judgments of the European Court. His Lordship went on to say that the jurisprudence of other jurisdictions where these rights are specifically set out,[4] may provide considerable assistance.

As has been rightly observed, these rights are at a crossroads (see Keane, A., *The Modern Law of Evidence*, 5th ed. (London: Butterworths, 2000), pp. 558–559). Parliament has sought to abrogate these rights in a number of areas and the Human Rights Act has created a new tension between these abrogations and the importance of these rights in Convention law.

17.2 THE RIGHT AGAINST SELF-INCRIMINATION

17.2.1 Compulsory questioning powers

A defendant in a criminal trial does not enjoy a privilege against self-incrimination in respect of the offence with which he is charged.[5] The privelege applies to witnesses and their refusal to answer questions in court or to produce requested items. The right against self-incrimination, however, principally arises in the field of compulsory questioning powers. These powers create offences for failing to respond to compulsory questioning under a range of statutory provisions. In *Saunders* v *UK* (1996) 23 EHRR 313[6] the applicant had been questioned by DTI inspectors using their compulsory powers of questioning under the Companies Act 1985, ss. 432(2), 436(3).[7] The applicant was subsequently charged with a number of criminal offences and at his trial the trial judge admitted in evidence answers obtained by the DTI inspectors under s. 431(5) of the 1985 Act.

The starting point for the European Court was the use that had been made of the interviews. Although the interviews did not contain admissions of guilt they included material that was deployed against the applicant at his trial (at paras 71, 72). There must, therefore, be a link between the material obtained and its use in

---

[4] For example, the Bill of Rights in chapter 2 of the Constitution of the Republic of South Africa.
[5] Criminal Evidence Act 1898, s. 1.
[6] See Cowell, 'The European Court and company investigations' [2000] 8 Archbold News 5.
[7] The European Court found a breach of Article 6 in the case of the other 'Guinness defendants': *IJL, GMR and AKP* v *UK* (2000) *The Times*, 13 October.

criminal proceedings. Compulsory powers which do not result in criminal proceedings do not necessarily breach Article 6.[8]

The European Court (at para. 74) did not accept the Government argument that the complexity of corporate fraud and the vital public interest in investigating such fraud could justify such a marked departure from basic principles of fair procedure as occurred in the instant case. The Court did not have to decide whether the right against self-incrimination was absolute[9] or whether infringements of it may be necessary in particular circumstances. The use of the applicant's compulsorily acquired answers at his trial amounted to a breach of Article 6.

In *Brown*, Lord Justice General Rodger outlined the way a court should approach a statutory provision under the HRA 1998 where it was alleged that the provision breached the right against self-incrimination. A three-stage process was involved. First, the court must test whether, on an ordinary construction, the provision is compatible with the Convention. If it is not, then secondly the court must see whether it can be read and given effect in a way which is compatible with the Convention. Only if it cannot be so read or given effect will s. 6(1) of the HRA 1998 mean that it falls to be disapplied (the third stage). The first two stages inevitably require the court to consider the scope of the Convention right in question. In *Brown* the court was concerned with the power under s. 172 of the Road Traffic Act 1988 requiring a suspected intoxicated driver to supply requested details on pain of a penalty. What allowed the court to read in the protection of the right against self-incrimination was the fact that the statute did not expressly provide for the admissibility of the compelled reply. This decision undoubtedly stretches the concept of reading a statute compatibly with the Convention to its outer limits. Why else would Parliament have provided for the power to compel a relevant reply unless it intended that answer to be used in evidence? Nevertheless, *Brown* does not render drink driving legislation impotent. As can be seen at 17.2.3, the Privy Council has now answered this question.

17.2.2 Derivative evidence

Two questions arise in respect of material obtained by the use of compulsory powers. First, does such material fall within the privilege against self-incrimination? Secondly, if it does not, can the judicial discretion to exclude evidence be used in respect of it? The European Court in *Saunders* observed (para. 69) that the right not to incriminate oneself was primarily concerned with the will of the accused. This right did not, however, extend to the use in criminal proceedings of material which may be obtained from the accused through the use of compulsory

---

[8] *Abas v Netherlands* [1997] EHRLR 418; *K v Austria* (1993) A/255-B.
[9] The right to silence is not absolute: *John Murray v UK* (1996) 22 EHRR 29 at paras 47, 49–50; *Condron v UK* (2000) 8 BHRC 290 at para. 56.

powers but which has 'an existence independent of the will of the subject' (para. 69) such as, *inter alia*, documents acquired pursuant to a warrant, breath, blood and urine samples and bodily tissue for the purpose of DNA testing. The distinction is therefore drawn between oral or written self-incrimination where an emission from the will of the accused incriminates himself, and physical material that is independent of the accused's will.

Without explicitly saying so this distinction appeared to contradict the decision of the European Court in *Funke* v *France* (1993) 16 EHRR 297. In *Funke* the European Court held that the privilege against self-incrimination extended to the handing over of potentially incriminating documents. As the dissenting opinion of Judges Martens and Kuris in *Saunders* points out ((1996) 23 EHRR 313 at p. 354), the court appears to overrule *Funke* without providing cogent reasons for so doing. Moreover, they believe it is open to 'grave doubt' as to whether the distinction between oral and physical self-incrimination is a sound one (at p. 355). As they say: 'Why should a suspect be free from coercion to make incriminating statements but not from coercion to co-operate to furnish incriminating data?' (ibid). They go on to point out that in both cases 'the will of the accused is not respected in that he is forced to bring about his own conviction' (ibid).

In *R* v *Central Criminal Court, ex parte the Guardian, the Observer and Bright and others* [2000] UKHRR 796, Judge LJ, in a strongly worded dissenting judgment on this point, sought to draw a further distinction. His Lordship began by saying that the principles to be found in the Convention are 'bred in the bone of the common law' (p. 814). The starting point was to see if a statutory provision expressly breached the privilege against self-incrimination. Powers that permit the seizure of material involve the police taking material as opposed to an accused being compelled to hand over material or provide access to it. The latter situations go beyond mere passivity on the part of the accused and infringe the privilege against self-incrimination (p. 820). Judge LJ added that even if his interpretation was wrong, a trial judge could still use s. 78 of PACE to exclude evidence so obtained (p. 820).

Both of the other two judges in *Bright*[10] took the view that the provision under consideration[11] did expressly breach the right against self-incrimination but this was permissible as the privilege was not absolute.

A different approach from Judge LJ was also taken in *Brown* v *Procurator Fiscal, Dunfermline* [2000] UKHRR 239 at pp. 257–8. Lord Justice General Rodger classified the privilege as being one of 'testimonial immunity': a protection from being forced to speak or give evidence against oneself. His Lordship went on to point out that the taking of samples does not involve the accused in saying anything and so the privilege is not breached. Similarly, if the

---

[10] Maurice Kay J (p. 830) and Gibbs J (p. 832).
[11] Section 9, PACE 1984 (production orders).

accused is forced to produce documents or to permit a search, that again involves 'an act rather than any speech' on the part of the accused.[12]

The section of the judgment in *Saunders* concerning derivative evidence must be approached with a degree of caution. In stating the general principle in relation to material which exists independent of the will of the accused, the court simply listed examples without any analysis of the relevant power to obtain the material. As Judge LJ pointed out in *Bright*, the seizure of material without the involvement of the accused does not involve a breach of the privilege. But what of the case where access to the material is gained by oral agreement which itself has been obtained by threat of a penalty? The distinguishing feature is that on the one hand material can be seized irrespective of the consent of the accused, and on the other hand the material which cannot be seized without the consent of the suspect but that consent has been obtained by threat of penalty. Clearly the seizure of material pursuant to a search warrant does not require the consent of the suspect. In contrast, the taking of breath samples from drivers suspected of driving with excess alcohol under ss. 6 and 7 of the Road Traffic Act 1988 does require such consent. The document that sets out the procedure for obtaining the specimen of breath[13] warns the suspect that they are required to provide two specimens of breath. The suspect is told that a failure to provide either of the specimens will render him or her liable to prosecution. Finally, the suspect is asked: 'Do you agree to provide two specimens of breath for analysis?' and the reply is recorded on the form. As judges Martens and Kuris pointed out in their dissenting opinion in *Saunders*: 'can it really be said that the results of a breath test to which a person suspected of driving under the influence has been compelled have an existence independent of the will of the suspect?'[14]

What would appear to be the decisive factor is whether the accused's reply is used at court. As Lord Justice General Rodger pointed in *Brown*,[15] the prosecution would rely on the answer under s. 172 at trial, whereas in *Tora Tolmos* v *Spain* (App. No. 23816/94, 17 May 1995) (a speed camera case) the accused's reply as to whether he was the driver of a speeding car was not used against him at trial. In the case of driving with excess alcohol the driver's compelled reply is merely an evidential step to obtaining incriminating material as opposed to being inherently incriminating.

The court in *Brown* did not deal with the fact that in domestic law the court would be entitled to consider the lawfulness by which such material had been

---

[12] See also *Thomson Newspapers Ltd* v *Canada* [1990] 1 SCR 425.

[13] Form MG DD/A (2 February 1999).

[14] At p. 355. The European Commission has declared inadmissible a case concerning blood samples: *Cartledge* v *UK* (App. No. 30551/96, 9 April 1997).

[15] At p. 253. *Brown* was applied at first instance to an allegation of dangerous driving captured on video where the alleged offenders were served a notice under s. 172, RTA 1988 and a notice of intended prosecution under s. 1 of the same Act: *R* v *Chauhan and Hollingsworth* (13 July 2000, unreported, Birmingham Crown Court).

obtained in order to determine admissibility under ss. 76 and 78 of PACE 1984. In *R* v *Hertfordshire County Council, ex parte Green Enviromental Industries Ltd and another* [2000] 2 WLR 373 at p. 380, Lord Hoffman recognised that the advent of the HRA 1998 meant that judges in criminal trials will have to ask whether Article 6 requires them to exercise their discretion to exclude such evidence. It has been recognised by the Constitutional Court of South Africa that discretionary exclusionary powers may be used to exclude material that is derived from compelled testimony ('derivative evidence') (*Ferreira* v *Levin*; *Vryenhoek* v *Powell* (6 December 1995, unreported, Constitutional Court); *State* v *Nombewu* 1996 (12) BCLR 1635 (E), High Court Eastern Cape Division (Erasmus J); *S* v *M* 2000 (8) BCLR 930 (N) High Court Natal Provisional Division (Nicholson J)). It is submitted that the discretionary powers to exclude evidence apply to both the evidence of the compelled testimony and any evidence derived from the compelled testimony. The use of discretionary powers must always involve a consideration of the principle underpinning the HRA 1998: the preservation of Parliamentary sovereignty. If a statute explicitly infringes a Convention right and cannot be read compatibly with the Convention, then a declaration of incompatibility should be sought under s. 4. As Lord Irvine has observed:[16]

> Thus the Act, while significantly changing the nature of the interpretative process, does not confer on the courts a licence to construe legislation in a way which is so radical and strained that it arrogates to the judges a power completely to rewrite existing law: that is the task for Parliament and the executive.

17.2.3 *Brown* at the Privy Council

In *Brown* v *Stott (Procurator Fiscal, Dunfermline)* [2001] 2 All ER 97, the Privy Council considered the prosecution appeal. After an extensive review of both domestic and Convention case law, Lord Bingham, in a judgment with which the other Board members agreed, considered *Tolmos* and two analogous Commission decisions.[17] His Lordship pointed out that, although in all three cases there was no reliance at trial on incriminating answers compulsorily obtained at an earlier stage, the cases were not irrelevant. The choice facing the applicants in those cases was the same as that facing Mrs Brown: answer the question and be prosecuted for the substantive offence or refuse to answer it and be penalised for that refusal.

Lord Bingham pointed out that, although the right against self-incrimination is an important right, it is an implied one and there is no treaty provision which expressly governs the effect or extent of what is to be implied. Limited

---

[16] 'Activism and Restraint: Human Rights and the Interpretative Process' [1999] 4 EHRLR 350 at 367.
[17] *DN* v *Netherlands* (App. No. 6170/73, 26 May 1975); *JP, KR and GH* v *Austria* (App. Nos 15135/89, 15136/89 and 15137/89, 5 September 1989).

qualification of such rights is acceptable 'if reasonably directed by national authorities towards a clear and proper public objective and if representing no greater qualification than the situation calls for'. Lord Bingham observed that Convention jurisprudence has recognised the need for a fair balance between the general interest of the community and the personal rights of the individual. There was a clear public interest in the enforcement of road traffic legislation and the crucial question for Lord Bingham was whether s. 172 was a disproportionate response or one that undermines a defendant's right to a fair trial.

Lord Bingham did not think that s. 172 was a disproportionate response to a serious social problem or its use undermined the right to a fair trial. The reasons for this conclusion were as follows:

(a) The answer to the question under s. 172 cannot of itself incriminate the suspect, since it is not without more an offence to drive a car. The use of the section, in contrast to the situation in *Saunders*, does not sanction prolonged questioning and the penalty for declining to answer the question was moderate and non-custodial. There was nothing in the present case to say that the use of s. 172 involved improper coercion or oppression such as might give rise to an unreliable confession. If there were such a suggestion then a trial judge has ample powers to exclude such evidence.

(b) While the High Court was entitled to distinguish between the giving of an answer under s. 172 and the provision of physical samples, this distinction should not be 'pushed too far'. Lord Bingham said that it was not easy to see why a requirement to answer a question was objectionable and a requirement to undergo a breath test was not.

(c) All of those who drive cars know that by so doing they subject themselves to a regulatory regime which does not apply to members of the public who do not drive. Section 172 did not represent a disproportionate legislative response to the problem of maintaining road safety.

While Lord Bingham agreed with much of the judgment of the High Court, the High Court came 'very close to treating the right not to incriminate oneself as absolute, describing it as a 'central right' which permitted no gradations of fairness depending on the seriousness of the charge or the circumstances of the case'. Lord Bingham went on to say that the High Court had interpreted the decision in *Saunders* as laying down a more absolute standard than he thought the European Court intended. The judgment of the High Court was also absent of any consideration of the question of proportionality. Lord Steyn agreed that the High Court had come very close to saying that the privilege against self-incrimination was an absolute Convention right and that no interference with it could ever be justified.

The proportionality test is not the sole consideration in Convention jurisprudence when assessing the compatibility of a statutory provision with the Convention. Any measure which interferes with a Convention right must be both proportionate and must not extinguish 'the very essence'[18] of the Convention right. If the essence of the Convention right is extinguished then proportionality or public interest will not legitimise such extinction. Thus in *Brogan, Murray, Heaney* and *Quinn* (see footnote 18) the threat to society posed by terrorism did not ensure compliance with the Convention, and in *Saunders* the public importance of tackling corporate fraud could not excuse the breach of the applicant's rights.

To return to the specific, what runs through the Convention case law on self-incrimination and silence is the distinction between direct and indirect compulsion. Direct compulsion destroys the essence of the right whereas indirect compulsion preserves the right but permits adverse inferences to potentially flow from the exercise of the right. Sections 34 and 35 of the Criminal Justice and Public Order Act 1994 provide, respectively, for adverse inferences from a failure to answer questions or to testify. The provisions do not compel a defendant to answer questions or testify and in not so doing only involve indirect compulsion.

Accepting proportionality and pubic interest, the question in *Brown* should have been whether s. 172 involved direct compulsion and did such compulsion destroy the essence of the right. Undoubtedly there was direct compulsion in *Brown* but the contentious point will be whether the penalty that flowed from a refusal to comply with the request was sufficiently severe to destroy the essence of the right (see also *DPP* v *Wilson* (2001) *The Times*, 21 March).

17.2.4   *Heaney and McGuinness v Ireland*

In *Heaney and McGuinness* v *Ireland* (App. No. 34720/97, 21 December 2000), both applicants were arrested in the Republic of Ireland as suspected terrorists under s. 30 of the Offences Against the State Act 1939. Although they were cautioned that they had a right to remain silent in the course of interviews, the terms of s. 52 of the Act were read to the applicants. This provision entitles a police officer to demand from a suspect a full account of his movements and actions during a specified time and to provide all information in his possession in relation to the commission or intended commission by another of acts of terrorism. By virtue of s. 52(2) a suspect's failure or refusal to give such an account or information or giving such an account or information which is false or misleading constitutes a criminal offence which carries a maximum sentence of six months' imprisonment.

---

[18] *Belgian Linguistic Case* (1968) 1 EHRR 252 at 281; *Ashingdane* v *UK* (1985) 7 EHRR 528; *Mathieu-Mohin* v *Belgium* (1987) 10 EHRR 1 at 16; *Brogan and others* v *UK* (1989) 11 EHRR 117; *John Murray* v *UK* (1996) 22 EHRR 29; *Saunders* v *UK*; *Condron* v *UK*; *Rowe and Davis* v *UK* (2000) 30 EHRR 1; *Heaney and McGuinness* v *Ireland* (App. No. 34720/97, 21 December 2000); *Quinn* v *Ireland* (App. No. 36887/97, 21 December 2000).

The European Court rejected the argument that the nature of the sanction was important and said that the only relevant factor was that the sanction was criminal in nature. Any protections inherent in the statutory provision are only relevant if they 'could effectively and sufficiently reduce the degree of compulsion imposed by section 52 of the 1939 Act to the extent that the essence of the rights at issue would not be impaired by that domestic provision' (para. 51). Section 52 'destroyed the very essence of [the] privilege against self incrimination and [the] right to remain silent' (para. 55). The European Court also rejected the Irish Government argument that security and public order concerns meant that s. 52 was a proportionate response to the threat of terrorism (paras 56–58). The Court noted that it had rejected similar arguments in *Saunders* v *UK* (1996) 23 EHRR 313 at para. 74 and *Brogan and others* v *UK* (1988) 11 EHRR 117 and said that such concerns could not justify a provision which 'extinguishes the very essence of the applicants' rights to silence and against self-incrimination' (para. 58).

Heaney and McGuinness is a salient reminder that any statutory incursion into the right to silence or the privilege against self-incrimination must not have such a degree of compulsion that the very essence of the rights is destroyed. Such a situation will normally arise where a provision goes beyond permitting an adverse inference arising from the exercise of the right and providing a criminal sanction for the exercise of the right. A judgment to the same effect was delivered on the same day in *Quinn* v *Ireland* (App. No. 36887/97, 21 December 2000).

17.2.5 The effect of *Saunders*

At common law incriminating answers obtained during compulsory examination were admissible in subsequent criminal proceedings if the statute explicitly or implicitly so provided.[19] The domestic courts held, following *Saunders*, that even though a statutory power to compel an answer might amount to a breach of Article 6, the domestic court was powerless to act in the face of a clearly worded statute.[20] Following the decision in *Saunders*, the Government formed and applied a policy of not using against an accused in criminal proceedings evidence obtained by compulsory questioning whether before or after charge.[21] This policy applied to questioning under the Companies Act 1985, the Insolvency Act 1986, the Financial Services Act 1986, the Banking Act 1987, the Criminal Justice Act 1987 and analogous powers under other provisions.[22] The policy restricted the use of compulsorily acquired answers in cross-examination during a subsequent criminal trial unless the defendant introduced the questioning; or the defendant had been the subject of a statutory duty to provide answers in the course of an

---

[19] *Commrs of Customs and Excise* v *Harz and Power* [1967] 1 AC 760, HL.
[20] *R* v *Staines* [1997] 2 Cr App R 426; *R* v *Saunders* [1996] 1 Cr App R 463.
[21] *R* v *Secretary of State for Trade and Industry, ex parte McCormick* [1998] BCC 379.
[22] See Hansard, HC vol. 305, cols 639–40.

administrative or regulatory procedure, or had been required to answer truthfully in the course of judicial proceedings, and the subsequent prosecution is based on: (a) a failure or refusal to answer; (b) an omission to disclose a material fact that should have been disclosed; or (c) the giving of an untruthful answer.[23]

Statutory effect is given to this policy by the Youth Justice and Criminal Evidence Act 1999. Section 59 of the Act gives effect to sch. 3 to the Act, which effects a series of amendments to a number of statutory provisions concerning compulsory powers.[24]

17.2.6 Conclusion

The amendments effected by the Youth Justice and Criminal Evidence Act 1999 have ensured that the importance of compulsorily acquired interviews in criminal trials has all but disappeared. The new challenge will be the compatibility of relying upon material derived from such interviews at trial with Article 6. Also, following *Brown*, any statutory provision infringing the right against self-incrimination will have to be viewed against the principles set out in the case.

17.3 THE RIGHT TO SILENCE

17.3.1 Background

Prior to the introduction of the Criminal Justice and Public Order Act (CJPOA) 1994 juries and magistrates could not draw adverse inferences from an accused's exercise of his right to silence in interview[25] but such a position had been the subject of judicial criticism.[26] Prior to the CJPOA 1994 the prosecution were prohibited from commenting on a defendant's failure to testify[27] and judicial comment was restricted.[28] In 1972 the Criminal Law Revision Committee (CLRC)[29] recommended radical reform in these areas but their proposals were rejected by two subsequent Royal Commissions.[30] The reforms introduced by the CJPOA 1994 were based principally on the draft Bill attached to the report of the CLRC and the Criminal Evidence (Northern Ireland) Order 1988.[31] In *R* v *Bowden*

---

[23] Examples of such offences are the Perjury Act 1911, s. 1 (perjury), the Companies Act 1985, s. 451 (furnishing false information), the Insolvency Act 1986, s. 353 (non-disclosure), the Banking Act 1987, s. 94 (false and misleading information) and the Criminal Justice Act 1987, s. 2(14) (making a false or misleading statement). The guidance is set out in full at 148 NLJ 208.

[24] Including those provisions listed above. The section came into force on 14 April 2000: Youth Justice and Criminal Evidence Act 1999 (Commencement No. 2) Order 2000 (SI 2000/1034).

[25] *R* v *Gilbert* (1977) 66 Cr App R 237.

[26] Ibid; *R* v *Alladice* (1988) 87 Cr App R 380.

[27] Criminal Evidence Act 1898, s. 1(b).

[28] *R* v *Bathurst* [1968] 2 QB 99; *R* v *Martinez-Tobon* (1994) 98 Cr App R 375.

[29] Eleventh Report: *Evidence* (Cm. 4991).

[30] Cm. 8092 (1981); Cm. 2263 (1993).

[31] SI 1988/1987 (NI 20). Sections 36 and 37 of the CJPOA 1994 were based on provisions in the Republic of Ireland's Criminal Justice Act 1984.

[1999] 2 Cr App R 176 at p. 181, Lord Bingham CJ said that since these provisions 'restrict rights recognised at common law as appropriate to protect defendants against the risk of injustice they should not be construed more widely than the statutory language requires'.

17.3.2 The Criminal Justice and Public Order Act 1994

17.3.2.1 Section 34

Section 34 concerns an accused's failure to mention facts when questioned or charged which he later relies on in his defence. In *R* v *Argent* [1997] 2 Cr App R 27 at pp. 32–3, Lord Bingham CJ indicated that there were six formal conditions to be met before s. 34 could apply:

(a) there had to be proceedings against a person for an offence;
(b) the failure to answer had to occur before a defendant was charged (this is subject to s. 34(1)(b));
(c) the failure had to occur during questioning under caution by a constable or other person within s. 34(4);
(d) the questioning had to be directed to trying to discover whether or by whom the offence had been committed;
(e) the failure had to be to mention any fact relied on in the person's defence in those proceedings;
(f) the fact the defendant failed to mention had to be one which, in the circumstances existing at the time of interview, he could reasonably be expected to mention when so questioned.

As a result of an amendment to s. 34,[32] a seventh condition needs to be added. An adverse inference cannot arise in respect of a person who is at an authorised place of detention and who has not been allowed an opportunity to consult a solicitor prior to interview.

Additional protections for suspects are that the failure to mention the fact must relate to a positive fact rather than a theory, a possibility or speculation[33] and the prosecution must prove that the defendant was aware of the fact at the time of the alleged failure.[34] A court must look at the circumstances at the time of the failure to mention the fact and not look at the circumstances restrictively.[35] The court must also ask whether the defendant acted reasonably in his decision to remain silent and this involves a subjective test.

---

[32] Section 34(2A). This provision will be considered in detail below at 17.3.2.1.1.
[33] *R* v *Nickolson* [1999] Crim LR 61.
[34] *R* v *B (MT)* [2000] Crim LR 181.
[35] *R* v *Argent* [1997] 2 Cr App R 27 at p. 33.

John Murray v UK

In *John Murray* v *UK* (1996) 22 EHRR 29, the European Court reviewed the compatibility of the scheme for drawing adverse inferences under the Criminal Evidence (Northern Ireland) Order 1988[36] with Article 6. Although not mentioned in Article 6, the right to silence is a generally recognised international standard lying at the heart of the notion of a fair procedure under Article 6 (para. 45). By providing the accused with protection against improper compulsion, the right to silence contributes towards avoiding miscarriages of justice and to securing the aims of Article 6.

The right to silence was not an absolute right (para. 47). It was self-evident that it was incompatible with the right to silence to base a conviction 'wholly or mainly' on an accused's silence (para. 47). Nevertheless, it was equally obvious that the right to silence should not prevent the accused's silence, in situations which clearly called for an explanation from him, from being taken into account in assessing the persuasiveness of the evidence adduced by the prosecution. Whether the drawing of adverse inferences from silence infringes Article 6 is a matter to be determined in the light of all the circumstances of the case, 'having particular regard to the situations where inferences may be drawn, the weight attached to them by the national courts in their assessment of the evidence and the degree of compulsion inherent in the situation' (para. 47). The essence of the right to silence was preserved in the provisions in question inasmuch as the defendant could remain silent and no penalty would flow from his exercise of his right to silence. Although there was indirect compulsion this feature by itself was not decisive. The European Court said that the national court had to concentrate instead on the role played by the inference in the proceedings against the defendant and especially in his conviction.

The European Court noted that the proceedings in *Murray* were proceedings without a jury, the trier of fact being an experienced judge (para. 51). In the European Commission Nicolas Bratza[37] in his partly concurring, partly dissenting opinion, had dealt with this feature in greater detail. In finding there had been no violation of the Convention he attached 'considerable importance' to the fact that the adverse inferences had been drawn by a judge sitting without a jury (para. 53). Not only was a judge by his training and legal experience likely to be better equipped than a lay juryman to draw only such adverse inferences as are necessary from a suspect's silence but he must also give a reasoned judgment as to what inferences he drew and what weight he attached to them. Mr Bratza added: 'The same safeguards against unfairness do not appear to me to exist in the case of jury trial' (para. 53) and also said that the risk of unfairness was 'substantially increased' in trial by jury (para 54).

---

[36] SI 1988/1987 (NI 20). The English provisions are based on this Order and the draft Bill attached to the Eleventh Report of the Criminal Law Revision Committee (Cm. 4991 (1972)).

[37] Sir Nicolas Bratza is now a judge of the European Court.

After noting the fact of trial by a single judge, the European Court went on to point out 'a series of important safeguards designed to respect the rights of the defence and to limit the extent to which reliance can be placed on inferences' (1996) 22 EHRR 29 at para. 51). These safeguards are:

(a) appropriate warnings must have been given to the accused as to the legal effects of maintaining silence. The caution to suspects upon arrest and prior to interview[38] is such an appropriate warning;[39]

(b) a judge has a discretion as to whether adverse inferences should be drawn. A judge who had doubts about whether the accused understood the nature of the warning would not invite the jury to draw an adverse inference;

(c) the prosecution must first establish a prima facie case, i.e. a case consisting of direct evidence which, if believed and combined with legitimate inferences based upon it, could lead a properly directed jury to be satisfied beyond reasonable doubt that each of the essential elements is proved.[40] The prosecution evidence must be 'sufficiently strong' to require an answer (para. 51) and only common-sense inferences can be drawn;

(d) an accused cannot be convicted on the basis of silence alone;[41]

(e) a judge in Northern Ireland must explain the reasons for his decision to draw adverse inferences and the weight attached to them. The exercise of the discretion in this respect was subject to review by the appellate courts.

In view of the 'formidable case' against John Murray, his refusal to explain his presence at the scene of the crime meant that the drawing of adverse inferences was a matter of common sense and was not unfair or unreasonable in the circumstances (para. 54). The Northern Ireland scheme for drawing adverse inferences represented a 'formalised system which aims at allowing common-sense implications to play an open role in the assessment of evidence' (para. 54).

Condron v *UK*[42]

Karen and William Condron were admitted heroin addicts and were arrested for supplying drugs. At the police station the police medical examiner noted that they were both exhibiting signs of withdrawal symptoms but he determined that both were fit for interview. The Condrons' solicitor expressed concern that they were not fit for interview. At interview they both made no comment following legal

---

[38] PACE Code of Practice C:10.4. See Archbold (2001) 15-295.

[39] *Condron* v *UK* (2000) 8 BHRC 290 at para. 59.

[40] See further, *Murray* v *DPP* (1993) 97 Cr App R 151.

[41] See s. 38(3), CJPOA 1994.

[42] (2000) 8 BHRC 290. For the wider effects of the decision, see Jennings, Ashworth and Emmerson, 'Silence and Safety: the Impact of the Human Rights Act 1998' [2000] Crim LR 879 and *R* v *Francom and others* (2000) *The Times*, 24 October.

advice. At trial the trial judge permitted the jury to draw inferences from their failure to mention matters relied on in their defence at trial. Both defendants were convicted and subsequently had their appeals against conviction dismissed in the Court of Appeal.

The European Court noted that 'particular caution' (para. 60) was required before a domestic court should invoke an accused's silence against him. The Court noted in a later decision that, although the purpose of the provisions was to limit ambush defences, 'the extent to which adverse inferences can be drawn from an accused's failure to respond to police questioning must be necessarily limited'.[43] The European Court pointed out that there were a number of features that distinguished the Condrons' case from that of John Murray: the Condrons gave evidence at trial and explained the reasons for their silence and they were tried by a jury who had to be directed in respect of the potential adverse inferences.

The applicants in *Condron* v *UK* had argued that the fact that they had been tried by a jury meant that it was impossible to ascertain the significance of their silence in the jury's decision to convict. The European Court rejected this argument saying that trial by jury was not by itself incompatible with the Convention but was a 'relevant consideration' in determining fairness (para. 58). Where trial by jury was of particular importance was when a trial judge's directions were defective. The trial judge had failed to direct the jury that if they were satisfied that the applicants' silence in interview could not sensibly be attributed to their having no answer, or none that would stand up to cross-examination, then they should not draw an adverse inference (para. 61). This omission meant that the jury were left at liberty to draw an adverse inference notwithstanding that they might have been satisfied as to the plausibility of the applicants' explanation for silence. This did not strike the required balance between the right to silence and the drawing of adverse inferences. This direction was not merely 'desirable', as the Court of Appeal had said ([1997] 1 Cr App R 185 at 195), but its omission was incompatible with the right of silence ((2000) 8 BHRC at para. 62).

The imperfection could not be remedied on appeal (para. 66) because the Court of Appeal had no means of ascertaining whether or not the applicants' silence played a significant role in the jury's decision to convict (para. 63). The Court of Appeal had regard to the weight of the evidence against the applicants. However, it was in no position to assess properly whether the jury considered this to be conclusive of their guilt.

Because of the European Court's determination that the Condrons had not received a fair trial, the Court did not have to consider two other challenges to the terms of the specimen directions (para. 67). First, the absence of the direction,

---

[43] *Averill* v *UK* (2000) 8 BHRC 430 at para. 47.

identified in *Murray* as a safeguard, that an adverse inference could only arise once the prosecution had established a prima facie case.[44] Secondly, the absence of a direction that silence could not be the main basis of a defendant's conviction.[45] This first criticism has now been incorporated in the specimen directions.[46] It is submitted that this latter safeguard should be included in the specimen direction. As Lord Bingham CJ warned in *R* v *Birchall* [1999] Crim LR 311, unless these provisions are the subject of very carefully framed directions it was very possible that breaches of the Convention would occur.

17.3.2.1.1   Access to legal advice   In *Murray* v *UK*, the European Court held that denial of access to legal advice, in the context of a system which permitted the drawing of adverse inferences from an accused's silence, violated the right to a fair trial under Article 6. The Court described the right to legal advice as being of 'paramount importance' and held that to deny access to legal advice, 'whatever the justification', was incompatible with Article 6 (para. 66).[47]

Following the decision in *Murray*, guidance was provided to the police and prosecutors by the Home Office[48] and the Attorney General.[49] Prosecutors were advised not to seek to rely on adverse inferences from silence until an accused has been granted access to legal advice. Section 58 of the Youth Justice Criminal Evidence Act 1999 gives statutory effect to this guidance by amending s. 34.

17.3.2.1.2   Legal advice to remain silent   In *R* v *Condron and Condron* [1997] 1 Cr App R 185 at 191, the Court of Appeal said that legal advice could not automatically prevent an adverse inference from being drawn otherwise section 34 would be rendered wholly nugatory. Legal advice was one of the factors taken into account in deciding if an adverse inference should be drawn.[50]

In *Condron* v *UK* (2000) 8 BHRC 290 at para. 60, the European Court said that the fact that an accused has been advised by his lawyer to remain silent must be given 'appropriate weight' by the domestic court. As has been noted earlier, the jury must not be able to draw an adverse inference notwithstanding that it may have been satisfied as to the plausibility of the defendant's explanation for silence. Does this mean that legal advice by itself can prevent an adverse inference from being drawn? Jennings, Ashworth and Emmerson[51] have argued that *Condron* has

---

[44] This is now part of the Judicial Studies Board specimen direction.

[45] This is being considered by the Judicial Studies Board as an additional direction.

[46] See Archbold (2001), 15-404. There must be a case for the defendant to meet. Lord Bingham CJ in *R* v *Birchall* [1999] Crim LR 311 described this as a sufficiently compelling case for the defendant to meet.

[47] See also *Magee* v *UK* (2000) 8 BHRC 646; *Averill* v *UK* (2000) 8 BHRC 430.

[48] HO Circular 53/1998. Set out in full at 163 JPN 18.

[49] 163 JPN 40.

[50] *R* v *Argent* [1997] 2 Cr App R 27.

[51] 'Silence and Safety: the Impact of the Human Rights Act 1998' [2000] Crim LR 879.

created a two-stage test: (i) the jury must take into account the fact that the defendant has been advised by his legal representative to remain silent; (ii) if the defendant's resulting silence was or may have been because of the reason provided, then no adverse inference should be drawn. This formula would allow a jury who believed that a defendant had only latched on to the fact that he had been advised to remain silent because he had no explanation or none that would stand up to scrutiny, to draw an adverse inference. Conversely, if a jury thought that the reason for a defendant's silence was genuinely because he was following legal advice, then no adverse inference should be drawn. Cross and Tapper[52] have pointed to a certain inconsistency in the approach of the European Court:

> It certainly seems odd to elevate the privilege against self-incrimination, the right to silence and access to a lawyer as amongst the most fundamental of human rights, and then to condone the exercise of those rights on the advice of the lawyer as grounds for a conviction.

17.3.2.2   Sections 36 and 37

Section 36 is concerned with an accused's failure or refusal to account for objects, substances or marks on his person, clothing, possession or in any place in which he is at the time of his arrest. Section 37 is concerned with an accused's failure or refusal to account for his presence at a particular place. These provisions have yet to be tested under the Convention. They lack a number of the safeguards set out or implied in s. 34. It is submitted that the effect of ss. 2 and 3 of the HRA 1998 is that, as these safeguards are not explicitly excluded by the provisions, they should be read into the sections. A jury will therefore have to take account of, *inter alia*, the circumstances at the time of the refusal or failure, whether that course was reasonable, whether the defendant had been advised by his legal representative to refuse to provide an explanation and whether the prosecution has made out a case to answer.

17.3.2.3   Section 35

A court may draw such inferences as are proper from a defendant's failure to give evidence or his refusal, without good cause, to answer any question in the course of giving evidence. The section does not apply where the defendant's guilt is not in issue or it appears to the court that the physical or mental condition of the accused makes it 'undesirable' for him to give evidence. Until 30 September 1998 s. 35 did not apply to defendants under the age of 14.[53] A defendant cannot be convicted solely on the basis of an adverse inference.[54] As with s. 34, it is

---

[52] *Evidence*, 9th edn (London: Butterworths, 1999), p. 629.
[53] The amendment to the section was brought about by s. 35, Crime and Disorder Act 1998.
[54] CJPOA 1994, s. 38(3).

submitted that silence also cannot be the main basis of a conviction.[55] The adverse inference only arises if the jury conclude that the reason for the defendant's silence was because he had no explanation or answer to give, or none that could have stood up to questioning. Although it has been held that once the prosecution establish a prima facie case then the adverse inference may be one of guilt,[56] the domestic specimen directions from the Judicial Studies Board have not gone this far. The direction indicates that an adverse inference from a failure to testify is 'some additional support for the prosecution case'.

In *R* v *Cowan* [1996] QB 373, Lord Taylor CJ pointed out that s. 35 was not limited to exceptional cases and indeed the exceptional cases would be those in which s. 35 did not apply. Before a judge should exercise his discretion to advise a jury not to draw an adverse inference, there should be some evidential basis for so doing or some exceptional factors.

In *Murray* v *UK* (1996) 22 EHRR 29, the European Court did not seek to distinguish between ss. 34 and 35 although s. 35 is clearly of much broader application. Nevertheless, the safeguards identified in *Murray* apply equally to s. 35. There is therefore no reason why a jury should not take into account, provided that there is an evidential basis for so doing, the fact that a defendant has been advised by his legal advisers not to give evidence. Although the statutory bar preventing adverse inferences in respect of defendants under 14 years has been removed, the fact that a defendant is under 14 must be a legitimate factor in the decision as to whether an adverse inference direction should be given.[57]

17.3.2.4 Conclusion

The adverse inference provisions have been substantially eroded since their introduction. An essential part of this has been the importance attached by the European Court to legal advice to remain silent. Nevertheless, domestic decisions have also curtailed the ambit of the provisions. In *R* v *Mountford* [1999] Crim LR 575 it was held that if the 'fact' not revealed in interview was the defence, then the resolution of the defence would resolve the issue of the fact. If the s. 34 issue could not be resolved independently of the question of guilt, then there was no mileage in the s. 34 point. As Professor Birch observed in her commentary, 'the present decision rather cleverly deprives [s. 34] of much of its potency' (at p. 576).[58] In *R* v *Milford* (21 December 2000, unreported) the Court of Appeal gave the word 'fact' a broad interpretation encompassing reasons and explanations for the defendant's involvement in the particular event observed which, if true, would

---

[55] This point will be considered in respect of s. 35 in *Owen* v *UK* (App. No. 3783/97).
[56] *Murray* v *DPP* (1993) 97 Cr App R 151.
[57] See the importance of age in trying young offenders in *T and V* v *UK* (1999) 30 EHRR 121.
[58] *Mountford* was the subject of criticism in *R* v *Hearne* [2000] 6 Archbold News 2 but confirmed in *R* v *Gill* [2000] Crim LR 922. For a consideration of *Gill*, see Jennings, All England Legal Opinion, Issue 2. See also *R* v *Milford* (21 December 2000, unreported).

absolve him from the suspicion of criminal intent or involvement which might otherwise arise. The Court also preferred to follow the authority which said that *Mountford* was not a case of general application (*R* v *Hearne* [2000] 6 Archbold News 2).[59] Although the Court accepted that the Court of Appeal had followed *Mountford* in *R* v *Gill* [2000] All ER (D) 1036, the Court preferred the reasoning in *Hearne*. What was not drawn to the Court's attention, supportive of the argument that *Mountford* is a case of general application, was that Henry LJ was the presiding judge in both *Mountford* and *Gill*. Further erosions of the effectiveness of the adverse inference provisions will undoubtedly occur. Sections 34, 36 and 37 remain the most vulnerable sections of the 1994 Act. Section 35 stands in a different position. The adverse inference there only arises once a defendant has had the case against him disclosed, has tested the evidence and had full access to legal advice.

17.3.3   Other statutory infringements of the right to silence

17.3.3.1   *Intimate samples*
Under PACE, s. 62(10), an adverse inference can be drawn from an accused's refusal, without good cause, to provide an intimate sample. Once again, in order to ensure compliance with Article 6, the '*Murray* safeguards' will have to be read into this and similar statutory infringements of the right to silence.

17.3.3.2   *Failure to call witnesses or provide evidence*
In appropriate circumstances a jury may take into account a defendant's failure to call a particular witness but only if there is no good reason for such a failure.[60] Such comment is usually reserved for 'ambush cases' where the relevance of the witness is only revealed by the evidence of the defendant. It may be inappropriate to make a comment in circumstances where the witness could have been called by the prosecution.[61]

17.3.3.3   *Failure of the spouse of the accused to testify*
The prosecution are prohibited from commenting on a failure of the accused to call his spouse as a witness[62] but the trial judge may comment.[63] This comment should normally be made with a great deal of circumspection. Although not covered by the statutory prohibition, similar circumspection should be shown in respect of co-habitees.[64]

---

[59] This was also the approach of the Court of Appeal in *R* v *Coady* (30 March 2000, unreported).

[60] *R* v *Gallagher* [1974] 1 WLR 1204; *R* v *Wilmot* (1989) 89 Cr App R 341; *R* v *Couzens* [1992] Crim LR 822; *R* v *Forsyth* [1997] 2 Cr App R 299.

[61] *R* v *Wheeler* (1968) 52 Cr App R 28.

[62] PACE, s. 80(8).

[63] *R* v *Naudeer* [1984] 3 All ER 1036. See also *R* v *Whitton* [1998] Crim LR 492.

[64] *R* v *Weller* [1994] Crim LR 856.

17.3.3.4 *Defendant's lies and/or untrue alibi*

A lie by a defendant can strengthen the case for the prosecution if it is deliberate, it relates to a material issue and there is no innocent explanation for it.[65] The same position exists in relation to false alibis.[66] The obligation to disclose an alibi is now governed by the Criminal Procedure and Investigations Act 1996 (see below at 17.3.4).

17.3.3.5 *Membership of a proscribed organisation*

In determining if a defendant is a member of a proscribed organisation under s. 2 of the Prevention of Terrorism (Temporary Provisions) Act 1989, a court may draw inferences from the defendant's failure to mention a fact material to the offence.[67] The section only bites once the defendant has been permitted to consult a solicitor (s. 2A(4)(a), (b)). Although the section is wider than s. 34 of CJPOA 1994 by means of the expression 'a fact which is material to the offence', the use of the word 'material' arguably strengthens the protections for the defendant. A defendant cannot be convicted solely on the basis of the inference (s. 2A(6)(b) of the 1989 Act). From a date to be appointed, this section is replaced by s. 109 of the Terrorism Act 2000.

17.3.4 Inferences from a failure to comply with disclosure requirements

Once the prosecution have complied or purported to comply with 'primary disclosure',[68] the defendant must give a defence statement to the prosecutor (s. 5). The defence statement must set out the nature of the defence and the matters with which the defendant takes issue. A court may draw an adverse inference if the defence (s. 11):

(a) fail to give a defence statement;
(b) gives a defence statement outside the prescribed period;
(c) set out inconsistent defences in the defence statement;
(d) put forward a defence at trial that is inconsistent with that contained in the defence statement;
(e) adduce evidence at trial of an alibi which has not been mentioned in the defence statement;
(f) call an alibi witness at trial without having provided details of that witness in the defence statement.

Section 11 also applies to voluntary disclosure by an accused under s. 6 of the Act. In deciding if a defendant has put forward different defences, the court must have

---

[65] *R* v *Lucas* [1981] QB 720; *R* v *Goodway* (1994) 98 Cr App R 11.
[66] *R* v *Lesley* [1996] 1 Cr App R 39; *R* v *Drake* [1996] Crim LR 109.
[67] Section 2A of the 1989 Act added by Criminal Justice (Terrorism and Conspiracy) Act 1998, s. 1.
[68] CPIA 1996, s. 3.

regard to the extent of the difference and whether there is any justification for it (s. 11(4)). A defendant cannot be convicted solely in respect of such inferences (s. 11(5)). There is no specimen direction in respect of s. 11 so it is unclear whether judges should give an adapted s. 34 direction or a '*Lucas*' direction.[69] Whatever direction is given it is submitted that it should include the '*Murray*' safeguards.

In one respect s. 11 of the 1996 Act is narrower than s. 34 of the CJPOA 1994. The former section is not applicable in determining if there is a case for the defendant to meet.[70] However, s. 5 is a form of direct compulsion and may give rise to problems concerning the privilege against self-incrimination. If, as has been argued elsewhere in this book,[71] defence statements are susceptible to challenge under the HRA 1998, then s. 11 of the 1996 Act is equally vulnerable.

17.3.5   Conclusion

All of the above disparate statutory provisions will have to have the '*Murray*' safeguards read into them to ensure compatibility with the Convention.

---

[69] *R* v *Lucas* [1981] QB 720.
[70] Section 11(3)(b) restricts the section to a determination of a defendant's guilt.
[71] Chapter 13.

Chapter Eighteen

Sentence

Michelle Strange

18.1 INTRODUCTION

The incorporation of the Convention into domestic law has already brought about some change in our sentencing and appeal procedures. The Convention has been the basis of successful challenges to domestic law, including the passing of 'automatic' life sentences and the setting of tariff periods for young people detained at Her Majesty's pleasure. Other challenges are pending at the time of writing.

Sentencing does not sit neatly under a single heading, and it is possible for a single sentence to engage a number of Articles of the Convention. These include Article 3 (prohibition of torture), Article 4 (prohibition of forced labour), Article 5 (right to liberty), Article 6 (right to a fair trial), Article 7 (prohibition of retroactive penalties), Article 8 (right to family life) and Article 14 (prohibition of discrimination). These issues will be considered below.

18.2 PUNITIVE AND PREVENTATIVE SENTENCES

In order to understand the case law in respect of individual Articles of the Convention and sentence, it is useful to review the case law of the European Court and Commission upon different types of sentence. Three have been identified:

(a) Punitive sentences imposed on principles of retribution and proportional punishment for the crime committed. These will usually involve fixed sentences 'to a period of imprisonment imposed by the court as appropriate to the case'.[1] Under the Convention there is no right to review or release before the end of the period prescribed by the sentencing court.[2] The Court has ruled that the mandatory life sentence can be viewed as wholly punitive.[3]

(b) Preventative sentences based purely or predominantly on circumstances or characteristics of the offender, including mental disorder[4] and dangerousness and unpredictability.[5] These sentences are imposed for preventative and rehabilitative objectives, and the continuing detention must be justified with reference to these purposes. Article 5(4) requires periodic review of the detention to determine whether the pre-conditions for further detention remain valid.[6]

(c) Mixed sentences, which are partly retributive and partly preventative. Domestic sentences with this dual purpose are the discretionary life sentence, and detention at Her Majesty's pleasure.[7] In both cases the sentences contain a punitive 'tariff' element, followed by a post-tariff preventative stage, where there are rights to review under Article 5(4).

18.3   ARTICLE 3 ISSUES AND SENTENCING

The European Court has shown itself to be reluctant to become involved in complaints about the nature or length of any sentence imposed after conviction for a criminal offence. It is, however, possible for an unduly harsh sentence to engage Article 3, the prohibition of inhuman or degrading treatment or punishment. The threshold for violation of Article 3 is nonetheless extremely high[8] and the Commission has said that 'only in exceptional circumstances could the length of a sentence be relevant under Article 3'.[9]

In the case of adult offenders who have no mental health problems, it is unlikely that domestic law would be found to violate this Article of the Convention, however long the sentence passed. Considerations are different in the sentencing

---

[1] *Van Droogenbroeck* v *Belgium* (1982) 4 EHRR 433.

[2] Although failure to follow accepted procedure on release could make continued detention arbitrary and in violation of Article 5(1)(a).

[3] *Wynne* v *UK* (1994) 19 EHRR 333. The reasoning has been reluctantly extended to detention at Her Majesty's pleasure: see below at 18.3.1.

[4] See above at 18.3.1.

[5] *Weeks* v *UK* (1987) 10 EHRR 293.

[6] See for example *X* v *UK* (1982) 4 EHRR 188; *Thynne, Wilson and Gunnell* v *UK* (1990) 13 EHRR 666; *Hussain* v *UK* (1996) 22 EHRR 1; *Johnson* v *UK* (1997) 27 EHRR 296, and chapter 20.

[7] Strictly speaking, the list should include extended sentences under s. 2(2)(b), Criminal Justice Act 1991. It is arguable that any court passing such a sentence should perform a tariff-setting exercise to indicate clearly what the punitive and preventative components are.

[8] See for example, *Herczegfalvy* v *Austria* (1992) 15 EHRR 437; *Soering* v *UK* (1989) 11 EHRR 439, *Selmouni* v *France* (1999) 29 EHRR 403.

[9] *C* v *Germany* (1986) 46 DR 179.

of young offenders and the mentally ill, and the UK Government has been held to be in violation on a number of occasions.

18.3.1 Juveniles

The United Kingdom has one of the youngest ages of criminal responsibility in the world.[10] Under the UN Convention on the Rights of the Child[11] and the Beijing Rules,[12] the welfare of the child is a primary consideration when he or she is being sentenced.[13] In contrast, the principal aim of the youth justice system in this country is 'to prevent offending by children and young persons'.[14] Although every court dealing with a child or young person should 'have regard to [their] welfare',[15] the difference in emphasis is obvious, and there is much scope for our system to come into conflict with the Convention.

That said, there is nothing under the Convention to prevent the passing of a lengthy custodial sentence for the protection of the public. In the case of a young person, the sentence may violate Article 3 if its purpose is to punish. In *Weeks* v *UK* (1988) 13 EHRR 435 at para. 47 the European Court held that to sentence a 17-year-old to life imprisonment by means of punishment for an offence of robbery was capable of violating Article 3. The principle was extended in *Hussain* v *UK* (1996) 22 EHRR 1 in which the European Court held that if detention for life of a juvenile for murder was interpreted as punitive rather than preventative, this would also be capable of breaching Article 3.

In *T and V* v *UK* (1999) 30 EHRR 121 it was argued that the automatic detention of two 10-year-olds at Her Majesty's pleasure, following their convictions for murder, was in breach of Article 3 because the tariff element of the sentence necessarily involved a punitive element. The Court said (at para. 98):

... states have a duty under the Convention to take measures for the protection of the public from violent crime. It does not consider that the punitive element inherent in the tariff approach itself gives rise to a breach of Article 3, or that the Convention prohibits states from subjecting a child or young person convicted of a serious crime to an indeterminate sentence allowing for the offender's continued detention or recall to detention following release where necessary for the protection of the public.

---

[10] In most European countries the age is between 13 and 16. A Committee on the Rights of the Child report on the United Kingdom in 1995 recommended that the UK give serious concern to raising the age of criminal responsibility.

[11] Article 37(b) provides that 'no child shall be deprived of his or her liberty unlawfully or arbitrarily. The arrest, detention or imprisonment of a child shall be in conformity with the law and shall be used only as a measure of last resort and for the shortest appropriate period of time.'

[12] United Nations Standard Minimum Rules for the Administration of Juvenile Justice, Rule 17(1).

[13] Rule 17(1)(d), Beijing Rules specifically provides that 'the well-being of the juvenile shall be the guiding factor in the consideration of her or his case'.

[14] Section 37, Crime and Disorder Act 1998.

[15] Section 44, Children and Young Persons Act 1933.

The ruling was by a majority, and no fewer than seven judges were of the view that the sentencing process had breached Article 3. The dissenting judges[16] were particularly concerned about the indeterminacy of the sentence, questioning whether it was ever acceptable in the case of an 11-year-old child. In the light of the 'living instrument' principle, and a tendency among contracting parties to raise the age of criminal responsibility, the sentencing of children in England is likely to be the subject of future review.

18.3.2   Mentally disordered offenders

The existence of mental illness or handicap does not in itself mean that there are no grounds for the sentence to contain a punitive element. Where, however, there is an acceptance by a court that a treatment, rather than punishment model is appropriate, it may be a breach of Article 3 to pass a sentence which contains an element of punishment (for example, life imprisonment). This is of some relevance to the passing of automatic life sentences upon the mentally ill.[17]

Under s. 109, Powers of Criminal Courts (Sentencing) Act (PCC(S)A) 2000, an offender will automatically receive a life sentence for a second serious offence unless the court is satisfied that there are 'exceptional circumstances relating to either of the offences or to the offender which justify its not doing so' (s. 109(2)).

Section 109, PCC(S)A 2000 replaced s. 2(2), Crime (Sentences) Act 1997, which had amended s. 37(1), Mental Health Act 1983.[18] The section now reads:

> Where a person is convicted before the court of an offence punishable with imprisonment other than an offence the sentence for which is fixed by law, or falls to be imposed under section 2(2), Crime (Sentences) Act 1997 ... and [the medical requirements are satisfied] ... the court may by order authorise his admission to and detention in such hospital as may be specified in the order or, as the case may be, place him [under guardianship] ...

In *R* v *Newman* [2000] 1 Cr App R 471 the Court of Appeal held that s. 37(1) expressly excluded the making of a hospital order where the defendant fulfilled the conviction requirements of the Crime (Sentences) Act 1997, s. 2(2). It further held that acute mental illness cannot in itself amount to an exceptional circumstance under the Act.

This authority was decided before the case of *R* v *Offen* [2001] 2 All ER 154 (see also 18.4) and it is of dubious weight. In *Offen*, the Court of Appeal said that it was permissible to look to the intention of Parliament when construing the meaning of the words 'exceptional circumstances' — they agreed that Parliament

---

[16] See joint, partly dissenting opinion, of Judges Pastor Ridruejo, Ress, Makarczyk, Tulkens and Butkevych.

[17] See chapter 20 for fuller discussion.

[18] And s. 45A(1)(b), which deals with hospital and limitation directions.

had intended for a life sentence to be the norm in cases where the offender had been convicted of serious offences on two or more occasions, but thought that it could not have been the intention of Parliament to impose a life sentence where the offender presented no ongoing risk to the public. Applying the same purposive construction in cases where the offender is mentally ill, it could be argued that Parliament could not have intended to place partially punitive sentences on mentally disordered offenders, where the sentencing court felt that punishment (as opposed to treatment) would be inappropriate. The transcript of *Newman* does not suggest that these arguments were raised before the Court of Appeal.

Passing a punitive sentence in these circumstances may be in breach of Article 3,[19] and it is submitted that mental illness should be capable of being an exceptional circumstance. It would also be in breach of Article 5(1)(c) (see 20.3) to detain the person in prison. The words 'where sentence falls to be imposed' in section 37(1) can be construed to include 'in the absence of exceptional circumstances'. Thus, where there are exceptional circumstances no sentence would fall to be imposed under the PCC(S)A 2000 and the court would be free to make a hospital order if it saw fit.

18.4 ARTICLE 5

Article 5 provides:

> Everyone has the right to liberty and security of person. No one shall be deprived of his liberty save in the following cases and in accordance with a procedure prescribed by law:
>
> (1) the lawful detention of a person after conviction by a competent court;
>
> . . .
>
> (4) everyone who is deprived of his liberty by arrest or detention shall be entitled to take proceedings by which the lawfulness of his detention shall be decided speedily by a court and his release ordered if the detention is not lawful.

The provisions of Article 5 have been discussed in detail elsewhere in this book (see chapter 11), but have particular application in terms of sentence. Although detention following conviction is lawful, it must be in accordance with a procedure prescribed by law, which means that it must not be arbitrary,[20] in the sense that it must comply with domestic law, with the Convention, and must be clear and predictable.

The European Court has upheld the automatic imposition of fixed penalties and punitive sentences where no specific consideration is given to the circumstances

---

[19] See *Weeks* v *UK* (1987) 10 EHRR 293 at para. 47; *Hussain* v *UK* (1996) 22 EHRR 1; *T and V* v *UK* (1999) 30 EHRR 121.

[20] See *Winterwerp* v *Netherlands*.

of the offender,[21] but this would appear to be confined to cases at the very top and bottom of the scale of offending. The provisions for passing an 'automatic' life sentence under s. 109, PCC(S)A 2000 (formerly s. 2(2), Crime (Sentences) Act 1997) were vulnerable to challenge under Article 5. Under the provisions, a life sentence will follow a second conviction for a serious offence in the absence of 'exceptional circumstances'. A line of authorities from the Court of Appeal interpreted the term restrictively, so that it was permissible for a person to receive a life sentence under s. 2(2) when they presented no ongoing risk to the public.[22] In *R* v *Offen* [2001] 2 All ER 154 it was argued that the imposition of a life sentence in these circumstances would be in breach of Article 5, in that it was arbitrary to pass a sentence which contained a preventive element in respect of an offender who presented no danger to the public.

The Court of Appeal accepted the argument. Giving the judgment of the Court, the Lord Chief Justice said that when construing the phrase 'exceptional circumstances', it was appropriate to look at the context in which the term was created — in this case, the intention of Parliament to protect the public from a person who had committed two serious offences (para. 88). With this in mind, the Court could nevertheless assume that the section was not created to protect the public from a person who did not present any danger. Considering the compatibility of the provision with Article 5, the Lord Chief Justice said:

> Section 2 [Crime (Sentences) Act 1997)] will not contravene Convention rights if courts apply the section so that it does not result in offenders being sentenced to life imprisonment when they do not constitute a significant risk to the public.

The section therefore appears to create a presumption of dangerousness, which can be rebutted in an individual case.

18.4.1   Article 5(4)

Article 5(4) entitles a detained person to judicial scrutiny of the continued lawfulness of the detention (see chapter 11). Where the domestic court imposes a fixed sentence of imprisonment for the purposes of punishment, the supervision required by Article 5(4) is incorporated within that decision.[23] Where the detention is indeterminate, and has a preventative element, Article 5(4) will be engaged at the 'post-tariff' stage. Thus in discretionary or automatic life

---

[21] For example *Wynne* v *UK* (1994) 19 EHRR 333 (mandatory life term for murder); *T and V* v *UK* (1999) 30 EHRR 121 (mandatory detention at Her Majesty's pleasure for the same offence); *Malige* v *France* (1998) 28 EHRR 578 (fixed tariff of penalty points for speeding).

[22] See *R* v *Kelly* [2000] QB 198 for a statement of the authorities prior to *Offen*.

[23] *De Wilde, Ooms and Versyp* v *Belgium* (1971) 1 EHRR 373 at para. 76. See also *Wynne* v *UK* (1994) 19 EHRR 333 at para. 35.

sentences,[24] the prisoner has a right to periodic review of detention once the tariff has been served.[25]

Prior to the European Court's ruling in *T and V v UK* (1999) 30 EHRR 121 it was the practice in England where defendants had received a mandatory life sentence, or detention at Her Majesty's pleasure, for the Home Secretary to determine the appropriate tariff or punitive element to be served. In that case the European Court found a violation of Article 5(4), on the basis that the Home Secretary was not independent of the executive. As a result, the law has been changed to allow the appropriate tariff to be set by the judiciary. A similar challenge to the Home Secretary's power to set the tariff in life sentences is pending at the time of writing.

18.5   ARTICLE 6 AND SENTENCE

As discussed in chapter 14, when looking at whether a trial has been fair, the European Court will look at proceedings as a whole. The 'determination of a criminal charge' under Article 6(1) includes sentence as well as the trial itself.[26]

This does not mean that the Strasbourg bodies are keen to intervene and adjudicate upon the appropriate type or level of sentence imposed.[27] Article 6 does, however, require that some of the procedural safeguards continue to apply at the sentencing stage. In practice, these may be limited: for obvious reasons the presumption of innocence no longer applies. The sentencing court is entitled to take into account evidence which was inadmissible at trial at the sentencing stage, for example, previous convictions.[28] It is permissible for the court to give credit for a plea of guilty,[29] but where the degree of inducement is too great, Article 6 may be engaged.

18.6   ISSUES UNDER ARTICLE 7

The second limb of Article 7(1) prohibits the imposition of a 'heavier penalty ... than the one that was applicable at the time the criminal offence was committed': sentences are therefore within the principle of non-retroactivity. Although Article 7(2) creates an exception for war crimes, the prohibition within Article 7(1) is

---

[24] In *Wynne* v *UK* (1994) 19 EHRR 333 the European Court held that the mandatory life sentence for murder was wholly punitive. The decision may no longer be good law, and should be read in the light of *T and V v UK* (1999) 30 EHRR 121, which reached different conclusions for sentences at Her Majesty's pleasure, and *R* v *Secretary of State, ex parte Pierson* [1997] 3 WLR 492, in which the House of Lords recognised a preventative element in a mandatory life sentence.

[25] The right of review is contained within s. 28, Crime (Sentences) Act 1997.

[26] *X* v *UK* (1972) 2 Digest 766.

[27] *Engel* v *Netherlands* (1976) 1 EHRR 647.

[28] *Albert and le Compte* v *Belgium* (1983) 5 EHRR 533.

[29] *X* v *UK* (1975) 3 DR 10.

absolute if the applicant succeeds in establishing that the measure to which he has been subjected is in fact a penalty.

There is surprisingly little case law on Article 7. It is clear that, like the terms 'criminal charge' and 'civil rights and obligations', 'penalty' must be construed autonomously.[30] The European Court will use domestic classification as a starting point only, and take into account such factors as whether the measure is imposed after a criminal offence, the nature and purpose of the measure, and the procedure involved in its creation and implementation. Severity will be relevant but not determinative.[31]

In *Welch* v *UK* (1995) 20 EHRR 247, a confiscation order was made under the provisions of the Drug Trafficking Offences Act 1986,[32] which had not been in force at the time the applicant committed the offences. The European Court held that the confiscation amounted to a penalty, rejecting an argument by the Government that the measure was preventative rather than punitive. As the measure had retroactive effect, Article 7(1) had been breached.

Other domestic provisions are capable of retroactive application,[33] and it is difficult to predict whether the European Court would consider them to be penalties for the purposes of Article 7. A distinction has been drawn, which has been seized upon by our domestic courts, between provisions which are preventative and those which are punitive. In *Ibbotson* v *UK* [1999] Crim LR 153, the Commission declared inadmissible a complaint that the requirement of notification under the Sex Offenders Act 1997 amounted to a retroactive penalty to which he could not have been subject at the time of the offence. The Commission was satisfied that the provisions were preventative only.[34] The position was also considered in the case of *In re B* (4 April 2000) by the Court of Appeal. Similar reasoning has been used domestically in the classification of proceedings as civil or criminal.

The principle of non-retroactivity has been considered on a number of occasions in the domestic courts. In *R* v *Secretary of State, ex parte Pierson* [1997] 3 WLR 492 the House of Lords held that a mandatory lifer's tariff cannot be increased after fixing. In *R* v *Secretary of State for the Home Department, ex parte Francois* [1999] AC 43 the Divisional Court took a narrower view. The applicant was a short-term prisoner who received a sentence for a further offence which had the effect of transforming him into a long-term prisoner. This delayed his eligibility date for release under the first sentence. Giving the judgment of the

---

[30] See *Engel* v *Netherlands* (1976) 1 EHRR 647 at para. 82; *Pierre-Bloch* v *France* (1996) 26 EHRR 202 at para. 53.

[31] *Welch* v *UK* (1995) 20 EHRR 247 at paras 27–32. See also *Malige* v *France* (1998) 28 EHRR 578.

[32] The provisions have now been replaced by the Drug Trafficking Act 1997.

[33] For example, notification requirements under s. 1(3), Sex Offenders Act 1997, banning orders under s. 1, Football Spectators Act 2000.

[34] It may be of relevance to note that s. 1(3) only applied to offenders subject to an order, sentence or licence at the time the 1997 Act came into force.

court, Lord Slynn said that this did not amount to an increase in sentence but a postponement of a period of early release.[35]

A more contentious decision was reached in the case of *R* v *Alden* (15 February 2001). The defendants were convicted of buggery and indecent assault on boys at an approved school, which had occurred many years before the allegations were made. They argued that the sentences applied were in breach of Article 7, as they were higher than the sentencing tariff operating at the time the offences were committed. The Court of Appeal was not persuaded by the argument, and said that any changes to the tariff were irrelevant, as the maximum penalty for the offences had remained the same. The Court apparently quoted the case of *SW and CR* v *UK* (1995) 21 EHRR 363, where the European Court upheld a prosecution for marital rape, on the basis that the common law had developed to a point where the law was sufficiently clear for the applicant to predict the risk of a prosecution for the offence. It is difficult to square the two judgments, and this case is unlikely to be the last word on the subject.

18.7   ARTICLE 4 AND SENTENCE

Article 4(2) of the Convention provides that 'no one shall be required to perform forced or compulsory labour'. Article 4(3)(a) excludes from this definition 'any work required to be done in the ordinary course of detention imposed according to the provisions of Article 5 of this Convention or during conditional release from such detention'. The European Court has interpreted this exception to mean only work which is directed to the rehabilitation of the prisoner.[36]

Prior to the implementation of s. 38, Crime (Sentences) Act 1997, community service and probation orders could not be imposed without the consent of the offender. Section 38 removed the need for consent, unless a probation order contained a condition of psychiatric treatment, or treatment for alcohol or drug dependency.[37] Although it has been argued[38] that such an order would be in breach of Article 4(2), the European Court has adopted a flexible approach to the provisions, stressing that the notion of compulsory labour is changeable, and should be interpreted 'in the light of the notions currently prevailing in democratic states'.[39] In practice, it is unlikely that the provisions violate the Convention in

---

[35] The approach of the Court of Appeal in *R* v *Parker* (2000) Archbold News Issue 4, 9 May is more generous. The Court of Appeal held that where imposing a sentence on a serving prisoner who will become a long-term prisoner as a result, the sentencer may make a reduction in the further sentence to avoid an unduly long time served.

[36] *De Wilde, Ooms and Versyp* v *Belgium* (1971) 1 EHRR 373.

[37] Powers of Criminal Courts Act 1973, sch. 1A, para. 6(4)(b). Similar provisions apply to young people who are over 14 when the court imposes psychiatric conditions on a supervision order: s. 12B(2)(b), Children and Young Persons Act 1933.

[38] See David Thomas on the subject.

[39] *Van der Mussele* v *Belgium* (1983) 6 EHRR 163. See also Starmer, K., *European Human Rights Law* (London: LAG, 1999), chapter 28.

circumstances where the order imposed is a realistic alternative to a sentence of custody, and can be seen to have a rehabilitative aim.

18.8   ARTICLE 14 AND SENTENCE

Article 14 of the Convention prohibits discrimination 'on any ground such as sex, race, colour, language, religion, political or other opinion, national or social origin, association with a national minority, property, birth or other status'. The right is not free-standing and can only be used in tandem with another Convention right. This does not mean that there must be a breach of that other Convention right before a breach under Article 14 can be found.[40]

In the area of sentence, the conjunctive Convention right is most likely to be Article 5(1)(a). In *Nelson* v *UK* (1986) 49 DR 170 the Commission said 'where a settled sentencing policy appears to affect individuals in a discriminatory fashion ... this may raise issues under Article 5 read in conjunction with Article 14'.

The clearest scope for arguing a breach in domestic law relates to pre-trial remands into custody of young people. Under s. 23(5), Children and Young Persons Act 1969[41] it is permissible to remand 14-year-old boys to local authority accommodation, but not girls of the same age. Under the Convention there is a strong argument that these provisions are discriminatory, and any attempt to remand a 14-year-old boy in these circumstances will be subject to challenge under Articles 5(1)(c) and 14.

Other arguments about discrimination may arise at the sentencing stage. It is possible to envisage a situation where, by reason of an offender's sex, religion, or problems with English, he or she is denied access to a non-custodial alternative or treatment programme which would otherwise be available. Lawyers should be alert to Article 14 issues in circumstances where a defendant may be placed higher up the sentencing tariff because of unavailability of appropriate resources.

---

[40] See *Belgian Linguistic Case (No. 2)* (1968) 1 EHRR 252 at para. 9.
[41] Read in conjunction with the Secure Remands and Committals (Prescribed Description of Children and Young Persons) Order 1999 (SI 1999/1265).

Chapter Nineteen

Appeals

Michelle Strange

19.1 INTRODUCTION

Article 6 does not guarantee a right of appeal against either conviction or sentence. Article 2 of Protocol 7 provides:

> 1. Everyone convicted of a criminal offence by a tribunal shall have the right to have his conviction or sentence reviewed by a higher tribunal. The exercise of this right, including the grounds on which it may be exercised, shall be governed by law.
> 2. This right may be subject to exceptions in regard to offences of a minor character, as prescribed by law, or in cases in which the person concerned was tried in the first instance by the highest tribunal or was convicted following an appeal against conviction.

Protocol 7 has not been incorporated within the Human Rights Act 1998, but in the White Paper *Rights Brought Home*[1] the Government indicated its intention to ratify and incorporate Protocol 7, and stated (at para. 4.15) that the provisions of Protocol 7 'reflect principles already inherent in our law'.

In practice, the incorporation of Protocol 7 would have a limited effect on domestic law, as domestic law provides a comprehensive appeal system, and the European Court has stated that where a right of appeal is provided, the trial process is extended and Article 6 continues to apply. In *Delcourt* v *Belgium* (1969) 1 EHRR 355[2] the Court said:

---

[1] (1997) Cm. 3782.
[2] See also *Tolstoy Miloslavsky* v *UK* (1995) 20 EHRR 442.

a criminal charge is not really 'determined' as long as the verdict of acquittal or conviction has not become final. Criminal proceedings form an entity and must, in the ordinary way, terminate in an enforceable decision . . . the Convention does not, it is true, compel the Contracting States to set up courts of appeal or of cassation. Nevertheless, a State which does institute such courts is required to ensure that persons amenable to the law shall enjoy before these courts the fundamental guarantees in Article 6.

In keeping with the European Court's general approach to Article 6, it will look at the entirety of the proceedings, including the role of the appellate courts, when determining if the defendant has had a fair trial.[3] It is clear from the authorities that not all Article 6 rights can be read into the appeal stage. The special features of the appeal procedure, and the non-applicability of the presumption of innocence may mean that evidence and legal argument is presented in a different manner from that used at trial.

Accordingly, some Article 6 guarantees, such as the right of the defendant to be present and participate, are considered less important by the European Court at the appeal stage. Where there has been an unfair trial, however, the European Court is unsympathetic to the argument that the defect can be cured on appeal.[4]

19.2   LIMITS ON THE RIGHT TO APPEAL

Although reasonable time limits can be applied to appeal proceedings,[5] the state bears the responsibility of keeping the applicant informed about what these are. In *Vacher* v *France* (1996) 24 EHRR 482 the applicant was not informed of a time limit for filing his notice of appeal, and was not told of the date of the hearing. The European Court held that as Article 6(3) continued to apply at the appeal stage, the onus was on the state, and not the convicted appellant, to ensure that he learned the information. The state should also be mindful of delay in hearing the appeal: appeal proceedings form part of the period considered under Article 5(3) when the court determines whether time spent in custody amounts to a reasonable time.[6]

In *Omar* v *France* (1998) 29 EHRR 210 the European Court held that a condition that an appellant must first surrender to custody to be entitled to pursue an appeal was in breach of Article 6, saying 'while restrictions on an appeal are legitimate, they must not be disproportionate nor must they destroy the essence of the right in question'. In *Krombach* v *France* (13 February 2001) the Court held that, where the accused absconds, he will not be taken to have waived rights to appeal in the absence of a clear withdrawal of instructions: the lawyers may continue an appeal in his absence (see *R* v *Jones* 55 Cr App R 321).

---

[3] *Ekbatani* v *Sweden* (1988) 13 EHRR 504 at para. 26.
[4] See for example, *Condron* v *UK*, below at 19.8.2.
[5] *Bricmont* v *Belgium* (1986) 48 DR 106.
[6] *B* v *Austria* (1990) 13 EHRR 20.

Where the offence is minor, the imposition of an automatic sentence is unlikely to offend the Convention. In *Malige* v *France* (1998) 28 EHRR 578 the applicant challenged penalties under domestic provisions which automatically deducted points from his driving licence on commission of speeding offences. The applicant claimed that Article 6(1) was violated by the failure of the domestic system to provide any avenue of appeal against the penalty.[7] The European Court held that, because the driver is informed about the penalty in the event of a conviction, he is at the time of notification of the charge given the opportunity to contest the basis for the later deduction of points (para. 47).

19.3 LEGAL AID

Provision of legal aid has been discussed in detail elsewhere in this book (see chapter 12), but has particular relevance at the appeal stage. Where there is a genuine issue to be determined on appeal, or where the appellant has received a substantial term of custody, it appears from the case law that Article 6(3)(c) requires the appellant to be provided with representation in the interests of justice.

Although the leave to appeal stage is part of the whole trial process, and falls within the ambit of Article 6, this does not mean that legal representation should automatically be provided to an appellant who wishes to continue with an appeal against the advice of his trial lawyers.[8] The process of granting legal aid for representation should nonetheless be reviewed by the courts.

In *Granger* v *UK* (1990) 12 EHRR 469 the applicant was convicted of perjury and sentenced to five years' imprisonment. His trial counsel, who had been provided under the legal aid scheme, advised against an appeal, but the applicant's solicitor believed that there were valid grounds. The solicitor had assisted in preparing statements for the applicant to read at the appeal hearing. The relevant legal aid committee refused legal aid on the basis that it was not satisfied that there were substantial grounds for appealing. The European Court refused to substitute its own decision for that of the committee, but held that in the circumstances of the case the interests of justice required that legal aid should have been granted. The European Court said that the consideration of what was in the interests of justice included looking at the case as a whole, particularly where the applicant's liberty was at stake. As the applicant had not been able to present his case fully or deal with complex legal arguments, the European Court thought that the Court of Appeal should have reconsidered whether legal aid should be granted.[9]

---

[7] The applicant did have a right to deny that he had committed the speeding offence: see para. 48 of the judgment.

[8] *Monnell and Morris* v *UK* (1987) 10 EHRR 205.

[9] Similar reasoning was applied in the Scottish case of *Bullock* v *Her Majesty's Advocate* 1999 JC 260.

In *Maxwell* v *UK* (1994) 19 EHRR 97, the European Court stressed that legal aid should be provided even in relatively straightforward cases where the consequences might be grave for the appellant. The important issue was whether the appellant was in fact capable of representing himself effectively. Similar reasoning was used in *Twalib* v *Greece* [1998] HRCD 632, where an appellant was a foreign national who spoke little Greek, and so had little chance of presenting his case on appeal. The European Court has also held[10] that even when an appellant has been given notice but fails to appear, he or she is entitled to be represented by a lawyer in appeal proceedings.

19.4   THE RIGHT TO ORAL ARGUMENT AND A PUBLIC HEARING AT THE APPEAL STAGE

As the appeal stage forms part of the trial process, the convicted appellant has in principle a right to attend a public hearing.[11] In practice, the right is subject to qualification at the appeal stage, and the European Court has been slow to find breaches of Article 6 when applicants have not been present on appeal, unless their presence might have influenced the outcome of the case. The position was most recently stated in *Prinz* v *Austria* (8 February 2000), where the applicant had been detained in a mental hospital following trial, and was not present at the appeal. The European Court said (at para. 34):[12]

> ... a person charged with a criminal offence should, as a general principle based on the notion of a fair trial, be entitled to be present at the first-instance hearing. However, the personal attendance of the defendant does not necessarily take on the same significance for an appeal hearing ... even where an appellate court has full jurisdiction to review the case on questions both of fact and law, Article 6 does not always entail rights to a public hearing and to be present in person. Regard must be had in assessing this question to, *inter alia*, the special features of the proceedings involved and that manner in which the defence's interest are presented and protected before the appellate court, particularly in the light of the issues to be decided by it and their importance for the applicant.

Where the appeal court is simply reviewing findings of fact below, and no new evidence is adduced nor is there a prospect of the sentence being increased, the European Court has held that there is no duty on the authorities to secure the appellant's presence at the hearing, particularly when he or she is represented.[13]

Where there is a question of fact to be determined by the appeal court, however, the appellant should generally be present. In *Ektabani* v *Sweden* (1988) 13 EHRR

---

[10] *Geysegham* v *Belgium* [1999] EHRLR 337.
[11] See for example, *Werner* v *Austria* (1998) 26 EHRR 310.
[12] See also *Belziuk* v *Poland* (1998) 30 EHRR 614.
[13] *Prinz* v *Austria*, at para. 44. See also *Axen* v *Germany* (1983) 6 EHRR 195.

504 the appeal court had to assess the appellant's credibility where the main ground of appeal was that he had not committed the act of which he had been convicted. The European Court found that in the circumstances the applicant had a right to be present. The European Court used similar reasoning in *Cooke* v *Austria* (8 February 2000, merits), in which the applicant had been convicted of murder and given a sentence of 20 years. Part of the appeal proceedings involved an argument by the prosecution that the sentence should be increased to life, but the applicant was not present. The European Court held that, since the sentence could be increased, and the determination of that issue involved reassessment of his mental state at the time of the killing, his presence and participation at the hearing was essential (para. 42).[14] The fact that he was represented by a lawyer did not cure a breach of Article 6 (para. 42).

Where the appellate court has a power to substitute a conviction with an offence other than that with which the appellant was charged at trial, the appellant must be given an opportunity to deal with the alternative charge. In *Pélissier* v *France* (1999) 30 EHRR 715 the court of appeal substituted a conviction for the principal offence with aiding and abetting. The European Court held that the failure to give the applicant an opportunity to deal with what was effectively a new allegation was a breach of Article 6.

In the light of the above, there is limited scope for challenge to domestic law. The appellant has a right to be present when issues of fact are to be decided,[15] and the Court of Appeal may only increase sentence on an Attorney-General's reference. The defendant has a right to be present, and if necessary produced from custody at any substantive hearing where sentence may be increased.[16] The Court of Appeal may only substitute a conviction where the jury could, on the indictment, have found the appellant guilty of the alternative charge[17] at trial.

19.5   A PUBLIC HEARING

There are similar qualifications upon the right for a hearing to be heard in public. In *Axen* v *Germany* (1983) 6 EHRR 195 the first instance trial had been held in public, but the appeal hearing, which considered only points of law, was not. The European Court held that it was unnecessary for the hearing to take place in public, and that handing down a written copy of the judgment would suffice.

---

[14] The decision has implications for s. 23(2), Criminal Appeals Act 1968, which provides that a person in custody may not be present without leave of the court when he or she is in custody because of a verdict of not guilty by reason of insanity or a finding of disability.
[15] Criminal Appeals Act 1968, s. 23(2).
[16] Criminal Justice Act 1988, sch. 3, para. 6.
[17] Criminal Appeals Act 1968, s. 3.

19.6   REASONS AT THE APPEAL STAGE

It appears that the unsuccessful appellant has a limited right to a reasoned judgment at the appeal stage. In *Webb* v *UK* (1997) 24 EHRR CD 73 the Commission found that a failure of the Privy Council to give reasons for refusing leave to appeal against conviction did not violate Article 6. Appeals to the Privy Council can only be brought when there is a point of general importance, or a grave injustice, and the Commission thought refusal of leave could only mean that the applicant had failed to satisfy the court that he or she came within that test.

Following the decision in *Condron* v *UK* (2000) 8 BHRC 290[18] it can be argued that the Court of Appeal should be providing full reasons in any appeal against conviction.[19] The judgment compels the Court of Appeal to examine the fairness of the proceedings, rather than resort to an impressionistic judgment on guilt or innocence. It is submitted that any decision of the Court of Appeal without any reasons might be subject to further challenge (see *R* v *Crown Court sitting in Inner London, ex parte London Borough of Lambeth* (7 December 1999); cf. *R* v *Doubtfire* (2000) *The Times*, 28 December).

19.7   NEW EVIDENCE AND REFERENCES BACK TO THE COURT OF APPEAL

The European Court has not dealt with the question of new evidence which emerges post-conviction. In an early case[20] the Commission took a robust line, saying:

> ... Article 6 does not apply to proceedings for reopening a trial given that someone who applies for his case to be reopened and whose sentence has become final, is not someone 'charged with a criminal offence' within the meaning of the said article.

Applying similar reasoning in the civil context, the Commission declined to read a right to a rehearing into Article 6 where it emerged after the end of the trial that there was doubt about the impartiality of an expert witness.[21] It is not clear whether this reasoning would hold if similar doubts were voiced about criminal proceedings, at a stage where the defendant was still serving a sentence of imprisonment. Such a sentence would fall within Article 5(1)(a), and it could be argued that if grounds existed to show that the conviction was not by 'a competent court', a right of review might follow under Article 5(4).

Where a procedure is provided for referring the case back to an appeal court, Article 6 does apply.[22] This does not mean that, where there is fresh evidence, a

---

[18] For full discussion on the case, and its effect on the 'safety' test on appeal, see below at 19.8.2.
[19] There is domestic authority that full reasons should still be given at an appeal hearing in the Crown Court: *R* v *Canterbury Crown Court, ex parte Howson-Ball* (9 November 2000).
[20] *X* v *Austria* (1962) 9 EHRR CD 17.
[21] *X* v *Austria* (1978) 14 DR 171.
[22] For example, by the Criminal Cases Review Commission.

retrial before a jury should inevitably follow, and failure to order a new trial may only be a breach of Article 6 if the appellate court declines to hear new evidence. In *Callaghan* v *UK* (1989) 60 DR 296 the Commission was satisfied by the Court of Appeal hearing fresh evidence and submissions by counsel, and then going on to determine if the convictions were safe and satisfactory.

19.8 CHALLENGES TO DOMESTIC LAW AND PROCEDURE

English law and practice has been challenged in the area of hearings for leave to appeal and loss of time directions, and in the application of the 'safety test' used by the Court of Appeal when considering appeal against conviction.

19.8.1 Proceedings for leave to appeal

Under English law, the appellant has no right to be present at an application for leave to appeal,[23] and a power exists to order that the time served to the date of the leave application can be discounted in calculating the period to be served in the sentence.[24]

The procedure was considered by the European Court in *Monnell and Morris* v *UK* (1987) 10 EHRR 205 where the applicants complained that they had not been present at the hearing for the application for leave to appeal. The European Court found no violation of Article 6, although the leave hearing may involve mixed issues of fact and law, because it does not involve rehearing the case on the facts, or the hearing of live witnesses. The issue to be determined at the leave stage is whether arguable grounds exist for an appeal, and in the European Court's judgment Article 6 did not require oral argument at a public hearing or the personal appearance of the applicants.

In *Monnell and Morris* the Court of Appeal had made a 'loss of time' direction, but the European Court remained unpersuaded that there should have been oral argument. Whilst recognising that the 'loss of time' direction meant a further period in custody, and therefore fell within Article 5(1)(a), the European Court was impressed by the fact that it was imposed for the policy reason of deterring unmeritorious appeals. At the leave stage the prosecution did not appear, and the applicants' interests were sufficiently safeguarded by receipt of legal advice of their prospects of appeal, and the opportunity of making legal submissions.

The Court of Appeal has on a number of occasions stated that the fact that grounds of appeal were drafted by counsel should not prevent the court ordering loss of time where an application for leave is renewed to the full court following refusal by the single judge. There are no reported cases of loss of time being ordered in these circumstances. It should be noted that *Monnell and Morris*

---

[23] Criminal Appeals Act 1968, s. 23(2).
[24] Criminal Appeals Act 1968, s. 29(1); *Practice Direction (Crime: Sentence: Loss of Time)* [1980] 1 WLR 250, following *Practice Direction* (1970) 54 Cr App R 280.

concerned an application for leave when counsel had advised against pursuing an appeal. Where counsel has advised in favour of an appeal, a loss of time direction would probably be in breach of the Convention. It is difficult to see how holding the appellant responsible for shortcomings in his or her lawyer's advice is either compatible with the right to effective representation under Article 6(3)(c), or with the power being exercised giving 'appropriate weight'[25] to a lawyer's advice. It may be that a more appropriate course in such a case would be for the Court to take up the matter with counsel.

19.8.2   The 'safety' test

Under section 2 of the Criminal Appeals Act 1968, as amended, the Court of Appeal must allow an appeal against conviction if it thinks the conviction is 'unsafe'. The section, as originally worded[26] provided that the court should allow an appeal if the conviction was unsafe or unsatisfactory, based on a decision which was wrong in law, or where there had been a material irregularity in the course of the trial.

The narrowing of the test is significant, and gives rise to issues under Article 6. The omission of the word 'unsatisfactory', and the ground of material irregularity suggested at the outset that the new test did not permit the quashing of a conviction where there had been procedural irregularities in an otherwise strong case. In *R* v *Chalkley and Jeffries* [1998] 2 Cr App R 79 the Court of Appeal held that a conviction should not be quashed merely because of procedural irregularity, abuse of process or a failure of justice being seen to be done. In other words, the Court of Appeal accepted that its role included an evaluation of all the material in the case to determine whether the conviction was in fact a safe one, whatever the shortcomings of the trial at first instance.

The case was at odds with another Court of Appeal decision in the case of *R* v *Mullen* [1999] 2 Cr App R 143. In that case a conviction was quashed because an application to stay proceedings should have been allowed, on the basis that it was impossible for the defendant to have had a fair trial. In the event there was no suggestion that the trial had in fact been unfair, or any grounds for doubting the defendant's guilt.

For some time it appeared that the reasoning in *Chalkley and Jeffries* was likely to prevail.[27] This approach to the safety test nevertheless sat uncomfortably with the provisions of Article 6, as it required the Court of Appeal to ignore defects in the trial process by making a judgment about the appellant's guilt. In *Condron* v *UK* (2000) 8 BHRC 290 the European Court considered the relationship between this test and the right to a fair trial under Article 6. The applicants were drug

---

[25] *Condron* v *UK*, above.

[26] Prior to amendment by the Criminal Appeals Act 1995.

[27] See for example, Archbold (2000), para. 7-46a, in which it is suggested that *Mullen* was wrongly decided.

addicts, who had been advised by their lawyer to remain silent in interview because he thought they were incapable of providing coherent answers, as they were withdrawing from heroin. The trial judge permitted the jury to draw such inference as they thought fit from the silence, and the applicants were convicted. The Court of Appeal ([1997] 1 Cr App R 135) adopted a robust approach, considering that inadequate judicial directions had no effect on the safety of the conviction where there was 'substantial, almost overwhelming evidence of drug supply'. The European Court disagreed with this approach, saying (at paras 65 and 66):

> ... the Court of Appeal was concerned with the safety of the applicants' conviction, not whether they had in the circumstances received a fair trial. In the Court's opinion, the question whether or not the rights of the defence guaranteed to an accused under Article 6 of the Convention were secured in any given case cannot be assimilated to a finding that his conviction was safe in the absence of any enquiry into the issue of fairness.
> ... it was the function of the jury, properly directed, to decide whether or not to draw an adverse inference from the applicants' silence ... the jury was not properly directed and the imperfection in the direction could not be remedied on appeal. Any other conclusion would be at variance with the fundamental importance of the right to silence, a right which, as observed earlier, lies at the heart of the notion of a fair procedure guaranteed by Article 6. On that account the Court concludes that the applicants did not receive a fair hearing within the meaning of Article 6 § 1 of the Convention.

The European Court specifically distinguished between cases where the Court of Appeal has reviewed the fairness of the trial below, and where there can be an objective assessment of the impact of the irregularity on the jury's verdict. This is in keeping with the judgment in *Khan* v *UK* (12 May 2000)[28] where the European Court raised no criticism of the appeal procedures in the Court of Appeal and House of Lords, because review of the trial judge's decision not to exclude the evidence under section 78 necessarily involved consideration of the fairness of proceedings (at paras 37–40). In practice, the distinction is hard to draw, and recent authorities of the Court of Appeal have shown a much less robust approach to the safety test.[29] In *R* v *Davis, Rowe and Johnson* (2000) *The Times*, 24 April (a reference back to the Court of Appeal) the European Court had already held that there had been a breach of Article 6.[30] The European Court had made similar observations that the appeal hearing was insufficient to remedy the breaches at the trial stage (*Rowe and Davis* v *UK* (2000) 30 EHRR 1 at para. 65).

In the second appeal hearing, the Court of Appeal reverted to the *Mullen* approach, saying:

---

[28] See also *Edwards* v *UK* (1992) 15 EHRR 417.

[29] See for example, *R* v *Vasilou* (2000) Archbold News Issue 4, p. 1, where the defence had not been told about the previous convictions of a key witness, and may have decided, had they known, to attack his credibility. The case was decided before *Davis, Rowe and Johnson*.

[30] *Rowe and Davis* v *UK* (2000) 30 EHRR 1.

A conviction can never be safe if there is a doubt about guilt. However, the converse is not true. A conviction may be unsafe even where there is no doubt about guilt but the trial process had been 'vitiated by serious unfairness or significant legal misdirection ...'

The Court of Appeal allowed the appeal in spite of the strength of the evidence against the appellants (in *Rowe*'s case, it was described as 'formidable'). Although the European Court stopped short of equating breaches of Article 6 with an unsafe conviction, the gap between the right to a fair trial procedure and the right to have an unsafe conviction quashed has closed considerably. Unless the Court of Appeal is able to determine the impact of a breach objectively without speculating as to the jury's reasoning, or to the effect it would have had on the conduct of the trial, it is likely that a conviction obtained in breach of Article 6 will be unsafe, whatever the quantity or strength of the evidence.

There is some evidence that the Court of Appeal is moving back from this position. In *R* v *Craven* (8 December 2000) the Court found several irregularities in the course of the trial, but found that the conviction was safe in the light of new DNA evidence from which they inferred guilt. Arguably, the Court of Appeal usurped the function of a jury, and it is difficult to square the authority with the European Court's judgment in *Condron*. See also *R* v *Williams* (2001) *The Times*, 30 March, where the Court of Appeal reasoned that where there was a material misdirection as to the ingredients of an offence charged, a conviction may arguably not have been obtained 'according to law' within Article 6(2). Nonetheless, it did not automatically follow that the conviction was 'unsafe'.

Chapter Twenty

Mental Health and Crime
Michelle Strange

20.1 INTRODUCTION

There are several areas in which Convention law may provide additional rights to the mentally ill defendant in criminal proceedings. This chapter will focus upon the following issues:

- the detention of people who are mentally ill under Article 5 (the right to liberty);
- specific issues arising under Article 6 (the right to a fair trial);
- conditions of detention and treatment under Article 3 (prohibition on inhuman and degrading treatment);
- confidentiality and compulsory treatment and Article 8 (the protection of private life).

Much of the Convention jurisprudence relates to the detention of mentally ill people under civil provisions, and has limited relevance to the criminal defendant at the pre-trial stage. Although in many instances domestic law provides greater safeguards for the mentally ill, there remains scope for challenge to several areas of domestic law and practice, most notably at the post-trial stage. Areas of domestic law which may need to be changed to comply with the Convention are discussed below.

20.2 DETENTION UNDER ARTICLE 5

The Convention contains only one specific reference to mental health within the text of Article 5(1)(e). This creates a specific exception to the right to liberty by providing for:

the lawful detention of persons for the prevention of the spreading of infectious diseases, of persons of unsound mind, alcoholics or drug addicts and vagrants.

The provision is designed to stand alone, and will generally cover the detention of mentally ill persons under domestic civil provisions. In criminal cases, the mentally ill defendant may be detained as a result of bail being withdrawn at the pre-trial stage, or as a result of a sentence of imprisonment.[1] Article 5(1)(e) will, however, apply in criminal cases, either in substitution for or in addition to other parts of Article 5(1), in the following situations:

- where a defendant is remanded to a psychiatric wing of a prison or to a hospital before or during trial;
- where a defendant has been found guilty or to have committed the acts alleged but to be absolved of responsibility and the question arises of whether a punitive sentence or treatment should follow;
- where a defendant is transferred to a psychiatric hospital from a prison in the course of a sentence of imprisonment;
- in all of the above situations, on review of the question of whether release should be ordered.

It is clear from the text of Article 5(1)(e) that three pre-conditions must be met in order to justify detention under this head: the state must establish (a) that the person is 'of unsound mind'; (b) that the detention is in accordance with procedure prescribed by law; and (c) that he or she is detained on a lawful basis. Each of these concepts has been considered by the European Court, and will be considered below.

20.2.1 'Unsound mind'

Although the European Court has stressed that the concept of 'unsound mind' does not extend to an individual whose 'views or behaviour deviate from norms prevailing in a particular society',[2] it has resisted any attempt to define the term further. In the landmark case of *Winterwerp v Netherlands* (1979) 2 EHRR 387 the Court explained:

> this term is not one that can be given a definitive interpretation … it is a term whose meaning is continually evolving as research in psychiatry progresses, an increasing flexibility in treatment is developing and society's attitude to mental illness changes, in particular so that a greater understanding of the problem of mental patients is becoming more widespread.

---

[1] In these cases, Article 5(1)(c) (detention for trial) and 5(1)(a) (detention for sentence) will be relevant.

[2] *Winterwerp v Netherlands* (1979) 2 EHRR 387 at para. 37.

The European Court's reluctance is understandable. There are few areas in which the 'living instrument' principle is likely to have greater application,[3] and where contracting states will be given a greater margin of discretion in interpreting the term. To date, there have been no successful applications to Strasbourg challenging the existence of a mental illness.

20.2.2 'Prescribed by law'

There is a general requirement that persons detained under Article 5 should be detained 'in accordance with a procedure prescribed by law', and the principles adopted by the European Court in interpreting this phrase have been discussed in detail in chapter 11 and are relevant under this head. The phrase has been interpreted to mean that any domestic procedure should be strictly followed. In *Winterwerp* v *Netherlands* (para. 45) the Court said that the authorities should follow:

> a fair and proper procedure, namely that any measure depriving a person of his liberty should issue from and be executed by an appropriate authority and should not be arbitrary.

In *Winterwerp* itself the European Court was nevertheless more concerned with substantive than procedural irregularity. In *Van der Leer* v *Netherlands* (1990) 12 EHRR 567 a stricter approach was taken where the domestic court had ordered detention in the absence of a psychiatric report or any hearing at which the applicant was present. The European Court said that both Article 5(1)(e) and *Winterwerp* required conformity with both substantive and procedural law.

20.2.3 'Detained on a lawful basis'

Article 5(1)(e) also states in terms that the detention should be 'lawful'. In *Winterwerp*, the European Court set out the minimum criteria for detention under Article 5(1)(e):

(a) a true mental disorder must be found before a competent authority on the basis of objective medical expertise;
(b) the disorder must be of a kind or degree warranting compulsory detention;
(c) the validity of the confinement depends upon the persistence of the disorder.

In *Ashingdane* v *UK* (1985) 7 EHRR 528[4] the European Court added that the detention must be in a hospital, clinic or other appropriate institution.

---

[3] See for example, *X* v *Germany* (1976) 19 Yearbook 276 where the Commission did not criticise a decision of German authorities to admit a man for compulsory treatment on the ground that he was homosexual — a ruling which would be inconceivable today.
[4] For a recent application of the principle, see *Aerts* v *Belgium* (1998) 29 EHRR 50.

20.2.3.1   *A true mental disorder before a competent authority*
It is unclear what sort of 'objective medical expertise' is needed,[5] although the
term implies some specialisation in matters of mental health. Notes of the medical
expert will be deemed to be objective unless the applicant can prove otherwise.[6]
The assessment should where possible be current rather than based on past
events,[7] and there is in principle a need to have the defendant examined
personally, although it may be lawful to delay an examination until after
admission where there is an emergency. In *X* v *UK* (1981) 4 EHRR 188 the recall
of a restricted patient was found to be lawful when there had been no examination
of the applicant; the European Court held that the emergency admission was
justified in the absence of the usual guarantees of Article 5(1)(e) because of the
risk to the applicant's wife and to the public.

20.2.3.2   *Detention in a hospital, clinic or other appropriate institution*
In *Ashingdane* v *UK* (1985) 7 EHRR 528 the European Court held that for
detention to be lawful under Article 5(1)(e) it should take place in an appropriate
therapeutic setting. The issue was revisited by the European Court in *Aerts* v
Belgium (1998) 29 EHRR 50, where the applicant was charged with an assault on
his ex-wife. He was found to have committed the acts alleged, but not to have been
criminally responsible by reason of his mental illness. The national court ordered
that he be detained in the psychiatric wing of a prison pending a decision by the
Mental Health Board to transfer him to a psychiatric institution. The decision was
duly taken, but no bed was available in that facility, and he remained on the
psychiatric wing for some seven months. The conditions in that wing were poor
(see 20.7) and conceded by all not to be therapeutic. The European Court found
that there had been no 'conviction' and that only Article 5(1)(e) applied (para. 45).
The failure to transfer him for treatment therefore rendered his detention unlawful
as it was not in a hospital, clinic or other appropriate institution.[8]

The decision is significant in this country, where it is common for defendants
to remain in prison in the absence of a suitable hospital bed,[9] and where a prison
sentence may be justified under s. 37(4) of the Mental Health Act 1983 on the sole
ground that no bed is available (see 20.5.1 below).

---

[5] In *Schuurs* v *Netherlands* (1985) 41 DR 186 a friendly settlement was reached where complaint was
made of a certificate of detention which had been issued by a general practitioner. Domestically, a
practitioner approved under s. 12(2), Mental Health Act 1983 would no doubt suffice.
[6] *Winterwerp* v *Netherlands* (1979) 2 EHRR 387.
[7] *Varbanov* v *Bulgaria* (5 October 2000).
[8] *Ashingdane* v *UK* (1985) 7 EHRR 528. It remains to be seen whether a prison psychiatric wing in
this country would satisfy the requirement.
[9] Criminal Procedure (Insanity and Unfitness to Plead) Act 1991, s. 5, sch. 1, para. 1(4) which provide
that a hospital order following a finding that the accused has done the acts charged, must be carried
out within two months. Where a hospital order is sought to be made after plea or conviction there
is no bar to repeated adjournments until a bed is available.

20.2.3.3   *Of a kind and degree warranting compulsory detention*

Not all mental illness warrants detention, and not all mental illness is capable of improvement through treatment. The European Court has avoided questions as to the suitability of treatment[10] and has adopted a generous approach to the detaining authorities where issues of public safety are involved. Public safety may be taken into account in deciding whether the mental disorder warrants detention. In the case of *Guzzardi* v *Italy* (1980) 3 EHRR 333 the European Court said:[11]

> The reason why the Convention allows [persons of unsound mind, alcoholics and drug addicts], all of whom are socially maladjusted, to be deprived of their liberty is not only that they have to be considered as occasionally dangerous for pubic safety but also that their own interests necessitate detention.[12]

Continued detention on these grounds is unlikely to offend Article 5 unless it is arbitrary or unreasonable.[13] Thus, the fact that a treatment may give no obvious benefit to the particular offender may not offend the Convention, and the concept of 'unsound mind' has been held to embrace untreatable personality disorders which cannot be said to amount to mental illness.[14]

It is unclear whether detention will be lawful under Article 5(1)(e) when there is no convincing argument that it benefits the detainee. The *Goddi* judgment (*Goddi* v *Italy* (1984) 6 EHRR 457) suggests that the detention must be in the person's 'own interests' to continue. The Scottish courts have nonetheless accepted that there has been some watering down of the principle recently,[15] by the European Court's decision in *Litwa* v *Poland* (4 April 2000). *Litwa* involved another limb of Article 5(1)(e), the detention of 'alcoholics', and the Polish authorities sought to justify detention for six hours under that limb on the basis that the applicant had been drunk and offensive, and needed to sober up.[16] There was no suggestion that he was an 'alcoholic', but the European Court said:

---

[10] See below at 20.7 on Article 3.

[11] At para. 98. The applicant, who was connected with the Mafia, succeeded because the authorities had failed to demonstrate that he was a 'vagrant' under Article 5(1)(e). There was no suggestion that he was mentally ill.

[12] See also *E* v *Norway* (1990) 17 EHRR 29, where similar assumptions were made. But see also *Roux* v *UK* [1997] EHRLR 102.

[13] Domestic law is in theory more protective of the defendant. Under s. 37, Mental Health Act 1983, hospital orders may be made only on the condition that the defendant needs to be detained in hospital for treatment which is likely to alleviate or prevent a deterioration of his condition. In practice, however, the term has been widely interpreted: see *R* v *Canons Park MHRT, ex parte A* [1994] 2 All ER 659; *Reid* v *Secretary of State for Scotland* [1999] 1 All ER 481.

[14] *X* v *Germany* (1981) 6 DR 182: the application alleging that personality disorder did not fit within the concept of 'unsound mind' was declared to be manifestly ill-founded.

[15] *Anderson and others* v *The Scottish Ministers and the A-G for Scotland* (16 June 2000).

[16] In England, the detention would be no doubt be covered by Article 5(1)(c), following an arrest for a breach of the peace or under the Public Order Act 1986.

... the expression 'alcoholics' should be understood in the light of the object and purpose of Article 5(1)(e) ... It ... cannot be interpreted as only allowing the detention of 'alcoholics' in the limited sense of persons in a clinical state of 'alcoholism'. The Court considers that, under Article 5(1)(e) of the Convention, persons who are not medically diagnosed as 'alcoholics' *but whose conduct and behaviour under the influence of alcohol pose a threat to public order or themselves, can be taken into custody for the protection of the public or their own interests, such as their health or personal safety.* (emphasis supplied)

The Court of Sessions in Scotland cited *Litwa* in the case of *Anderson and others v Scottish Ministers and the Advocate-General for Scotland* (16 June 2000), ruling that an amendment of the Mental Health (Scotland) Act 1984 to allow for continued detention of restricted patients who derived no benefit from treatment was not in breach of the Convention, when those people represented a danger to the public. The court said any mentally disordered person was a person whose interests 'in principle' might justify detention, and that *Litwa* showed that the European Court is willing to adopt a purposive construction of Article 5(1)(e) to protect the public as well as the person detained, and that these interests may be in the alternative.[17] The Scottish case shows a questionable interpretation of the European Court's judgment.

20.3   THE PRACTICAL APPLICATION OF ARTICLE 5(1)(e)

Where there has been a plea or a conviction, both Article 5(1)(a) and (e) will apply, even if the defendant is then committed to hospital for treatment rather than a penal sanction being imposed.[18] Where the defendant is given a prison sentence and then transferred to hospital, both subparagraphs will continue to apply whilst he remains in hospital. Where there is no criminal responsibility,[19] the detention will be covered by Article 5(1)(e) only, and give additional rights to the defendant to be detained in a hospital, and to insist upon release if the *Winterwerp* criteria are no longer satisfied.[20]

In *X v UK* (1981) 4 EHRR 188 the applicant was convicted of wounding with intent, and received the equivalent of a restriction order under the Mental Health Act 1959. He was conditionally discharged, and remained at liberty for nearly three years before the Home Secretary recalled him to hospital because of concerns about his mental health. The European Commission found that when a

---

[17] On the facts of *Litwa* it is inconceivable that the European Court did not think it in the applicant's interests to be detained: he was blind, and very drunk.

[18] English law recognises a similar distinction — although the hospital order will be a 'sentence' for the purpose of an appeal, the hospitalised defendant will be in the same position as a civil patient: see *R v Birch* (1989) 11 Cr App R (S) 202 at 210.

[19] For example, where there is an acquittal by reason of insanity.

[20] See *Aerts v Belgium* (1998) 29 EHRR 50, above.

convicted person is sent to a mental hospital for treatment rather than to prison, Article 5(1)(e) applied to the exclusion of Article 5(1)(a). The European Court disagreed (at para. 39), finding that both provisions were applicable to a hospital order. The European Court specifically left open the point of whether Article 5(1)(a) continued to apply to situations where the applicant had been at liberty for some time before being taken back into custody.[21]

20.4 REVIEW OF DETENTION UNDER ARTICLE 5(4)

Article 5(4) provides that:

> Everyone who is deprived of his liberty by arrest or detention shall be entitled to take proceedings by which the lawfulness of his detention shall be decided speedily by a court and his release ordered if the detention is not lawful.

This has particular relevance in mental health cases because of the *Winterwerp* requirement that the continuation of the detention depends on the persistence of the condition. Read literally, the detainee has an immediate right to release if the criteria for detention are no longer satisfied, although in practice this right is subject to qualification.

Article 5(4) envisages the following minimum procedural rights:

(a) the right to 'take proceedings at reasonable intervals' to challenge the detention;[22]

(b) that the review be undertaken by a court, or judicial body with 'court-like' attributes, which has the power both to assess the applicant's mental state and to order release;[23]

(c) that the procedure followed has a judicial character and a number of safeguards for the applicant. How extensive these rights are will depend upon the circumstances,[24] but they may not be the full fair trial rights under Article 6 (see above at text to, and footnote 22);

(d) representation by a lawyer, whether or not the applicant has asked for representation.[25]

---

[21] The European Court did find that the failure to have periodic reviews of the detention was a breach of Article 5(4). The decision prompted the enactment of the Mental Health Act 1983, which gave mental health review tribunals wider powers of discharge. See also *M v Germany* (App. No. 10272/83).

[22] *Magyeri v Germany* (1992) 15 EHRR 584 at para. 22.

[23] *X v UK* (1981) 4 EHRR 188 which prompted the granting of greater powers to Mental Health Review Tribunals.

[24] *Wassink v Netherlands* (1990) A/185-A.

[25] *Magyeri v Germany* (1993) 15 EHRR 584.

In considering whether the proceedings to challenge the legality of the detention take place sufficiently 'speedily', the European Court will take into account the fact that mental health cases may take more time to resolve,[26] but it has observed that this does not absolve the authorities from their obligation to consider release.

20.4.1 Release

Although the *Winterwerp* guidelines appear to provide for the immediate release of any person to whom the criteria no longer apply, the European Court has adopted a cautious approach to release. In *Luberti* v *Italy* (1984) 6 EHRR 440 the European Court accepted that delays to release may be inevitable, observing (at para. 29):

> the termination of the confinement of an individual who has previously been found by a court to be of unsound mind and to present a danger to society is a matter that concerns, as well as that individual, the community in which he will live if released.

Release which is conditional on taking medication is unlikely to breach the Convention. In *W* v *Sweden* (1988) 59 DR 158 the European Commission found that attaching conditions to release did not constitute a deprivation of liberty under Article 5. In *L* v *Sweden* (1986) 8 EHRR 269 it found that a condition to take medication was not in breach of Article 8, because it was justified under Article 8(2) for the protection of the applicant's health.

In *Johnson* v *UK* (1997) 27 EHRR 296 the Mental Health Review Tribunal had already held that the applicant was no longer suffering from a mental illness, but he remained in hospital for almost three years without a suitable hostel being found. The applicant was for a long time uncooperative with the process of finding an alternative place to live. The European Court rejected an argument that unconditional release should immediately follow where it has been found that there is no persisting mental illness, saying (at para. 61):

> it does not automatically follow from a finding by an expert authority that the mental disorder which justified a patient's compulsory confinement no longer persists, the latter must be immediately and unconditionally released. Such a rigid approach to the interpretation of that condition would place an unacceptable degree of constraint on the responsible authority's exercise of judgment to determine . . . whether the interests of the patient and the community . . . would in fact be best served by this course of action . . .

The Court added (at para. 63) that the domestic authority 'should be able to retain some measure of supervision over the progress of the person once he is released

---

[26] *Musial* v *Poland* (25 March 1999) at para. 47; *Matter* v *Slovakia* (5 July 1999) at para. 55. See also *Vodenicarov* v *Slovakia* (21 December 2000).

into the community and to that end make his discharge subject to conditions'. The European Court did, however, find a breach of Article 5(1)(e) because the release had been delayed unreasonably, and because the tribunal had no power to order that suitable hostel accommodation be made available.

20.5   DETENTION UNDER DOMESTIC LAW AND THE CONVENTION

Domestic mental health legislation is unlikely to offend the Convention in most respects, and in many cases provides a more comprehensive set of rights and safeguards for the mentally disordered person. There remain, however, several areas where it is arguable that domestic law violates the Convention. A non-exhaustive list can be made:

(a)   where the trial judge decides that the requirements are satisfied for the making of a hospital order under s. 37, Mental Health Act 1983, but the hospital vetoes the order under s. 37(4);

(b)   where the magistrates' court has a power to make a hospital order without convicting the accused, under s. 37(3), Mental Health Act 1983;

(c)   s. 51(5), Mental Health Act 1983, which empowers a court to make a hospital order with or without restrictions when there has been no determination of the charge alleged;

(d)   where a person with mental illness receives an automatic sentence under the Crime (Sentences) Act 1997;

(e)   where a mentally ill person is fit to plead to the charge but is not able to participate effectively in the trial process.

20.5.1   Where hospitals refuse to provide a place for a defendant who satisfies the requirements for a hospital order

Under s. 37(4), Mental Health Act 1983 hospitals can veto admission even where the court finds on medical evidence that the requirements of a hospital order are made out. This position probably breaches the Convention in two respects: first, it allows for the passing of a punitive sentence for a person who may not be criminally responsible, and secondly, it lends legislative support to a position where the defendant would be sent to prison although it has already been accepted on the evidence that he should be detained in a hospital.[27]

---

[27] See *Ashingdane* v *UK* (1985) 7 EHRR 528 and *Aerts* v *Belgium* (1998) 29 EHRR 50 above at 20.2.3.2. It may be possible to avoid this outcome by inviting the judge to request information about available beds from the health authority under s. 39, MHA 1983, and then judicially reviewing the response given.

20.5.2   Section 37(3), Mental Health Act 1983

Under this section the magistrates' court has a power to make a hospital order without convicting the accused, if it is satisfied that he did the act or made the omission charged. Domestic law recognises the disposal as a conviction,[28] which is sensible as power to make a hospital order cannot be exercised without having regard to the facts of the offence.[29] There is no statutory provision to govern how the magistrates satisfy themselves that the acts were committed, but there is domestic authority suggesting that it may be circumvented by the consent of those acting for the accused.[30] More alarmingly, there is authority that the power can be used even where the accused has elected trial on indictment.[31] It is submitted that both of these propositions probably breach the fair trial rights of the accused and the presumption of innocence, and that it will be necessary under the Convention for magistrates to hear the prosecution evidence before making any order.

20.5.3   Section 51(5), Mental Health Act 1983

Section 51(5) is a similar provision which empowers the trial court to make a hospital order (with or without restriction) in the absence of a trial on the facts, without the defendant being present, when it is 'impracticable or inappropriate to bring the detainee before the court'. The court may make such an order on the evidence of two practitioners that detention in hospital is appropriate, and when it feels after consideration of the prosecution case that it is 'proper' to do so (s. 51(6)).

The section effectively gives the judge the discretion to dispense with any trial on the facts, or the need to make any enquiry under the Criminal Procedure (Insanity) Act 1964 as to whether the defendant did the facts alleged. The limited case law highlights the problems of the power by saying that the trial judge need not embark on an 'elaborate fact finding exercise: the outcome was inevitable ...'.[32] As under section 37(3) above, the decision whether to make an order and whether to add restrictions requires careful consideration of the facts of the prosecution case. To proceed to disposal of the matter without hearing the evidence would probably breach Article 6.

---

[28] See *R* v *Thames Magistrates' Court, ex parte Ramadan* [1999] COD 19.

[29] Section 37(2)(b), MHA 1983.

[30] *R* v *Lincolnshire (Kesteven) Justices, ex parte O'Connor* [1983] 1 WLR 335. See also Samuels, A., 'Hospital Orders without Conviction' [1995] Crim LR 220.

[31] *R* v *Ramsgate Justices, ex parte Kazmarek* (1985) 80 Cr App R 366.

[32] *R* v *Kingston Crown Court, ex parte Mason* (27 July 1998). In that case, the judge held that the defendant could not be tried because of his aversion to women, but this did not presumably make it unnecessary or impossible for trial counsel to test the Crown case before a jury.

20.5.4   Automatic life sentences

Article 5(1)(a) specifically allows for the 'lawful detention of a person after conviction by a competent court'. Such a sentence will nonetheless be in breach of Article 5 if it results from an arbitrary process. Under s. 109, PCC(S)A 2000 an offender will automatically receive a life sentence for a second serious offence unless the court is satisfied that there are 'exceptional circumstances relating to either of the offences or to the offender which justify its not doing so'.

Section 109 replaced s. 2(2), Crime (Sentences) Act 1997, which amended s. 37(1), Mental Health Act 1983.[33] The section now reads:

> Where a person is convicted before the court of an offence punishable with imprisonment other than an offence the sentence for which is fixed by law, or falls to be imposed under section 2(2), Crime (Sentences) Act 1997 ... and [the medical requirements are satisfied] ... the court may by order authorise his admission to and detention in such hospital as may be specified in the order or, as the case may be, place him [under guardianship] ...

In *R* v *Newman* [2000] 1 Cr App R 471, the Court of Appeal held that s. 37(1) expressly excludes the making of a hospital order where the defendant fulfils the conviction requirements for an automatic sentence. It further held that acute mental illness cannot in itself amount to an exceptional circumstance under the 1997 Act.

It is unclear if *Newman* remains good law after *R* v *Offen* [2001] 2 All ER 154, but it is submitted that the reasoning is erroneous, and that the ruling is capable of giving rise to violations of the Convention. An automatic life sentence is a mixed sentence which contains both a punitive and preventative element, and the court is obliged to set a punitive tariff which reflects the gravity of the offence. The exclusion of situations where s. 109, PCC(S)A 2000 applies would appear to oblige the court to pass a punitive sentence on a mentally ill defendant even where it considers that punishment would be inappropriate.

Passing a punitive sentence in these circumstances may be in breach of Article 3 (inhuman or degrading treatment),[34] and it is submitted that mental illness should be capable of being an exceptional circumstance. The words 'where sentence falls to be imposed' in s. 37(1) can be construed to include 'in the absence of exceptional circumstances': where there are exceptional circumstances (including mental illness) no sentence would fall to be imposed under the PCC(S)A 2000 and the court would be free to make a hospital order if it saw fit.

---

[33] And s. 45A(1)(b) which deals with hospital and limitation directions.
[34] See *Weeks* v *UK* (1988) 13 EHRR 435 at para. 47; *Hussain* v *UK* (1996) 22 EHRR 1; *T and V* v *UK* (1999) 30 EHRR 121.

20.5.5　Effective participation for the mentally ill or vulnerable defendant

In the case of *T and V v UK* (1999) 30 EHRR 121 the European Court held that there had been a breach of Article 6 because the child defendants had been unable to participate effectively in their trial. The European Court said that where children were tried in an adult court, they should be 'dealt with in a manner which takes full account of age, level of maturity, intellectual and emotional capabilities' (para. 84). A failure to address these issues was not capable of being cured by effective legal representation. Although the judgment focused more on the youth than the undoubted mental health problems of the two applicants, it has significant implications for the trials of some people with mental health problems. It is not advocated that all mentally ill defendants should form a category, or should be treated on a par with juveniles, but where it appears that any condition makes effective participation difficult, or that the proceedings will be more of an ordeal because of problems in understanding or concentration, then lawyers should argue that the trial court should adapt its procedure to secure a fair trial to the individual defendant. There may be strong grounds for arguing, for example, that a defendant who is an in-patient at the time of trial, who is nonetheless fit to plead, should be tried in a court on one level, sit near his lawyers rather than in a dock, and not be confronted by lawyers in wigs and gowns. Domestically, the *Practice Direction (Crown Court: Young Defendants)* [2000] 1 WLR 659 should provide persuasive guidance to trial courts where the welfare of a vulnerable defendant is at stake.

Where a defendant is unfit to plead to the charge, and is incapable of giving coherent instructions, what is 'effective participation'?[35] It may be unrealistic to argue that a defendant in these circumstances can never have a fair trial, but significant allowances in procedure may have to be made. It is difficult to imagine that Article 6 would be satisfied where lawyers fail to test the strength of the prosecution case, or concede involvement in the offence where no instructions are received. Effective participation must mean that the defence lawyers assert the defendant's minimum rights, including the presumption of innocence. Accordingly, domestic authority suggesting that the defence lawyers can abrogate the trial process by agreement (above at 20.5.3) must be questionable in the light of Article 6.

20.6　PSYCHIATRIC EXAMINATIONS

Unwarranted psychiatric examinations can be a breach of Article 8 (right to privacy),[36] and the requirement of a court to force someone to undergo one could

---

[35] For a flagrant breach of Article 6 in this regard, see *Vaudelle v France* (30 January 2001), where a mentally handicapped man was tried in his absence when he failed to appear after he (but not his guardian) had been notified of the hearing.

[36] *X v Germany* (1981) 24 DR 103.

in some circumstances also be a breach of Article 6. It is for the state authorities to justify the need for such action. In practice, the European Court has adopted a cautious approach where the interests of the defendant and protection for the public may be at stake. In *Matter* v *Slovakia* (5 July 1999)[37] the European Court held that compulsory psychiatric examination to ascertain whether an individual should be afforded legal status can be justified under Article 8 of the Convention.

20.7   CONDITIONS OF DETENTION AND ARTICLE 3

Article 3 provides that 'no one shall be subjected to torture or to inhuman or degrading treatment or punishment'. The European Court has been very cautious in finding particular treatment regimes to be in breach of Article 3. This is because there is a high threshold before the Article is engaged,[38] and in any event the European Court has found that its powers of review under Article 5(1)(e) are 'not in principle concerned with suitable treatment or conditions'.[39]

The case law relating to the mentally ill is disappointing. In *Grare* v *France* (1993) 15 EHRR CD 100 the European Commission held that unpleasant side-effects from medication fell short of Article 3 because these were insufficiently serious. In *Herczegfalvy* v *Austria* (1992) 15 EHRR 437 the applicant was detained under civil provisions, and handcuffed, isolated and force-fed for four weeks. The European Court found no breach of Article 3, saying that its role was to consider whether the programme conformed to accepted psychiatric standards. In at least one case, however, in the general medical sphere, the European Commission declared admissible a claim under Article 3 where the applicant had received treatment of an experimental nature without consent.[40]

Failure to provide medical treatment can in principle give rise to a violation of Article 3, but the European Court has required similarly high standards. The matter was considered again in *Aerts* v *Belgium* (1998) 29 EHRR 50, where the applicant had been detained in the psychiatric wing of a prison for some seven months after a decision had been taken to transfer him to a psychiatric institution. The reason for the delay was the absence of a bed, and it was accepted by the authorities that the applicant should not have been on the wing. Conditions on the wing had been the subject of much criticism in Belgium, and the court accented that the applicant 'had literally been left to his own devices and had not received any regular medical or psychiatric attention' (at para. 61). Despite reports and a decision of a Mental Health Board that further detention in prison would harm the

---

[37] At paras 71–2. The applicant had indicated that he wished to be viewed as a person with legal capacity, but refused to see the psychiatrist. At the time the examination was ordered the applicant had not had legal capacity for around four years.
[38] *Ireland* v *UK* (1978) 2 EHRR 25.
[39] *Ashingdane* v *UK* (1985) 7 EHRR 528 at para. 44. See also *Buckley* v *UK* (1997) 23 EHRR CD 129.
[40] *X* v *Denmark* (1983) 32 DR 282.

applicant, the European Court found there was no breach of Article 3, as the applicant had not established conclusively that the treatment he received had been sufficiently severe to engage Article 3.[41]

A more creative approach was adopted in *Cruz Varas* v *Sweden* (1991) 14 EHRR 1, where the applicant alleged that his post-traumatic stress disorder would be exacerbated if he were deported to Chile. The European Court held that the knowledge of such facts by the authorities could in principle engage Article 3.[42] In *D* v *UK* (1997) 24 EHRR 423 the court found that the removal of a convicted drug trafficker to St Kitts, in circumstances where he was dying of AIDS and had no hope of treatment or financial support there, amounted to a breach of Article 3.

---

[41] See also *Passanante* v *Italy* (1998) 26 CD 153 where the European Commission found that excessive delay by a public health service in providing a medical service to which the patient was entitled, where a deterioration in health occurred, could raise an issue under Article 8(1).

[42] See also *Chahal* v *UK* (1996) 23 EHRR 413; *BB* v *France* [1998] EHRLR 620.

Chapter Twenty-One

Victims

Quincy Whitaker

The HRA 1998 is likely to have both a direct and an indirect effect on victims. Many of the decisions regarding a defendant's fair trial rights will have involved balancing rights of victims and witnesses as the criminal courts themselves will be under a duty to ensure that such rights are respected. In addition the Convention creates positive obligations on the state to prevent the violation of one individual's rights by another, stemming from the obligation under Article 1 to *secure Convention rights to those within their jurisdiction.*

21.1 THE DUTY TO PROVIDE EFFECTIVE PROTECTION FOR CONVENTION RIGHTS

The state must provide adequate and effective deterrents against crime by means of enacting adequate legislation and by providing a means of recourse through the courts if a criminal act is committed. In *X and Y v Netherlands* (1985) 8 EHRR 235 the European Court considered the case of Y who was sexually abused in a home for the mentally disabled in which she lived. She was over 16 but incapable of filing a rape complaint and Dutch law did not permit a complaint to be filed on her behalf by her father, thus preventing any prosecution taking place. Y and her father complained to Strasbourg that her rights under Article 8 had been breached. The European Court held that 'the state's positive obligations may involve measures designed to secure respect for private life even in the sphere of relations between individuals themselves'. Relying on civil remedies was insufficient in a case involving a sexual assault as 'effective deterrence is indispensable in this area and it can be achieved only by criminal law provisions; indeed it is by such provisions that the matter is normally regulated' (para. 27). However this principle does not mean that where criminal laws are already in place there must be unlimited access to civil remedies.[1]

21.2   THE DUTY TO TAKE PREVENTATIVE MEASURES

In certain well-defined circumstances there is a positive obligation on the authorities to take preventative operational steps to protect an individual whose life is at risk from another. In the case of *Osman* v *UK* [1999] EHRLR 228 the Osman family challenged the failure of the Metropolitan Police to protect them from a sustained campaign of harassment by the schoolteacher of their son which had culminated in a shooting in which the father was killed and his son was wounded. At domestic law there was a blanket immunity on the grounds of public policy against suing the police for negligence in the way they conducted their investigations. The European Court held that this blanket immunity amounted to an unjustifiable restriction on the right to have a determination of the family's arguable claim for negligence and thus amounted to a violation of Article 6. The European Court found no violation of Article 2 in the circumstances as the police had attempted to arrest the teacher, but it did recognise the existence of a positive duty in an appropriate case. The duty requires that authorities must do all that can reasonably be expected of them to avoid a 'real and immediate' risk to life — however, it was precisely this inquiry that had not taken place in the domestic courts as a result of the immunity. The European Court's finding in relation to Article 2 may therefore be the result of not wishing to prejudge the outcome of the claim for negligence without a proper domestic evidential hearing.

The duty to take preventative measures, however, cannot be used as a mechanism for restricting the Convention rights of others. The court stated in *Osman* that (at para. 116):

> another relevant consideration is the need to ensure that the police exercise their powers to control and prevent crime in a manner which fully respects the due process and other guarantees which legitimately place restraints on the scope of their action to investigate crime and bring offenders to justice, including the guarantees contained in Articles 5 and 8 of the Convention.

Where an individual is at risk of paramilitary attack, there may be a duty to provide protection but not for an indefinite period. In the case of *X* v *Ireland* (1973) 16 Yearbook 388 at 392 the European Commission held that 'Article 2 cannot be interpreted as imposing a duty on a state to give protection of this nature, at least not for an indefinite period' and in the case of *W* v *UK* (1983)

---

[1] *Stubbings* v *UK* (1996) 23 EHRR 213.

32 DR 190 at 200 the European Commission stated that 'a positive obligation to exclude any possible violence cannot be read into Article 2'.

The positive obligations under Article 8 can extend to protection of employees in the workplace. In a recent Scottish case involving unwanted sexual letters being sent by one employee to another, it was held that Article 8 obliges the relevant authorities to protect individuals at work from deliberate persecution and harassment.[2]

The positive obligations of the state may be breached through overly wide defences. In *A* v *UK* (1999) 27 EHRR 611 it was held that the UK had failed to protect a child's rights under Article 3 where that child had been beaten by his stepfather using a garden cane (so that welts were caused to his back). A's stepfather was prosecuted for an offence of causing actual bodily harm but acquitted by the jury on the defence of 'reasonable chastisement'. The European Court held that the provision of the defence in such circumstances meant that the law did not provide adequate protection for A. However, it is a question of degree and there may be methods of protection other than a criminal prosecution which a person may be required to pursue, such as civil injunctions, depending on the level of interference. In *Whiteside* v *UK* (App. No. 20367/92, 7 March 1994) it was held that although the level of harassment was such that state responsibility was engaged, Ms Whiteside had failed to exhaust her domestic remedies such as an action for nuisance or an application for an injunction.

21.3 EFFECTIVE SYSTEM FOR INVESTIGATION OF CRIME

In addition to the substantive criminal law providing protection, there must also exist a proper and effective system for the investigation of crime. In *Aydin* v *Turkey* (1997) 25 EHRR 251 the applicant, a Turkish Kurd, was subjected to horrific treatment including beating and rape while in police custody. Unsurprisingly the European Court found that this treatment violated the applicant's rights under Article 3. However, in addition the European Court held that the failure to carry out an effective investigation by the authorities amounted to a separate violation of Article 3. The European Court considered the failure of the public prosecutor to question police at the police station, to seek out witnesses or to obtain proper medical evidence in the context of Article 6 and Article 13. It held that the wholly inadequate investigation had deprived the applicant of any prospect of gaining redress in the civil courts and thus her right to an effective remedy had been violated. Where serious crime is alleged and it affects fundamental rights, there is a duty on the relevant authority to respond diligently and effectively: '[what is required is] a thorough and effective investigation capable of leading to the identification and punishment of those responsible and

---

[2] *Janice Ward* v *Scotrail Railways Ltd* (27 November 1998, HC), p. 5

including effective access for the relatives to the investigatory procedure'.[3] The duty will not be fulfilled where the investigating authorities fail to ascertain possible eyewitnesses, fail to question suspects at a sufficiently early stage, fail to search for corroborating evidence or adopt an over-deferential attitude to authority.[4]

Article 2 also requires that the state establish a procedure to investigate unlawful killings,[5] particularly when state officials may have been involved in the death. The duty requires that there be 'some form of official investigation'. In *McCann*, a case concerning three IRA suspects who were shot dead by the SAS in Gibraltar, a challenge to the UK inquest system failed. In particular, the European Court relied upon the fact that the applicants were legally represented and their lawyers were able to cross-examine all the key witnesses and the inquest involved a detailed review of the events surrounding the killing. It follows therefore that an inquest where the scope of the inquiry was limited would not necessarily survive a challenge.[6] The granting of an amnesty to those suspected of homicide, however, will not necessarily breach the Convention provided there is a legitimate basis and a proper balance is struck between competing interests.[7]

21.4 VICTIMS AND THE CRIMINAL TRIAL PROCESS

The decisions of Strasbourg in relation to hearsay testimony and anonymous witnesses demonstrate the extent to which a defendant's fair trial rights must be balanced against those of victims and witnesses. The complainant has Article 3 and Article 8 rights but no Article 6 rights in regard to the determination of the criminal proceedings (as it is not a determination 'against him'). However, the operation of these rights will necessarily impact upon the defendant's rights under Article 6. In *Doorson* v *Netherlands* (1996) 22 EHRR 330 the European Court held that the defendant's rights under Article 6(3)(d) were not violated through the use of anonymous witnesses who feared for their safety (at para. 70):

> It is true that Article 6 does not explicitly require the interests of witnesses in general ... to be taken into account. However their life, liberty or security of person may be at stake, as may interests coming generally within the ambit of Article 8 ... Against this background, principles of fair trial also require that in appropriate cases the interests of the defence are balanced against those of witnesses or victims called upon to testify.

---

[3] *Aksoy* v *Turkey* (1996) 23 EHRR 553 at para 98; *Aydin* v *Turkey* (1997) 25 EHRR 251 at para. 103; *Kaya* v *Turkey* (1998) 28 EHRR 1 at para. 107; *Kurt* v *Turkey* (1998) 27 EHRR 373 at para. 140.
[4] *Aksoy* v *Turkey* (1996) 23 EHRR 553 at paras 104–9.
[5] *McCann* v *UK* (1995) 21 ECHR 97.
[6] See also *Taylor, Crampton, Gibson and King* v *UK* (1994) 79-A DR 127 concerning the minimum requirements of a mechanism to investigate deprivation of life.
[7] *Dujardin* v *France* (App. No. 16734/90, 2 September 1991).

The European Court has also upheld the use in the UK of screens to shield witnesses from the defendant and the public where the witnesses were journalists giving evidence concerning a murder in Northern Ireland[8] although the position is different with regard to police witnesses.[9] The interests of victims and vulnerable witnesses are particularly important where the proceedings might be seen as an ordeal in themselves, such as those involving sexual offences. The European Commission has stated that it 'accepts that in criminal proceedings concerning sexual abuse certain measures may be taken for the purpose of protecting the victim, provided that such measures can be reconciled with an adequate and effective exercise of the rights of the defence'.[10] In that case the European Commission held that there was no violation of Article 6 where the defendant was able to confront but not question the complainant in a rape trial. The Commission was particularly influenced by the fact that the defendant had not taken the opportunity to put written questions to her, applied to the court to hear her or submitted blood and DNA tests. In the light of this decision it seems that s. 34 of the Youth Justice and Criminal Evidence Act 1999, which prohibits a defendant charged with a sexual offence from cross-examining the complainant in person, is unlikely to lead to a finding that Article 6 is violated provided there was no less restrictive measure that was open to the authorities.[11] In this context, however, the option of permitting counsel to undertake cross-examination of the complainant while the defendant otherwise represents himself or herself would appear to be a less restrictive alternative.

21.5 DISCLOSURE OF MEDICAL RECORDS

In the case of *Z* v *Finland* (1997) 25 EHRR 371 the European Court considered the issue of the rights of a third party in a criminal trial. The case concerned the trial of Z's former husband on a charge of engaging in sexual acts knowing that he was HIV positive. When the defendant declined to give evidence the Finnish authorities seized Z's medical files and ordered her medical adviser to give evidence with a view to establishing the defendant's date of knowledge. The court ordered that the judgment convicting the defendant remain confidential for 10 years and this was upheld in the Court of Appeal although Z was identified in the judgment which was then faxed to the press. The European Court was of the view that 'any state measures compelling communication or disclosure of such information without the consent of the patient calls for the most careful scrutiny on the part of the Court' (at para. 96). However, the public interest in the

---

[8] *X and Y* v *UK* (1993) 15 EHRR CD 113.
[9] See *Van Mechelen and others* v *Netherlands* (1997) 25 EHRR 647.
[10] *Baegen* v *Netherlands* (1995) A/327-B.
[11] See also *Her Majesty's Advocate* v *Nulty* 2000 SLT 528.

prosecution of crime and the public interest in the publicity of court proceedings can outweigh medical confidentiality but only in limited circumstances and with other safeguards to protect the interests of patients. On the facts of *Z*, the European Court held the compulsory disclosure did not amount to a violation of Article 8. However, her Article 8 rights were violated by the 10-year order which the European Court considered to be too short and by the disclosure of the applicant's name in the Court of Appeal judgment.[12]

---

[12] See also Canadian decisions holding that a balance may have to be struck in sensitive cases: *R v Mills* (1999) 3 SCR 668; *M(A) v Ryan* (1997) 1 SCR 157.

Appendix One

Human Rights Act 1998

CHAPTER 42

ARRANGEMENT OF SECTIONS

HUMAN RIGHTS ACT 1998

1998 CHAPTER 42

An Act to give further effect to rights and freedoms guaranteed under the European Convention on Human Rights; to make provision with respect to holders of certain judicial offices who become judges of the European Court of Human Rights; and for connected purposes. [9th November 1998]

BE IT ENACTED by the Queen's most Excellent Majesty, by and with the advice and consent of the Lords Spiritual and Temporal, and Commons, in this present Parliament assembled, and by the authority of the same, as follows:—

Introduction

1. The Convention Rights

(1) In this Act 'the Convention rights' means the rights and fundamental freedoms set out in—

(a) Articles 2 to 12 and 14 of the Convention,

(b) Articles 1 to 3 of the First Protocol, and

(c) Articles 1 and 2 of the Sixth Protocol,

as read with Articles 16 to 18 of the Convention.

(2) Those Articles are to have effect for the purposes of this Act subject to any designated derogation or reservation (as to which see sections 14 and 15).

(3) The Articles are set out in Schedule 1.

(4) The Secretary of State may by order make such amendments to this Act as he considers appropriate to reflect the effect, in relation to the United Kingdom, of a protocol.

(5) In subsection (4) 'protocol' means a protocol to the Convention—

(a) which the United Kingdom has ratified; or

(b) which the United Kingdom has signed with a view to ratification.

(6) No amendment may be made by an order under subsection (4) so as to come into force before the protocol concerned is in force in relation to the United Kingdom.

2. Interpretation of Convention rights

(1) A court or tribunal determining a question which has arisen in connection with a Convention right must take into account any—

(a) judgment, decision, declaration or advisory opinion of the European Court of Human Rights,

(b) opinion of the Commission given in a report adopted under Article 31 of the Convention,

(c) decision of the Commission in connection with Article 26 or 27(2) of the Convention, or

(d) decision of the Committee of Ministers taken under Article 46 of the Convention,

whenever made or given, so far as, in the opinion of the court or tribunal, it is relevant to the proceedings in which that question has arisen.

(2) Evidence of any judgment, decision, declaration or opinion of which account may have to be taken under this section is to be given in proceedings before any court or tribunal in such manner as may be provided by rules.

(3) In this section 'rules' means rules of court or, in the case of proceedings before a tribunal, rules made for the purposes of this section—

(a) by the Lord Chancellor or the Secretary of State, in relation to any proceedings outside Scotland;

(b) by the Secretary of State, in relation to proceedings in Scotland; or

(c) by a Northern Ireland department, in relation to proceedings before a tribunal in Northern Ireland—

(i) which deals with transferred matters; and

(ii) for which no rules made under paragraph (a) are in force.

Legislation

3. Interpretation of legislation

(1) So far as it is possible to do so, primary legislation and subordinate legislation must be read and given effect in a way which is compatible with the Convention rights.

(2) This section—

(a) applies to primary legislation and subordinate legislation whenever enacted;

(b) does not affect the validity, continuing operation or enforcement of any incompatible primary legislation; and

(c) does not affect the validity, continuing operation or enforcement of any incompatible subordinate legislation if (disregarding any possibility of revocation) primary legislation prevents removal of the incompatibility.

4. Declaration of incompatibility

(1) Subsection (2) applies in any proceedings in which a court determines whether a provision of primary legislation is compatible with a Convention right.

(2) If the court is satisfied that the provision is incompatible with a Convention right, it may make a declaration of that incompatibility.

(3) Subsection (4) applies in any proceedings in which a court determines whether a provision of subordinate legislation, made in the exercise of a power conferred by primary legislation, is compatible with a Convention right.

(4) If the court is satisfied—

(a) that the provision is incompatible with a Convention right, and

(b) that (disregarding any possibility of revocation) the primary legislation concerned prevents removal of the incompatibility, it may make a declaration of that incompatibility.

(5)   In this section 'court' means—

(a)   the House of Lords;

(b)   the Judicial Committee of the Privy Council;

(c)   the Courts-Martial Appeal Court;

(d)   in Scotland, the High Court of Justiciary sitting otherwise than as a trial court or the Court of Session;

(e)   in England and Wales or Northern Ireland, the High Court or the Court of Appeal.

(6)   A declaration under this section ('a declaration of incompatibility')—

(a)   does not affect the validity, continuing operation or enforcement of the provision in respect of which it is given; and

(b)   is not binding on the parties to the proceedings in which it is made.

5.   Right of Crown to intervene

(1)   Where a court is considering whether to make a declaration of incompatibility, the Crown is entitled to notice in accordance with rules of court.

(2)   In any case to which subsection (1) applies—

(a)   a Minister of the Crown (or a person nominated by him),

(b)   a member of the Scottish Executive,

(c)   a Northern Ireland Minister,

(d)   a Northern Ireland department,

is entitled, on giving notice in accordance with rules of court, to be joined as a party to the proceedings.

(3)   Notice under subsection (2) may be given at any time during the proceedings.

(4)   A person who has been made a party to criminal proceedings (other than in Scotland) as the result of a notice under subsection (2) may, with leave, appeal to the House of Lords against any declaration of incompatibility made in the proceedings.

(5)   In subsection (4)—

'criminal proceedings' includes all proceedings before the Courts-Martial Appeal Court; and

'leave' means leave granted by the court making the declaration of incompatibility or by the House of Lords.

Public authorities

6.   Acts of public authorities

(1)   It is unlawful for a public authority to act in a way which is incompatible with a Convention right.

(2)   Subsection (1) does not apply to an act if—

(a)   as the result of one or more provisions of primary legislation, the authority could not have acted differently; or

(b)   in the case of one or more provisions of, or made under, primary legislation which cannot be read or given effect in a way which is compatible with the Convention rights, the authority was acting so as to give effect to or enforce those provisions.

(3)   In this section 'public authority' includes—

(a)   a court or tribunal, and

(b)   any person certain of whose functions are functions of a public nature, but does not include either House of Parliament or a person exercising functions in connection with proceedings in Parliament.

(4)   In subsection (3) 'Parliament' does not include the House of Lords in its judicial capacity.

(5)   In relation to a particular act, a person is not a public authority by virtue only of subsection (3)(b) if the nature of the act is private.

(6)   'An act' includes a failure to act but does not include a failure to—

(a)   introduce in, or lay before, Parliament a proposal for legislation; or

(b)   make any primary legislation or remedial order.

7. Proceedings

(1)   A person who claims that a public authority has acted (or proposes to act) in a way which is made unlawful by section 6(1) may—

(a)   bring proceedings against the authority under this Act in the appropriate court or tribunal, or

(b)   rely on the Convention right or rights concerned in any legal proceedings,
but only if he is (or would be) a victim of the unlawful act.

(2)   In subsection (1)(a) 'appropriate court or tribunal' means such court or tribunal as may be determined in accordance with rules; and proceedings against an authority include a counterclaim or similar proceeding.

(3)   If the proceedings are brought on an application for judicial review, the applicant is to be taken to have a sufficient interest in relation to the unlawful act only if he is, or would be, a victim of that act.

(4)   If the proceedings are made by way of a petition for judicial review in Scotland, the applicant shall be taken to have title and interest to sue in relation to the unlawful act only if he is, or would be, a victim of that act.

(5)   Proceedings under subsection (1)(a) must be brought before the end of—

(a)   the period of one year beginning with the date on which the act complained of took place; or

(b)   such longer period as the court or tribunal considers equitable having regard to all the circumstances,
but that is subject to any rule imposing a stricter time limit in relation to the procedure in question.

(6)   In subsection (1)(b) 'legal proceedings' includes—

(a) proceedings brought by or at the instigation of a public authority; and

(b) an appeal against the decision of a court or tribunal.

(7) For the purposes of this section, a person is a victim of an unlawful act only if he would be a victim for the purposes of Article 34 of the Convention if proceedings were brought in the European Court of Human Rights in respect of that act.

(8) Nothing in this Act creates a criminal offence.

(9) In this section 'rules' means—

(a) in relation to proceedings before a court or tribunal outside Scotland, rules made by the Lord Chancellor or the Secretary of State for the purposes of this section or rules of court,

(b) in relation to proceedings before a court or tribunal in Scotland, rules made by the Secretary of State for those purposes,

(c) in relation to proceedings before a tribunal in Northern Ireland—

(i) which deals with transferred matters; and

(ii) for which no rules made under paragraph (a) are in force,

rules made by a Northern Ireland department for those purposes,

and includes provision made by order under section 1 of the Courts and Legal Services Act 1990.

(10) In making rules, regard must be had to section 9.

(11) The Minister who has power to make rules in relation to a particular tribunal may, to the extent he considers it necessary to ensure that the tribunal can provide an appropriate remedy in relation to an act (or proposed act) of a public authority which is (or would be) unlawful as a result of section 6(1), by order add to—

(a) the relief or remedies which the tribunal may grant; or

(b) the grounds on which it may grant any of them.

(12) An order made under subsection (11) may contain such incidental, supplemental, consequential or transitional provision as the Minister making it considers appropriate.

(13) 'The Minister' includes the Northern Ireland department concerned.

8. Judicial remedies

(1) In relation to any act (or proposed act) of a public authority which the court finds is (or would be) unlawful, it may grant such relief or remedy, or make such order, within its powers as it considers just and appropriate.

(2) But damages may be awarded only by a court which has power to award damages, or to order the payment of compensation, in civil proceedings.

(3) No award of damages is to be made unless, taking account of all the circumstances of the case, including—

(a) any other relief or remedy granted, or order made, in relation to the act in question (by that or any other court), and

(b) the consequences of any decision (of that or any other court) in respect of that act,
the court is satisfied that the award is necessary to afford just satisfaction to the person in whose favour it is made.

(4) In determining—
(a) whether to award damages, or
(b) the amount of an award,
the court must take into account the principles applied by the European Court of Human Rights in relation to the award of compensation under Article 41 of the Convention.

(5) A public authority against which damages are awarded is to be treated—
(a) in Scotland, for the purposes of section 3 of the Law Reform (Miscellaneous Provisions) (Scotland) Act 1940 as if the award were made in an action of damages in which the authority has been found liable in respect of loss or damage to the person to whom the award is made;
(b) for the purposes of the Civil Liability (Contribution) Act 1978 as liable in respect of damage suffered by the person to whom the award is made.

(6) In this section—
'court' includes a tribunal;
'damages' means damages for an unlawful act of a public authority; and
'unlawful' means unlawful under section 6(1).

9. Judicial acts

(1) Proceedings under section 7(1)(a) in respect of a judicial act may be brought only—
(a) by exercising a right of appeal;
(b) on an application (in Scotland a petition) for judicial review; or
(c) in such other forum as may be prescribed by rules.

(2) That does not affect any rule of law which prevents a court from being the subject of judicial review.

(3) In proceedings under this Act in respect of a judicial act done in good faith, damages may not be awarded otherwise than to compensate a person to the extent required by Article 5(5) of the Convention.

(4) An award of damages permitted by subsection (3) is to be made against the Crown; but no award may be made unless the appropriate person, if not a party to the proceedings, is joined.

(5) In this section—
'appropriate person' means the Minister responsible for the court concerned, or a person or government department nominated by him;
'court' includes a tribunal;
'judge' includes a member of a tribunal, a justice of the peace and a clerk or other officer entitled to exercise the jurisdiction of a court;

'judicial act' means a judicial act of a court and includes an act done on the instructions, or on behalf, of a judge; and

'rules' has the same meaning as in section 7(9).

Remedial action

10. Power to take remedial action

(1)   This section applies if—

(a)   a provision of legislation has been declared under section 4 to be incompatible with a Convention right and, if an appeal lies—

(i)   all persons who may appeal have stated in writing that they do not intend to do so;

(ii)   the time for bringing an appeal has expired and no appeal has been brought within that time; or

(iii)   an appeal brought within that time has been determined or abandoned; or

(b)   it appears to a Minister of the Crown or Her Majesty in Council that, having regard to a finding of the European Court of Human Rights made after the coming into force of this section in proceedings against the United Kingdom, a provision of legislation is incompatible with an obligation of the United Kingdom arising from the Convention.

(2)   If a Minister of the Crown considers that there are compelling reasons for proceeding under this section, he may by order make such amendments to the legislation as he considers necessary to remove the incompatibility.

(3)   If, in the case of subordinate legislation, a Minister of the Crown considers—

(a)   that it is necessary to amend the primary legislation under which the subordinate legislation in question was made, in order to enable the incompatibility to be removed, and

(b)   that there are compelling reasons for proceeding under this section, he may by order make such amendments to the primary legislation as he considers necessary.

(4)   This section also applies where the provision in question is in subordinate legislation and has been quashed, or declared invalid, by reason of incompatibility with a Convention right and the Minister proposes to proceed under paragraph 2(b) of Schedule 2.

(5)   If the legislation is an Order in Council, the power conferred by subsection (2) or (3) is exercisable by Her Majesty in Council.

(6)   In this section 'legislation' does not include a Measure of the Church Assembly or of the General Synod of the Church of England.

(7)   Schedule 2 makes further provision about remedial orders.

Other rights and proceedings

11. Safeguard for existing human rights

A person's reliance on a Convention right does not restrict—

(a) any other right or freedom conferred on him by or under any law having effect in any part of the United Kingdom; or

(b) his right to make any claim or bring any proceedings which he could make or bring apart from sections 7 to 9.

12. Freedom of expression

(1) This section applies if a court is considering whether to grant any relief which, if granted, might affect the exercise of the Convention right to freedom of expression.

(2) If the person against whom the application for relief is made ('the respondent') is neither present nor represented, no such relief is to be granted unless the court is satisfied—

(a) that the applicant has taken all practicable steps to notify the respondent; or

(b) that there are compelling reasons why the respondent should not be notified.

(3) No such relief is to be granted so as to restrain publication before trial unless the court is satisfied that the applicant is likely to establish that publication should not be allowed.

(4) The court must have particular regard to the importance of the Convention right to freedom of expression and, where the proceedings relate to material which the respondent claims, or which appears to the court, to be journalistic, literary or artistic material (or to conduct connected with such material), to—

(a) the extent to which—

(i) the material has, or is about to, become available to the public; or

(ii) it is, or would be, in the public interest for the material to be published;

(b) any relevant privacy code.

(5) In this section—

'court' includes a tribunal; and

'relief' includes any remedy or order (other than in criminal proceedings).

13. Freedom of thought, conscience and religion

(1) If a court's determination of any question arising under this Act might affect the exercise by a religious organisation (itself or its members collectively) of the Convention right to freedom of thought, conscience and religion, it must have particular regard to the importance of that right.

(2) In this section 'court' includes a tribunal.

Derogations and reservations

14. Derogations

(1)   In this Act 'designated derogation' means—

   (a)   the United Kingdom's derogation from Article 5(3) of the Convention; and

   (b)   any derogation by the United Kingdom from an Article of the Convention, or of any protocol to the Convention, which is designated for the purposes of this Act in an order made by the Secretary of State.

(2)   The derogation referred to in subsection (1)(a) is set out in Part I of Schedule 3.

(3)   If a designated derogation is amended or replaced it ceases to be a designated derogation.

(4)   But subsection (3) does not prevent the Secretary of State from exercising his power under subsection (1)(b) to make a fresh designation order in respect of the Article concerned.

(5)   The Secretary of State must by order make such amendments to Schedule 3 as he considers appropriate to reflect—

   (a)   any designation order; or

   (b)   the effect of subsection (3).

(6)   A designation order may be made in anticipation of the making by the United Kingdom of a proposed derogation.

15. Reservations

(1)   In this Act 'designated reservation' means—

   (a)   the United Kingdom's reservation to Article 2 of the First Protocol to the Convention; and

   (b)   any other reservation by the United Kingdom to an Article of the Convention, or of any protocol to the Convention, which is designated for the purposes of this Act in an order made by the Secretary of State.

(2)   The text of the reservation referred to in subsection (1)(a) is set out in Part 11 of Schedule 3.

(3)   If a designated reservation is withdrawn wholly or in part it ceases to be a designated reservation.

(4)   But subsection (3) does not prevent the Secretary of State from exercising his power under subsection (1)(b) to make a fresh designation order in respect of the Article concerned.

(5)   The Secretary of State must by order make such amendments to this Act as he considers appropriate to reflect—

   (a)   any designation order; or

   (b)   the effect of subsection (3).

16. Period for which designated derogations have effect

(1)   If it has not already been withdrawn by the United Kingdom, a designated derogation ceases to have effect for the purposes of this Act—

    (a)   in the case of the derogation referred to in section 14(1)(a), at the end of the period of five years beginning with the date on which section 1(2) came into force;

    (b)   in the case of any other derogation, at the end of the period of five years beginning with the date on which the order designating it was made.

(2)   At any time before the period—

    (a)   fixed by subsection (1)(a) or (b), or

    (b)   extended by an order under this subsection,

comes to an end, the Secretary of State may by order extend it by a further period of five years.

(3)   An order under section 14(1)(b) ceases to have effect at the end of the period for consideration, unless a resolution has been passed by each House approving the order.

(4)   Subsection (3) does not affect—

    (a)   anything done in reliance on the order; or

    (b)   the power to make a fresh order under section 14(1)(b).

(5)   In subsection (3) 'period for consideration' means the period of forty days beginning with the day on which the order was made.

(6)   In calculating the period for consideration, no account is to be taken of any time during which—

    (a)   Parliament is dissolved or prorogued; or

    (b)   both Houses are adjourned for more than four days.

(7)   If a designated derogation is withdrawn by the United Kingdom, the Secretary of State must by order make such amendments to this Act as he considers are required to reflect that withdrawal.

17. Periodic review of designated reservations

(1)   The appropriate Minister must review the designated reservation referred to in section 15(1)(a)—

    (a)   before the end of the period of five years beginning with the date on which section 1(2) came into force; and

    (b)   if that designation is still in force, before the end of the period of five years beginning with the date on which the last report relating to it was laid under subsection (3).

(2)   The appropriate Minister must review each of the other designated reservations (if any)—

    (a)   before the end of the period of five years beginning with the date on which the order designating the reservation first came into force; and

(b)   if the designation is still in force, before the end of the period of five years beginning with the date on which the last report relating to it was laid under subsection (3).

(3)   The Minister conducting a review under this section must prepare a report on the result of the review and lay a copy of it before each House of Parliament.

Judges of the European Court of Human Rights

18.   Appointment to European Court of Human Rights

(1)   In this section 'judicial office' means the office of—

(a)   Lord Justice of Appeal, Justice of the High Court or Circuit judge, in England and Wales;

(b)   judge of the Court of Session or sheriff, in Scotland;

(c)   Lord Justice of Appeal, judge of the High Court or county court judge, in Northern Ireland.

(2)   The holder of a judicial office may become a judge of the European Court of Human Rights ('the Court') without being required to relinquish his office.

(3)   But he is not required to perform the duties of his judicial office while he is a judge of the Court.

(4)   In respect of any period during which he is a judge of the Court—

(a)   a Lord Justice of Appeal or Justice of the High Court is not to count as a judge of the relevant court for the purposes of section 2(1) or 4(1) of the Supreme Court Act 1981 (maximum number of judges) nor as a judge of the Supreme Court for the purposes of section 12(1) to (6) of that Act (salaries etc.);

(b)   a judge of the Court of Session is not to count as a judge of that court for the purposes of section 1(1) of the Court of Session Act 1988 (maximum number of judges) or of section 9(1)(c) of the Administration of Justice Act 1973 ('the 1973 Act') (salaries etc.);

(c)   a Lord Justice of Appeal or judge of the High Court in Northern Ireland is not to count as a judge of the relevant court for the purposes of section 2(1) or 3(1) of the Judicature (Northern Ireland) Act 1978 (maximum number of judges) nor as a judge of the Supreme Court of Northern Ireland for the purposes of section 9(1)(d) of the 1973 Act (salaries etc.);

(d)   a Circuit judge is not to count as such for the purposes of section 18 of the Courts Act 1971 (salaries etc.);

(e)   a sheriff is not to count as such for the purposes of section 14 of the Sheriff Courts (Scotland) Act 1907 (salaries etc.);

(f)   a county court judge of Northern Ireland is not to count as such for the purposes of section 106 of the County Courts Act (Northern Ireland) 1959 (salaries etc.).

(5)   If a sheriff principal is appointed a judge of the Court, section 11(1) of the Sheriff Courts (Scotland) Act 1971 (temporary appointment of sheriff principal) applies, while he holds that appointment, as if his office is vacant.

(6)   Schedule 4 makes provision about judicial pensions in relation to the holder of a judicial office who serves as a judge of the Court.

(7)   The Lord Chancellor or the Secretary of State may by order make such transitional provision (including, in particular, provision for a temporary increase in the maximum number of judges) as he considers appropriate in relation to any holder of a judicial office who has completed his service as a judge of the Court.

Parliamentary procedure

19.   Statements of compatibility

(1)   A Minister of the Crown in charge of a Bill in either House of Parliament must, before Second Reading of the Bill—

(a)   make a statement to the effect that in his view the provisions of the Bill are compatible with the Convention rights ('a statement of compatibility'); or

(b)   make a statement to the effect that although he is unable to make a statement of compatibility the government nevertheless wishes the House to proceed with the Bill.

(2)   The statement must be in writing and be published in such manner as the Minister making it considers appropriate.

Supplemental

20.   Orders etc. under this Act

(1)   Any power of a Minister of the Crown to make an order under this Act is exercisable by statutory instrument.

(2)   The power of the Lord Chancellor or the Secretary of State to make rules (other than rules of court) under section 2(3) or 7(9) is exercisable by statutory instrument.

(3)   Any statutory instrument made under section 14, 15 or 16(7) must be laid before Parliament.

(4)   No order may be made by the Lord Chancellor or the Secretary of State under section 1(4), 7(11) or 16(2) unless a draft of the order has been laid before, and approved by, each House of Parliament.

(5)   Any statutory instrument made under section 18(7) or Schedule 4, or to which subsection (2) applies, shall be subject to annulment in pursuance of a resolution of either House of Parliament.

(6)   The power of a Northern Ireland department to make—

(a)   rules under section 2(3)(c) or 7(9)(c), or

(b)   an order under section 7(11),

is exercisable by statutory rule for the purposes of the Statutory Rules (Northern Ireland) Order 1979.

(7) Any rules made under section 2(3)(c) or 7(9)(c) shall be subject to negative resolution; and section 41(6) of the Interpretation Act (Northern Ireland) 1954 (meaning of 'subject to negative resolution') shall apply as if the power to make the rules were conferred by an Act of the Northern Ireland Assembly.

(8) No order may be made by a Northern Ireland department under section 7(11) unless a draft of the order has been laid before, and approved by, the Northern Ireland Assembly.

21. Interpretation etc.

(1) In this Act—

'amend' includes repeal and apply (with or without modifications);

'the appropriate Minister' means the Minister of the Crown having charge of the appropriate authorised government department (within the meaning of the Crown Proceedings Act 1947);

'the Commission' means the European Commission of Human Rights;

'the Convention' means the Convention for the Protection of Human Rights and Fundamental Freedoms, agreed by the Council of Europe at Rome on 4th November 1950 as it has effect for the time being in relation to the United Kingdom;

'declaration of incompatibility' means a declaration under section 4;

'Minister of the Crown' has the same meaning as in the Ministers of the Crown Act 1975;

'Northern Ireland Minister' includes the First Minister and the deputy First Minister in Northern Ireland;

'primary legislation' means any—

    (a) public general Act;
    (b) local and personal Act;
    (c) private Act;
    (d) Measure of the Church Assembly;
    (e) Measure of the General Synod of the Church of England;
    (f) Order in Council—
      (i) made in exercise of Her Majesty's Royal Prerogative;
      (ii) made under section 38(1)(a) of the Northern Ireland Constitution Act 1973 or the corresponding provision of the Northern Ireland Act 1998; or
      (iii) amending an Act of a kind mentioned in paragraph (a), (b) or (c);

and includes an order or other instrument made under primary legislation (otherwise than by the National Assembly for Wales, a member of the Scottish Executive, a Northern Ireland Minister or a Northern Ireland department) to the extent to which it operates to bring one or more provisions of that legislation into force or amends any primary legislation;

'the First Protocol' means the protocol to the Convention agreed at Paris on 20th March 1952;

'the Sixth Protocol' means the protocol to the Convention agreed at Strasbourg on 28th April 1983;

'the Eleventh Protocol' means the protocol to the Convention (restructuring the control machinery established by the Convention) agreed at Strasbourg on 11th May 1994;

'remedial order' means an order under section 10;

'subordinate legislation' means any—

    (a)   Order in Council other than one—

        (i)   made in exercise of Her Majesty's Royal Prerogative;

        (ii)   made under section 38(1)(a) of the Northern Ireland Constitution Act 1973 or the corresponding provision of the Northern Ireland Act 1998; or

        (iii)   amending an Act of a kind mentioned in the definition of primary legislation;

    (b)   Act of the Scottish Parliament;

    (c)   Act of the Parliament of Northern Ireland;

    (d)   Measure of the Assembly established under section 1 of the Northern Ireland Assembly Act 1973;

    (e)   Act of the Northern Ireland Assembly;

    (f)   order, rules, regulations, scheme, warrant, byelaw or other instrument made under primary legislation (except to the extent to which it operates to bring one or more provisions of that legislation into force or amends any primary legislation);

    (g)   order, rules, regulations, scheme, warrant, byelaw or other instrument made under legislation mentioned in paragraph (b), (c), (d) or (e) or made under an Order in Council applying only to Northern Ireland;

    (h)   order, rules, regulations, scheme, warrant, byelaw or other instrument made by a member of the Scottish Executive, a Northern Ireland Minister or a Northern Ireland department in exercise of prerogative or other executive functions of Her Majesty which are exercisable by such a person on behalf of Her Majesty;

'transferred matters' has the same meaning as in the Northern Ireland Act 1998; and

'tribunal' means any tribunal in which legal proceedings may be brought.

(2)   The references in paragraphs (b) and (c) of section 2(1) to Articles are to Articles of the Convention as they had effect immediately before the coming into force of the Eleventh Protocol.

(3)   The reference in paragraph (d) of section 2(1) to Article 46 includes a reference to Articles 32 and 54 of the Convention as they had effect immediately before the coming into force of the Eleventh Protocol.

(4)   The references in section 2(1) to a report or decision of the Commission or a decision of the Committee of Ministers include references to a report or

decision made as provided by paragraphs 3, 4 and 6 of Article 5 of the Eleventh Protocol (transitional provisions).

(5)   Any liability under the Army Act 1955, the Air Force Act 1955 or the Naval Discipline Act 1957 to suffer death for an offence is replaced by a liability to imprisonment for life or any less punishment authorised by those Acts; and those Acts shall accordingly have effect with the necessary modifications.

22.   Short title, commencement, application and extent

(1)   This Act may be cited as the Human Rights Act 1998.

(2)   Sections 18, 20 and 21(5) and this section come into force on the passing of this Act.

(3)   The other provisions of this Act come into force on such day as the Secretary of State may by order appoint; and different days may be appointed for different purposes.

(4)   Paragraph (b) of subsection (1) of section 7 applies to proceedings brought by or at the instigation of a public authority whenever the act in question took place; but otherwise that subsection does not apply to an act taking place before the coming into force of that section.

(5)   This Act binds the Crown.

(6)   This Act extends to Northern Ireland.

(7)   Section 21(5), so far as it relates to any provision contained in the Army Act 1955, the Air Force Act 1955 or the Naval Discipline Act 1957, extends to any place to which that provision extends.

SCHEDULES

Section 1(3)   SCHEDULE 1
                                            THE ARTICLES

PART I
THE CONVENTION

RIGHTS AND FREEDOMS

Article 2
Right to life

1.   Everyone's right to life shall be protected by law. No one shall be deprived of his life intentionally save in the execution of a sentence of a court following his conviction of a crime for which this penalty is provided by law.

2.   Deprivation of life shall not be regarded as inflicted in contravention of this Article when it results from the use of force which is no more than absolutely necessary:

(a)   in defence of any person from unlawful violence;

(b)   in order to effect a lawful arrest or to prevent the escape of a person lawfully detained;

(c)   in action lawfully taken for the purpose of quelling a riot or insurrection.

Article 3
Prohibition of torture

No one shall be subjected to torture or to inhuman or degrading treatment or punishment.

Article 4
Prohibition of slavery and forced labour

1.   No one shall be held in slavery or servitude.

2.   No one shall be required to perform forced or compulsory labour.

3.   For the purpose of this Article the term 'forced or compulsory labour' shall not include:

(a)   any work required to be done in the ordinary course of detention imposed according to the provisions of Article 5 of this Convention or during conditional release from such detention;

(b)   any service of a military character or, in case of conscientious objectors in countries where they are recognised, service exacted instead of compulsory military service;

(c)   any service exacted in case of an emergency or calamity threatening the life or well-being of the community;

(d)   any work or service which forms part of normal civic obligations.

Article 5
Right to liberty and security

1.   Everyone has the right to liberty and security of person. No one shall be deprived of his liberty save in the following cases and in accordance with a procedure prescribed by law:

(a)   the lawful detention of a person after conviction by a competent court;

(b)   the lawful arrest or detention of a person for non-compliance with the lawful order of a court or in order to secure the fulfilment of any obligation prescribed by law;

(c)   the lawful arrest or detention of a person effected for the purpose of bringing him before the competent legal authority on reasonable suspicion of having committed an offence or when it is reasonably considered necessary to prevent his committing an offence or fleeing after having done so;

(d)   the detention of a minor by lawful order for the purpose of educational supervision or his lawful detention for the purpose of bringing him before the competent legal authority;

(e)   the lawful detention of persons for the prevention of the spreading of infectious diseases, of persons of unsound mind, alcoholics or drug addicts or vagrants;

(f)   the lawful arrest or detention of a person to prevent his effecting an unauthorised entry into the country or of a person against whom action is being taken with a view to deportation or extradition.

2.   Everyone who is arrested shall be informed promptly, in a language which he understands, of the reasons for his arrest and of any charge against him.

3.   Everyone arrested or detained in accordance with the provisions of paragraph 1(c) of this Article shall be brought promptly before a judge or other officer authorised by law to exercise judicial power and shall be entitled to trial within a reasonable time or to release pending trial. Release may be conditioned by guarantees to appear for trial.

4.   Everyone who is deprived of his liberty by arrest or detention shall be entitled to take proceedings by which the lawfulness of his detention shall be decided speedily by a court and his release ordered if the detention is not lawful.

5.   Everyone who has been the victim of arrest or detention in contravention of the provisions of this Article shall have an enforceable right to compensation.

Article 6
Right to a fair trial

1.   In the determination of his civil rights and obligations or of any criminal charge against him, everyone is entitled to a fair and public hearing within a reasonable time by an independent and impartial tribunal established by law. Judgment shall be pronounced publicly but the press and public may be excluded from all or part of the trial in the interest of morals, public order or national security in a democratic society, where the interests of juveniles or the protection of the private life of the parties so require, or to the extent strictly necessary in the opinion of the court in special circumstances where publicity would prejudice the interests of justice.

2.   Everyone charged with a criminal offence shall be presumed innocent until proved guilty according to law.

3.   Everyone charged with a criminal offence has the following minimum rights:

(a)   to be informed promptly, in a language which he understands and in detail, of the nature and cause of the accusation against him;

(b)   to have adequate time and facilities for the preparation of his defence;

(c)   to defend himself in person or through legal assistance of his own choosing or, if he has not sufficient means to pay for legal assistance, to be given it free when the interests of justice so require;

(d)   to examine or have examined witnesses against him and to obtain the attendance and examination of witnesses on his behalf under the same conditions as witnesses against him;

(e)   to have the free assistance of an interpreter if he cannot understand or speak the language used in court.

Article 7
No punishment without law

1.   No one shall be held guilty of any criminal offence on account of any act or omission which did not constitute a criminal offence under national or international law at the time when it was committed. Nor shall a heavier penalty be imposed than the one that was applicable at the time the criminal offence was committed.

2.   This Article shall not prejudice the trial and punishment of any person for any act or omission which, at the time when it was committed, was criminal according to the general principles of law recognised by civilised nations.

Article 8
Right to respect for private and family life

1.   Everyone has the right to respect for his private and family life, his home and his correspondence.

2.   There shall be no interference by a public authority with the exercise of this right except such as is in accordance with the law and is necessary in a democratic society in the interests of national security, public safety or the economic well being of the country, for the prevention of disorder or crime, for the protection of health or morals, or for the protection of the rights and freedoms of others.

Article 9
Freedom of thought, conscience and religion

1.   Everyone has the right to freedom of thought, conscience and religion; this right includes freedom to change his religion or belief and freedom, either alone or in community with others and in public or private, to manifest his religion or belief, in worship, teaching, practice and observance.

2.   Freedom to manifest one's religion or beliefs shall be subject only to such limitations as are prescribed by law and are necessary in a democratic society in the interests of public safety, for the protection of public order, health or morals, or for the protection of the rights and freedoms of others.

Article 10
Freedom of expression

1.   Everyone has the right to freedom of expression. This right shall include freedom to hold opinions and to receive and impart information and ideas without interference by public authority and regardless of frontiers. This Article shall not prevent States from requiring the licensing of broadcasting, television or cinema enterprises.

2. The exercise of these freedoms, since it carries with it duties and responsibilities, may be subject to such formalities, conditions, restrictions or penalties as are prescribed by law and are necessary in a democratic society, in the interests of national security, territorial integrity or public safety, for the prevention of disorder or crime, for the protection of health or morals, for the protection of the reputation or rights of others, for preventing the disclosure of information received in confidence, or for maintaining the authority and impartiality of the judiciary.

Article 11
Freedom of assembly and association

1. Everyone has the right to freedom of peaceful assembly and to freedom of association with others, including the right to form and to join trade unions for the protection of his interests.

2. No restrictions shall be placed on the exercise of these rights other than such as are prescribed by law and are necessary in a democratic society in the interests of national security or public safety, for the prevention of disorder or crime, for the protection of health or morals or for the protection of the rights and freedoms of others. This Article shall not prevent the imposition of lawful restrictions on the exercise of these rights by members of the armed forces, of the police or of the administration of the State.

Article 12
Right to marry

Men and women of marriageable age have the right to marry and to found a family, according to the national laws governing the exercise of this right.

Article 14
Prohibition of discrimination

The enjoyment of the rights and freedoms set forth in this Convention shall be secured without discrimination on any ground such as sex, race, colour, language, religion, political or other opinion, national or social origin, association with a national minority, property, birth or other status.

Article 16
Restrictions on political activity of aliens

Nothing in Articles 10, 11 and 14 shall be regarded as preventing the High Contracting Parties from imposing restrictions on the political activity of aliens.

Article 17
Prohibition of abuse of rights

Nothing in this Convention may be interpreted as implying for any State, group or person any right to engage in any activity or perform any act aimed at the destruction of any of the rights and freedoms set forth herein or at their limitation to a greater extent than is provided for in the Convention.

Article 18
Limitation on use of restrictions on rights

The restrictions permitted under this Convention to the said rights and freedoms shall not be applied for any purpose other than those for which they have been prescribed.

PART II
THE FIRST PROTOCOL

Article 1
Protection of property

Every natural or legal person is entitled to the peaceful enjoyment of his possessions. No one shall be deprived of his possessions except in the public interest and subject to the conditions provided for by law and by the general principles of international law.

The preceding provisions shall not, however, in any way impair the right of a State to enforce such laws as it deems necessary to control the use of property in accordance with the general interest or to secure the payment of taxes or other contributions or penalties.

Article 2
Right to education

No person shall be denied the right to education. In the exercise of any functions which it assumes in relation to education and to teaching, the State shall respect the right of parents to ensure such education and teaching in conformity with their own religious and philosophical convictions.

Article 3
Right to free elections

The High Contracting Parties undertake to hold free elections at reasonable intervals by secret ballot, under conditions which will ensure the free expression of the opinion of the people in the choice of the legislature.

PART III
THE SIXTH PROTOCOL

Article 1
Abolition of the death penalty

The death penalty shall be abolished. No one shall be condemned to such penalty or executed.

Article 2
Death penalty in time of war

A State may make provision in its law for the death penalty in respect of acts committed in time of war or of imminent threat of war; such penalty shall be applied only in the instances laid down in the law and in accordance with its provisions. The State shall communicate to the Secretary General of the Council of Europe the relevant provisions of that law.

SCHEDULE 2
REMEDIAL ORDERS

Orders

1.—(1)   A remedial order may—

(a)   contain such incidental, supplemental, consequential or transitional provision as the person making it considers appropriate;

(b)   be made so as to have effect from a date earlier than that on which it is made;

(c)   make provision for the delegation of specific functions;

(d)   make different provision for different cases.

(2)   The power conferred by sub-paragraph (1)(a) includes—

(a)   power to amend primary legislation (including primary legislation other than that which contains the incompatible provision); and

(b)   power to amend or revoke subordinate legislation (including subordinate legislation other than that which contains the incompatible provision).

(3)   A remedial order may be made so as to have the same extent as the legislation which it affects.

(4)   No person is to be guilty of an offence solely as a result of the retrospective effect of a remedial order.

Procedure

2.   No remedial order may be made unless—

(a)   a draft of the order has been approved by a resolution of each House of Parliament made after the end of the period of 60 days beginning with the day on which the draft was laid; or

(b)   it is declared in the order that it appears to the person making it that, because of the urgency of the matter, it is necessary to make the order without a draft being so approved.

Orders laid in draft

3.—(1)   No draft may be laid under paragraph 2(a) unless—

(a)   the person proposing to make the order has laid before Parliament a document which contains a draft of the proposed order and the required information; and

(b)   the period of 60 days, beginning with the day on which the document required by this sub-paragraph was laid, has ended.

(2)   If representations have been made during that period, the draft laid under paragraph 2(a) must be accompanied by a statement containing—

(a)   a summary of the representations; and

(b)   if, as a result of the representations, the proposed order has been changed, details of the changes.

Urgent cases

4.—(1)   If a remedial order ('the original order') is made without being approved in draft, the person making it must lay it before Parliament, accompanied by the required information, after it is made.

(2)   If representations have been made during the period of 60 days beginning with the day on which the original order was made, the person making it must (after the end of that period) lay before Parliament a statement containing—

(a)   a summary of the representations; and

(b)   if, as a result of the representations, he considers it appropriate to make changes to the original order, details of the changes.

(3)   If sub-paragraph (2)(b) applies, the person making the statement must—

(a)   make a further remedial order replacing the original order; and

(b)   lay the replacement order before Parliament.

(4)   If, at the end of the period of 120 days beginning with the day on which the original order was made, a resolution has not been passed by each House approving the original or replacement order, the order ceases to have effect (but without that affecting anything previously done under either order or the power to make a fresh remedial order).

Definitions

5.   In this Schedule—

'representations' means representations about a remedial order (or proposed remedial order) made to the person making (or proposing to make) it and includes any relevant Parliamentary report or resolution; and

'required information' means—

(a)   an explanation of the incompatibility which the order (or proposed order) seeks to remove, including particulars of the relevant declaration, finding or order; and

(b)   a statement of the reasons for proceeding under section 10 and for making an order in those terms.

Calculating periods

6.   In calculating any period for the purposes of this Schedule, no account is to be taken of any time during which—

(a)   Parliament is dissolved or prorogued; or

(b)   both Houses are adjourned for more than four days.

SCHEDULE 3
DEROGATION AND RESERVATION

PART I
DEROGATION

The 1988 notification

The United Kingdom Permanent Representative to the Council of Europe presents his compliments to the Secretary General of the Council, and has the honour to convey the following information in order to ensure compliance with the obligations of Her Majesty's Government in the United Kingdom under Article 15(3) of the Convention for the Protection of Human Rights and Fundamental Freedoms signed at Rome on 4 November 1950.

There have been in the United Kingdom in recent years campaigns of organised terrorism connected with the affairs of Northern Ireland which have manifested themselves in activities which have included repeated murder, attempted murder, maiming, intimidation and violent civil disturbance and in bombing and fire raising which have resulted in death, injury and widespread destruction of property. As a result, a public emergency within the meaning of Article 15(1) of the Convention exists in the United Kingdom.

The Government found it necessary in 1974 to introduce and since then, in cases concerning persons reasonably suspected of involvement in terrorism connected with the affairs of Northern Ireland, or of certain offences under the legislation, who have been detained for 48 hours, to exercise powers enabling further detention without charge, for periods of up to five days, on the authority of the Secretary of State. These powers are at present to be found in Section 12 of the Prevention of Terrorism (Temporary Provisions) Act 1984, Article 9 of the Prevention of Terrorism (Supplemental Temporary Provisions) Order 1984 and Article 10 of the Prevention of Terrorism (Supplemental Temporary Provisions) (Northern Ireland) Order 1984.

Section 12 of the Prevention of Terrorism (Temporary Provisions) Act 1984 provides for a person whom a constable has arrested on reasonable grounds of suspecting him to be guilty of an offence under Section 1, 9 or 10 of the Act, or to be or to have been involved in terrorism connected with the affairs of Northern Ireland, to be detained in right of the arrest for up to 48 hours and thereafter, where the Secretary of State extends the detention period, for up to a further five days. Section 12 substantially re-enacted Section 12 of the Prevention of Terrorism (Temporary Provisions) Act 1976 which, in turn, substantially re-enacted Section 7 of the Prevention of Terrorism (Temporary Provisions) Act 1974.

Article 10 of the Prevention of Terrorism (Supplemental Temporary Provisions) (Northern Ireland) Order 1984 (SI 1984/417) and Article 9 of the Prevention of Terrorism (Supplemental Temporary Provisions) Order 1984 (SI 1984/418) were both made under Sections 13 and 14 of and Schedule 3 to the 1984 Act and substantially re-enacted powers of detention in Orders made under the 1974 and 1976 Acts. A person who is being examined under Article 4 of either Order on his arrival in, or on seeking to leave, Northern Ireland or Great Britain for the purpose of determining whether he is or has been involved in terrorism connected with the affairs of Northern Ireland, or whether there are grounds for suspecting that he has committed an offence under Section 9 of the 1984 Act, may be detained under Article 9 or 10, as appropriate, pending the conclusion of his examination. The period of this examination may exceed 12 hours if an examining officer has reasonable grounds for suspecting him to be or to have been involved in acts of terrorism connected with the affairs of Northern Ireland.

Where such a person is detained under the said Article 9 or 10 he may be detained for up to 48 hours on the authority of an examining officer and thereafter, where the Secretary of State extends the detention period, for up to a further five days.

In its judgment of 29 November 1988 in the Case of *Brogan and Others*, the European Court of Human Rights held that there had been a violation of Article 5(3) in respect of each of the applicants, all of whom had been detained under Section 12 of the 1984 Act. The Court held that even the shortest of the four periods of detention concerned, namely four days and six hours, fell outside the constraints as to time permitted by the first part of Article 5(3). In addition, the Court held that there had been a violation of Article 5(5) in the case of each applicant.

Following this judgment, the Secretary of State for the Home Department informed Parliament on 6 December 1988 that, against the background of the terrorist campaign, and the over-riding need to bring terrorists to justice, the Government did not believe that the maximum period of detention should be reduced. He informed Parliament that the Government were examining the matter with a view to responding to the judgment. On 22 December 1988, the Secretary of State further informed Parliament that it remained the Government's wish, if it could be achieved, to find a judicial process under which extended detention might be reviewed and where appropriate authorised by a judge or other judicial officer. But a further period of reflection and consultation was necessary before the Government could bring forward a firm and final view.

Since the judgment of 29 November 1988 as well as previously, the Government have found it necessary to continue to exercise, in relation to terrorism connected with the affairs of Northern Ireland, the powers described above enabling further detention without charge for periods of up to 5 days, on the authority of the Secretary of State, to the extent strictly required by the exigencies of the situation to enable necessary enquiries and investigations properly to be completed in order to decide whether criminal proceedings should be instituted. To the extent that the exercise of these powers may be inconsistent with the obligations imposed by the Convention the Government has availed itself of the right of derogation conferred by Article 15(1) of the Convention and will continue to do so until further notice.

Dated 23 December 1988.

The 1989 notification

The United Kingdom Permanent Representative to the Council of Europe presents his compliments to the Secretary General of the Council, and has the honour to convey the following information.

In his communication to the Secretary General of 23 December 1988, reference was made to the introduction and exercise of certain powers under section 12 of the Prevention of Terrorism (Temporary Provisions) Act 1984, Article 9 of the Prevention of Terrorism (Supplemental Temporary Provisions) Order 1984 and Article 10 of the Prevention of Terrorism (Supplemental Temporary Provisions) (Northern Ireland) Order 1984.

These provisions have been replaced by section 14 of and paragraph 6 of Schedule 5 to the Prevention of Terrorism (Temporary Provisions) Act 1989, which make comparable provision. They came into force on 22 March 1989. A copy of these provisions is enclosed.

The United Kingdom Permanent Representative avails himself of this opportunity to renew to the Secretary General the assurance of his highest consideration.

23 March 1989.

PART II
RESERVATION

At the time of signing the present (First) Protocol, I declare that, in view of certain provisions of the Education Acts in the United Kingdom, the principle affirmed in the second sentence of Article 2 is accepted by the United Kingdom only so far as it is compatible with the provision of efficient instruction and training, and the avoidance of unreasonable public expenditure.

Dated 20 March 1952. Made by the United Kingdom Permanent Representative to the Council of Europe.

SCHEDULE 4
JUDICIAL PENSIONS

Duty to make orders about pensions

1.—(1) The appropriate Minister must by order make provision with respect to pensions payable to or in respect of any holder of a judicial office who serves as an ECHR judge.

(2)   A pensions order must include such provision as the Minister making it considers is necessary to secure that—

(a)   an ECHR judge who was, immediately before his appointment as an ECHR judge, a member of a judicial pension scheme is entitled to remain as a member of that scheme;

(b)   the terms on which he remains a member of the scheme are those which would have been applicable had he not been appointed as an ECHR judge; and

(c)   entitlement to benefits payable in accordance with the scheme continues to be determined as if, while serving as an ECHR judge, his salary was that which would (but for section 18(4)) have been payable to him in respect of his continuing service as the holder of his judicial office.

Contributions

2.   A pensions order may, in particular, make provision—

(a)   for any contributions which are payable by a person who remains a member of a scheme as a result of the order, and which would otherwise be payable by deduction from his salary, to be made otherwise than by deduction from his salary as an ECHR judge; and

(b)   for such contributions to be collected in such manner as may be determined by the administrators of the scheme.

Amendments of other enactments

3.   A pensions order may amend any provision of, or made under, a pensions Act in such manner and to such extent as the Minister making the order considers necessary or expedient to ensure the proper administration of any scheme to which it relates.

Definitions

4.   In this Schedule—

'appropriate Minister' means—

(a)   in relation to any judicial office whose jurisdiction is exercisable exclusively in relation to Scotland, the Secretary of State; and

(b)   otherwise, the Lord Chancellor;

'ECHR judge' means the holder of a judicial office who is serving as a judge of the Court;

'judicial pension scheme' means a scheme established by and in accordance with a pensions Act;

'pensions Act means—

(a)   the County Courts Act (Northern Ireland) 1959;

(b)   the Sheriffs' Pensions (Scotland) Act 1961;

(c)   the Judicial Pensions Act 1981; or

(d)   the Judicial Pensions and Retirement Act 1993; and

'pensions order' means an order made under paragraph 1.

Appendix Two

European Convention on Human Rights

CONVENTION FOR THE PROTECTION OF HUMAN RIGHTS AND
FUNDAMENTAL FREEDOMS AS AMENDED BY PROTOCOL NO. 11
(Date of entry into force 1 November 1998)

The governments signatory hereto, being members of the Council of Europe,

Considering the Universal Declaration of Human Rights proclaimed by the General Assembly of the United Nations on 10th December 1948;

Considering that this Declaration aims at securing the universal and effective recognition and observance of the Rights therein declared;

Considering that the aim of the Council of Europe is the achievement of greater unity between its members and that one of the methods by which that aim is to be pursued is the maintenance and further realisation of human rights and fundamental freedoms;

Reaffirming their profound belief in those fundamental freedoms which are the foundation of justice and peace in the world and are best maintained on the one hand by an effective political democracy and on the other by a common understanding and observance of the human rights upon which they depend;

Being resolved, as the governments of European countries which are like-minded and have a common heritage of political traditions, ideals, freedom and the rule of law, to take the first steps for the collective enforcement of certain of the rights stated in the Universal Declaration,

Have agreed as follows:

Article 1
Obligation to respect human rights

The High Contracting Parties shall secure to everyone within their jurisdiction the rights and freedoms defined in Section I of this Convention.

Section I — Rights and freedoms

Article 2
Right to life

1   Everyone's right to life shall be protected by law. No one shall be deprived of his life intentionally save in the execution of a sentence of a court following his conviction of a crime for which this penalty is provided by law.

2   Deprivation of life shall not be regarded as inflicted in contravention of this article when it results from the use of force which is no more than absolutely necessary:

a   in defence of any person from unlawful violence;

b   in order to effect a lawful arrest or to prevent the escape of a person lawfully detained;

c   in action lawfully taken for the purpose of quelling a riot or insurrection.

Article 3
Prohibition of torture

No one shall be subjected to torture or to inhuman or degrading treatment or punishment.

Article 4
Prohibition of slavery and forced labour

1   No one shall be held in slavery or servitude.

2   No one shall be required to perform forced or compulsory labour.

3   For the purpose of this article the term 'forced or compulsory labour' shall not include:

a   any work required to be done in the ordinary course of detention imposed according to the provisions of Article 5 of this Convention or during conditional release from such detention;

b   any service of a military character or, in case of conscientious objectors in countries where they are recognised, service exacted instead of compulsory military service;

c   any service exacted in case of an emergency or calamity threatening the life or well-being of the community;

d   any work or service which forms part of normal civic obligations.

Article 5
Right to liberty and security

1   Everyone has the right to liberty and security of person. No one shall be deprived of his liberty save in the following cases and in accordance with a procedure prescribed by law:

a   the lawful detention of a person after conviction by a competent court;

    b the lawful arrest or detention of a person for non-compliance with the lawful order of a court or in order to secure the fulfilment of any obligation prescribed by law;

    c the lawful arrest or detention of a person effected for the purpose of bringing him before the competent legal authority on reasonable suspicion of having committed an offence or when it is reasonably considered necessary to prevent his committing an offence or fleeing after having done so;

    d the detention of a minor by lawful order for the purpose of educational supervision or his lawful detention for the purpose of bringing him before the competent legal authority;

    e the lawful detention of persons for the prevention of the spreading of infectious diseases, of persons of unsound mind, alcoholics or drug addicts or vagrants;

    f the lawful arrest or detention of a person to prevent his effecting an unauthorised entry into the country or of a person against whom action is being taken with a view to deportation or extradition.

2   Everyone who is arrested shall be informed promptly, in a language which he understands, of the reasons for his arrest and of any charge against him.

3   Everyone arrested or detained in accordance with the provisions of paragraph 1.c of this article shall be brought promptly before a judge or other officer authorised by law to exercise judicial power and shall be entitled to trial within a reasonable time or to release pending trial. Release may be conditioned by guarantees to appear for trial.

4   Everyone who is deprived of his liberty by arrest or detention shall be entitled to take proceedings by which the lawfulness of his detention shall be decided speedily by a court and his release ordered if the detention is not lawful.

5   Everyone who has been the victim of arrest or detention in contravention of the provisions of this article shall have an enforceable right to compensation.

Article 6
Right to a fair trial

1   In the determination of his civil rights and obligations or of any criminal charge against him, everyone is entitled to a fair and public hearing within a reasonable time by an independent and impartial tribunal established by law. Judgment shall be pronounced publicly but the press and public may be excluded from all or part of the trial in the interests of morals, public order or national security in a democratic society, where the interests of juveniles or the protection of the private life of the parties so require, or to the extent strictly necessary in the opinion of the court in special circumstances where publicity would prejudice the interests of justice.

2   Everyone charged with a criminal offence shall be presumed innocent until proved guilty according to law.

3   Everyone charged with a criminal offence has the following minimum rights:

a   to be informed promptly, in a language which he understands and in detail, of the nature and cause of the accusation against him;

b   to have adequate time and facilities for the preparation of his defence;

c   to defend himself in person or through legal assistance of his own choosing or, if he has not sufficient means to pay for legal assistance, to be given it free when the interests of justice so require;

d   to examine or have examined witnesses against him and to obtain the attendance and examination of witnesses on his behalf under the same conditions as witnesses against him;

e   to have the free assistance of an interpreter if he cannot understand or speak the language used in court.

Article 7
No punishment without law

1   No one shall be held guilty of any criminal offence on account of any act or omission which did not constitute a criminal offence under national or international law at the time when it was committed. Nor shall a heavier penalty be imposed than the one that was applicable at the time the criminal offence was committed.

2   This article shall not prejudice the trial and punishment of any person for any act or omission which, at the time when it was committed, was criminal according to the general principles of law recognised by civilised nations.

Article 8
Right to respect for private and family life

1   Everyone has the right to respect for his private and family life, his home and his correspondence.

2   There shall be no interference by a public authority with the exercise of this right except such as is in accordance with the law and is necessary in a democratic society in the interests of national security, public safety or the economic well-being of the country, for the prevention of disorder or crime, for the protection of health or morals, or for the protection of the rights and freedoms of others.

Article 9
Freedom of thought, conscience and religion

1   Everyone has the right to freedom of thought, conscience and religion; this right includes freedom to change his religion or belief and freedom, either alone or in community with others and in public or private, to manifest his religion or belief, in worship, teaching, practice and observance.

2   Freedom to manifest one's religion or beliefs shall be subject only to such limitations as are prescribed by law and are necessary in a democratic society in the interests of public safety, for the protection of public order, health or morals, or for the protection of the rights and freedoms of others.

Article 10
Freedom of expression

1   Everyone has the right to freedom of expression. This right shall include freedom to hold opinions and to receive and impart information and ideas without interference by public authority and regardless of frontiers. This article shall not prevent States from requiring the licensing of broadcasting, television or cinema enterprises.

2   The exercise of these freedoms, since it carries with it duties and responsibilities, may be subject to such formalities, conditions, restrictions or penalties as are prescribed by law and are necessary in a democratic society, in the interests of national security, territorial integrity or public safety, for the prevention of disorder or crime, for the protection of health or morals, for the protection of the reputation or rights of others, for preventing the disclosure of information received in confidence, or for maintaining the authority and impartiality of the judiciary.

Article 11
Freedom of assembly and association

1   Everyone has the right to freedom of peaceful assembly and to freedom of association with others, including the right to form and to join trade unions for the protection of his interests.

2   No restrictions shall be placed on the exercise of these rights other than such as are prescribed by law and are necessary in a democratic society in the interests of national security or public safety, for the prevention of disorder or crime, for the protection of health or morals or for the protection of the rights and freedoms of others. This article shall not prevent the imposition of lawful restrictions on the exercise of these rights by members of the armed forces, of the police or of the administration of the State.

Article 12
Right to marry

Men and women of marriageable age have the right to marry and to found a family, according to the national laws governing the exercise of this right.

Article 13
Right to an effective remedy

Everyone whose rights and freedoms as set forth in this Convention are violated shall have an effective remedy before a national authority notwithstanding that the violation has been committed by persons acting in an official capacity.

Article 14
Prohibition of discrimination

The enjoyment of the rights and freedoms set forth in this Convention shall be secured without discrimination on any ground such as sex, race, colour, language, religion, political or other opinion, national or social origin, association with a national minority, property, birth or other status.

Article 15
Derogation in time of emergency

1   In time of war or other public emergency threatening the life of the nation any High Contracting Party may take measures derogating from its obligations under this Convention to the extent strictly required by the exigencies of the situation, provided that such measures are not inconsistent with its other obligations under international law.

2   No derogation from Article 2, except in respect of deaths resulting from lawful acts of war, or from Articles 3, 4 (paragraph 1) and 7 shall be made under this provision.

3   Any High Contracting Party availing itself of this right of derogation shall keep the Secretary General of the Council of Europe fully informed of the measures which it has taken and the reasons therefor. It shall also inform the Secretary General of the Council of Europe when such measures have ceased to operate and the provisions of the Convention are again being fully executed.

Article 16
Restrictions on political activity of aliens

Nothing in Articles 10, 11 and 14 shall be regarded as preventing the High Contracting Parties from imposing restrictions on the political activity of aliens.

Article 17
Prohibition of abuse of rights

Nothing in this Convention may be interpreted as implying for any State, group or person any right to engage in any activity or perform any act aimed at the destruction of any of the rights and freedoms set forth herein or at their limitation to a greater extent than is provided for in the Convention.

Article 18
Limitation on use of restrictions on rights

The restrictions permitted under this Convention to the said rights and freedoms shall not be applied for any purpose other than those for which they have been prescribed.

Section II — European Court of Human Rights

Article 19
Establishment of the Court

To ensure the observance of the engagements undertaken by the High Contracting Parties in the Convention and the Protocols thereto, there shall be set up a European Court of Human Rights, hereinafter referred to as 'the Court'. It shall function on a permanent basis.

Article 20
Number of judges

The Court shall consist of a number of judges equal to that of the High Contracting Parties.

Article 21
Criteria for office

1   The judges shall be of high moral character and must either possess the qualifications required for appointment to high judicial office or be jurisconsults of recognised competence.

2   The judges shall sit on the Court in their individual capacity.

3   During their term of office the judges shall not engage in any activity which is incompatible with their independence, impartiality or with the demands of a full-time office; all questions arising from the application of this paragraph shall be decided by the Court.

Article 22
Election of judges

1   The judges shall be elected by the Parliamentary Assembly with respect to each High Contracting Party by a majority of votes cast from a list of three candidates nominated by the High Contracting Party.

2   The same procedure shall be followed to complete the Court in the event of the accession of new High Contracting Parties and in filling casual vacancies.

Article 23
Terms of office

1   The judges shall be elected for a period of six years. They may be re-elected. However, the terms of office of one-half of the judges elected at the first election shall expire at the end of three years.

2   The judges whose terms of office are to expire at the end of the initial period of three years shall be chosen by lot by the Secretary General of the Council of Europe immediately after their election.

3   In order to ensure that, as far as possible, the terms of office of one-half of the judges are renewed every three years, the Parliamentary Assembly may decide, before proceeding to any subsequent election, that the term or terms of office of one or more judges to be elected shall be for a period other than six years but not more than nine and not less than three years.

4   In cases where more than one term of office is involved and where the Parliamentary Assembly applies the preceding paragraph, the allocation of the terms of office shall be effected by a drawing of lots by the Secretary General of the Council of Europe immediately after the election.

5   A judge elected to replace a judge whose term of office has not expired shall hold office for the remainder of his predecessor's term.

6   The terms of office of judges shall expire when they reach the age of 70.

7   The judges shall hold office until replaced. They shall, however, continue to deal with such cases as they already have under consideration.

Article 24
Dismissal

No judge may be dismissed from his office unless the other judges decide by a majority of two-thirds that he has ceased to fulfil the required conditions.

Article 25
Registry and legal secretaries

The Court shall have a registry, the functions and organisation of which shall be laid down in the rules of the Court. The Court shall be assisted by legal secretaries.

Article 26
Plenary Court

The plenary Court shall

    a   elect its President and one or two Vice-Presidents for a period of three years; they may be re-elected;

    b   set up Chambers, constituted for a fixed period of time;

    c   elect the Presidents of the Chambers of the Court; they may be re-elected;

    d   adopt the rules of the Court, and

    e   elect the Registrar and one or more Deputy Registrars.

Article 27
Committees, Chambers and Grand Chamber

1   To consider cases brought before it, the Court shall sit in committees of three judges, in Chambers of seven judges and in a Grand Chamber of seventeen judges. The Court's Chambers shall set up committees for a fixed period of time.

2   There shall sit as an *ex officio* member of the Chamber and the Grand Chamber the judge elected in respect of the State Party concerned or, if there is

none or if he is unable to sit, a person of its choice who shall sit in the capacity of judge.

3 The Grand Chamber shall also include the President of the Court, the Vice-Presidents, the Presidents of the Chambers and other judges chosen in accordance with the rules of the Court. When a case is referred to the Grand Chamber under Article 43, no judge from the Chamber which rendered the judgment shall sit in the Grand Chamber, with the exception of the President of the Chamber and the judge who sat in respect of the State Party concerned.

Article 28
Declarations of inadmissibility by committees

A committee may, by a unanimous vote, declare inadmissible or strike out of its list of cases an application submitted under Article 34 where such a decision can be taken without further examination. The decision shall be final.

Article 29
Decisions by Chambers on admissibility and merits

1 If no decision is taken under Article 28, a Chamber shall decide on the admissibility and merits of individual applications submitted under Article 34.

2 A Chamber shall decide on the admissibility and merits of inter-State applications submitted under Article 33.

3 The decision on admissibility shall be taken separately unless the Court, in exceptional cases, decides otherwise.

Article 30
Relinquishment of jurisdiction to the Grand Chamber

Where a case pending before a Chamber raises a serious question affecting the interpretation of the Convention or the protocols thereto, or where the resolution of a question before the Chamber might have a result inconsistent with a judgment previously delivered by the Court, the Chamber may, at any time before it has rendered its judgment, relinquish jurisdiction in favour of the Grand Chamber, unless one of the parties to the case objects.

Article 31
Powers of the Grand Chamber

The Grand Chamber shall

a determine applications submitted either under Article 33 or Article 34 when a Chamber has relinquished jurisdiction under Article 30 or when the case has been referred to it under Article 43; and

b consider requests for advisory opinions submitted under Article 47.

Article 32
Jurisdiction of the Court

1   The jurisdiction of the Court shall extend to all matters concerning the interpretation and application of the Convention and the protocols thereto which are referred to it as provided in Articles 33, 34 and 47.

2   In the event of dispute as to whether the Court has jurisdiction, the Court shall decide.

Article 33
Inter-State cases

Any High Contracting Party may refer to the Court any alleged breach of the provisions of the Convention and the protocols thereto by another High Contracting Party

Article 34
Individual applications

The Court may receive applications from any person, non-governmental organisation or group of individuals claiming to be the victim of a violation by one of the High Contracting Parties of the rights set forth in the Convention or the protocols thereto. The High Contracting Parties undertake not to hinder in any way the effective exercise of this right.

Article 35
Admissibility criteria

1   The Court may only deal with the matter after all domestic remedies have been exhausted, according to the generally recognised rules of international law, and within a period of six months from the date on which the final decision was taken.

2   The Court shall not deal with any application submitted under Article 34 that

     a   is anonymous; or

     b   is substantially the same as a matter that has already been examined by the Court or has already been submitted to another procedure of international investigation or settlement and contains no relevant new information.

3   The Court shall declare inadmissible any individual application submitted under Article 34 which it considers incompatible with the provisions of the Convention or the protocols thereto, manifestly ill-founded, or an abuse of the right of application.

4   The Court shall reject any application which it considers inadmissible under this Article. It may do so at any stage of the proceedings.

Article 36
Third party intervention

1   In all cases before a Chamber of the Grand Chamber, a High Contracting Party one of whose nationals is an applicant shall have the right to submit written comments and to take part in hearings.

2   The President of the Court may, in the interest of the proper administration of justice, invite any High Contracting Party which is not a party to the proceedings or any person concerned who is not the applicant to submit written comments or take part in hearings.

Article 37
Striking out applications

1   The Court may at any stage of the proceedings decide to strike an application out of its list of cases where the circumstances lead to the conclusion that

  a   the applicant does not intend to pursue his application; or
  b   the matter has been resolved; or
  c   for any other reason established by the Court, it is no longer justified to continue the examination of the application.

However, the Court shall continue the examination of the application if respect for human rights as defined in the Convention and the protocols thereto so requires.

2   The Court may decide to restore an application to its list of cases if it considers that the circumstances justify such a course.

Article 38
Examination of the case and friendly settlement proceedings

1   If the Court declares the application admissible, it shall

  a   pursue the examination of the case, together with the representatives of the parties, and if need be, undertake an investigation, for the effective conduct of which the States concerned shall furnish all necessary facilities;
  b   place itself at the disposal of the parties concerned with a view to securing a friendly settlement of the matter on the basis of respect for human rights as defined in the Convention and the protocols thereto.

2   Proceedings conducted under paragraph 1.b shall be confidential.

Article 39
Finding of a friendly settlement

If a friendly settlement is effected, the Court shall strike the case out of its list by means of a decision which shall be confined to a brief statement of the facts and of the solution reached.

Article 40
Public hearings and access to documents

1   Hearings shall be in public unless the Court in exceptional circumstances decides otherwise.

2   Documents deposited with the Registrar shall be accessible to the public unless the President of the Court decides otherwise.

Article 41
Just satisfaction

If the Court finds that there has been a violation of the Convention or the protocols thereto, and if the internal law of the High Contracting Party concerned allows only partial reparation to be made, the Court shall, if necessary afford just satisfaction to the injured party.

Article 42
Judgments of Chambers

Judgments of Chambers shall become final in accordance with the provisions of Article 44, paragraph 2.

Article 43
Referral to the Grand Chamber

1   Within a period of three months from the date of the judgment of the Chamber, any party to the case may, in exceptional cases, request that the case be referred to the Grand Chamber.

2   A panel of five judges of the Grand Chamber shall accept the request if the case raises a serious question affecting the interpretation or application of the Convention or the protocols thereto, or a serious issue of general importance.

3   If the panel accepts the request, the Grand Chamber shall decide the case by means of a judgment.

Article 44
Final judgments

1   The judgment of the Grand Chamber shall be final.

2   The judgment of a Chamber shall become final

   a   when the parties declare that they will not request that the case be referred to the Grand Chamber; or

   b   three months after the date of the judgment, if reference of the case to the Grand Chamber has not been requested; or

   c   when the panel of the Grand Chamber rejects the request to refer under Article 43.

3   The final judgment shall be published.

Article 45
Reasons for judgments and decisions

1   Reasons shall be given for judgments as well as for decisions declaring applications admissible or inadmissible.

2   If a judgment does not represent, in whole or in part, the unanimous opinion of the judges, any judge shall be entitled to deliver a separate opinion.

Article 46
Binding force and execution of judgments

1   The High Contracting Parties undertake to abide by the final judgment of the Court in any case to which they are parties.

2   The final judgment of the Court shall be transmitted to the Committee of Ministers, which shall supervise its execution.

Article 47
Advisory opinions

1   The Court may, at the request of the Committee of Ministers, give advisory opinions on legal questions concerning the interpretation of the Convention and the protocols thereto.

2   Such opinions shall not deal with any question relating to the content or scope of the rights or freedoms defined in Section I of the Convention and the protocols thereto, or with any other question which the Court or the Committee of Ministers might have to consider in consequence of any such proceedings as could be instituted in accordance with the Convention.

3   Decisions of the Committee of Ministers to request an advisory opinion of the Court shall require a majority vote of the representatives entitled to sit on the Committee.

Article 48
Advisory jurisdiction of the Court

The Court shall decide whether a request for an advisory opinion submitted by the Committee of Ministers is within its competence as defined in Article 47.

Article 49
Reasons for advisory opinions

1   Reasons shall be given for advisory opinions of the Court.

2   If the advisory opinion does not represent, in whole or in part, the unanimous opinion of the judges, any judge shall be entitled to deliver a separate opinion.

3   Advisory opinions of the Court shall be communicated to the Committee of Ministers.

Article 50
Expenditure on the Court

The expenditure on the Court shall be borne by the Council of Europe.

Article 51
Privileges and immunities of judges

The judges shall be entitled, during the exercise of their functions, to the privileges and immunities provided for in Article 40 of the Statute of the Council of Europe and in the agreements made thereunder.

Section III — Miscellaneous provisions

Article 52
Inquiries by the Secretary General

On receipt of a request from the Secretary General of the Council of Europe any High Contracting Party shall furnish an explanation of the manner in which its internal law ensures the effective implementation of any of the provisions of the Convention.

Article 53
Safeguard for existing human rights

Nothing in this Convention shall be construed as limiting or derogating from any of the human rights and fundamental freedoms which may be ensured under the laws of any High Contracting Party or under any other agreement to which it is a Party.

Article 54
Powers of the Committee of Ministers

Nothing in this Convention shall prejudice the powers conferred on the Committee of Ministers by the Statute of the Council of Europe.

Article 55
Exclusion of other means of dispute settlement

The High Contracting Parties agree that, except by special agreement, they will not avail themselves of treaties, conventions or declarations in force between them for the purpose of submitting, by way of petition, a dispute arising out of the interpretation or application of this Convention to a means of settlement other than those provided for in this Convention.

Article 56
Territorial application

1   Any State may at the time of its ratification or at any time thereafter declare by notification addressed to the Secretary General of the Council of Europe that

the present Convention shall, subject to paragraph 4 of this Article, extend to all or any of the territories for whose international relations it is responsible.

2   The Convention shall extend to the territory or territories named in the notification as from the thirtieth day after the receipt of this notification by the Secretary General of the Council of Europe.

3   The provisions of this Convention shall be applied in such territories with due regard, however, to local requirements.

4   Any State which has made a declaration in accordance with paragraph 1 of this article may at any time thereafter declare on behalf of one or more of the territories to which the declaration relates that it accepts the competence of the Court to receive applications from individuals, non-governmental organisations or groups of individuals as provided by Article 34 of the Convention.

Article 57
Reservations

1   Any State may, when signing this Convention or when depositing its instrument of ratification, make a reservation in respect of any particular provision of the Convention to the extent that any law then in force in its territory is not in conformity with the provision. Reservations of a general character shall not be permitted under this article.

2   Any reservation made under this article shall contain a brief statement of the law concerned.

Article 58
Denunciation

1   A High Contracting Party may denounce the present Convention only after the expiry of five years from the date on which it became a party to it and after six months' notice contained in a notification addressed to the Secretary General of the Council of Europe, who shall inform the other High Contracting Parties.

2   Such a denunciation shall not have the effect of releasing the High Contracting Party concerned from its obligations under this Convention in respect of any act which, being capable of constituting a violation of such obligations, may have been performed by it before the date at which the denunciation became effective.

3   Any High Contracting Party which shall cease to be a member of the Council of Europe shall cease to be a Party to this Convention under the same conditions.

4   The Convention may be denounced in accordance with the provisions of the preceding paragraphs in respect of any territory to which it has been declared to extend under the terms of Article 56.

Article 59
Signature and ratification

1   This Convention shall be open to the signature of the members of the Council of Europe. It shall be ratified. Ratifications shall be deposited with the Secretary General of the Council of Europe.

2   The present Convention shall come into force after the deposit of ten instruments of ratification.

3   As regards any signatory ratifying subsequently, the Convention shall come into force at the date of the deposit of its instrument of ratification.

4   The Secretary General of the Council of Europe shall notify all the members of the Council of Europe of the entry into force of the Convention, the names of the High Contracting Parties who have ratified it, and the deposit of all instruments of ratification which may be effected subsequently.

Done at Rome this 4th day of November 1950, in English and French, both texts being equally authentic, in a single copy which shall remain deposited in the archives of the Council of Europe.

The Secretary General shall transmit certified copies to each of the signatories.

PROTOCOL [NO. 1] TO THE CONVENTION FOR THE PROTECTION OF HUMAN RIGHTS AND FUNDAMENTAL FREEDOMS, AS AMENDED BY PROTOCOL NO. 11

The governments signatory hereto, being members of the Council of Europe,

Being resolved to take steps to ensure the collective enforcement of certain rights and freedoms other than those already included in Section I of the Convention for the Protection of Human Rights and Fundamental Freedoms signed at Rome on 4 November 1950 (hereinafter referred to as 'the Convention'),

Have agreed as follows:

Article 1
Protection of property

Every natural or legal person is entitled to the peaceful enjoyment of his possessions. No one shall be deprived of his possessions except in the public interest and subject to the conditions provided for by law and by the general principles of international law.

The preceding provisions shall not, however, in any way impair the right of a State to enforce such laws as it deems necessary to control the use of property in accordance with the general interest or to secure the payment of taxes or other contributions or penalties.

Article 2
Right to education

No person shall be denied the right to education. In the exercise of any functions which it assumes in relation to education and to teaching, the State shall respect the right of parents to ensure such education and teaching in conformity with their own religious and philosophical convictions.

Article 3
Right to free elections

The High Contracting Parties undertake to hold free elections at reasonable intervals by secret ballot, under conditions which will ensure the free expression of the opinion of the people in the choice of the legislature.

Article 4
Territorial application

Any High Contracting Party may at the time of signature or ratification or at any time thereafter communicate to the Secretary General of the Council of Europe a declaration stating the extent to which it undertakes that the provisions of the present Protocol shall apply to such of the territories for the international relations of which it is responsible as are named therein.

Any High Contracting Party which has communicated a declaration in virtue of the preceding paragraph may from time to time communicate a further declaration modifying the terms of any former declaration or terminating the application of the provisions of this Protocol in respect of any territory.

A declaration made in accordance with this article shall be deemed to have been made in accordance with paragraph 1 of Article 56 of the Convention.

Article 5
Relationship to the Convention

As between the High Contracting Parties the provisions of Articles 1, 2, 3 and 4 of this Protocol shall be regarded as additional articles to the Convention and all the provisions of the Convention shall apply accordingly.

Article 6
Signature and ratification

This Protocol shall be open for signature by the members of the Council of Europe, who are the signatories of the Convention; it shall be ratified at the same time as or after the ratification of the Convention. It shall enter into force after the deposit of ten instruments of ratification. As regards any signatory ratifying subsequently, the Protocol shall enter into force at the date of the deposit of its instrument of ratification.

The instruments of ratification shall be deposited with the Secretary General of the Council of Europe, who will notify all members of the names of those who have ratified.

Done at Paris on the 20th day of March 1952, in English and French, both texts being equally authentic, in a single copy which shall remain deposited in the archives of the Council of Europe. The Secretary General shall transmit certified copies to each of the signatory governments.

PROTOCOL NO. 4 TO THE CONVENTION FOR THE PROTECTION OF HUMAN RIGHTS AND FUNDAMENTAL FREEDOMS, SECURING CERTAIN RIGHTS AND FREEDOMS OTHER THAN THOSE ALREADY INCLUDED IN THE CONVENTION AND IN THE FIRST PROTOCOL THERETO, AS AMENDED BY PROTOCOL NO. 11

The governments signatory hereto, being members of the Council of Europe,

Being resolved to take steps to ensure the collective enforcement of certain rights and freedoms other than those already included in Section 1 of the Convention for the Protection of Human Rights and Fundamental Freedoms signed at Rome on 4th November 1950 (hereinafter referred to as the 'Convention') and in Articles 1 to 3 of the First Protocol to the Convention, signed at Paris on 20th March 1952,

Have agreed as follows:

Article 1
Prohibition of imprisonment for debt

No one shall be deprived of his liberty merely on the ground of inability to fulfil a contractual obligation.

Article 2
Freedom of movement

1   Everyone lawfully within the territory of a State shall, within that territory, have the right to liberty of movement and freedom to choose his residence.

2   Everyone shall be free to leave any country, including his own.

3   No restrictions shall be placed on the exercise of these rights other than such as are in accordance with law and are necessary in a democratic society in the interests of national security or public safety, for the maintenance of *ordre public*, for the prevention of crime, for the protection of health or morals, or for the protection of the rights and freedoms of others.

4   The rights set forth in paragraph 1 may also be subject, in particular areas, to restrictions imposed in accordance with law and justified by the public interest in a democratic society.

Article 3
Prohibition of expulsion of nationals

1   No one shall be expelled, by means either of an individual or of a collective measure, from the territory of the State of which he is a national.

2   No one shall be deprived of the right to enter the territory of the state of which he is a national.

Article 4
Prohibition of collective expulsion of aliens

Collective expulsion of aliens is prohibited.

Article 5
Territorial application

1   Any High Contracting Party may, at the time of signature or ratification of this Protocol, or at any time thereafter, communicate to the Secretary General of the Council of Europe a declaration stating the extent to which it undertakes that the provisions of this Protocol shall apply to such of the territories for the international relations of which it is responsible as are named therein.

2   Any High Contracting Party which has communicated a declaration in virtue of the preceding paragraph may, from time to time, communicate a further declaration modifying the terms of any former declaration or terminating the application of the provisions of this Protocol in respect of any territory.

3   A declaration made in accordance with this article shall be deemed to have been made in accordance with paragraph 1 of Article 56 of the Convention.

4   The territory of any State to which this Protocol applies by virtue of ratification or acceptance by that State, and each territory to which this Protocol is applied by virtue of a declaration by that State under this article, shall be treated as separate territories for the purpose of the references in Articles 2 and 3 to the territory of a State.

5   Any State which has made a declaration in accordance with paragraph 1 or 2 of this Article may at any time thereafter declare on behalf of one or more of the territories to which the declaration relates that it accepts the competence of the Court to receive applications from individuals, non-governmental organisations or groups of individuals as provided in Article 34 of the Convention in respect of all or any of Articles 1 to 4 of this Protocol.

Article 6
Relationship to the Convention

As between the High Contracting Parties the provisions of Articles 1 to 5 of this Protocol shall be regarded as additional Articles to the Convention, and all the provisions of the Convention shall apply accordingly.

Article 7
Signature and ratification

1   This Protocol shall be open for signature by the members of the Council of Europe who are the signatories of the Convention; it shall be ratified at the same time as or after the ratification of the Convention. It shall enter into force after the deposit of five instruments of ratification. As regards any signatory ratifying subsequently, the Protocol shall enter into force at the date of the deposit of its instrument of ratification.

2   The instruments of ratification shall be deposited with the Secretary General of the Council of Europe, who will notify all members of the names of those who have ratified.

In witness whereof the undersigned, being duly authorised thereto, have signed this Protocol.

Done at Strasbourg, this 16th day of September 1963, in English and in French, both texts being equally authoritative, in a single copy which shall remain deposited in the archives of the Council of Europe. The Secretary General shall transmit certified copies to each of the signatory states.

PROTOCOL NO. 6 TO THE CONVENTION FOR THE PROTECTION OF HUMAN RIGHTS AND FUNDAMENTAL FREEDOMS CONCERNING THE ABOLITION OF THE DEATH PENALTY, AS AMENDED BY PROTOCOL NO. 11

The member States of the Council of Europe, signatory to this Protocol to the Convention for the Protection of Human Rights and Fundamental Freedoms, signed at Rome on 4 November 1950 (hereinafter referred to as 'the Convention'),

Considering that the evolution that has occurred in several member States of the Council of Europe expresses a general tendency in favour of abolition of the death penalty;

Have agreed as follows:

Article 1
Abolition of the death penalty

The death penalty shall be abolished. No-one shall be condemned to such penalty or executed.

Article 2
Death penalty in time of war

A State may make provision in its law for the death penalty in respect of acts committed in time of war or of imminent threat of war; such penalty shall be applied only in the instances laid down in the law and in accordance with its provisions. The State shall communicate to the Secretary General of the Council of Europe the relevant provisions of that law.

Article 3
Prohibition of derogations

No derogation from the provisions of this Protocol shall be made under Article 15 of the Convention.

Article 4
Prohibition of reservations

No reservation may be made under Article 57 of the Convention in respect of the provisions of this Protocol.

Article 5
Territorial application

1   Any State may at the time of signature or when depositing its instrument of ratification, acceptance or approval, specify the territory or territories to which this Protocol shall apply.

2   Any State may at any later date, by a declaration addressed to the Secretary General of the Council of Europe, extend the application of this Protocol to any other territory specified in the declaration. In respect of such territory the Protocol shall enter into force on the first day of the month following the date of receipt of such declaration by the Secretary General.

3   Any declaration made under the two preceding paragraphs may, in respect of any territory specified in such declaration, be withdrawn by a notification addressed to the Secretary General. The withdrawal shall become effective on the first day of the month following the date of receipt of such notification by the Secretary General.

Article 6
Relationship to the Convention

As between the States Parties the provisions of Articles 1 to 5 of this Protocol shall be regarded as additional articles to the Convention and all the provisions of the Convention shall apply accordingly.

Article 7
Signature and ratification

The Protocol shall be open for signature by the member States of the Council of Europe, signatories to the Convention. It shall be subject to ratification, acceptance or approval. A member State of the Council of Europe may not ratify, accept or approve this Protocol unless it has, simultaneously or previously, ratified the Convention. Instruments of ratification, acceptance or approval shall be deposited with the Secretary General of the Council of Europe.

Article 8
Entry into force

1   This Protocol shall enter into force on the first day of the month following the date on which five member States of the Council of Europe have expressed their consent to be bound by the Protocol in accordance with the provisions of Article 7.

2   In respect of any member State which subsequently expresses its consent to be bound by it, the Protocol shall enter into force on the first day of the month following the date of the deposit of the instrument of ratification, acceptance or approval.

Article 9
Depositary functions

The Secretary General of the Council of Europe shall notify the member States of the Council of:

a   any signature;

b   the deposit of any instrument of ratification, acceptance or approval;

c   any date of entry into force of this Protocol in accordance with Articles 5 and 8;

d   any other act, notification or communication relating to this Protocol.

In witness whereof the undersigned, being duly authorised thereto, have signed this Protocol.

Done at Strasbourg, this 28th day of April 1983, in English and in French, both texts being equally authentic, in a single copy which shall be deposited in the archives of the Council of Europe. The Secretary General of the Council of Europe shall transmit certified copies to each member State of the Council of Europe.

PROTOCOL NO. 7 TO THE CONVENTION FOR THE PROTECTION OF HUMAN RIGHTS AND FUNDAMENTAL FREEDOMS, AS AMENDED BY PROTOCOL NO. 11

The member States of the Council of Europe signatory hereto,

Being resolved to take further steps to ensure the collective enforcement of certain rights and freedoms by means of the Convention for the Protection of Human Rights and Fundamental Freedoms signed at Rome on 4 November 1950 (hereinafter referred to as 'the Convention'),

Have agreed as follows

Article 1
Procedural safeguards relating to expulsion of aliens

1   An alien lawfully resident in the territory of a State shall not be expelled therefrom except in pursuance of a decision reached in accordance with law and shall be allowed:

   a   to submit reasons against his expulsion,

   b   to have his case reviewed, and

   c   to be represented for these purposes before the competent authority or a person or persons designated by that authority.

2   An alien may be expelled before the exercise of his rights under paragraph 1.a, b and c of this Article, when such expulsion is necessary in the interests of public order or is grounded on reasons of national security.

Article 2
Right of appeal in criminal matters

1   Everyone convicted of a criminal offence by a tribunal shall have the right to have his conviction or sentence reviewed by a higher tribunal. The exercise of this right, including the grounds on which it may be exercised, shall be governed by law.

2   This right may be subject to exceptions in regard to offences of a minor character, as prescribed by law, or in cases in which the person concerned was tried in the first instance by the highest tribunal or was convicted following an appeal against acquittal.

Article 3
Compensation for wrongful conviction

When a person has by a final decision been convicted of a criminal offence and when subsequently his conviction has been reversed, or he has been pardoned, on the ground that a new or newly discovered fact shows conclusively that there has been a miscarriage of justice, the person who has suffered punishment as a result of such conviction shall be compensated according to the law or the practice of the State concerned, unless it is proved that the non-disclosure of the unknown fact in time is wholly or partly attributable to him.

Article 4
Right not to be tried or punished twice

1   No one shall be liable to be tried or punished again in criminal proceedings under the jurisdiction of the same State for an offence for which he has already been finally acquitted or convicted in accordance with the law and penal procedure of that State.

2   The provisions of the preceding paragraph shall not prevent the reopening of the case in accordance with the law and penal procedure of the State concerned, if there is evidence of new or newly discovered facts, or if there has been a fundamental defect in the previous proceedings, which could affect the outcome of the case.

3   No derogation from this Article shall be made under Article 15 of the Convention.

Article 5
Equality between spouses

Spouses shall enjoy equality of rights and responsibilities of a private law character between them, and in their relations with their children, as to marriage, during marriage and in the event of its dissolution. This Article shall not prevent States from taking such measures as are necessary in the interests of the children.

Article 6
Territorial application

1   Any State may at the time of signature or when depositing its instrument of ratification, acceptance or approval, specify the territory or territories to which the Protocol shall apply and state the extent to which it undertakes that the provisions of this Protocol shall apply to such territory or territories.

2   Any State may at any later date, by a declaration addressed to the Secretary General of the Council of Europe, extend the application of this Protocol to any other territory specified in the declaration. In respect of such territory the Protocol shall enter into force on the first day of the month following the expiration of a period of two months after the date of receipt by the Secretary General of such declaration.

3   Any declaration made under the two preceding paragraphs may, in respect of any territory specified in such declaration, be withdrawn or modified by a notification addressed to the Secretary General. The withdrawal or modification shall become effective on the first day of the month following the expiration of a period of two months after the date of receipt of such notification by the Secretary General.

4   A declaration made in accordance with this Article shall be deemed to have been made in accordance with paragraph 1 of Article 56 of the Convention.

5   The territory of any State to which this Protocol applies by virtue of ratification, acceptance or approval by that State, and each territory to which this Protocol is applied by virtue of a declaration by that State under this Article, may be treated as separate territories for the purpose of the reference in Article 1 to the territory of a State.

6   Any State which has made a declaration in accordance with paragraph 1 or 2 of this Article may at any time thereafter declare on behalf of one or more of the

territories to which the declaration relates that it accepts the competence of the Court to receive applications from individuals, non-governmental organisations or groups of individuals as provided in Article 34 of the Convention in respect of Articles 1 to 5 of this Protocol.

Article 7
Relationship to the Convention

As between the States Parties, the provisions of Article 1 to 6 of this Protocol shall be regarded as additional Articles to the Convention, and all the provisions of the Convention shall apply accordingly.

Article 8
Signature and ratification

This Protocol shall be open for signature by member States of the Council of Europe which have signed the Convention. It is subject to ratification, acceptance or approval. A member State of the Council of Europe may not ratify, accept or approve this Protocol without previously or simultaneously ratifying the Convention. Instruments of ratification, acceptance or approval shall be deposited with the Secretary General of the Council of Europe.

Article 9
Entry into force

1 This Protocol shall enter into force on the first day of the month following the expiration of a period of two months after the date on which seven member States of the Council of Europe have expressed their consent to be bound by the Protocol in accordance with the provisions of Article 8.

2 In respect of any member State which subsequently expresses its consent to be bound by it, the Protocol shall enter into force on the first day of the month following the expiration of a period of two months after the date of the deposit of the instrument of ratification, acceptance or approval.

Article 10
Depositary functions

The Secretary General of the Council of Europe shall notify all the member States of the Council of Europe of:

a any signature;
b the deposit of any instrument of ratification, acceptance or approval;
c any date of entry into force of this Protocol in accordance with Articles 6 and 9;
d any other act, notification or declaration relating to this Protocol.

In witness whereof the undersigned, being duly authorised thereto, have signed this Protocol.

Done at Strasbourg, this 22nd day of November 1984, in English and French, both texts being equally authentic, in a single copy which shall be deposited in the archives of the Council of Europe. The Secretary General of the Council of Europe shall transmit certified copies to each member State of the Council of Europe.

PROTOCOL NO. 12 TO THE CONVENTION FOR THE PROTECTION OF HUMAN RIGHTS AND FUNDAMENTAL FREEDOMS

The member states of the Council of Europe signatory hereto,

Having regard to the fundamental principle according to which all persons are equal before the law and are entitled to the equal protection of the law;

Being resolved to take further steps to promote the equality of all persons through the collective enforcement of a general prohibition of discrimination by means of the Convention for the Protection of Human Rights and Fundamental Freedoms signed at Rome on 4 November 1950 (hereinafter referred to as 'the Convention');

Reaffirming that the principle of non-discrimination does not prevent States Parties from taking measures in order to promote full and effective equality, provided that there is an objective and reasonable justification for those measures,

Have agreed as follows:

Article 1
General prohibition of discrimination

1   The enjoyment of any right set forth by law shall be secured without discrimination on any ground such as sex, race, colour, language, religion, political or other opinion, national or social origin, association with a national minority, property, birth or other status.

2   No one shall be discriminated against by any public authority on any ground such as those mentioned in paragraph 1.

Article 2
Territorial application

1   Any state may, at the time of signature or when depositing its instrument of ratification, acceptance or approval, specify the territory or territories to which this Protocol shall apply.

2   Any state may at any later date, by a declaration addressed to the Secretary General of the Council of Europe, extend the application of this Protocol to any other territory specified in the declaration, in respect of such territory the Protocol shall enter into force on the first day of the month following the expiration of a period of three months after the date of receipt by the Secretary General of such declaration.

3   Any declaration made under the two preceding paragraphs may, in respect of any territory specified in such declaration, be withdrawn or modified by a notification addressed to the Secretary General. The withdrawal or modification shall become effective on the first day of the month following the expiration of a period of three months after the date of receipt of such notification by the Secretary General.

4   A declaration made in accordance with this article shall be deemed to have been made in accordance with paragraph 1 of Article 56 of the Convention.

5   Any state which has made a declaration in accordance with paragraph 1 or 2 of this article may at any time thereafter declare on behalf of one or more of the territories to which the declaration relates that it accepts the competence of the Court to receive applications from individuals, non-governmental organisations or groups of individuals as provided by Article 34 of the Convention in respect of Article 1 of this Protocol.

Article 3
Relationship to the Convention

As between the States Parties, the provisions of Articles 1 and 2 of this Protocol shall be regarded as additional articles to the Convention, and all the provisions of the Convention shall apply accordingly.

Article 4
Signature and ratification

This Protocol shall be open for signature by member states of the Council of Europe which have signed the Convention. It is subject to ratification, acceptance or approval. A member state of the Council of Europe may not ratify, accept or approve this Protocol without previously or simultaneously ratifying the Convention. Instruments of ratification, acceptance or approval shall be deposited with the Secretary General of the Council of Europe.

Article 5
Entry into force

1   This Protocol shall enter into force on the first day of the month following the expiration of a period of three months after the date on which ten member states of the Council of Europe have expressed their consent to be bound by the Protocol in accordance with the provisions of Article 4.

2   In respect of any member state which subsequently expresses its consent to be bound by it, the Protocol shall enter into force on the first day of the month following the expiration of a period of three months after the date of the deposit of the instrument of ratification, acceptance or approval.

Article 6
Depositary functions

The Secretary General of the Council of Europe shall notify all the member states of the Council of Europe of:

a   any signature;

b   the deposit of any instrument of ratification, acceptance or approval;

c   any date of entry into force of this Protocol in accordance with Articles 2 and 5;

d   any other act, notification or communication relating to this Protocol.

In witness whereof the undersigned, being duly authorised thereto, have signed this Protocol.

Done at ...., this .... day of .... 2000, in English and French, both texts being equally authentic, in a single copy which shall be deposited in the archives of the Council of Europe. The Secretary General of the Council of Europe shall transmit certified copies to each member state of the Council of Europe.

Index

Index

BLACKSTONE'S HUMAN RIGHTS SERIES

TITLES IN THE SERIES

Criminal Justice, Police Powers & Human Rights
Employment Law & Human Rights
Family Law & Human Rights
Immigration, Asylum & Human Rights
Local Authorities & Human Rights
Media Law & Human Rights
Property Law & Human Rights
Taking a Case to the European Court of Human Rights